In 1981 the Brookings Institution, with the financial support of the U.S. Department of Health and Human Services, began a series of studies to examine the economic consequences of aging and the effects of public and private programs that aid the aged. This book presents findings of the first round of these studies.

Four labor supply papers are presented first. Douglas A. Wolf and Frank Levy apply innovative statistical techniques to estimate the effect of private pension programs on job turnover over workers' lifetimes. Robert H. Haveman, Barbara L. Wolfe, and Jennifer L. Warlick examine the effects of the disability insurance program on male labor force participation. Within a new analytical framework, Peter A. Diamond and Jerry A. Hausman estimate the effects of health, social security, and spells of unemployment on the timing of retirement. Gary Burtless and Robert A. Moffitt develop a new model with which to analyze the trade-off between the timing of retirement and post-retirement labor supply; with this model they estimate the effect on labor supply of various changes in the social security system.

The next three papers examine specific aspects of post-retirement living standards. Sheldon Danziger, Eugene Smolensky, Jacques van der Gaag, and Michael K. Taussig present estimates of the incomes necessary for the elderly to achieve the same living standards as the nonelderly and then compare the living standards of the elderly and nonelderly. Sally R. Merrill analyzes the mobility patterns of older households and the importance of owner-occupied housing for living standards of the elderly. Saul Schwartz, Eugene Smolensky, and Sheldon Danziger examine the factors that influence the decisions of elderly persons to live alone or with younger relatives.

The book concludes with three papers analyzing behavior relevant to determining the consequences of trends and policies that alter the economic status of the elderly. Alan J. Auerbach and Laurence J. Kotlikoff present simulations of the effects of demographic changes on real wages, saving, labor supply, and other economic variables within a closed model based on rational expectations. Paul N. Courant, Edward M. Gramlich, and John P. Laitner apply a life-cycle model to data from the Panel Study of Income Dynamics to measure saving behavior. Sheila R. Zedlewski projects the incomes that the elderly will receive from private pensions and social security through the year 2020.

Henry J. Aaron and Gary Burtless are senior fellows in the Brookings Economic Studies program; Aaron is also professor of economics at the University of Maryland. This volume is the twenty-fourth in the Brookings Studies in Social Economics series.

Jacket design by Susan Foster

Studies in Social Economics

TITLES PUBLISHED

STUDIES IN SOCIAL ECONOMICS

Henry J. Aaron and Gary Burtless, Editors

Retirement and Economic Behavior

THE BROOKINGS INSTITUTION
Washington, D.C.

Library of Congress Cataloging in Publication data:
Main entry under title:
Retirement and economic behavior.

(Studies in social economics)
Includes bibliographical references.
1. Retirement—Economic aspects—United States—
addresses, essays, lectures. 2. Aged—United States—
economic conditions—Addresses, essays, lectures.
3. Retirement income—United States—Addresses, essays,
lectures. I. Aaron, Henry J. II. Burtless, Gary T.,
1950– . III. Series.
HQ1062.R43 1984   306′.38   83-45961
ISBN 0-8157-0036-9
ISBN 0-8157-0035-0 (pbk.)

9 8 7 6 5 4 3 2 1

Foreword

A central policy concern for U.S. society is the care and support of the retired elderly. The cost of public programs that provide income to the elderly is already high and will increase greatly in the next century when the baby boom generation retires. The cost of medical care is now rising because of technological advances and, to a lesser extent, because the number of the very elderly—people 75 and older—is increasing.

Policymakers and social scientists are concerned not only with the cost of programs for the elderly but also with their effects. Social security and private pensions affect the timing of retirement and the amount of work done by people who have retired from full-time jobs. Medicare greatly affects the amount of medical care received by the aged. But public policies aimed specifically at the retired also affect the behavior of the working and nonelderly populations. For example, many economists have concluded that social security has reduced the amount of private savings set aside for retirement.

Public concern about policies toward retirees has inspired a large and rapidly growing economic literature on retirement. In recent years analysts have investigated the economic and other determinants of retirement, the income status, consumption patterns, and living arrangements of the elderly, and the economic effects of policies affecting the aged. This research carries implications for policymaking, though only a few of the most important analyses have received much public attention.

The papers in this volume treat many of the issues. They are based on research supported by a grant to Brookings from the U.S. Department of Health and Human Services. Each paper represents an original contribution to knowledge rather than a summary of prior contributions. The papers were presented at a conference held at Brookings on October

21–22, 1982. Though much of the research was highly technical, the authors and editors have sought to state the policy significance of the findings clearly. The introduction includes a summary of each paper and its main conclusions.

Shortly after the conference, Congress and the President revised the old-age and survivors insurance program to reduce its short- and long-term deficit. The effects of these changes on average retirement age, the consumption levels of retirees, and saving among the nonelderly will not be known for many years, but the papers in this volume constitute a basis for evaluating some of them.

Henry J. Aaron and Gary Burtless are senior fellows in the Brookings Economic Studies program; Aaron is also a professor of economics at the University of Maryland. Joseph A. Pechman, former director of Economic Studies at Brookings, played a valuable role in organizing the conference at which the papers in this volume were presented. Thomas A. Gustafson and Anthony J. Pellechio of the Department of Health and Human Services assisted with the selection of topics and participants for the conference.

Dana Lane edited the manuscript, Penelope Schmitt verified its factual content, Nancy Snyder did the proofreading, and Florence Robinson prepared the index. The Brookings computation staff, especially Paul E. Morawski and Carole H. Newman, provided valuable assistance in preparing data tapes for some of the projects.

The views expressed here are those of the authors and discussants and should not be ascribed to the Department of Health and Human Services, or to the trustees, officers, or other staff members of the Brookings Institution.

BRUCE K. MACLAURY
President

February 1984
Washington, D.C.

Contents

Index   347

Tables

Contents

Figures

Henry J. Aaron and Gary Burtless

Introduction and Summary

Retirement is a phenomenon of growing importance in economic life. With the establishment of social security in 1935, the rise of private pensions after World War II, and the general increase in living standards since the Depression, an extended period of retirement has come to be viewed as normal. Longevity has been increasing, and retirement ages have been declining. As a result, retired people represent a growing proportion of the population. When the baby boom generation retires, starting around 2005, this proportion will rise sharply. Trends in retirement have raised important questions about the financial soundness of some of the main institutions that provide income to retirees and their families: social security, other public and private pension plans, and medicare.

Public concern about the future of social security and public and private pensions has stimulated a growing body of research on retirement, aging, and the problems of the elderly. This research covers many topics: lifetime savings and employment patterns, illness and disability and their economic consequences, the income status and living arrangements of the elderly, and the macroeconomic effects of pensions, social security, and demographic change. Many of these issues are treated in one or more of the papers in this volume.

It was not our intention when commissioning research studies to provide an encyclopedic treatment of all important issues. Because research on many of the subjects examined in this book began only in the 1970s, such a systematic survey of the issues is not yet warranted. We asked authors to try to contribute to knowledge, not to summarize the existing literature within their areas of expertise. The result is a diverse set of original research papers that touch on a variety of related subjects of interest to both policymakers and social scientists. Each of these papers should be regarded as a progress report, not as the definitive

1

treatment of a given subject area. The continuing research in each area is too vigorous for any "definitive" summary to remain valid for long. But individually and collectively, these studies extend one's knowledge of the determinants of retirement and the economic behavior that is affected by retirement.

Pension Coverage and Job Tenures

In recent years there has been growing interest in private pension plans and their effect on aggregate savings and labor market performance. Pensions are a popular form of compensation among workers because of their substantial tax advantage over straight money wages. Employers are probably interested in offering pensions because they can provide powerful inducements to discourage employee turnover at younger ages, when productivity is still rising, and to encourage employee retirement at older ages, when productivity may be declining. In their study in this volume, Douglas A. Wolf and Frank Levy are particularly concerned with pension effects at younger ages. The main characteristic of a pension plan they consider is its vesting rule. The vesting rule establishes a minimum tenure requirement—say, five years—for a worker to become eligible to receive benefits under the plan. This device obviously provides a strong incentive for employees to work at least the required minimum number of years before seeking other employment.

Wolf and Levy are careful to point out that a pension plan actually has two kinds of effects on younger workers. First, potential employees who plan on remaining steadily employed for a number of years would be more attracted to a firm that offers pensions than would potential workers who plan on a transitory or casual attachment. Workers with different preferences would therefore sort themselves among employers on the basis of planned job attachment, and firms offering pensions could attract a more stable work force. Second, workers in a firm offering pensions might be induced to change their tenure patterns as a result of the specific features of the pension plan, for example, its vesting rule. In his comment on the paper, Anthony J. Pellechio points out that pensions also may be a more natural form of pay in industries where long job attachments are common. In those industries pension plans arise because they are a convenient form of compensation both for workers and their employers. It should be obvious from this discussion that workers covered by pensions should have longer average tenures than do uncovered workers. But not all of the difference in tenures is caused by the pensions, since to some extent workers with differing preferences for job stability simply sort themselves into jobs with and without pensions.

A large part of the Wolf and Levy study is devoted to the problem of estimating the relation between pension coverage and average length of job tenure. Like the study by Peter Diamond and Jerry Hausman, which we consider below, the work of Wolf and Levy is based on the hazard, or the time-to-failure, model that has recently received wide application in the economic and sociological literatures. This model is applied in estimating how the probability of job leaving varies depending on the length of a worker's tenure, his coverage by a pension plan, and the characteristics of that pension plan. As the authors point out, an ideal data set for this purpose would include start and end dates as well as pension characteristics for all jobs held over the work life for a representative sample of the population. Because existing data sets fall well short of this ideal, the estimation problem is formidable. Wolf and Levy use a 1979 Census Bureau survey that asked workers about their tenure on current jobs as well as their status under a pension plan. They then supplement this survey information with data on the rate of entry into jobs since 1950 in order to establish the completed tenure distribution of different types of jobs since that year. (Because data on job entry are limited to manufacturing, the authors restrict their analysis to manufacturing jobs.)

The basic conclusions of the study can be summarized briefly. As expected, workers covered by pensions have substantially lower job-exit rates than uncovered workers, especially during the first few years on a job. Wolf and Levy find, not surprisingly, that job-exit rates tend to jump immediately after workers become vested in a pension but fall thereafter. Workers covered by shorter vesting requirements tend to have higher exit probabilities than workers covered by more stringent requirements, even during the first few years on a job when the prospects for becoming vested must seem remote in a job with a long vesting period. The job-exit probabilities can be translated to show how long, on average, a new worker can be expected to remain on a job. For a newly hired 25-year-old, Wolf and Levy find that an uncovered worker will remain an average of 3.2 years, a worker covered by a plan with a 1-year vesting requirement will remain 3.5 years, and a worker under a 10-year vesting requirement will remain about 13 years. Thus pension coverage and longer vesting requirements are associated with considerably greater job stability.

The paper concludes with a simulation exercise to see how worker turnover might be affected by provisions in federal laws pertaining to pension plan vesting requirements. The 1974 ERISA (Employment Retirement Income Security Act) standards caused some employers to reduce the stringency of their vesting requirements and probably contributed to a modest shortening of the average length of time required to become vested. According to the authors' simulation results, this change has caused a slight increase in employee turnover: the average manufacturing worker now holds 5.4 jobs over his lifetime rather than the 5.0 he held before the passage of ERISA; and the average duration of a job has fallen from 6.84 years to 6.48 years. We should add that these simulation results provide an upper-bound estimate of the effect of pension plan provisions on the aggregate job tenure distribution. Nonetheless, they suggest that there is scope for affecting job stability in U.S. manufacturing through regulation of pension plans and pension vesting requirements.

Disability Transfers and Early Retirement

The explosive rise in disability insurance rolls during the 1970s spurred intensive study of the effect of disability transfers on labor supply. One economist has suggested that the social security disability insurance program is the main reason for the sharp decline in labor force participation rates among men between 45 and 59 after 1957.[1] It is true that liberalization in disability payments during the 1960s and 1970s permitted workers with health impairments to accept early retirement. But just how much the program has affected work behavior remains a topic of spirited controversy.

Robert H. Haveman, Barbara L. Wolfe, and Jennifer L. Warlick examine the controversy and provide some new estimates of the effects of disability insurance. First they point out that the rise in disability

---

1. Donald Parsons, "Racial Trends in Male Labor Force Participation," *American Economic Review*, vol. 70 (December 1980), pp. 911–20.

benefits was not the only event that coincided with the drop in male participation rates. During the 1970s unemployment rates were generally higher than in the 1950s and 1960s, and women and youths joined the labor market in unprecedented numbers. Both trends have probably hurt the employment opportunities of older men. The authors then offer an economic model to explain the choice between work, on the one hand, and disability benefits, on the other. The basis for this model is a comparison between the income stream available from continued work and the potential stream available after cessation of work and commencement of disability transfer payments. Each older worker is presumed to consider these two potential income streams and then to select the one that offers greatest satisfaction.

There are some technical problems in estimating this kind of model, simple though it might appear. A major problem is that for most workers the exact income streams from only one of the two alternatives is known. If a worker decides against taking early retirement and applying for disability transfers, one does not know whether his application would have been accepted and, if accepted, how large the benefit would have been. Similarly, only imperfect information exists about the amount of wage income that could be earned by a disability transfer recipient should he return to work. Haveman, Wolfe, and Warlick propose a solution to this problem that involves statistical imputation of potential income streams. They use information on incomes of working men to infer the potential incomes that would be available to disability transfer recipients if the latter were workers, and they use information on incomes of disability recipients to infer the potential disability incomes available to working men. In their predictive equations the authors employ a statistical correction procedure to account for the selected samples used in obtaining their estimates.

Using their estimates of expected income flows under the two labor market alternatives, the authors then estimate the effect of the two income flows on workers' choices of employment status. They consider choices of men surveyed in the 1978 wave of the Michigan Panel Study of Income Dynamics.

The authors' findings are in marked contrast to those reported in some earlier studies. They find that though the increase in social security disability benefits has had an important and statistically significant effect on male labor force participation, the effect is much smaller than that reported earlier and accounts for only a small part of the decline in participation rates observed in recent years. For example, in the ten years after 1968, the labor force participation rates of men aged 55 through 64 declined by 12 percentage points while social security disability benefits per recipient rose 43 percent. The authors conclude that less than 2 percentage points of the decline in participation rates was caused by increases in disability insurance. In commenting on the paper, Joseph P. Newhouse agrees that this finding casts considerable doubt on the reliability of earlier estimates of the effects of disability insurance. He argues, however, that the statistical procedures used in the paper, particularly those controlling for sample selection problems, are subject to serious criticism. For that reason he advises skepticism in accepting the exact estimates reported.

The final section of the paper provides estimates of the impact of a variety of disability insurance reforms. The authors are particularly concerned with the effects of program cutbacks on net family income, taking into account the fact that some people who are denied benefits may be able to earn some wages on their own. They examine the effects of denying benefits to people with specific ailments (such as back problems) or socioeconomic characteristics (such as a high level of education). As was pointed out in the discussion of this paper, these kinds of reforms are not realistic. However, the simulation findings do illustrate the impact of some draconian budget cuts. The authors conclude that many affected individuals could not replace the lost disability benefits through increases in their wage earnings. Even taking account of the work effort response, they find that net family income in the affected groups would drop by one-third to almost one-half after the cut in disability benefits. One can conclude from this study that drastic reductions in the disability program are unlikely to have a great effect on labor force participation but can be expected to cause substantial income reductions among an important fraction of affected families.

Retirement and Unemployment

Although older workers usually have general plans for their retirement, its exact timing is often a matter of chance. Men and women who would prefer to work longer find themselves the victims of involuntary unemployment, disability, or sudden illness. Peter A. Diamond and Jerry A. Hausman focus on these sources of uncertainty in their examination of the retirement patterns of older men. The central contribution of their study is to introduce new statistical procedures for analyzing the retirement process and to provide new estimates of the effect of health, unemployment, permanent income, and social security benefits on the timing of retirement.

Diamond and Hausman propose two different statistical procedures, the first to explain the observed distribution of retirement ages in the National Longitudinal Survey of Older Men (NLS) and the second to evaluate the impact of involuntary unemployment on the timing of retirement. Their first procedure—an adaptation of the hazard model—is conceptually simple, though it has only recently begun to be applied to economic and sociological problems. The idea behind the model is that for a person with a particular set of characteristics there is an inherent probability during each month or year that retirement will take place. The estimation procedure is designed to show how the retirement hazard (or probability) is affected by important individual characteristics like marital status, education, and race. Diamond and Hausman modify the basic hazard model in order to estimate the effect of variables that change over time, such as pension and social security entitlements, age, and health status. The hazard model is then estimated on the basis of retirements observed between 1966 and 1978 in the NLS older-men sample. The model has the important advantage of using information on all men who were surveyed, including men who did not retire during the twelve-year interval covered by the NLS. This aspect of the model is probably the main reason that results in the paper differ from those reported in earlier studies where sample selection issues were treated less carefully.

Diamond and Hausman find that the probability of retirement is strongly associated with a worker's permanent income, especially at very low and very high income levels. Workers with high permanent incomes tend to retire earlier, undoubtedly because they can afford to do so. Not surprisingly, the onset of bad health is found to markedly increase the chances of early retirement. The authors compute that a transition from good to poor health has roughly the same effect on the probability of retirement as a sudden increase in pension entitlement equal to about $540 per month. The findings in the paper with the greatest policy interest are those on the effect of social security benefits. Diamond and Hausman interpret their statistical results to show that the elimination of early social security awards (made between ages 62 and 64) and the delay of the normal retirement age to 68 would increase the average working life by about seven months. Although this represents a significant delay in retirements, it would still cause a substantial drop in monthly social security benefits for retirees. (Under the proposed reform, retirement would have to be postponed nearly three years for the monthly benefit to remain unchanged.)

The second part of the paper introduces a novel statistical treatment of unemployment among older workers. Diamond and Hausman wish to examine all cases of involuntary, permanent job loss among older men in their sample to determine how the spells of unemployment end. In the case of younger men, such spells ordinarily end with the unemployed worker finding a new job. Older workers have another option: they can retire. For example, 36 percent of discharged men aged 60 through 64 fail to find another job and choose instead to retire. Diamond and Hausman estimate a "competing risks" statistical model to evaluate the choice between retirement and job finding. This model estimates the influence of such factors as social security benefits, age, and health on the choice between the two options as well as their influence on the average length of a spell of unemployment. Not surprisingly, higher levels of pensions, social security benefits, and wealth all tend to cause discharged workers to retire rather than to obtain new jobs, as do poor health and advanced age. For workers who obtain new jobs, the spell of unemployment is especially prolonged for workers in poor health and of advanced age.

One striking finding in the paper is contained in tabulations of the delay between the onset of retirement or disability and the start of retirement income. For example, nearly one-quarter of the retired men in the NLS survey waited two or more years after their retirements for retirement income to begin, and of that fraction roughly half waited five or more years. These delays in retirement income, as well as the substantial effects of involuntary unemployment and bad health on timing of retirement, indicate that the incentive effects of pensions and social security are not important to many retirees. The authors conclude that though social security reform could indeed reduce present incentives to retire, many workers who are in poor health or who have been permanently discharged from their jobs would simply face longer periods without retirement income or lower retirement incomes if social security benefits were reduced.

Social Security Benefits and Labor Supply

The retirement behavior of older Americans is an important determinant of the total labor supply available to the economy. It is widely believed that social security benefits as well as private pensions have had a great influence on the retirement age since World War II. Between 1950 and 1979 the labor force participation rate of men 65 and over fell by more than half, from 46 percent to 20 percent. For men aged 55 through 64 the rate fell from 87 percent to 73 percent, with all of the decline occuring after 1961, when early social security retirement benefits were first extended to men between 62 and 65. These declines in labor force participation during a period in which real social security benefits were rising strongly are often cited as evidence that the social security program encourages early retirement. Critics of the program also argue that it discourages work effort after retirement because the earnings test imposes a high marginal tax on postretirement earnings.

Gary Burtless and Robert A. Moffitt devote their paper to a careful study of these issues. In the first substantive section of their paper they discuss the specific incentives that social security provides to encourage early retirement and discourage postretirement labor supply. They point out that the program raises lifetime incomes because retirement benefits typically exceed prior tax contributions by a substantial margin. This rise in lifetime income should induce workers to retire earlier if retirement is a normal good. In addition the program affects workers' discounted wages, since each year of added work can affect both the annual amount and the expected duration of social security benefits. The authors show that the effect of social security on discounted wages may somewhat offset its effect on lifetime income, so that the net effect of the program on retirement ages is ambiguous, at least until workers reach age 65, when social security clearly encourages workers to retire. They then show how the earnings test affects not only the incentive to work after retirement but also the timing of retirement itself.

The authors derive and estimate a formal economic model of retirement and postretirement work effort. Data for the study were obtained from the Retirement History Survey and cover the retirement patterns of nondisabled older men over the period 1969 through 1977. Many of their findings echo those of earlier researchers who used less elaborate economic models. For example, Burtless and Moffitt find that health status, lack of schooling, and race play important roles in the timing of retirement.

The more interesting findings pertain to the effect of social security and other types of retirement income. The results in the paper generally conform to theoretical expectations, but Burtless and Moffitt find a somewhat smaller overall effect of social security on early retirement than some earlier researchers found. They also conclude, however, that after about age 60 one dollar of potential social security benefits seems to have an appreciably larger effect on retirement behavior than does a dollar of other types of retirement income. The reason may be that social security benefits are indexed to inflation, making their value far more certain than income from such other sources as pension plans and savings. If an average worker's expected retirement income were raised by $125 per month (in 1982 dollars), his age of retirement would drop by six weeks. But if the same worker's expected social security grant were raised by $125 a month, his retirement age would drop by twice as much—twelve weeks. Although the effect of social security benefits on the retirement age is much greater than the effect of other types of income, it is nonetheless small in relation to the typical length of the work life. Burtless and Moffitt estimate, for example, that if the normal retirement age in the social security program were advanced from 65 to 68, lifetime benefits would fall about 15 percent, but an average married male would postpone his retirement by only four and one-half months, which is less than 1 percent of the average work life and 2.5 percent of the average length of retirement.

The paper also examines the effect of social security on postretirement work effort. About one in five new male retirees works, and the amount of weekly work effort is quite low. The authors find that the relative effect of social security on work effort is quite large, though the absolute effect is unimpressive because of the small number of labor force participants among new retirees. Thus the authors estimate that elimination of the earnings test might raise weekly hours among new retirees over 62 by about one-third, or about 1.0 to 1.5 hours per week on average.

One of the main conclusions of the paper is that the retirement age is not particularly sensitive to basic changes in the social security formula. Burtless and Moffitt consider the effect of a variety of changes in the benefit formula that have been suggested to reduce social security outlays. None of the reforms is found to cause as much as a half-year delay in the average male's retirement. One implication of this finding is that social security benefit cutbacks will result primarily in reductions in consumption during retirement rather than delays in the timing of retirement. If the normal retirement age is advanced from 65 to 67, as it is scheduled to do under current law, workers will not delay their retirements by two years in order to obtain an unchanged monthly social security benefit. An average worker will delay his retirement by less than four months and choose to accept the implied reduction in his social security check. If this conclusion is correct, an important question for future research is how much retirement savings will rise in order to offset the resulting decline in social security income.

Relative Economic Status

That the elderly have less income than the nonelderly has been well known for many years. The reason is clear enough. Most people derive most of their income from earnings, and the elderly are usually retired. But the meaning of the dry statistics is more obscure. Studies show that the elderly typically have fewer family responsibilities and pay fewer taxes than the nonelderly, and that they have had time to pay off mortgages on the homes in which they live; some of the same studies that show that the elderly have less income also show that they have more assets than the nonelderly. Sheldon Danziger, Jacques van der Gaag, Eugene Smolensky, and Michael K. Taussig try to take account of several of these sources of information to portray the relative economic status of the elderly.

They report that incomes of elderly families average less than two-thirds those of nonelderly families. But this ratio was nearly one-third higher in 1981 than it was in 1966. The proportion of the elderly in poverty, roughly twice that of the general population in 1966, had fallen to approximately the same level by 1981.

The authors apply detailed adjustments to data on incomes in 1973 to compare the economic status of the elderly with that of the nonelderly. They begin by noting that in that year the cash income of elderly households averaged 48.6 percent of that of the nonelderly. They then adjust this statistic in several ways: for the possession of consumer durable goods, for variation in direct taxes, for differences in family size, and for the fact that some elderly persons reside in units headed by nonelderly persons. If all these factors are taken into account, the elderly had 90 percent as much income as the nonelderly in 1973. And these adjustments do not consider that the elderly have more nonhousing wealth per capita than the nonelderly. In thinking about the current economic status of the elderly, one should also keep in mind that in the decade following 1973, social security benefits, a major source of income of the elderly, rose more rapidly than wages.

The authors then show the effects on the economic status of the elderly of alternative reductions in social security benefits. They show that a decision to include half of all social security benefits in income subject to personal income tax would produce a far different pattern of reductions than would an across-the-board cut in social security benefits. Making half of social security benefits taxable would have no effect on the incomes of the poor elderly and less effect than the general reduction on the bottom half of the elderly income distribution. Elderly persons with higher-than-average incomes, by contrast, would lose more from taxability than from a benefit cut. Neither of these changes would have much effect on global measures of income inequality.

In addition to these applied results, the paper reports the results of an extended effort to develop improved "equivalency" scales. These scales, or ratios, are used to measure the relative incomes that families of different sizes and compositions need to achieve equivalent living standards. For example, the authors find that a single elderly woman can achieve the same standard of living as a four-person family consisting of a couple and two children, one age 6 to 11, one age 12 to 17, if she has 37 percent as much income as the family.

Home Equity and the Elderly

A high proportion of older families own their own homes. The savings that are tied up in these homes often represent a large fraction of all savings accumulated over a lifetime. Yet it is not easy to draw on this type of accumulation to provide for consumption during old age. Savings invested in owner-occupied homes are not liquid, so that old people who wish to consume some of the savings tied up in their homes must usually sell them and move to new establishments. This can be a wrenching experience for elderly families with many years' residence in the same place.

In view of the special characteristics of housing that distinguish it from other forms of saving, the question of how home equity holdings rise and fall over the lifetime is an interesting one. Sally R. Merrill examines this question for a group of people who turned 60 in the late 1960s and early 1970s. Since the data set she uses failed to include information about housing accumulation patterns early in people's lifetimes, she considers housing accumulation and decumulation only among the elderly, over the eight-year period between 1969 and 1977. The economic framework for her analysis is provided by a simple version of the life-cycle consumption model. According to this model, families or individuals over the course of their working lives accumulate retirement savings that are used up during retirement. Annual consumption remains relatively steady over lifetimes, but family asset holdings follow a hump-backed pattern over the years, with a decline in asset holdings beginning about the time of retirement. Of course this model has no direct implications for the various components of asset holdings, such as stocks or home equity, but instead yields predictions only about the pattern of total wealth holdings. It nonetheless seems plausible that home equity, as a major component of asset holdings, would begin to decline around the age of retirement.

The evidence assembled in Merrill's paper fails to support this hypothesis. In fact, the author finds that during the eight-year period under review, the elderly families in her sample actually *increased* their home equity holdings by about 12 percent in constant dollar terms. Notwithstanding the fact that most household heads retired over the period and family incomes fell by about one-third, homeowning families appeared to be reluctant to move. Homeowners who remained in the same houses usually realized substantial capital gains and paid off some portion of their remaining housing debt. At a time of rapid inflation of housing values, the equity gains of this group of families should hardly be surprising. However, a real surprise in the study is the finding that even among *movers* in the sample, gains in home equity tended to be important. For example, there were nearly twice as many renting families in 1969 that became homeowning families by 1977 as there were home-owning families in 1969 that sold their houses to become renters by 1977.

Even among homeowning families that moved between 1969 and 1977, but nonetheless remained homeowners, the average real value of a home was higher in 1977 than in 1969. On balance, families that changed residence between 1969 and 1977 actually increased their home equity holdings, contrary to expectation.

Merrill suggests several reasons that individuals continued to raise their holdings of home equity during their sixties, even as their incomes were dropping. Many older people may have reasoned (correctly as it turned out) that housing was a safer store of value than other forms of wealth. Families with strong emotional attachments to their homes might have resisted selling them and then received large capital gains as an unanticipated consequence of their immobility. In his comment on the paper, Raymond J. Struyk cautions that Merrill's main findings may not be applicable to other elderly populations or to other time periods. First, she restricted her analysis to people aged 66 through 71 in 1977, and these people are the comparatively "young" elderly. Among all elderly families, housing survey data show that 75 percent of families that switch tenure status become renters rather than homeowners, contrary to Merrill's findings for the 66-through-71-year-old subgroup. Second, the period covered by the study was one in which housing was an unusually attractive investment. During more normal times the home equity holdings of even the "young" elderly might decline rather than rise.

Whether or not they can be generalized, Merrill's findings raise interesting questions about the role of home equity for consumption patterns over retirement. Merrill finds that many families have home equity holdings that are high relative to their incomes. Homeowning families with low incomes that wish to increase their consumption of nonhousing items might benefit from reverse annuities or other home equity conversion schemes. Under such schemes the older family sells its house in exchange for a regular annuity payment and the lifetime right to reside in the house. Merrill finds that this kind of scheme would benefit some but by no means all low-income homeowning families. The problem for many poor, "illiquid" families is that the value of their homes is low—less than $25,000 or $30,000 in most cases. If home values are very low, families clearly cannot obtain a large supplement to their monthly incomes through reverse annuities. For many poor homeowning families, then, the main problem is lack of assets, not the concentration of asset holdings in housing.

Living Arrangements and the Elderly

Americans are accustomed to think of the elderly as a disadvantaged and relatively impoverished population. Yet the rise of social security, private pensions, and medicare benefits over the past three decades has substantially increased the money and in-kind incomes of older people. This rise in retirement income has made it possible for an increasing share of elderly families and individuals to live apart from their children. Consequently, more of the elderly now live in households with relatively low incomes, and many measures of income inequality are perversely affected by this trend. Although older people and their children presumably prefer the present living arrangements to the former ones, the relatively low incomes of households headed by older persons give the impression of continuing hardship among the elderly.

Saul Schwartz, Sheldon Danziger, and Eugene Smolensky carefully examine the determinants of living arrangements among the elderly, with special attention to the effects of health and income. They begin with the hypothesis that elderly families would prefer to live independently and will share living quarters with children or other relatives only if compelled to do so by poor health or very low income. An elderly family is considered to be living alone if it shares living quarters with no other persons except minor children under age 21. The authors use longitudinal information from the Retirement History Survey to estimate their model. Families in this survey were headed by a man or woman aged 60–65 when the analysis period began in 1971, and aged 66–71 when the analysis period ended in 1977. The focus of the study is thus on changes in living arrangements during the crucial years when many of the families are retiring from full-time work. The authors examine these changes for both single people and married couples.

Rather surprisingly, Schwartz, Danziger, and Smolensky find that their hypothesis is borne out only for singles, not for married couples. In the case of singles, the authors estimate that a $1,000 rise in income from the 1971 average income ($4,000 per year) leads to a 1.3 percentage point rise in the probability of living alone (from 53.0 percent to 54.3 percent). The onset of a health disability leads to a 1 percentage point decline in the probability of living alone, and retirement from work leads to a 2 percentage point decline. But the pattern for married couples when both spouses survive over the six-year period is markedly different. Among this group a $1,000 rise in income from the 1971 average ($9,800) leads to about a 3 percentage point *decline* in the probability of living alone. The authors surmise that older couples whose incomes are rising may be attracting their less affluent children to live with them. To test this conjecture, one would need better information about the incomes of independent children than is currently available.

In interpreting the findings of this study, we should note that the population examined consists of the relatively young elderly, that is, those still in their sixties. Only 3 percent of the sample that was living independently in 1971 had become dependent in a larger household by 1977. Thus disability, retirement, or death of a spouse had caused only a small proportion of these families to radically change their living arrangements by the end of the analysis period. Obviously, these events may have much more serious consequences for people in their seventies and eighties, and the findings of this study probably do not apply to that population.

Social Security and the Demographic Transition

The large impact that the baby boom generation will have on the social security system is widely recognized. The retirement of the baby boom generation will sharply increase the payroll tax on cohorts then in the labor force unless tax rates on the baby boomers are increased sufficiently to build up large reserves. But these demographic shifts will cause other shifts as well. When smaller cohorts follow the baby boom generation, labor will become scarcer, and that will tend to boost wages. Changes in wage rates will affect saving and hence the capital stock and will alter the amount each person wants to work. What will happen when all these effects work themselves out simultaneously?

Alan J. Auerbach and Laurence J. Kotlikoff apply a special model of the economy to answer these questions. Applying recent work in economic theory, the authors build into their model the assumption that people form expectations rationally about future events. They exclude from their model any randomness or uncertainty about the future. Accordingly, people at each time have available to them enough information to formulate accurate forecasts about all the conditions to which they and their offspring will be subject. The practical problem for

Auerbach and Kotlikoff was how to solve a model so that the rational behavior of individuals cumulated to aggregate economic conditions consistent with the assumed outcomes on which the individuals based their decisions.

The authors find that the roughly 50 percent permanent reduction in fertility rates that occurred after the postwar baby boom will require roughly a doubling in long-run social security tax rates if nothing else is done. In the long run, social security's tax rate is largely determined by demographic factors and the provisions of its benefit formula, such as the replacement rate and retirement age.

To avoid these tax increases, social security benefits in the long term could be cut 30 to 40 percent, assuming no changes in social security's retirement age or funding procedures. This reduction could be achieved by cutting social security's benefit replacement rate or by raising the age at which benefits are payable.

The long-run increase in the payment age needed to avoid tax rate increases ranges between three to five years. Since the model assumes a ten-year period of benefit receipt, a three- to five-year increase in the retirement age represents simply a different procedure to produce an equally significant long-term benefit cut.

An alternative to higher long-term social security tax rates that does not involve benefit reductions is the accumulation of a larger social security trust fund in the short run. The trust fund required to obviate long-run tax rate increases is roughly equal to 6.2 years of benefit payments, or roughly $1.4 trillion under current circumstances. This trust fund stands in contrast to social security's current reserves, which equal less than three months of benefit payments.

Even though long-term social security tax rates may double, economic welfare, as measured by per capita income or a combination of per capita consumption and leisure, may rise as a consequence of the demographic transition. The reduction in the number of nonproductive children per person in the economy means fewer mouths to feed for any given level of national output.

Depending on assumptions about government consumption per capita, the demographic transition can involve either small or quite large reductions in income tax rates. If per capita government consumption is constant, as might occur if all government consumption were for national defense, per adult government consumption would fall slightly as the ratio of adults to the total population increases. An alternative, extreme assumption is that government consumption is targeted primarily toward children, such as spending on education. Under such an assumption, government consumption per capita and per adult falls dramatically, permitting reductions in income tax rates by over 30 percent.

Individual Saving Behavior

Among the many factors influencing whether and when people retire, saving behavior is one of the most important and least understood. Economists have formulated a number of theories that do well in explaining the past course of aggregate saving. But none of these theories does a good job of predicting the future path of aggregate saving or of explaining variations in saving among individuals. At the individual level the problem is compounded by the fact that saving decisions taken in any one year depend not only on past experiences but on expectations about future events. Thus adequate data for the analysis of saving behavior at the individual level must cover many years. Such data do not exist and would be very expensive to gather.

Despite the inconclusiveness of the theoretical debate and the scarcity of data, one theory of saving behavior, the life-cycle model, has gained widespread acceptance among economists. According to this theory, people form expectations of the total wealth to which they will have access over their entire lives and base current consumption on that quantity, current and expected interest rates, and personal tastes. Among these tastes one of the most important is the rate at which people are willing to trade present for future consumption. It is normally assumed that people require more than $1 of future consumption to compensate them for $1 of forgone current consumption; this phenomenon is referred to as positive time preference.

Validation of the life-cycle model—or its replacement with a better model—would be useful for the formulation of retirement policy, as it would enable policymakers to understand how changes in taxes, pensions, or other public policies would affect saving, the timing of retirement, and the economic status of future retirees. Paul N. Courant, Edward M. Gramlich, and John P. Laitner make such an attempt in the paper presented in this volume. Their analysis is based on data from the Panel Study of Income Dynamics, a unique source because it presents data on the same families for many years. It is deficient, however, in that it lacks direct information on assets other than housing or on saving. These shortcomings in the data force the authors to impute values for assets (based on reported asset income) and for saving. These imputations and the question of their reliability were the subject of extensive discussion at the conference (see the comment by John B. Shoven).

The authors allow for the fact that households learn more each year about their lifetime incomes and assets and adjust their consumption in the light of that new information. While such reprogramming is implied by the life-cycle model, most previous tests of the theory have been based on cross-sectional data for a single year, which obviates any explicit recognition of the need for families to revise their consumption plans.

One clear implication of the life-cycle model is that households should be indifferent among the possible forms a change in their lifetime wealth might take. Whether a household's lifetime wealth increases because of an increase in the value of an owner-occupied house, an increase in the size of a savings account, or growth of expected earnings, the effect on consumption should be the same if the effect on lifetime wealth is the same. If households face borrowing constraints, they might appear to consume larger shares of lifetime wealth in available assets than of lifetime wealth unavailable until earned.

Whatever the theoretical justification for this prediction, the empirical results of the analysis by Courant, Gramlich, and Laitner flatly contradict it. They divide lifetime wealth into three categories: equity in owner-occupied housing, all other assets, and the present value of estimated lifetime earnings. The last category is much the largest of the three. Based on these three wealth categories, the consumption function that the authors estimate implies that the rate of time preference based on lifetime earnings is large and negative, while that based on other assets is large and positive. The degree of statistical significance of the estimates does not allow for the possibility that they might be the same. These results suggest that an increase in assets other than owner-occupied housing would increase consumption more than an equally valuable increase in future earnings.

The authors examine several possible explanations for these results but in the end conclude that they have propounded a puzzle rather than solved one. The results of this study underscore the fact that the life-cycle model will remain a weakly supported hypothesis in the absence of accurate data on saving by individual households over an extended period of time.

Simulation of Private Pension Coverage and Benefits

Long-term projections are notoriously unreliable, in part because seemingly unrelated aspects of human behavior influence one another. Thus projections of the income of future cohorts of the elderly depend on whether the elderly have access to social security and private pensions. But the level and extent of these benefits depend on marriage patterns, labor supply behavior, and many other factors. To deal with these problems, Sheila R. Zedlewski applies the large-scale dynamic simulation model, DYNASIM, to project pension and social security benefits to the year 2020.

First, she projects individual earnings over each year from the present to 2020. The model takes account of births, deaths, marriages and divorces, education, disability, labor supply, unemployment, and wage rates in generating a synthetic earnings profile for workers with a representative range of personal characteristics. Second, she assigns these representative workers to particular jobs that may or may not be covered by social security and private pensions. Finally, she uses the combination of earnings history and pattern of jobs to calculate social security and pension benefits to which people will be entitled when they retire.

Zedlewski's simulations produce a number of striking results concerning access to private pensions and the level of benefits each person will receive. Under present pension rules, the proportion of older people who have private employer pensions will grow dramatically between 1982 and 2020, and retirement income from these pensions will more than double for people 65 and over. This is the base case.

Zedlewski then simulates the consequences of three changes in pension rules. Under one, all pensions would be adjusted automatically and completely for changes in the price level that occur after the pensioner claimed a benefit. Under a second, all private employers would be required to offer private pension plans; this option is referred to as universal coverage. Under a third, pension credits would be portable among employers. At present, a person who leaves a job that would ultimately lead to a pension may not receive any credit toward a pension if he or she leaves before the pension is vested. With portable credits only the total working life in covered jobs would count, not how long the worker spent in each job. The addition of price indexing to private pensions would increase real benefits significantly. For example, in 2020 the benefits of men 68 through 71 and men 72 and over would be 43 percent and 96 percent higher if they were fully indexed than they would be if the rules were not changed.

If pension coverage in private employment were made universal, women would benefit far more than men. In 2020, 60 percent of women 65 through 71 would receive a private employer pension if coverage were universal, compared with 40 percent under current rules. The comparable figures for men are 75 percent and 65 percent. However, most of those added to the pension rolls would receive modest benefits, which would cause the average benefit to decline.

If pension credits were made portable among employers, so that a worker would not lose accumulated credits when switching jobs, the proportion of workers eventually earning a pension would rise slightly, but the effect on the amount of benefits would be striking. The average benefit payable to men, for example, would rise from an estimated $3,809 (in 1980 dollars) in the base case to $6,756 if all pension credits were portable.

In her paper Zedlewski indicates a number of ways in which the accuracy of such projections could be improved. It would be desirable, for example, to incorporate into the DYNASIM model the relation between pension characteristics and job turnover, the issue examined in Wolf and Levy's paper in this book. The model lacks any explicit treatment of asset accumulation and government pensions, both of which would be expected to influence labor supply, particularly in the years just before or after retirement. Addition of modules that would permit simulation of asset accumulation and government pensions should be undertaken.

Conclusion

Several themes dominated the conference at which these papers were presented. One concerned the technical problems of modeling the process of retirement itself. These problems derive from the variety of motivations for retirement. In some cases physical or mental aging forces people out of the labor market. But most illnesses are unpredictable at the individual level and they differ greatly in severity. In other cases healthy people are forced to retire from jobs in which they would have liked to remain. And in still other cases people retire because they wish to do so.

The importance of economic factors is obviously different in each of these circumstances. It is difficult even to specify exactly what retirement is or when it occurs, because some people gradually reduce the number of hours they work, others leave one job and take another, and still other people resume work after a period of complete withdrawal from the labor market. In combination, the diversity of experience strains the capacities of economic theory and statistical technique. Of much greater importance, it creates enormous problems for legislators in designing programs for the elderly and for administrators in implementing them.

The papers at the conference also illustrated both the deferred consequences of economic, demographic, and other events on retirement behavior, and conversely, the pervasive importance of retirement policies on the nonelderly. Thus rules regarding private pensions influence job switching by the nonelderly. Policies that influence decisions of the elderly on living arrangements have important effects on nonelderly relatives. Changes in private pension rules that have indetectable effects for several years will significantly alter the level and distribution of benefits in the distant future. The papers have made valuable contributions to resolving some of the outstanding issues. In view of the importance and complexity of the issues involved, this is no small accomplishment.

Douglas A. Wolf and Frank Levy

Pension Coverage, Pension Vesting, and the Distribution of Job Tenures

In this paper we examine the relationship between pension coverage, pension-vesting rules, and job tenures. We focus on two policy-related questions. First, a number of authors have advanced the proposition that employers provide private pensions to increase employee tenure and reduce the costs of turnover. In this paper we examine the association, if any, between pension characteristics and job tenure. Second, the 1974 Employee Retirement Income and Security Act (ERISA) placed potentially significant limits on the freedom of pension plan sponsors to set vesting requirements. The vesting period is the length of time an employee can be required to work before he is guaranteed at least some benefits at retirement. In this paper we explore the effect of these limits on the distribution of job tenures.

Our investigation of these questions uses data from the May 1979 Pension Supplement to the Current Population Survey (CPS). This data set is a large cross-sectional survey that contains a moderately detailed set of questions about each person's pension coverage. Particularly important for our purposes are questions that locate each person in the pension cycle: whether he is covered; if covered, whether he is vested; if not vested, how many years he has to work until he becomes vested; and so on. Information at this level of detail is required to assess the possibility that a person's job-changing behavior varies as he approaches and then achieves the vesting of pension benefits.

At the same time, the May 1979 CPS data contain a serious liability.

We are grateful to Henry J. Aaron, Gary Burtless, Ralph Ginsberg, Robert A. Moffitt, and Anthony J. Pellechio for their comments on this paper; to Catherine Choisser and Vicki Aaronson for computational assistance; and to Terri Murray for secretarial services.

23

Because it is a cross-sectional survey, the CPS obtains information only about a person's tenure-to-date on his current job. For purposes of describing a person's career, we are not interested in tenure-to-date, but rather in completed job tenures. Therefore, we employ models from renewal theory that permit us to infer the distribution of completed job tenures from the distribution of job tenures-in-progress. Using this methodology, we can also examine the way in which the distribution of completed job tenures varies with the individual's pension and vesting status.

Our examination is contained in four sections. The first section discusses theories and evidence regarding both the distribution of job tenures and the association between pensions and job tenure. In this section we underline the difficulties in relating the two concepts empirically. The second section outlines the estimation of a hazard function model for job tenure, formulated in terms of data on job tenures-in-progress, data of the type contained in the CPS. The third section presents and interprets the hazard function estimates. The final section simulates work careers, using these estimates, to examine the way in which job tenure and turnover vary with pension coverage and vesting rules. It then focuses more explicitly on the way in which ERISA has helped shape the existing distribution of job tenures.

We wish to emphasize at the outset that although our findings indicate strong associations between pension characteristics and job tenures, they do not establish the nature of the underlying causal relationship between the two. In particular, we are unable to identify the extent to which pensions, and especially vesting rules, act as a "sorting" device in the labor market, encouraging workers with longer anticipated job tenure to accept employment in firms whose pension plan has substantially deferred vesting, while workers with shorter anticipated job tenure seek out employment in firms with quickly vested pensions, or no pensions at all. In addition to sorting effects, pensions may have a contrasting retention effect, operating upon the decision to remain on a particular job. That is, net of any built-in association between pension coverage (and vesting rules) and job tenure due to sorting effects, workers on pension-covered jobs may react differently from the way uncovered workers respond to unanticipated inflation, growth in alternative employment opportunities, or other factors influencing turnover decisions. Of course, pensions are likely to affect both sorting and retention effects. Our analysis is not designed to measure the relative strength of these two effects.

With this overall qualification in mind, our principal conclusions can be summarized as follows:

—Pension coverage matters. Among manufacturing jobs, we estimate the average completed job to last 6.48 years, with a median tenure of 2.56 years. If the current pension system were to be abolished and all jobs to be uncovered, we estimate the mean tenure in manufacturing would drop from 6.48 to 4.09 years with a drop in median tenure from 2.56 to 2.26 years.

—Within the pension system, the vesting rule matters. The probability of leaving a job with a ten-year vesting rule is about four times larger in the year after vesting than in the year before vesting. Thus the length of the vesting rule exerts an impact on the ability of a pension to reduce turnovers.

—ERISA matters a little. In practice, it appears that ERISA exerted a modest impact on reducing the average length of the vesting period, and our results suggest that this reduction may have had some impact on shortening job tenures. In particular, if three-quarters of pensions now under ten-year vesting rules were converted to fifteen-year vesting rules, our simulations predict that mean tenure in manufacturing jobs would rise from 6.48 years to 6.84 years while median tenure in all jobs would remain constant at 2.56 years.

Since one of the hypothesized effects of pensions is to self-select a work force with a potentially greater innate staying power on a job, it follows that the retention effects of pensions are created jointly by the pension system and the characteristics of the workers. Therefore, our simulation results should be regarded as an upper limit of pension effects per se. Nonetheless, our results are strongly consistent with the idea that pensions and work force behavior are associated in the hypothesized direction.

Job Tenures and Pensions

Within labor economics both the distribution of job tenures and the economic role of pensions have received wide attention in recent years. The analysis of job tenures has been characterized by a rapidly evolving empirical methodology while the analysis of the role of pensions has been characterized by a more stable theoretical consensus but some difficulty in estimating the important behavioral relationships suggested by the theory. We begin this paper by reviewing both areas briefly.

During the late 1960s and early 1970s, the investigation of job tenures was based on a generalized version of the dual labor market model. This model implied that job tenures were usually of modest length and that the proper focus of a study of careers was turnover and employment dynamics.[1] By 1980 this view had shifted radically toward a "Japanese" model that emphasized the relative importance of long-term or lifetime jobs and, for most people, little turnover through much of their careers.[2]

This dramatic turnabout occurred in part because questions of duration and turnover are particularly sensitive to the way in which they are posed. The typical career will involve a modest number of short-term jobs (when the young worker is job shopping) followed by one or two jobs of long duration. Thus if we ask the average duration of all jobs that begin in 1983, the answer is fairly short—perhaps as brief as three or four years. But if we define the significance of long-term jobs (for example, those jobs lasting fifteen years or more) in the context of a worker's career, we find them quite important in the sense that the typical worker will spend most of his working life in one or two such jobs. (Note, however, that these long-term jobs will not be an important fraction of the number of jobs the worker holds.)

Although this shifting perspective has now been well established, good estimates of the distribution of completed job tenures are still not available. The main problem is one alluded to in the introduction of this paper—very few data sets contain information on completed job tenures covering large numbers of people. Much more common are estimates of tenures-to-date at the time a particular survey was taken.[3] Thus existing estimates of completed job tenures are based on information covering tenures-in-progress and extrapolation techniques borrowed from demographic analysis.[4] In the next section we use the May 1979 CPS to

1. See Robert E. Hall, "Turnover in the Labor Force," *Brookings Papers on Economic Activity, 3:1972*, pp. 709–56; and George Perry, "Unemployment Flows in the U.S. Labor Market," *BPEA, 2:1972*, pp. 245–92.

2. George A. Akerlof and Brian G. M. Main, "Unemployment Spells and Job Tenures: Are They Long? Are They Short? Or, Are They Both?" University of California at Berkeley discussion paper, 1980; and Robert E. Hall, "The Importance of Lifetime Jobs in the U.S. Economy," *American Economic Review* (September 1982), pp. 716–24.

3. For a recent example, see Francis W. Horvath, "Job Tenure of Workers in January 1981," *Monthly Labor Review*, vol. 105 (September 1982), pp. 34–36.

4. Akerlof and Main, "Unemployment Spells and Job Tenures"; and Hall, "Importance of Lifetime Jobs in the U.S. Economy."

compute a new estimate of completed job tenures for manufacturing jobs based on the application of hazard function techniques.

While economists are now in substantial agreement on the distribution of completed job tenures, the impact of pensions on this distribution remains in doubt. The problem lies not in the theory of the impact of pensions—a subject on which there is some consensus—but in the lack of appropriate data sets containing information on both pensions and job tenure. Existing data sets have permitted analysts to examine the effect of pensions on a more restricted dependent variable—the probability that an employee will leave a job in the near future. The findings of these studies are generally consistent with the consensus theory of the impact of pensions on tenure.

There are two main elements in the consensus theory. The first is the idea that employees build up firm-specific human capital with increased tenure on the job.[5] Because a firm must expend resources to invest in a new employee, employee turnover can generate substantial costs to an employer. For this reason, a firm has an interest in designing compensation schemes that discourage such turnover. One such scheme is to pay rising wage rates with advances in an employee's tenure. Another is to offer pension plans that require minimum service requirements before the employer's contribution to that plan is vested in the employee.

A second element in the theory is that an employee's productivity begins to decline at some point in his career, but because of the customs of the internal labor market, a firm cannot reduce a long-term employee's wages. For this reason, a firm has an interest in encouraging employees to retire at certain ages. The retirement income provided by a pension facilitates such induced retirement.[6]

In summary, this theory holds that a firm has an interest in keeping employees both from leaving too soon and from staying too long. The provision of a pension plan has the potential to promote both objectives. The plan's vesting rule—the minimum time that an employee must work on the job before he becomes eligible for any benefits at retirement age—creates an incentive to complete job tenures in excess of some desired minimum. Other features of pension plans, such as the pension benefit

5. Gary S. Becker, *Human Capital: A Theoretical and Empirical Analysis, with Special Reference to Education,* 2d ed. (Columbia University Press, 1975).

6. For a theoretical treatment of this aspect of pensions, see Edward P. Lazear, "Severance Pay, Pensions, and Efficient Mobility," National Bureau of Economic Research Working Paper 854 (Cambridge, Mass.: NBER, February 1982).

formula, credit for work past the "normal" retirement age, early retirement provisions, and integration of benefits with social security, may be manipulated to encourage job exit among older workers.[7]

The theory just described suggests why employers would want to offer pensions. Less clear are the reasons why employees would accept pensions rather than higher current wages. One reason is that employees may be concerned about their own myopia and the way in which current financial pressures may undermine their plans to save for retirement out of current income. Enforced pension contributions shield current income from these pressures. A second reason for preferring pensions is the tax advantages they confer. Since no current taxes are owed on employer contributions to a qualified pension plan, the worker can defer paying taxes on part of his compensation until the retirement years when his pension is paid and marginal tax rates are typically low.[8]

At several points we have used the phrase "the impact of pensions on completed job tenures." The phrase implies that pension coverage in some way changes the employee's behavior. The implication is only partially correct. As noted in the introduction, it is more accurate to say that pensions influence job tenures in two distinct ways, which we have called sorting and retention effects.

By retention effect we refer to the way in which a pension induces an employee to remain on a job longer than he would without the pension.[9]

---

7. For many years the literature on the labor market effects of pensions focused upon the general proposition that pensions encourage job attachment while noting that vesting provisions should encourage job mobility. See, for example, *Private Pension Plans and Manpower Policy,* Bureau of Labor Statistics Bulletin 1358 (Government Printing Office, 1963); and *Studies in Public Welfare,* Paper 11: "The Labor Market Impacts of the Private Retirement System," by Robert Taggart, prepared for the Joint Economic Committee, 93 Cong. 1 sess. (GPO, 1973). Recently, increased attention has been given to the retirement incentives of pension plans, both private and public. See Richard Burkhauser and Joseph Quinn, "The Effect of Changes in Mandatory Retirement Rules on the Labor Supply of Older Workers"; and Gary Burtless and Jerry Hausman, " 'Double Dipping': The Combined Effects of Social Security and Civil Service Pensions on Employee Retirement," *Journal of Public Economics,* vol. 18 (July 1982), pp. 139–59.

8. In "Private Pensions and Public Pensions: Theory and Fact," NBER Working Paper 902 (June 1982), Alan S. Blinder argues that this tax shielding was unimportant before World War II, when federal income taxes were low, but became particularly important after the war, when federal income taxes grew substantially. Blinder suggests that this accounts, in part, for the rapid growth of pensions in the postwar period.

9. We mean to distinguish this kind of change from the prior decision to select one job over another. That decision is the sorting effect described below.

To the extent that such an effect occurs, it often involves the interaction of the pension plan and circumstances that the employee did not anticipate when he joined the firm. A good example of an unanticipated circumstance is the interaction between unanticipated inflation and the benefit formula of a defined benefit pension plan. In most cases, this formula bases an employee's retirement benefit on his years of service to the firm and his average wage in the last years he worked for the firm. In an inflationary period, an employee who has held one long job under a defined benefit plan will receive substantially higher retirement benefits than an employee who has held several different jobs even though each job was covered by similar defined benefit plans. If employees do not anticipate inflation (which is often the case), a period of inflation may cause an employee to stay with his current job somewhat longer than he had initially intended. In this way, the employee's behavior has been changed, and job tenures have been lengthened.

Probably more prominent than this retention effect is the sorting effect, an effect that arises from the matching of worker preferences and job characteristics. Sorting effects occur because of differences among workers in the length of time they expect (or desire) to remain on any job.[10] Employers who need to develop substantial firm-specific human capital will wish to encourage long employee tenures and will consequently attempt to attract employees with preferences for long-term jobs. Pensions are one potential device for attracting workers with greater expected job attachment; if this sorting is effective, the observed distribution of job tenures in that firm will be longer than at otherwise comparable firms not offering pensions. While this lengthening depends on the proper matching of workers and jobs, it does not depend on any change in worker behavior—that is, any change in the tenure that each worker desires.

Because in the present work we are unable to model underlying differences among workers in desired job tenures, we are unable to isolate the sorting effects of pension plans. It follows that our estimates (in the last two sections) of the impact of pensions on completed job tenures contain both sorting effects and the retention effects described

10. Differences across workers in anticipated job tenure are assumed in many labor market models. See Joanne Salop and Steven Salop, "Self-Selection and Turnover in the Labor Market," *Quarterly Journal of Economics,* vol. 90 (November 1976), pp. 619–27; and Peter T. Gottschalk, "Employer-Initiated Job Terminations," *Southern Economic Journal,* vol. 49 (July 1982), pp. 35–44.

above and so serve as upper-bound approximations of the impact of pensions on job tenure in the aggregate. This follows since sorting helps explain the distribution of workers but in no way affects the duration of job tenure either individually or in the aggregate.

If the theoretical effects of pensions are unambiguous, the empirical magnitudes of those effects are largely unknown. The problem lies in the data. As noted earlier, because pensions are only one of a variety of mechanisms developed to retain employees, a complete test of the impact of pensions on tenure would have to include the other mechanisms as well—for example, past and expected rates of wage change. The data would also have to include the full range of pension plan characteristics— that is, participation and vesting rules, benefit formulas, and retirement provisions—as well as employee perceptions of those characteristics since those perceptions, often containing misinformation, are the assumed basis of behavior. Finally, the data would have to contain at least some information on completed careers and not be restricted to careers (and jobs) in progress. Not surprisingly, no data set includes all these characteristics.

Existing empirical studies do not attempt to explain completed job tenures but do examine the probability that a worker will leave his current job within a particular period of time.[11] These studies share a common framework based essentially on repeated surveys. An initial survey collects information about the worker (age, education, years to date on the current job, and so forth) and his job (pension coverage, wage rate, health benefits, and so forth). A later survey is administered to the same worker, perhaps one year later, and records whether the worker changed jobs in the intervening year. The worker and job characteristics in the first survey are then used to explain whether a job change occurred in the intervening year.

The theory of pensions discussed above predicts that when all other things are held constant, workers covered by pensions should have lower rates of job change than uncovered workers. This prediction has

11. Ann P. Bartel, "Wages, Nonwage Job Characteristics, and Labor Mobility," *Industrial and Labor Relations Review*, vol. 35 (July 1982), pp. 578–89; Olivia S. Mitchell, "Fringe Benefits and Labor Mobility," *Journal of Human Resources*, vol. 17 (Spring 1982), pp. 286–98; Herbert S. Parnes and Gilbert Nestel, "Middle-Age Job Changes," in Parnes and others, *The Pre-Retirement Years: Five Years in the Work Lives of Middle-Aged Men* (Columbus, Ohio: Center for Human Resources Research, 1974); Bradley R. Schiller and Randall D. Weiss, "The Impact of Private Pensions on Firm Attachment," *Review of Economics and Statistics*, vol. 6 (August 1979), pp. 369–80; and Burtless and Hausman, "Double Dipping."

been confirmed by a number of studies.[12] In most cases, these studies have looked at pension coverage per se and have not investigated the impact of the vesting rule on persons who were covered but not vested. The one study that did investigate pension vesting found that longer periods before vesting tended to increase quit rates, presumably because the longer vesting period reduces the worker's perception that vesting can be attained.[13] This result seems unexpected since the presumed goal of vesting is to reduce employee turnover.

Each of the studies reviewed here takes account of tenure-to-date when estimating the effect of pensions upon job exit. They are nonetheless of little use for inferring the distribution of completed job tenures because several other variables also included in the analysis vary over time. As a result, the probability of remaining on the job in the future depends on the time path of values of every explanatory variable, beginning with the time of job entry and continuing into the future.[14]

In summary, existing studies using microdata have usually confirmed the idea that pension coverage should depress job-exit rates at least for young and middle-aged workers.[15] But little is known about the detailed effect of particular vesting rules. Moreover, the fact that researchers work in terms of impact on quit rates and not in job tenures makes it difficult to assess the overall significance of the estimated impact. A 10 percent reduction in a quit rate may be statistically significant but unimportant from a policy perspective if quit rates are low and tenures are long in any case. It is for this reason that we have framed our own investigation in the context of job tenures.

Estimation Methodology

Our primary econometric objective is to relate patterns of job tenure to pension coverage and vesting rules. We wish to examine both the

12. A typical result is found in Mitchell, "Fringe Benefits and Labor Mobility." Mitchell's results indicate that pension coverage reduces the probability that men will leave their job by about 10 percent during a four-year time interval.

13. Schiller and Weiss, "Impact of Private Pensions on Firm Attachment."

14. For an example of a model of the duration of employment with time-varying explanatory variables, see the paper by Peter A. Diamond and Jerry A. Hausman in this volume.

15. Various other studies have analyzed the effect of pensions upon quit rates using grouped data; for example, John H. Pencavel, *An Analysis of the Quit Rate in American Manufacturing Industry* (Princeton, N.J.: Princeton University, Industrial Relations Section, 1970).

Douglas A. Wolf and Frank Levy

Figure 1. Hypothetical Distribution of Completed Job Tenure

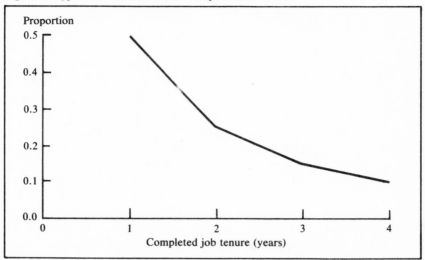

distribution of completed job tenures and the pattern of job attachment
at different tenures, each of which is hypothesized to vary by pension
status. Ideal data for our purposes would provide the starting and ending
dates, as well as the pension characteristics, of all jobs held over the
lifetime of a sample of workers. As noted earlier, available data files fall
short of this ideal in various respects. Our study is based upon data from
the May 1979 Current Population Survey, which is at present the largest
available data file containing information on both pension variables and
job tenure for a random sample of workers of all ages. Unfortunately,
the CPS tenure information is limited to tenure-in-progress on the job
held at the survey date. Thus, we use a modeling technique that permits
us to infer the distribution of completed tenure from the distribution of
partial tenures.[16]

Our estimation problem can be represented graphically. For purposes
of illustration, suppose that jobs of a certain type, which we shall call
type i (for example, manufacturing jobs that do not offer pension plans),
last exactly one, two, three, or four years, in the proportions shown in
figure 1. Assume also that the pattern shown in figure 1 holds regardless

16. Our approach is similar to that used to analyze the duration of spells of
unemployment in progress, in Stephen Nickell, "Estimating the Probability of Leaving
Unemployment," *Econometrica*, vol. 47 (September 1979), pp. 1249–66.

Figure 2. Time Profile of Job Entry for a Hypothetical Cohort

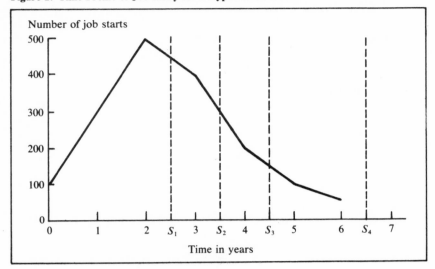

of a worker's age at job entry. Finally, suppose that within a well-defined cohort of people (for example, men born in a particular year), type i jobs are begun at the times and levels shown in figure 2. The time origin ($t = 0$) shown in figure 2 corresponds to the earliest age at which cohort members begin to work at type i jobs. The patterns shown in figures 1 and 2, while both simplified and exaggerated, nevertheless are illustrative of the actual patterns uncovered in our subsequent analysis.

Given the patterns depicted in figures 1 and 2, we can readily calculate the expected distributions by tenure-in-progress that would be found in surveys of our hypothetical cohort, taken at different times. For example, a midyear survey taken at time S_2 (that is, $t = 3.5$) would sample from a population in which all 400 of those beginning jobs at time $t = 3$ are still on the job (with tenure-in-progress equal to 0.5 years), one-half of the 500 that started jobs at time $t = 2$ are still on the job (with tenure-in-progress equal to 1.5 years), and so on. Similar calculations yield the proportionate distributions by tenure-in-progress at times S_1, S_3, and S_4 in figure 3. It is clear from figure 3 that the distribution of tenure-in-progress can differ greatly from the distribution of completed tenure shown in figure 1. If our information were confined to data such as those depicted in figure 3, we could say very little about the underlying pattern

Figure 3. Expected Distributions of Tenure-in-Progress for a Hypothetical Cohort, for Various Service Dates

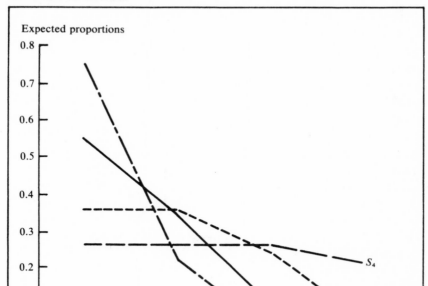

of completed job tenure.[17] However, with data of the type shown in figure 3, combined with data on the job-entry process pictured in figure 2, we can work backward, calculating the distribution of completed job

17. Completed-tenure distributions can be inferred from interrupted-tenure distributions in conditions of equilibrium, that is, conditions characterized by equal and stable patterns of inflow to and outflow from jobs, and tenure-in-progress distributions that remain constant over time. See Hyman B. Kaitz, "Analyzing the Length of Spells of Unemployment," *Monthly Labor Review,* vol. 93 (November 1970), pp. 11–20; Stephen W. Salant, "Search Theory and Duration Data: A Theory of Sorts," *Quarterly Journal of Economics,* vol. 91 (February 1977), pp. 39–57; and Robert H. Frank, "How Long Is a Spell of Unemployment?" *Econometrica,* vol. 46 (March 1978), pp. 285–302. In our hypothetical example, as well as in our subsequent analysis, we consider subgroups of the population defined with respect to narrow age intervals, for which the equilibrium assumption is clearly inappropriate. Even for broad age groups, we would hesitate to assume that the process generating job-tenure patterns is in equilibrium, given the observed changes over time in the pension and vesting characteristics of jobs.

tenures that is consistent with the observed tenure-in-progress distribution. Thus, to implement our analytic technique, we must supplement our CPS data with data showing the rate of entry into jobs over time. The job-entry data we use are described more fully below. A further analytic problem inherent in tenure-in-progress data can be illustrated with the aid of figures 1 to 3. Note that in the hypothetical completed-tenure distribution (figure 1), no jobs last longer than four years. This fact would go undetected in an analysis of data collected at times S_1 and S_2 (figure 2), both of which are less than four years after the earliest known job starts within the cohort being studied. With actual data, the problem of truncation of the tenure-in-progress variable is manifestly present. For young men, for example aged 25, we observe job tenures-in-progress of no more than eight or ten years, although the distribution of completed tenure on the jobs held at the survey date by these men will extend to thirty, forty, and even fifty years.

There are two basic ways to deal with the truncation problem, both of which are used in our analysis. The first is to assume a functional form for the completed-tenure distribution, allowing us, in effect, to extrapolate beyond the range of data contained in our sample. For reasons explained below, we use only those CPS observations for which tenure-in-progress is no more than twenty-seven years. Thus, we infer the shape of that portion of the completed-tenure distribution that lies beyond twenty-seven years by extrapolation of our estimated function. From our hypothetical example, it is evident that a sample of job tenures taken at time S_1, in combination with the information contained in figure 2, would allow us to infer the proportions of jobs ending after one year and after two years, as well as the proportion lasting more than two years. However, only by assuming some mathematical function to describe the distribution of completed tenures could we allocate completed job tenures in excess of two years to the categories three years, four years, and so on. In the example just given, if we had no basis for imposing the condition that no jobs last more than four years (the true state of affairs in our hypothetical illustration), we might erroneously adopt a mathematical model that encompasses completed job tenures of five or more years. A second modeling strategy, which we also employ, is to assume that the relative frequencies of completed job tenure found among older cohorts, for whom longer tenures-in-progress can be observed, will pertain as well to younger cohorts as they continue to age.

One final point concerning the use of tenure-in-progress data deserves mention. From the previous discussion of the hypothetical data shown in figures 1 to 3, it is clear that, given data collected at a particular survey date, we infer the probability that a job will last at least t years—denoting that probability $F(t)$—by combining information on the number of jobs that began t years ago with the number of jobs with current tenure equal to t. An identical procedure is used to compute the probabilities $F(t + 1)$, $F(t + 2)$, and so on. Our method obviously requires the assumption that the estimated values of $F(1)$, $F(2)$, . . . each of which is based on jobs of a different (single-year) vintage, held by workers in different (single-year) cohorts, all pertain to the same underlying completed-tenure distribution. In other words, we assume that the pattern of completed job tenure is stable during the time period, and across the birth cohorts, spanned by the data analyzed.

Fundamental to our model of completed job tenure is the hazard function, which describes the mathematical relationship between the job-exit rate and tenure-to-date on the job. We assume that the hazard function depends upon both job tenure itself (t) and variables representing worker and job attributes (x), such as the worker's age at job entry, pension coverage, and, as appropriate, the vesting rule. The hazard function is analogous to the demographic notion of age-specific death rates and the failure-rate concept used in reliability theory. Given a particular hazard function, we can calculate the other quantities of interest, for example, the probability, at job entry, that completed job tenure will exceed any specified value and the distribution of completed job tenures.[18]

In our study we have adopted a quadratic functional form for the hazard function,

(1) $$h(t, x) = \exp(a_x + b_x t + c_x t^2),$$

18. Formally, let $F(t, x)$ represent the cumulative distribution function for completed job tenures t for jobs with attributes x, while $\bar{F}(t, x) = 1 - F(t, x)$ represents the survivor function, or the probability that completed job tenure exceeds t. Finally, write $h(t, x)$ for the tenure-specific hazard function. These functions are related to one another by the equations

$$h(t, x) = \frac{dF(t, x)}{\bar{F}(t, x)},$$

$$\bar{F}(t,, x) = \exp\left[-\int_0^t h(z, x)\,dz\right].$$

For derivations of these relationships, see David R. Cox, *Renewal Theory* (London: Methuen, 1967), pp. 1–5; or John D. Kalbfleisch and Ross L. Prentice, *The Statistical Analysis of Failure Time Data* (Wiley, 1980), pp. 6–7.

with a, b, and c as unknown parameters to be estimated. The subscript x denotes the dependence of a parameter upon the attribute vector x. This functional form permits the tenure-specific job-exit rate to assume a variety of shapes, including the initially rising, and then declining, form predicted by recent models of employer-employee job matching and turnover.[19] We postulate the existence of two families of hazard functions, that is, two sets of the unknown coefficients a, b, and c to be estimated. One set pertains to jobs not covered by pension plans; the other, to jobs covered by pension plans. In the latter case, we adopt a specification whereby the hazard function can exhibit a discontinuous jump at the point of vesting, reflecting a sudden change in the degree of job attachment at that point.

We obtain our estimates of the unknown coefficients by maximum-likelihood methods.[20] While our hazard function model is formulated in continuous time, the CPS data record tenure-to-date in whole years. We assume that each respondent reports his job's tenure (t^*) as its "age at last anniversary" and construct an expression for the probability that, at the survey date, the respondent is on a type-x job with tenure-in-progress between t^* and $t^* + 1$ years. The numerator of this probability is the product of (1) the rate of entry into type-x jobs t^* years before the survey and (2) the probability that someone entering a type-x job t^* years ago will remain at that job at least t^* years. It is in the second of these components that the parameters of the hazard function appear. The denominator of the probability is the sum of terms of the same form as that appearing in the numerator, with t^* replaced by a series of numbers running from zero to the maximum possible value of tenure-in-progress (assumed in our study to be the respondent's current age minus fourteen years).

Our ability to infer the distribution of completed job tenures from information on partial job tenures—hence to identify the unknown parameters a_x, b_x, and c_x—depends critically upon having exogenous knowledge of the rate of entry into type-x jobs over time. However, knowledge of the rate of job entry over time is very difficult to obtain. In this paper our analysis is limited to manufacturing jobs that began after

19. See Boyan Jovanovic, "Job Matching and the Theory of Turnover," *Journal of Political Economy*, vol. 87 (October 1979), pp, 972–90.

20. The algorithm used in this study is that of Fletcher-Powell-Davidon, found in Gunnar T. Gruvaeus and Karl G. Joreskog, "A Computer Program for Minimizing a Function of Several Variables," Educational Testing Service Memorandum RB-70-14 (Princeton, N.J.: ETS, 1970).

1950 because we were able to construct annual rates of job entry only for such jobs. However, because manufacturing jobs were held by about 23 percent of all men aged 20 to 64 in the May 1979 CPS, our analysis pertains directly to a significant minority of the population. Because of the difficulty of obtaining information on job entry, by job attributes, over time, we consider only the following attributes: the worker's age, whether a job provides pension coverage, and, for jobs with pension coverage, the tenure requirement for vesting of benefits. Details on the job-entry data constructed for this study are presented in the appendix.

To clarify further the role of the job-entry rates in our model, we consider a man aged 25 at the time of the CPS survey. By assumption his maximum possible tenure is 11—that is, 25 minus 14. The probability that his reported tenure is t and that his current job offers no pension plan is the product of $r_{uc,25-t}(s - t)$—the rate of entry by $(25 - t)$-year-olds into uncovered jobs at time $(s - t)$—times the probability that an uncovered job begun at age $(25 - t)$ will last at least t years. This product is, in general, positive for $t = 0, 1, \ldots 11.$[21]

Before presenting our estimation results, we need to explain more fully certain limitations of the CPS data. First, many respondents do not know the details of their pension plans. Some respondents did not know if their employer offered a pension plan; others did not know whether they were participants. More commonly, workers who reported their participation in a plan did not know whether their benefits were vested or did not know the additional tenure required in order to become vested.[22] Cases were excluded from our analysis unless we were able to determine unambiguously that they were (1) not covered by a pension;

21. However, the corresponding probabilities for jobs covered by pension plans are somewhat more complicated and depend upon the plan's vesting requirement. Consider, for example, jobs with vesting after five years ($VRULE = 5$). Respondents with five-year vesting will be vested in their current job's pension plan ($VESTED = 1$) only if their current tenure exceeds five years. That is, the rate of entry into jobs with the *current* attributes $VRULE = 5$ and $VESTED = 1$ is zero for the five most recent years; before this, it is merely the rate of entry into jobs with five-year vesting rules. Similarly, the only admissible values of current job tenure for jobs with the attributes $VRULE = 5$ and $VESTED = 0$ are zero through four. These restrictions on the possible values of job tenure—given coverage, vesting rules, and vested status—are reflected in the job-entry data used in our estimation.

22. In addition, respondents were not asked directly about their plan's vesting rule. Instead, we inferred the rule by summing years of participation in the plan with the additional years required for vesting. Although this procedure yielded reasonable vesting rules for most cases, some cases with computed vesting rules exceeding fifteen years (the maximum permitted for full vesting under ERISA) were excluded.

(2) participating in a plan, with benefits not yet vested, and with a vesting requirement of fifteen years of tenure or less; or (3) participating in a plan with vested benefits.

Second, some CPS respondents evidently failed to distinguish partial from full vesting.[23] Under the alternative minimum vesting provisions permitted by ERISA, if gradual vesting is used, partial vesting must occur within five to ten years of participation, depending upon the participant's age and the particular vesting option chosen, leading to full vesting after no more than fifteen years of participation. Thus, CPS respondents with calculated vesting requirements in the range of eleven to fifteen years are evidently reporting full rather than partial vesting provisions. Some ambiguity is therefore introduced into our analysis through our use of calculated vesting rules that refer in some cases to partial, and in other cases to full, vesting.

Third, the CPS data do not permit us to reconstruct each worker's pension status for the lifetime of the job held at the survey date. Workers participating in a pension plan are asked the tenure of their participation, which is less than the tenure of their employment in many cases. In such cases, we are unable to determine whether the employer instituted the plan during the employee's job tenure or whether an existing plan imposed a tenure-based participation requirement. In the analyses reported here, we treat initial periods of nonparticipation as part of the vesting requirement of the pension plan. This measure greatly simplifies our estimation problem but may introduce some biases into the estimates since it ignores the possibility of unforeseen introduction of pension plans for previously uncovered jobs.

Fourth, a problem arises because CPS respondents who reported a vested benefit on their current job were not asked the point at which vesting was achieved. In such cases we know only that the tenure required for vesting is less than current tenure. This lack of complete knowledge introduces an indeterminacy to our estimates, as it precludes modeling the hypothesized shift in the job-exit hazard function at the vesting point for those already vested.

A final problem occurs because the CPS interview asked only about the existence of pension coverage and vesting requirements but did not

23. Respondents who were not yet eligible to receive ". . . some benefits at retirement" and for whom such ineligibility was due to insufficient tenure were asked, "How many *more* years must you be included in this plan in order to eventually receive *some* retirement benefit?"

obtain information about other pension characteristics. If a substantial variation exists in the generosity of the plans that cover our sample, we should expect a corresponding imprecision in our estimates of the ability of vested pension benefits (expressed as a yes-no condition) to affect job tenures.

It follows that our analysis, too, will have limitations. But the estimates that follow present a picture of the relationship between pension coverage, vesting rules, and the distribution of completed job tenures in ways that extend previous findings.

Results

Our model consists of two estimated job-exit or hazard functions, one each for uncovered and for covered manufacturing jobs. In each case we have estimated separate intercepts for several categories of age at job entry but a single set of "duration effect" parameters for all age groups.

For uncovered jobs, our estimated tenure hazard function, which depends upon age at job entry (AGE_0) and tenure itself, is

(2) $$h(t, AGE_0) = \exp(a - 0.084t),$$
$$(0.016)$$

in which $a = -0.715$ if $14 \leq AGE_0 < 20$,
$$(-0.110)$$
$\quad\quad a = -0.736$ if $20 \leq AGE_0 < 25$,
$$(-0.115)$$
$\quad\quad a = -0.943$ if $25 \leq AGE_0 < 30$,
$$(-0.124)$$
$\quad\quad a = -1.094$ if $30 \leq AGE_0 < 35$;
$$(-0.134)$$
$\quad\quad a = -1.035$ if $35 \leq AGE_0 \; 45$, and
$$(-0.120)$$
$\quad\quad a = -1.066$ if $45 \leq AGE_0 < 65$.
$$(-0.149)$$

Standard errors of the estimated parameters are shown in parentheses. Thus we find significant negative duration dependence for uncovered jobs—that is, rates of job exit that decrease as tenure increases.[24] We also find some evidence of age-at-entry effects, with higher exit rates out of jobs begun at younger ages. For example, the intercept of the job-exit hazard for jobs entered at ages 20 to 25 is $\exp(-0.736) = 0.48$ while the corresponding intercept for ages 30 to 35 is 0.33.

For covered jobs, our estimated hazard function is

$$
(3) \quad h(t, AGE_o) = \begin{cases} \exp\,[a + (0.265 - 0.045 VRULE)t] \text{ if } t < VRULE \\ \qquad\qquad (0.268) \quad (0.026) \\[2ex] \exp\,(a + 0.300t - 0.031t^2) \text{ if } t \geq VRULE, \\ \qquad\quad (0.107) \quad (0.008), \end{cases}
$$

in which $a = -1.389$ if $14 \leq AGE_o < 20$;

$\qquad\quad (-0.317)$

$\qquad a = -1.594$ if $20 \leq AGE_o < 25$;

$\qquad\quad (-0.323)$

$\qquad a = -1.587$ if $25 \leq AGE_o < 30$;

$\qquad\quad (-0.324)$

$\qquad a = -1.572$ if $30 \leq AGE_o < 65$.[25]

$\qquad\quad (-0.326)$

VRULE is the number of years of tenure required for vesting in the worker's pension plan. Attempts to estimate a fuller set of intercepts, representing more detailed entry-age effects, proved unsuccessful. We were also unable to estimate a quadratic duration effect prior to vesting, presumably owing to the inherently restricted range of tenure data prior to vesting. Finally, as explained earlier, the vesting rule is unknown for those already vested when interviewed for the CPS; therefore the VRULE variable does not appear in the postvesting hazard function.

As shown in the first line of equation 3, our model treats vesting requirements as a determinant of the duration-dependence parameter of the job-exit hazard function. According to these estimates, the rate of job leaving rises as tenure increases for vesting rules shorter than 5.9

24. When this equation is reestimated incorporating both linear and quadratic duration-dependence parameters—b and c in equation 1—neither parameter is statistically significant. The estimated parameters imply negative duration dependence for tenure in excess of 0.56 years, a pattern essentially captured by the simpler specification reported here.

25. Equations 2 and 3 are based on 550 and 1,410 observations, respectively.

Figure 4. Tenure-Specific Job-Exit Rates for Job Entry at Age 25

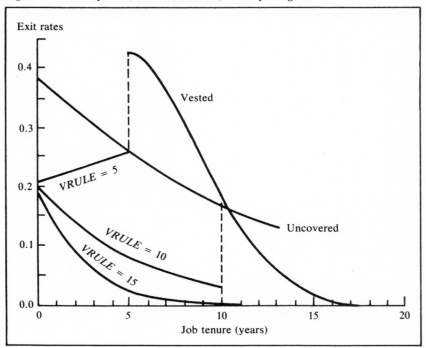

years ($\approx 0.265/0.045$) but declines as tenure increases for vesting rules longer than 5.9 years.[26] Moreover, the model implies that, at a given value of job tenure, job attachment is stronger—and, conversely, exit rates are lower—the larger the tenure requirement is for vesting of benefits.[27]

Job-exit rates associated with five-year, ten-year, and fifteen-year vesting rules are plotted in figure 4. For comparative purposes, the estimated exit rate for uncovered jobs is also shown. For each vesting rule shown, our model implies an increased rate of job exit upon attainment of vested benefits. The increase is shown as a dashed vertical line in figure 4. Statistical tests of the magnitude of the discrete shift in the job-exit hazard function—the discontinuities plotted in figure 4—

26. That is, $\partial h(t)/\partial t > 0$, for $0 < t < VRULE$, if $VRULE < 5.9$, while $\partial h(t)/\partial t < 0$, for $0 < t < VRULE$, if $VRULE > 5.9$.

27. That is, given $t = t'$, $\partial h(t')/\partial VRULE < 0$.

indicate that the shift is significant for $VRULE > 9$.[28] In particular, the shift is significant at $VRULE = 10$ ($t \approx 3.1$), where the majority of our sample is concentrated. This finding is consistent with the hypothesis that job mobility is increased after workers become vested in their pension plans. The pattern of job terminations shown also supports the notion that vesting provisions are an effective mechanism for encouraging employee attachment to the firm. However, as pointed out elsewhere in this paper, we are unable to infer the relative importance of selective matching of workers and firms with respect to expected tenure—the "sorting" effect. Hence our estimates cannot be used to infer impacts of pensions on the aggregate distribution of job tenure.

Our estimated job-exit hazard function can be used to compute the distribution of completed job tenures (see note 18). Three examples of such completed-tenure distributions are shown in figure 5. This figure shows completed-tenure distributions for (1) uncovered jobs, (2) covered jobs with five-year vesting, and (3) covered jobs with ten-year vesting; in each case, an entry age of 25 to 29 is assumed. Note that irrespective of pension coverage or the vesting rule, jobs most frequently end during their first year. However, many more uncovered than covered jobs are of short completed tenure. Moreover, there is a distinct bulge in the tenure distribution of covered jobs in the year immediately after vesting occurs.

In illustration of the association between vesting provisions and job-tenure patterns, the mean and median of the distribution of completed job tenure for covered jobs with vesting rules from one to fifteen years are shown in figure 6. Once again the age at job entry is assumed to be 25. This figure also shows the probability that a worker will become vested under each vesting rule. The means and medians were calculated using the assumption that no jobs last past age 65. The probability of

28. The tests were performed using a formula for the variance of an arbitrary function of a set of estimated parameters given in Harold Cramer, *Mathematical Methods of Statistics* (Princeton University Press, 1946), pp. 353–54. For a given vesting rule ($VRULE$) and intercept (a_o), the function giving the magnitude of the shift in the job-exit hazard is

$$d = \exp (a_o + b_2 VRULE + c_2 VRULE^2)$$
$$- \exp [a_o + (b_{10} + b_{11} VRULE)VRULE];$$

to approximate the variance of d, we calculate

$$\text{var} (d) = [\partial d/\partial a_o]^2 \, \text{var} (a_o) + \ldots$$
$$+ 2 \, [\partial d/\partial a_o] \, [\partial d/\partial b_2] \, \text{cov} (a_o, b_2) + \ldots.$$

Figure 5. Discrete Density of Completed Job Tenure for Job Entry at Age 25[a]

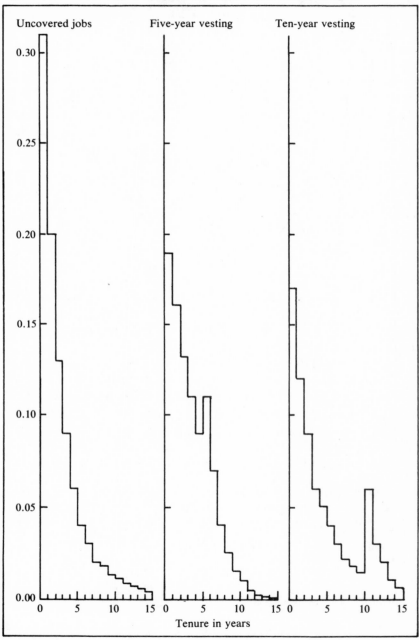

a. The vertical axis measures the proportion of workers who exit their jobs in the indicated year.

Figure 6. Mean and Median Tenure Vesting Probabilities for Job Entry at Age 25, by Vesting Requirement

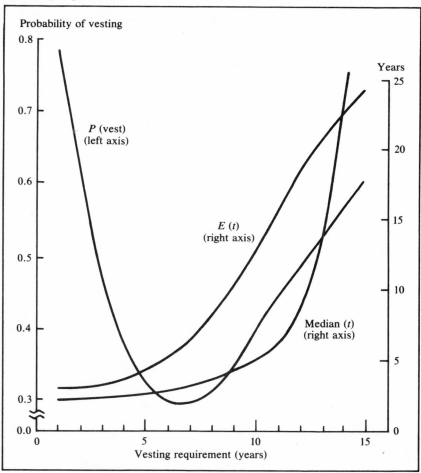

vesting is quite high on jobs with minimal tenure requirements but falls rapidly to a minimum at six-year vesting rules. An unexpected finding is the rising probability of vesting for vesting requirements in excess of seven years. It must be remembered that our findings are based upon a simple, continuous specification with linear dependence of the "duration-dependence" parameter upon the vesting rule. Alternative formulations of the vesting-rule effect have not been explored. In our data, a majority (60 percent) of the sample of covered workers faces ten-year vesting requirements; smaller concentrations are found at five, nine, eleven, and fifteen years, and traces are found at other reported vesting rules. One possible interpretation of the pattern of rising vesting probabilities as vesting requirements are raised above seven years is that stringent vesting rules more effectively select workers with expectations of long tenure. It is also possible that long vesting requirements are associated with more generous benefit formulas (in defined benefit plans) and more steeply sloped wage profiles, both of which would reduce the probability of job separation.

Figure 6 reveals steadily rising means and medians for longer vesting requirements. The effect of the vesting rule is pronounced, with the mean of the tenure distribution rising from about 3.5 years on one-year vesting jobs to nearly 25.0 years with fifteen-year vesting requirements. For purposes of comparison, the mean and median for uncovered jobs beginning at age 25 are 3.2 and 1.9 years, respectively.

Our discussion so far has focused exclusively on the tenure distribution for a single job, given the worker's age at job entry and the job's pension characteristics. Yet the high estimated probability of early job separation implies that a typical career will consist of several jobs rather than one. Moreover, to the extent that our findings reveal age effects on job mobility, we would expect these several jobs to be organized in a pattern of short jobs followed by one or two longer jobs. To consider job-tenure patterns in a context of a working life, we have devised a simple simulation model of career job-entry and exit patterns. In the last section of this paper, we describe our simulation model and its findings.

Simulation Results

To minimize complexity, in our comparisons we used a simulation model that embodies a number of simplifying features. First, the model is confined to data on males in the manufacturing sector, a restriction that follows from the sample used in our parameter estimation. Second, the model ignores the possibility of unemployment or labor force withdrawal and represents each career as an unbroken series of jobs from ages 20 to 65. This feature means that our model does not give sufficient attention to the impact on job tenures of college education at younger ages and early retirement or disability at older ages.

The actual workings of the model are summarized in the flow diagram pictured in figure 7. At age 20 the worker is initially assigned to any of four pension regimes: an uncovered job or a covered job with a five-year, ten-year, or fifteen-year vesting rule. These regimes are assigned randomly to conform with proportions observed in the May 1979 CPS. The person's tenure in the job is then determined by comparing a random draw on the (0,1) interval to the job survival probabilities calculated from the hazard functions described in the section on results. As noted there, these survival probabilities vary with both the age group of the worker and the regime of pension coverage.

At the end of the worker's job we tabulate the tenure of the job; whether the job was covered by a pension; if covered, whether vesting was attained; and the age of vesting (if any). These records are kept for each person and for the group as a whole as of certain benchmark years (for example, ages 25, 35, 45, and so on). Tenures-to-date are also kept for these benchmark ages to facilitate comparisons between the simulation results and published tenure-to-date data.

Having completed his first job, the worker is assigned to his second job in one of five pension regimes: an uncovered job, a covered job with a five-year, ten-year, or fifteen-year vesting rule, or a covered job with immediate vesting. The assignment is made in accordance with probabilities, which depend on the person's current age (three categories) and pension coverage and vesting status on previous jobs (three categories). Data for this transition matrix were derived from tabulations of recent job entrants in the May 1979 CPS. The matrix itself is reapplied at the end of each successive job up to retirement at age 65. Simulations were performed for two populations: an artificial cohort of 1,000 20-year-olds for whom a forty-five year career was simulated; and the men employed in manufacturing in the May 1979 CPS for whom the pension "regime" of the current job could be determined ($n = 1,869$) and for whom the remainder of a career ending at age 65 was simulated.[29]

---

29. The spirit of these simulations is close to the simulations developed by Izzet Sahin and Yves Balcer, but important differences exist. Sahin and Balcer are interested in how different pension rules affect pension benefits through the accumulation of years of pensionable service. For simplicity, they impose different kinds of pension rules on an unchanging set of behavioral assumptions. Thus in their simulation, the probability that a person leaves a job in a particular year depends on his age and his tenure-to-date on the job but *not* on his pension coverage or vesting status. Our central question—the way in which pension rules change job tenures—cannot be examined by their model. See Izzet Sahin and Yves Balcer, "Planning for the Future: Pensionable Service and Pension Benefits," *Journal of Risk and Insurance,* vol. 46 (March 1979), pp. 99–124, especially pp. 110 ff.

Figure 7. Flow Diagram of Simulation Model

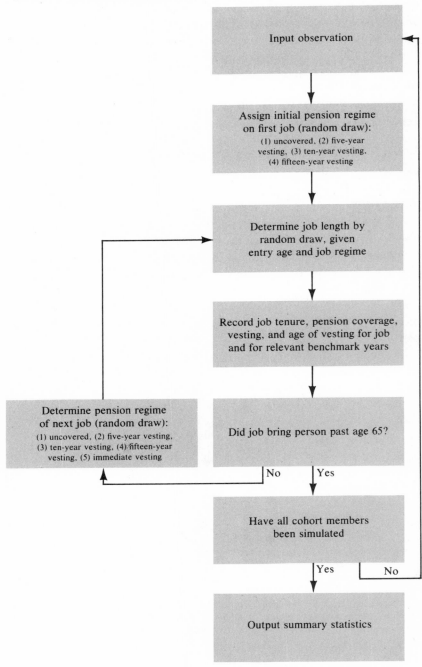

48

The Baseline Simulation

Our discussion of simulation results begins with a description of our baseline run. In this run our artificial cohort of young men passes through forty-five-year careers. Their probabilities of working in uncovered jobs and in covered jobs under immediate, five-year, ten-year, and fifteen-year vesting rules reflect the actual cross-sectional probabilities that existed for men in manufacturing jobs in 1979.

In fact, both pension coverage and vesting provisions were significantly more liberal in 1979 than in, for example, 1955. It follows that by the time one of our simulated workers reaches age 65 his career will have taken place under pension conditions that are more liberal than the conditions that faced an actual manufacturing worker who was 65 in May 1979. We shall return to this point at the end of this section.

The simulation is best described through the job tenures it generates, and these are summarized in figure 8 (solid line) and in table 1. Figure 8 portrays the distribution of *all* job tenures generated by the model. A comparison of the distribution's median, 2.56 years, with its mean, 6.48 years, suggests that it is consistent with the turnover-duration paradox described earlier, and this suggestion is correct. The mean and median number of jobs held by our typical worker are both about 5.35. If all of these jobs were of equal length, we would expect the typical job to last about 8.5 years. But the median job lasts 2.56 years while the median of the distribution of the *longest* job held by each worker is 25.6 years. Thus our baseline simulation describes a world in which a person experiences a fair amount of job shopping but, by age 40, has typically settled into a job that lasts until age 65.

How realistic are these results? The most readily available basis for comparison is the distributions of tenure-to-date published for various age-sex groups by the Bureau of Labor Statistics and tenure-to-date distributions generated by the model. This comparison appears in table 1, columns 1 and 2.[30] The comparisons suggest that the model produces

30. For purposes of comparison, the statistics from the Bureau of Labor Statistics have been modified in two respects. First, we have used linear interpolation to convert the age group data provided by the bureau into data for the single ages tabulated by the model. Second, the aggregate data for men of all ages suggest that median tenures-to-date are about 11 percent higher in manufacturing than for all industries as a whole. For this reason, we have inflated the age-specific data by 11 percent to provide a better basis for comparison.

Figure 8. Distribution of All Job Tenures under Various Scenarios

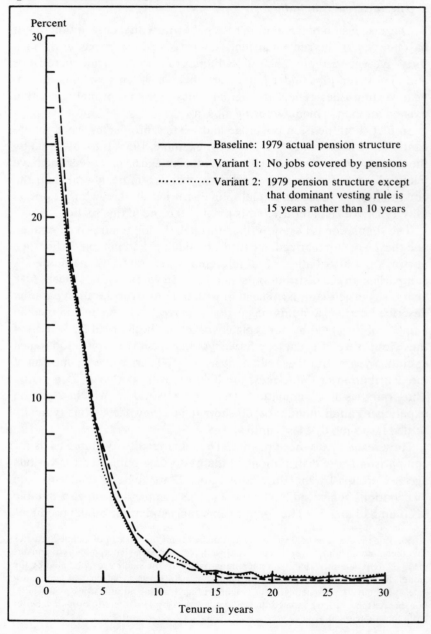

Table 1. Selected Tenure Statistics from Baseline Simulation and from the Bureau of Labor Statistics Survey, by Age

Age	Median tenure-to-date of current job for simulated cohort (1)	Adjusted median tenure-to-date of current job for men, 1978[a] (2)	Median completed tenure of current job for simulated cohort (3)
25	3.01	1.89; 2.78[b]	4.49
35	5.26	5.28	13.19
45	9.91	9.90	26.10
55	17.80	14.90	26.20
65	27.53	15.00	26.40

Sources: Columns 1 and 3, authors' calculations; column 2, authors' calculations based on U.S. Bureau of Labor Statistics, "Job Tenure Declines as Work Force Changes," Special Labor Force Report 235 (GPO, 1980).

a. See note 30 of the text for a discussion of these adjustments.

b. The first figure is the adjusted median tenure for men aged 25. The second is the adjusted median tenure for men aged 25 to 29.

quite realistic results for men at ages 35, 45, and 55 but estimates tenures-to-date that are too long for men at ages 25 and (in particular) 65.

The model's overestimation of tenure for men at age 25 arises from the fact that all men in our simulated cohort begin work histories at age 20 whereas many 25-year-old men in the Bureau of Labor Statistics sample began work histories only after completing several years of higher education.[31] Similarly, our serious overestimation of job tenures-to-date for men aged 65 (27.5 years versus a true value of 15.0 years) arises from the fact that our sample is restricted to men holding manufacturing jobs. Although few men retire completely before age 62, significant numbers of men leave their "main" jobs—the jobs from which they derived their pension coverage—and take other postretirement jobs. Typically these jobs will *not* be in manufacturing and, conversely, those older workers who are in manufacturing will be characterized by exceedingly long job tenures. Thus the model's results are realistic enough provided one recognizes they refer to manufacturing jobs rather than to all jobs.[32]

31. Note, for example, that the model's estimated tenure-to-date for 25-year-olds of 3.01 compares poorly with the interpolated value of 1.89 years. But the model's estimated tenure-to-date compares reasonably well with the adjusted Bureau of Labor Statistics figure of 2.78 years for men in the age group 25 to 29.

32. A more technical problem arises in our specification of the job-exit hazard function. For simplicity we have assumed that the job-leaving probabilities of different age groups shift up or down by a constant amount but have the same time dependence—that is, different age groups differ only in the a coefficient of equation 1 but share the

A final point to note in table 1 is the comparison between median tenures-to-date (which are readily available from published sources) and median completed tenures (which are not). These estimated completed tenures are contained in table 1, column 3. At age 25 tenure-to-date and completed tenure are relatively close: a typical worker will have already completed three years of what would be a 4.5-year job. By age 35 the statistics begin to diverge, with the worker having completed 5.25 years out of a 13.2-year job. And by age 45 the typical worker will have settled into what will be his longest job, the job from which he retires. Thus from age 45 on, the ultimate tenure of the job in progress remains constant at about twenty-six years while the tenure-to-date simply increases with age.

The Effect of the Pension System

Having described our baseline simulation, we turn to a second simulation that we use to assess the upper bound of the pension system's impact on job tenures. In this simulation all workers are assigned to uncovered jobs throughout their careers. When one uncovered job ends, they are reassigned to another. To the extent that uncovered jobs have lower survival probabilities than covered jobs, this procedure should result in shorter job tenures and weaker employee attachment.

We refer to this estimate as an upper bound because of the sorting effect described before. Recall that through this effect, an employer who offers a pension plan or other deferred compensation should attract workers with low job-exit probabilities—that is, workers with relatively high expected tenure on any job. To the extent that this unmeasured worker characteristic underlies job attachment, a portion of the upper tail of the tenure distribution would remain even if the pension system were abolished.

Figure 8 permits a comparison of the distribution of all jobs under our baseline simulation to the corresponding distribution from the no-pension simulation (variant 1). Although these plotted distributions

---

same b and c coefficients. This means that the time dependence of the entire model will be dominated by the behavior of nonretiring workers—for example, those aged 25 to 50—who make up the bulk of the sample. To the extent that retiring workers exhibit different patterns of time dependence, our estimating procedure will not capture it. This feature of our model may partly explain the divergence between the simulated medians and BLS median for 65-year-olds shown in the last line of table 1.

Table 2. Comparison of Simulated Summary Measures, Alternative Scenarios
Tenures in years

Item	Baseline (1)	No pensions (variant 1) (2)	Pre-ERISA (variant 2) (3)
Mean tenure, all jobs	6.48	4.08	6.84
Median tenure, all jobs	2.56	2.26	2.56
Median number of jobs held during career	5.40	10.10	5.00
Median tenure, longest job	25.60	11.05	28.20
Median tenure to date at age:			
25	3.01	2.36	3.14
35	5.26	3.16	5.91
45	9.91	3.54	10.98
55	17.25	4.53	19.71
65	27.00	5.39	29.71

Source: Authors' calculations.

appear similar, the accumulation of their small differences produces substantial overall differences. These overall differences are shown in table 2, which contains a comparison of the two distributions along several dimensions (see columns 1 and 2).

The comparison shows a significant weakening of job attachment in the absence of pensions. Without pensions, the median worker now holds about 10 jobs in his career (compared with a former 5.4); the median tenure of all jobs held falls to 2.26 years from 2.56 years; and the median tenure of the longest job held by each worker drops to 11.05 years from a previous 25.6 years. Together these figures suggest hypothetical career patterns in which lifetime jobs of twenty years or more are far less important than in the baseline run, which uses prevailing pension-coverage patterns. The hypothetical patterns suggest that firms interested in building up and retaining firm-specific human capital would require alternative mechanisms for doing so. Thus, these upper-bound limits suggest the current pension system may play an important part in encouraging worker attachment and long job tenures.

The Effect of ERISA

We turn next to the effect of ERISA on job tenures. Because the pension regimes in our baseline simulation are based on coverage and vesting-rule probabilities from the May 1979 CPS, the simulation represents behavior in a post-ERISA world. But the change from pre-ERISA to post-ERISA combines two different trends. The first is the continuous growth in pension coverage that occurred during the 1950s and the 1960s. The second is a trend toward more liberal (that is, shorter) vesting rules that had also been going on for some time but that ERISA accelerated. Our interest here is in the second factor. It is reasonable to suppose (and the results in our model confirm) that longer vesting periods lead to longer job tenures as people remain on the job at least long enough to vest some benefits. ERISA placed limits on vesting rules requiring that all pensions either vest full benefits after no more than ten years, or begin by ten years a process of graded vesting that leads to full vesting after no more than fifteen years. These limits raise two questions. First, were the limits binding in the sense that they induced changes in employer behavior? And second, to the extent that employer behavior was changed, was there a consequent weakening of employee job attachment?

The answer to the first question appears to be yes. Available data, although sketchy, indicate a long-run trend toward more liberal vesting provisions prior to 1974 when ERISA became law. For example, in 1952 only 25 percent of a group of 300 large collectively bargained pension plans had any sort of vesting provisions; by 1958 this figure had grown to 60 percent, with further growth to 70 percent of a much wider range of plans by 1967.[33] More relevant is the trend in worker coverage by plans with vesting provisions; this coverage grew from 60 percent in 1962 to 77 percent in 1969. In 1969, 11 percent of covered workers were in plans that provided vested benefits only after sixteen or more years of service.[34] But despite this trend, a substantial portion of workers were covered by vesting rules that would have had to be modified to conform to the new ERISA standards.[35]

To answer the second question within the context of the model, we

33. *Labor Mobility and Private Pension Plans: A Study of Vesting, Early Retirement, and Portability Provisions,* BLS Bulletin 1407 (GPO, 1964); and Donald M. Landay and Harry E. Davis, "Growth and Vesting Changes in Private Pension Plans," *Monthly Labor Review,* vol. 91 (May 1968), pp. 29–35.

34. Harry E. Davis and Arnold Strasser, "Private Pension Plans, 1960–1969—An Overview," *Monthly Labor Review,* vol. 93 (July 1970), pp. 45–56.

35. As of late 1974, 94 of the 149 plans regularly summarized in the Bureau of Labor Statistics' *Digest of Selected Pension Plans* series met none of the alternative minimum vesting standards of ERISA. See Evan L. Hodgens, "Key Changes in Major Pension Plans," *Monthly Labor Review,* vol. 98 (July 1975), pp. 22–27.

compare our baseline simulation to a third simulation that places more weight on an extended vesting rule. For example, our baseline simulation gives a new worker a 0.76 chance of being in an uncovered job, a 0.02 chance of being in either a five-year or a fifteen-year vesting rule, and a 0.20 chance of being in a ten-year vesting rule. The extended-vesting simulation reduces the chance of confronting a ten-year vesting rule from 0.20 to 0.05 while it increases the chance of confronting a fifteen-year vesting rule from 0.02 to 0.17. Similar changes are made in all subsequent pension regime assignments.

Results of this extended-vesting simulation run are presented in figure 8 (variant 2) and in table 2, column 3. The comparison suggests that the forced reduction to ten-year vesting rules has had a modest, negative impact on worker job attachment and job tenure. During his career the median worker held 5.0 jobs in the pre-ERISA simulation compared to 5.4 jobs in the baseline (post-ERISA) simulation. The mean length of all jobs held was 6.84 years in the pre-ERISA simulation compared to a baseline value of 6.48 years, and the median length of the longest job was 28.2 years compared to 25.6 years in the baseline simulation. But note that the median length of all jobs held was 2.56 years in both simulations.

These results follow from the fact that ten-year and fifteen-year vesting rules imply different behavior primarily after five or more years on the job (and particularly after vesting has occurred on ten-year rules). Abandoning the longer vesting rule means a modest decline in very long jobs and a modest increase in jobs of medium length—ten to fifteen years. But because the number of short jobs is relatively unaffected, the median tenure of all jobs remains unchanged. Thus our stylized ERISA does have a modest impact in reducing the number of very long jobs.

Conclusions

Theoretical analyses of labor market relationships often assume that pensions are a device whereby employers encourage desired patterns of employee attachment to the firm. Given the use of the pension mechanism, the choice of vesting rule is in theory an additional vehicle for control of the distribution of job tenures. Our findings support the notion that both coverage and the vesting rule affect mobility patterns and hence expected tenure at job entry.

Our econometric analysis of data on job tenures indicates substantial effects of coverage and vesting variables upon job-exit rates. We find that job-exit rates increase immediately after the attainment of vested benefit status. These job-exit rate patterns, in turn, imply substantial differences in the overall distribution of job tenures given different pension characteristics.

When we consider job-tenure patterns in a lifetime context, using simulation techniques, the effects of the pension system are less dramatic than when we consider the effect of pension variables on the expected tenure pattern for a particular job. Nonetheless, we conclude that the pension system as a whole contributes importantly to observed patterns of job tenure and turnover. Moreover, by constraining employers' ability to set vesting requirements, the 1974 ERISA legislation appears to have affected the overall distribution of completed job tenures in the economy.

We have stressed repeatedly that the associations we find between pension characteristics and job tenure reflect both a *sorting* effect—the use of pension characteristics to sort workers among firms, with respect to their preferred patterns of job attachment—and a causal association between pension status and the decision to change jobs—a *retention* effect. Because we are unable to identify the relative importance of the various effects of pensions, our inferences regarding the consequences of broad changes in the pension system should be regarded as upper-bound estimates. Nonetheless, our empirical results suggest that pension plans play an important role in allocating workers among firms with different pension offerings or inducing workers to remain longer on a job than they would otherwise choose to do.

Appendix: Construction of Annual Job-Entry Rate Series

This section documents the procedures used to create the crucial time series of annual job-entry rates required for our estimation method. We followed a two-part procedure, first calculating annual age-specific rates of job entry in manufacturing and then calculating the probability that a job beginning in a specified year would have each of several alternative pension characteristics. We now describe each of these steps in turn.

Age Profiles of Job Entry in Manufacturing

Our first object was to construct age profiles of job entry—that is, a series representing the number of job starts each year, working backwards from our reference point of May 1979. Data on job starts are not routinely tabulated by age. Therefore, we used the accessions data from the Bureau of Labor Statistics to provide the annual volume of manufacturing job starts by men. These job starts were then allocated to ages, using data on the age distribution of job starters in *all* industries, available for selected years only. The specific steps taken were as follows.

1. *Annual volume of job starts (accessions) in manufacturing.* These data are available for men for the years 1958 through 1968 and for both sexes combined in other years. Attempts to model the sex ratio of average annual accessions using time-series regression techniques proved unsuccessful. Therefore, for years before 1958 and since 1968, we simply multiplied annual total accessions by the average of the ratio of male accessions to total accessions during 1958 to 1968. Annual average accession *rates* were multiplied by the annual average employment *level* (also reported by the Bureau of Labor Statistics) to obtain the annual *number* of job starters.

2. *Age distribution of job starters.* For 1951, 1963, 1966, 1968, 1973, and 1978, the approximate age distribution of job starters was constructed from published data on job tenure, using the age distribution of those with job tenure of six months or less[36] For 1955 and 1961 the age distribution of job changers is available directly.[37] In the case of the tenure-based distributions, the data pertain only to those employed at the time of the survey and thus omit any workers who began a job in the indicated year but were unemployed at the time of the survey. Moreover, the distributions are for men in all industries, rather than just in manufacturing, because the published data are not simultaneously shown by narrow age categories and industry. Limited comparisons of the two distributions—manufacturing only and all industries—can be made for selected years using very broad age categories; for 1973 and 1968 the distributions are remarkably close while for 1966 and 1963 some differences are apparent.

The age distributions for all jobs, derived from tables published by

36. U.S. Bureau of Labor Statistics, "Job Tenure of American Workers," Special Labor Force Reports 36, 77, 112, 172 (title varies) (GPO, January 1963, 1966, 1968, 1973); BLS, "Job Tenure Declines as Work Force Changes," Special Labor Force Report 235 (GPO, 1980); and U.S. Bureau of the Census, *Current Population Reports*, series P-50, no. 36, "Experience of Workers at Their Current Jobs, January 1951" (GPO, 1951).

37. Bureau of the Census, *Current Population Reports*, series P-50, no. 70, "Job Mobility of Workers in 1955" (GPO, 1957); and BLS, "Job Mobility in 1961," Special Labor Force Report 35 (GPO, 1963).

Table 3. Age Distribution of Job Starters, All Industries, Selected Years, 1951–78

Percent

Age category	1978	1973	1966	1963	1961	1955	1951
Under 20	27.1	27.3	22.3	18.2	13.0	13.0	14.7
20–24	24.3	25.9	22.5	20.1	20.0	16.4	17.3
25–29	16.3	15.6	13.5	} 23.4	27.3	29.2	27.5
30–34	10.1	8.3	8.3				
35–39	6.1	5.5	7.5	} 17.5	20.5	18.4	18.9
40–44	4.8	5.0	6.6				
45–49	3.5	3.8	5.8	6.3	} 12.5	15.2	11.9
50–54	2.9	3.5	5.4	5.3			
55–59	2.3	2.4	4.2	4.0	} 4.9	6.0	7.1
60–64	1.4	1.5	2.2	3.0			
Over 64	1.2	1.2	2.1	2.1	1.8	1.8	2.6

Sources; See text notes 36 and 37.

the Bureau of the Census and the Bureau of Labor Statistics, are shown in table 3. The figures reveal fairly stable distributions in 1951, 1955, and 1961, with distinct increases in the proportion of young job starters and a corresponding decline in the proportion of older job starters since 1961.

Let $F_t(a)$ represent the cumulative age distribution of job starters in year t, points along which are observed by calculating partial sums of the columns of table 3 (that is, $F_{1978}[24] = 0.271 + 0.243 = 0.514$). We assume that no jobs begin before age 14. To fill in the gaps in our time series of entry-age distributions, we first interpolated cumulative proportions, at the ages shown in table 3, for the years not represented in the table. This procedure restricts our analysis to the period beginning in 1951. We then interpolated to single-year-of-age cumulative proportions within each derived annual distribution, using Aitken-Lagrange interpolation techniques.[38]

3. *Population at risk of job entry*. In order to convert the annual single-year-of-age job-entry frequencies into rates, the size of the population at risk must be determined. To do so, we interpolated between published age-distribution tables in the 1950, 1960, 1970, and 1980 decennial censuses.

4. *Derived job-entry rates*. The final job-entry rates are calculated simply as the ratio of the number of manufacturing job starts allocated to a specified age, in a given year, to the number of men of that age alive

38. Francis B. Hildebrand, *Introduction to Numerical Analysis*, 2d ed. (McGraw-Hill, 1973).

in that year, that is $[F_t(a + 1) - F_t(a)]ACC_t/R_t(a)$, for $a = 14, 15, \ldots 64$, and $t = 1951, \ldots 1978$; ACC_t is the number of accessions in year t (from step 1), and $R_t(a)$ is the frequency distribution of men by age in year t (from step 3).

Pension Attributes of Jobs

The procedures outlined above yield total rates of manufacturing job entry, by single year of age and by calendar year. However, our method requires that we partition these totals into components, reflecting the proportion of jobs covered and uncovered by pensions, and the distribution by vesting rule for covered jobs. Available data shed very little light on these proportions. Hence, we were required to adopt strong assumptions to use the few data that are available.

Recall that our job-tenure hazard functions distinguish job attributes at a single date—the survey date, at which tenure-in-progress is recorded—and that it is this limited set of attributes to which the partition of the job-entry rates must correspond. These attributes allow us to identify three pension "regimes": uncovered jobs; covered jobs that have already vested, in which case the vesting rule is unknown; and covered jobs that have not yet vested, in which case the vesting rule is known.

Thus our econometric model requires a three-way partition of each annual job-entry rate figure into (1) the proportion not covered by a pension, (2) the proportion covered by a pension, and for which vesting will be attained prior to 1979, and (3) the proportion covered by a pension, for which vesting will not be attained prior to 1979. The third category must be further partitioned into proportions representing each possible one-year vesting rule. Because of ERISA's vesting requirements, all covered jobs beginning before 1964, that is, fifteen years before the collection of the data we analyzed, must have fully vested benefits by 1979; thus for 1951 through 1963, category 3 is irrelevant. For $t = 1964$ through 1978, category 3 is relevant only if $VRULE$ exceeds the quantity $1979 - t$. Therefore, for 1978 we partition the job-entry rate into seventeen components: (1) the proportion uncovered; (2) the proportion covered, with immediate vesting (and hence vesting before 1979); (3) the proportion covered, with one-year vesting (and hence vesting not yet attained by 1979); ... (17) the proportion covered, with fifteen-year vesting (and, therefore, vesting not yet attained by 1979). Job-entry rates for 1977 are partitioned into only sixteen components, and so on, back to 1963 and before, which are partitioned into just two components, as explained above.

To determine the proportion of jobs beginning each year with and without coverage, we assumed that the coverage probability for a job beginning in year t equaled the proportion of all jobs covered by private pensions in year t.[39] This assumption undoubtedly introduces some error into our job-entry rates since coverage in manufacturing has been higher than in all private sector employment during much of the 1951–78 period.[40]

The final element of our partition of the job-entry rates is the assignment of proportions to each possible vesting rule, for jobs beginning in 1964 through 1978. As noted previously in the text, a long-run trend toward both more universal provision of vesting and more liberal vesting requirements has occurred; moreover, the enactment of ERISA led to a distinct shift in the distribution of vesting rules.[41] Nonetheless, published data do not permit the calculation of the frequency distribution of vesting rules for covered jobs beginning in *any* year during 1964 to 1978, much less the entire period. Therefore, we used the frequency distribution of $VRULE = 0, 1, \ldots 15$ based upon men in our May 1979 CPS sample and applied it to the job-entry rates for each year during the period 1964–78.

Application of Attribute-Specific Job-Entry Rates

The total job-entry rates described in the first section of this appendix are age-specific, while the proportions corresponding to pension attributes, described in the second section, are not age-specific. There is

39. The coverage proportions used (available for 1950 to 1979) were taken from Sylvester J. Schieber and Patricia M. George, *Retirement Income Opportunities in an Aging America*, vol. 1: *Coverage and Benefit Entitlement* (Washington, D.C.: Employee Benefit Research Institute, 1981), table III-1.

40. See, for example, Landay and Davis, *Growth and Vesting Changes in Private Pension Plans;* and Gayle Thompson Rogers, "Pension Coverage and Vesting among Private Wage and Salary Workers, 1979: Preliminary Estimates from the 1979 Survey of Pension Plan Coverage," Office of Research and Statistics Working Paper 16 (Social Security Administration, 1980).

41. U.S. General Accounting Office, *Effects of the Employee Retirement Income Security Act on Pension Plans with Fewer Than 100 Participants* (GAO, 1980); and Robert Frumkin and Donald Schmitt, "Pension Improvements since 1974 Reflect Inflation; New U.S. Law," *Monthly Labor Review*, vol. 102 (April 1979), pp. 32–37.

undoubtedly a relationship between a worker's age at job entry and the probability distribution over job attributes at job entry. However, taking account of this relationship is beyond the scope of the present study and in fact would require a behavioral model of life-cycle job choice. Thus we applied the annual job-attribute proportions just described to the appropriate annual job-entry rates of men of all ages. Our procedure, which assumes away any age effects on coverage probabilities and vesting attributes, may partially explain our general failure to detect age-at-entry effects in our econometric estimates, especially for covered jobs.

Comment by Anthony J. Pellechio

The central purpose of this paper is to infer the distribution of completed job tenures with information on the distribution of job tenures-in-progress reported in a recent cross-sectional survey. The authors then examine the impact that pensions may have on the distribution of completed job tenures. These impacts must be inferred from a cross-sectional survey because our available information on length of job tenures is so limited. The paper estimates detailed probability hazard functions from which the completed tenure distributions can be inferred.

The authors reach three major conclusions. First, pension coverage matters in determining job tenures, at least within the manufacturing sector; abolition of pensions might cause the average tenure in manufacturing jobs to decline by up to two and a half years. Second, within the pension-covered sector, the specific provisions of the vesting rule matter: workers covered by different vesting provisions appear to stay on a job different average lengths of time; furthermore, once a vesting requirement is attained, the probability that workers will leave a job is somewhat greater. Third, the authors find that the ERISA legislation of the mid-1970s has had a slight impact on provisions of pension plans and on the distribution of completed job tenures.

The formal analysis was done carefully and well. I will concentrate in my comments on some of the broader issues. A close reading of the paper reveals a major problem in inferring completed tenures from tenures-in-progress. The analysis depends very much on knowledge about the number of job beginnings in a particular year. Given this information, the authors must then make assumptions about the characteristics of jobs begun in each year. Hence, the analysis does depend heavily upon, and is very sensitive to, assumptions about the history of job starts. I am particularly concerned about the effect these assumptions have on our inferences about the pension coverage.

The authors take considerable pains to measure and describe the impact on a worker of becoming vested under a pension plan. I would like to point out that the size of this impact ordinarily should not be too large because the present value of pension wealth at the point of vesting is often quite small. The flow of pension income, after all, does not begin until many years in the future, and the amount of benefits for which a newly vested worker qualifies is typically quite small. You would expect, then, that the impact of this small change in pension wealth would be a small change in the probability of job leaving.

The basic finding of this paper is that jobs with pensions have higher average completed tenures. The authors give two explanations for this relationship. The first offered by the authors is that firms use pensions to sort out workers. Because some firms prefer to have workers with long average tenures, they use pensions to attract workers who plan on staying long enough to collect benefits under the pension. Another explanation is that workers who accept a job covered by a pension actually modify their behavior because of the incentives offered by the pension plan.

A third explanation that I would like to offer for the association between pensions and job tenure is that pensions grow where workers stay. Consider workers with a given set of preferences about how long they wish to stay on a given job in a particular kind of industry. If workers with particular kinds of preferences associate in particular industries and occupations, then it is conceivable that workers who prefer longer tenures might also prefer to receive a larger share of their compensation in the form of pensions. The fact that they are concentrated in certain industries and occupations makes it convenient for their employers to satisfy their preferences. Under this line of reasoning, a kind of reverse causality takes place between pensions and tenure: the long tenure on the job induces workers and firms to use pensions as an important component of compensation.

This correspondence raises important questions about the simulation results reported in the paper. The simulations make sense only if pensions are the cause of long tenures. The authors are careful to point out that the ''sorting'' impact of pensions does not really affect the aggregate

Retirement and Economic Behavior

Henry J. Aaron *AND* **Gary Burtless** *EDITORS*

distribution of job tenures, only the distribution of workers among firms with varying pension offerings. They therefore emphasize that their simulation results represent an upper-bound estimate of pension effects. But since it is possible that pensions grow where workers stay, I doubt whether pensions can be treated, even tentatively, as the cause of the current distribution of job tenure.

The comparison of the authors' simulation results with actual tenure distributions tabulated by the Bureau of Labor Statistics also raises questions. I wonder if some of the discrepancy is caused by the authors' assumption that people work until age 65 and then retire, an assumption at variance with recent statistics on labor force participation of the aged. Another issue in considering these results is the difference between defined benefit and defined contribution pension plans. As Bulow and others have shown, the change in present value of a defined pension benefit at the point of vesting is often quite small. For a defined contribution plan, by contrast, the value of an employer's contribution to the plan, at least for workers at younger ages, could be substantially larger. Hence, I expect that the jumps in the probability of leaving a job could be much higher after vesting for the defined contribution plan than for the defined benefit plan.

My last comment is a suggestion for future research. One of the most difficult issues faced in this paper is the technical problem of inferring completed tenure distributions on the basis of observed but not-yet-completed tenures at a single point in time. Although the analysis in this paper represents a considerable technical achievement, it is based on some highly specialized and perhaps unrealistic assumptions. By using longitudinal surveys such as the Retirement History Survey or the Panel Study of Income Dynamics, which contain information about completed tenures, a future researcher might be able to avoid some of the technical problems and specialized assumptions of the present study.

*Robert H. Haveman, Barbara L. Wolfe,
and Jennifer L. Warlick*

Disability Transfers, Early
Retirement, and Retrenchment

From 1968 to 1978, the social security disability insurance (SSDI) program experienced dramatic growth in caseload and costs. Expenditures grew from about $2 billion to nearly $13 billion, an average annual growth rate of nearly 20 percent. Over the same period the number of beneficiaries grew at an average annual rate of over 8 percent. Because of this growth a large portion of both the rapid decline in the labor force participation rate of older males and the financial problems of social security have been attributed to SSDI. Some analysts expect substantial benefits if the burden of SSDI can be reduced.[1]

Consider the relationship between SSDI growth and patterns of early retirement. From 1959 to 1980 the labor force participation rate of males aged 45–59 fell from 96 percent to 88.5 percent. On the basis of empirical analysis using data from the National Longitudinal Survey, Parsons asserts that the increased generosity of SSDI benefits is primarily

The authors gratefully acknowledge helpful comments by Dennis Aigner, Gary Chamberlain, Sheldon Danziger, Arthur Goldberger, Robert A. Moffitt, and Jacques van der Gaag. The first part of this paper is based on Robert H. Haveman and Barbara L. Wolfe, "Disability Transfers and Early Retirement: A Causal Relationship?" *Journal of Public Economics* (forthcoming).

1. In fact, growth in SSDI recipients has moderated substantially since 1978. The number of people receiving SSDI benefits has fallen by more than 400,000 in the past three years. See Mordechai E. Lando, Alice V. Farley, and Mary A. Brown, "Recent Trends in the Social Security Disability Insurance Program," *Social Security Bulletin*, vol. 45 (August 1982), pp. 3–14. A controversial government crackdown against alleged abuse in the SSDI program has contributed to this retarded growth. In 1982 alone, 180,000 people were removed from the rolls on the grounds that they were ineligible to receive benefits. Despite these recent trends in enrollments, the cost of the SSDI program has continued to rise rapidly. An expanding earnings base and the indexing of benefits to the CPI are the primary sources of increased costs.

responsible for the decline in work effort.[2] He concludes that high benefits have induced persons for whom the program is not intended to apply for disability insurance, thereby inflating total program costs. The implied policy action is the reduction of benefit levels (and replacement rates) and the identification and removal from the rolls of unintended beneficiaries.

The effects on individual economic status and program costs of reducing the number of beneficiaries have not been systematically evaluated. Until now, information on these effects has derived from individual case studies. Some of these suggest that many current beneficiaries could earn enough money to provide for themselves nearly as well as they are provided for on the rolls. Others argue that if beneficiaries are removed from the rolls, they will suffer extreme economic hardship, that there will be little in the way of labor supply adjustments by the affected individuals and their families, and that the availability of other government programs that could partially compensate for the income loss resulting from removal is limited.

In this paper, we pose two questions related to these incentive and economic status issues and provide empirical estimates in answer to them. First, are some of the prominent estimates suggesting that increasingly generous SSDI benefits have caused major reductions in older worker labor supply plausible?[3] Or do estimates based on alternative (and, we suggest, more adequate) data, statistical methods, and variable definitions suggest a different conclusion? Second, what would be the effect of SSDI cutbacks on program costs and on the economic status of current SSDI beneficiaries who are removed from the rolls by administrative action or reduced benefits? Will the work effort of the individual or his family, or other income transfers, adjust so that the loss of SSDI benefits will be largely compensated for, or will economic hardship result?

The second section of this paper deals with the first question. In it an empirical estimate of the work-disability transfer choice of older workers

2. Donald O. Parsons, "The Decline in Male Labor Force Participation," *Journal of Political Economy*, vol. 88 (February 1980), pp. 117–34; and Parsons, "Racial Trends in Male Labor Force Participation," *American Economic Review*, vol. 70 (December 1980), pp. 911–20.

3. See ibid.; and Jonathan S. Leonard, "The Social Security Disability Program and Labor Force Participation," National Bureau of Economic Research Working Paper 392 (Cambridge, Mass.: NBER, August 1979).

is presented. This estimate examines the extent to which increases in the benefit levels of disability transfers induce early retirement and decrease rates of labor force participation. The next section presents estimates of both the savings in program costs and the loss of economic status of individuals eliminated from SSDI rolls under various retrenchment strategies.

Do Disability Benefit Levels Cause Less Work?

During the 1970s real benefit levels in disability programs increased substantially.[4] And some evidence indicates that eligibility criteria have been applied more leniently. However, neither the change in benefit levels nor the increased availability of benefits is sufficient to attribute the decrease in the labor supply of older workers to the generosity and availability of disability benefits. Many other changes in the labor market for older workers have occurred during the same period that disability transfers were rising and labor force participation rates of older workers were falling: youths and women entered the labor market in unprecedented numbers; although labor demand rose rapidly throughout the period, unemployment remained high; the pressure on males to continue working decreased as spouses increased their contribution to household income; increasingly generous social security early retirement benefits freed savings for earlier retirement; and public attitudes became far more accepting of retirement before age 65. The observed decrease in older male labor force participation is explained by some complex interaction of these (and other) factors over the period.

In this section of the paper, we formulate an economic model to estimate the responsiveness of older male labor supply to the generosity of disability transfers. Our estimates are designed to test the assertion that the increased generosity of disability benefits is primarily responsible for the decreased work effort of older men.[5] Indeed, the estimates underlying this assertion imply that the SSDI program has induced a

4. From 1957 to 1978, the wage replacement rate in the social security disability insurance program rose from 30 percent to 41 percent for the average nonsupervisory manufacturing worker with no dependents; for the same worker with a wife and child, the rate rose from 57 percent to 68 percent.

5. Leonard, "Social Security Disability Program"; Parsons, "Decline in Male Labor Force Participation"; and Parsons, "Racial Trends in Male Labor Force Participation."

labor supply reduction equal to that of the social security retirement program, even though it is only one-sixth the size of the retirement program in number of recipients and level of expenditure.[6]

First, we present our model of the labor supply decision of older men. The model suggests that expected disability transfers and expected labor market income are primary determinants of the choice between work and transfer recipiency. Then, the data, specification, and results of the model are described. Finally, we interpret our results and relate them to those of others.

A Model of the Work Status Choice of Older Men

The public disability transfer system is large and complex.[7] Any eligible person can receive benefits from a number of programs. Benefits depend on the person's previous work history, the extent of his disability, his geographical region of residence, the number of his dependents, and the nature of his job or occupation. Modeling and measuring the responses of individuals to the incentives in this system must take into account the characteristics of the person, the structure of the system, and the nature of the labor market in which the person participates.

The model we use to estimate this labor supply response is an econometric model known as two-stage probit analysis. It and its econometric properties are described in appendix A. Here we briefly describe our general approach. We first identify the two basic choices available to a worker who is over 45 years of age but younger than 62. Because such a person is too young to qualify for social security early retirement benefits, he has the option of either continuing to work in the labor market or ceasing work and attempting to qualify for disability-related transfers. The person compares how well off he would be under each of these alternatives and then chooses the alternative he believes is superior.

6. Sheldon Danziger, Robert Haveman, and Robert Plotnick, "How Income Transfer Programs Affect Work, Savings, and the Income Distribution: A Critical Review," *Journal of Economic Literature,* vol. 19 (September 1981), pp. 975–1021.

7. The programs in this system include social security disability insurance with $14.9 billion expenditures and 4.7 million recipients in 1980; supplemental security income with $5 billion of expenditures and 2.3 million recipients in 1980; workers' compensation with $10.2 billion of expenditures in 1979 and 1.2 million recipients in 1975; and veterans' disability pensions with $8.1 billion of expenditures in 1980 and 3.3 million recipients in 1978. In addition, over twenty additional federal programs provide cash and in-kind benefits to the disabled.

The difficulty in making empirical estimates of the choices made by males aged 45–62 comes in determining how well off each person expects to be in each of the two options—the labor market alternative and the disability transfer alternative. We assume that each person forms his expectation of how well off he would be under each option by looking at the economic status of people who are just like him—in terms of health status, other personal characteristics, and labor market circumstances—and who have actually chosen that option. For example, his expected income in the labor market is taken to be the mean income of people with identical characteristics who are actually in the labor market. Similarly, his expected income if he chooses the disability transfer option is the average income of people like him who have chosen to be transfer recipients.

Estimates of both of these expected incomes are obtained from regression analysis, first on the group consisting of labor market participants and then on the group of disability transfer recipients. In performing these regressions, we adjust for the fact that those who are in each group, and who are thus included in the relevant regression, may be different from others in ways not captured by the measurable characteristics accounted for in the income regressions. The income flows are defined as the *total income flows* associated with each option, rather than as transfers from only one program, such as SSDI.

At this stage of the analysis, then, we have two expected income values for each person in the sample—expected income in the labor market option and expected income as a disability transfer recipient. Recalling the assumption that people will choose the option that leaves them best off, we can now analyze the choices made by a group of people on the basis of these two expected income terms. If our model is a good one, we will accurately predict the actual choices that people make. Moreover, we will also have the basis for estimating the extent to which people will modify their choice if expected income in either option is increased or decreased.

In the last step of our analysis, we determine how people respond in terms of work effort to changes in transfer benefit generosity or wages. Our model yields estimates of these responses in terms of elasticities. The larger the elasticity, the greater the responsiveness; the smaller the elasticity, the less people change their work effort in response to expected benefit changes or wage changes.

In statistically implementing this approach, we have followed fairly standard estimation procedures. The central relationship estimated is a

probit equation from which we infer the elasticity of labor force participation with respect to disability program generosity:

(1) $P(D_j = 1 \mid LE_j, DT_j) = \delta \widehat{LE}_j + \eta \widehat{DT}_j + \alpha'\underline{X} + \epsilon_j,$

where

$D_j = 1$ indicates that the individual is a labor market participant;

LE_j is total income flow associated with the labor market option;

DT_j is total income flow associated with the disability transfer option;

$\widehat{LE}_j$ is estimated value of LE_j;

$\widehat{DT}_j$ is estimated value of DT_j;

$\underline{X}$ are stigma and/or taste variables;

δ, η, α are parameters to be estimated; and

ϵ_j is the error term.

Because of the unobserved nature of either the labor market or
disability income flows for each person, we substitute estimated flows,
$\widehat{LE}_j$ and $\widehat{DT}_j$, for the unobserved actual flows. To obtain consistent
estimates of these flows, we first model the self-selection of people into
the labor market or disability groups by means of a reduced-form probit
equation (following the procedure developed by Heckman),[8] which
yields an inverse Mill's ratio. A reduced-form specification is used to
avoid simultaneous equation bias arising from the omission of any
important variables in the alternative structural equation model.

In the second stage, each income flow is modeled by a reduced-form,
ordinary least squares regression using the subgroup with observed
flows. The coefficients from these regression equations are then used to
provide estimates of expected income flows in the labor market and
disability transfer options for each individual in the sample.

The third step is to estimate the central probit equation presented
above, specified so that this sequential two-stage probit model will have
the properties of a full, maximum-likelihood estimation.[9]

8. James Heckman, "Shadow Prices, Market Wages, and Labor Supply," *Econometrica*, vol. 42 (July 1974), pp. 679–94; and Heckman, "Sample Selection Bias as a Specification Error," *Econometrica*, vol. 47 (January 1979), pp. 153–61.

9. The equivalence of this two-stage probit procedure with a maximum likelihood estimation is demonstrated in Lee, along with the alternative sets of error term restrictions required to guarantee equivalence. Lung-Fei Lee, "Identification and Estimation in Binary Choice Models with Limited (Censored) Dependent Variables," *Econometrica*, vol. 47 (July 1979), pp. 977–96.

Data and Model Specification

We estimate the model using data from the Michigan Panel Study of Income Dynamics on men who were aged 45–62 in 1978.[10] While the choice of work status in the latest year—1978—is the focus of the study, the panel character of the data allows construction of variables related to past earnings, occupational mobility (including downward changes), and the duration of disability status.

The disability measures we use are designed to capture both the duration and the intensity of impairment. The major disability transfer programs are designed to provide support for those unable to participate in "substantial gainful activity." Duration and intensity of health problems are also likely to influence earnings opportunities. The current extent of disability is likely to affect the probability both of working and of receiving disability transfers. It is measured by a variable indicating the percentage of lost functional capabilities. We base both measures of disability on information collected in eight of the eleven years of the survey. A labor market participant is defined as a person who has either earned income or unemployment benefits greater than zero and no disability-related transfers or a person who has disability transfers greater than zero but earnings in excess of $3,360.[11] A disability program participant is one with a disability transfer (except workers' compensation) greater than zero and earnings less than $3,360.[12]

The independent variables included in the first-stage probit equation explaining labor force participation, fit over all observations in the sample, reflect those demand- and supply-side characteristics of both the labor market and the disability transfer recipiency market likely to affect the presence of a person in either group. Past experience, educa-

10. We exclude workers older than 62 because most are eligible for social security early retirement benefits at that age. Inclusion of this group of workers would further complicate the estimation problem and mask the role of disability transfers in the early retirement decision. Evidence suggests that the availability of disability transfers is less likely to alter the work status choice of men below 45 years of age. Other researchers have also focused on this older age group.

11. The $3,360 cutoff was chosen because it is the annual equivalent of the monthly earnings limit in the dominant disability-related transfer program. In this group are 841 observations.

12. Disabilty-related transfers are defined to include benefits from SSDI, supplemental security income (a program of income-tested benefits directed at the blind and disabled), veterans' disability benefits, other disability pensions, and, if the person is disabled, a share of other welfare and help from relatives. In this group are 123 observations.

Table 1. First-Stage Probit Equation for Selectivity Correction, with Labor Market Participation as Dependent Variable

Explanatory variable	Coefficient	Asymptotic t-statistic
Constant	−346.80	−0.9
Long-term severe disability	−344.00	−3.1*
Long-term severe disability squared	0.65	0.5
Percent currently disabled	−1.59	−1.3
Percent currently disabled squared	0.08	0.1
Age	0.05	0.5
Age spline—age 52–59	0.04	0.4
Age spline—age 59–62	−0.35	−2.2*
Education	0.54	1.5
Education spline—8–11 years	0.03	0.2
Education spline—11 or more years	0.18	0.9
Race (white = 1)	0.28	1.1
Unemployment rate	0.003	0.1
Protestant (0,1)	−0.82	−2.0*
Catholic (0,1)	−0.66	−1.4
Jewish (0,1)	−0.41	−1.4
Decreasing occupational status (0,1)	−0.31	−1.3
Not married and no children under 18 (0,1)	−0.86	−2.2*
Married and no children under 18 (0,1)	−0.32	−1.1
Number of children under 18	−0.01	−0.1
Working spouse (0,1)	0.23	1.0
Wealthy parents (0,1)	−0.06	0.2
Income of others in household (thousands)	0.00003	1.5
South (0,1)	−0.38	−1.1
West (0,1)	0.05	0.1
North Central (0,1)	−0.06	−0.2
Veteran (0,1)	−0.42	−1.9*
Age times education	−0.01	−1.8
Professional (0,1)	70.27	0.9
Manager (0,1)	4.83	1.0
Clerical or sales (0,1)	7.47	0.9
Craftsperson (0,1)	46.28	0.9
Operative (0,1)	36.04	0.9
Farmer (0,1)	−259.90	−0.9
Other occupation (0,1)	39.12	0.9
Disability incidence in usual industry	29.67	0.9
Years of work experience in 1973	−0.01	−0.3
Two times log likelihood ratio	514.2	. . .
Number of observations	964	. . .

Source: Authors' calculations.
* Significant at the 5 percent level.

tion, and disability status reflect the person's potential work capacity and productivity, as does age. These variables also reflect important determinants of eligibility for disability transfers. Marital status and the presence of children reflect the income requirements of the household. The unemployment rate, downward occupational change, and geographical region are included to represent individual employment opportunities. These variables should affect the likelihood both of obtaining a job and of gaining eligibility for disability transfers. Geographical region is also included in our analysis because eligibility criteria for disability benefits may vary in different parts of the country. Veteran status indicates eligibility for military-related disability benefits. Race enters to capture the effect of potential labor market discrimination as a constraint on employment opportunities and as a determinant of eligibility for disability transfers. Religion is entered as a taste variable.

The results for the first-stage probit equation are shown in table 1. Not surprisingly, persons with greater intensity and duration of disability are less likely to have earned income. Most of the other included variables are insignificant, except age above 59, veteran status, and a dummy variable indicating the person is single and has no dependent children. Each of these variables is negatively related to the probability that a person is a labor market participant. Religion, as a proxy for taste, also has a significant influence on the probability of having labor income.

The second-stage equations are estimated by ordinary least squares procedures. To predict expected labor market income, our dependent variable is labor market income flow, and our sample includes all labor market participants. To predict expected disability income, our dependent variable is disability income flow, and our sample includes individuals who chose the disability option. The independent variables in these equations are the same ones used in the first-step probit, except the taste-toward-work variables, unemployment rate, and downward occupational change. In addition, the appropriate inverse Mill's ratio calculated from the step-one probit equation is included to deal with possible sample selectivity that might otherwise bias the second-stage estimates (see appendix A).

The reduced-form equations used to estimate expected income in each status are shown in table 2. For predicting income if one is a disability transfer recipient, the extent of current disability has a large, though not quite significant, positive effect. Duration and intensity of disability are not significant, suggesting that once one is found to be

Table 2. Second-Stage Least Squares Regressions for Predicting Income Flows under the Labor Market and Disability Transfer Recipiency Options

Explanatory variable	Labor market option		Disability transfer recipiency option	
	Coefficient	t-statistic	Coefficient	t-statistic
Constant	−6,492.2	−0.4	26,239.7	2.4*
Long-term severe disability	−8,599.4	−0.8	−3,370.6	−1.0
Long-term severe disability squared	−768.3	−0.04	1,643.5	0.6
Percent currently disabled	−3,604.3	−0.7	7,164.1	1.4
Percent currently disabled squared	416.7	0.1	−5,328.0	−1.3
Age	203.2	0.7	−445.5	−2.1*
Age spline—age 52–59	−193.0	−0.6	430.2	1.5
Age spline—age 59–62	−498.7	−0.7	−620.9	−1.3
Education	2,208.7	2.2*	−2,047.2	−2.1*
Education spline—8–11 years	−3,031.0	−0.5	200.1	0.6
Education spline—11 years or more	2,002.2	3.9*	258.3	0.4
Race (white = 1)	976.2	1.0	1,578.8	2.6*
Not married and no children under 18 (0,1)	−5,706.3	−3.5*	−2,366.6	−2.4*
Married and no children under 18 (0,1)	1,285.9	1.3	−2,139.2	−2.6*
Number of children under 18	182.5	0.5	−332.3	−1.3
Working spouse (0,1)	−2,223.9	−2.9*	−5.0	−0.01
Wealthy parents (0,1)	3,823.3	3.4*	2,600.5	0.3
Income of others in household (thousands)	−0.03	−0.6	−0.02	−0.3
South (0,1)	−1,752.3	−1.8	−1,753.8	−2.5*
West (0,1)	−425.78	−0.4	−1,818.1	−1.4
North Central (0,1)	548.6	0.6	−293.7	−0.3
Veteran (0,1)	297.7	0.4	349.8	0.6
Age times education	−36.4	−2.1*	38.8	2.2*
Professional (0,1)	4,793.0	2.6*	221.5	0.1
Manager (0,1)	9,383.6	5.8*	652.8	0.5
Clerical or sales (0,1)	4,647.9	2.6*	2,554.7	2.0*
Craftsperson (0,1)	5,556.7	3.8*	1,377.8	1.5
Operative (0,1)	4,479.5	3.0*	1,923.7	2.3*
Farmer (0,1)	−2,293.1	−1.0	−2,110.4	−1.5
Other occupation (0,1)	5,998.9	1.8	4,371.7	2.9*
Years of experience in 1973	123.1	1.2	44.3	1.1
Selectivity correction variable	3,863.0	1.1	−365.3	−0.4
Number of observations	841	. . .	123	. . .
R^2	0.36	. . .	0.62	. . .

Source: Authors' calculations.
* Significant at the 5 percent level.

eligible for benefits, current inability to function in the labor market is the main factor in determining the amount of transfers. The nonlinear relationship of current disability to transfers may indicate that those with severe handicaps have a reduced likelihood of earning more than the income cutoff. Lesser need (as measured by being either married or unmarried and without dependent children) has the expected negative sign. Benefits are, in part, based on family size. Prior earnings, as measured by usual occupation, have some influence.[13] Race is significant in predicting disability-related income flows, suggesting either racial differences in application propensity or discrimination in benefit awards, or differences in earlier earnings experience not captured in our specifications. Age is also important, possibly reflecting prior earnings. The significant negative coefficient on the South dummy indicates that lower disability benefits are paid in the South, that more stringent eligibility rules are applied there, or that prior earnings on which some transfer benefits depend are lower in that region. Finally, the negative coefficient on education suggests that eligibility determination is based in part on vocational opportunities. The selectivity term is not significant.

The labor market income equation has few unexpected coefficients. The positive impact of education and of having wealthy parents and the pattern of occupation results are all consistent with economic theory (or common sense). The negative effects of having a working spouse and being in the South are also expected. The insignificance of disability is somewhat surprising; however, the sign is negative, as expected. Again, the selectivity term is not significant.

The third-stage probit estimates in table 3 indicate the role of disability transfers—their accessibility and level—and labor income in affecting the work status choice of older men. Results are based on the measure of the expected income flow in each status and on the additional variables used in the first-stage probit equation but not included in the second-stage regressions.[14]

Table 3 presents results from both a simple and an extended form of the model. In the simple form, only the two expected incomes are assumed to influence the work status choice along with taste toward work (as proxied by religion), decline in occupational status, riskiness

13. The other occupation category includes police and firemen, who tend to have extensive disability pension plans.
14. This procedure ensures consistency with the underlying maximum-likelihood estimation model.

Table 3. Third-Stage Probit Estimates of the Determinants of Work Status Choice

Item	Simple model[a]		Extended model[a]		Dependent variable[b]	
	Co-effi-cient	Asymptotic t-statistic	Co-effi-cient	Asymptotic t-statistic	$\overline{X}$	σ
Expected labor market income	0.45	10.7*	0.42	8.9*	14,695c	8,550c
Expected disability transfer recipiency income	−0.49	−7.6*	−0.41	−5.7*	6,067c	2,729c
Percent currently disabled	. . .	. . .	−0.87	−2.8*	0.17	0.35
Age	. . .	. . .	−0.02	−0.9	52.9	5.0
Not married and number children under 18 (0,1)	. . .	. . .	0.77	1.97*	0.081	0.27
Constant	0.83	1.0	2.30	1.2	. . .	. . .
Two times log likelihood function	596	. . .	612	. . .	. . .	. . .

Source: Authors' calculations.
* Significant at the 5 percent level.
a. Both models also include a set of six variables included in the first-stage probit equation but not included in the income regressions. These variables are Protestant (0,1), Catholic (0,1), Jewish (0,1), decreasing occupational status (0,1), disability incidence in usual industry, and unemployment rate.
b. $\overline{X}$ = 0.872; σ = 0.33.
c. Dollars.

of job, and unemployment rate. The extended model also introduces stigma-related variables (age, disability status, and marital status) along with the expected income variables. These proxies for the stigma costs of not working imply that the extent of stigma is greater the younger the worker, the less severe his health problem, and the greater the number of persons dependent on him. Expected income in the disability transfer option is negatively and significantly related to the decision to participate in the labor market in both versions of the model. The extent of disability—which captures a form of stigma costs—has the expected sign and is statistically significant. The role of dependents, probably capturing both stigma and need, also has the expected sign and is statistically significant.

Results in table 3 can be used to compute the elasticity of labor force participation with respect to expected disability transfers. This elasticity is small in both models. In the simpler model, the elasticity is −0.0005 (t-statistic = 7.6); in the extended model it is even smaller, −0.0003 (t-statistic = 5.7). Thus, while the response to the incentives implicit in disability transfers—increased leniency in eligibility or more generous benefits—is verified and found to be statistically significant, its quantitative magnitude is not very large in any of the models.

Table 4. Simulated Effect of Changes in Social Security Disability Transfer Generosity on the Work Effort Choice

Percent change in expected SSDI benefits	Labor force participation rate	Disability recipiency rate
−20	92.41	7.59
0	91.37	8.63
+20	90.73	9.27

Source: Authors' calculations.

These estimated elasticities are much smaller than those found in previous studies. For this reason, tests of the validity of our estimates are in order. By comparing the predicted results with the actual participation-nonparticipation decision of the older workers in the sample, we can provide one measure of the accuracy of our estimates. Of the 841 observations in the sample who are labor-force participants, 821 are predicted by the third-stage probit equation to have a probability of more than 0.5 of being participants. Of the 123 nonparticipants in the labor force (recipients of disability transfers) in the sample, 108 have a predicted probability of more than 0.5 of being nonparticipants (receiving disability transfers). Thus our predictions are correct for 96.4 percent of the sample. Our estimate of the labor force participation rate in the sample is also accurate. The actual weighted rate in our sample is 91.37 percent, and the predicted rate is 91.3. The predicted value deviates from the actual by less than a tenth of one percent. The implied accuracy of the predictions suggests that our model does accurately distinguish the significant determinants of the labor force participation decision.[15] And it lends confidence to our conclusion that an increase in expected disability benefits is a significant determinant of the decrease in labor force participation of older workers, but that this factor accounts for only a relatively small portion of the decrease.

To obtain a rough estimate of the contribution of disability program generosity to early retirement, we simulate the effect of a plus or minus 20 percent change in expected SSDI benefits (including dependents' benefits) in the transfer option of each individual in the sample. The results, reported in table 4, show that a 20 percent change in expected disability income would elicit a change in the labor force participation rate of 0.64 to 1.04 percentage points.

This response can be placed in a historical perspective. From 1968 to

15. We use the model in its extended form for this exercise.

Table 5. Elasticities of Expected Labor Market Income and Disability Transfer Recipiency Income

Setting of variables	Expected labor market income	Expected disability transfer recipiency income
Simple equation at means	0.0012	−0.0005
Extended equation at means[a]	0.0007	−0.0003
Percent currently disabled = 0	0.0004	−0.0001
Percent currently disabled = 100	0.0095	−0.0039
Age = 45	0.0003	−0.0001
Age = 59	0.0012	−0.0005
Expected earnings + σ	0.0000	0.0000
Expected earnings − σ	1.3948	−1.3593
Expected earnings + σ; percent currently disabled = 0	0.0000	0.0000
Expected earnings − σ; percent currently disabled = 100	2.5370	−2.4727

Source: Authors' calculations.
a. Other variables in extended equation set at their means.

1978 the labor force participation rate of males aged 55–64 decreased by about 12 percentage points; the labor force participation rate for males aged 45–54 fell 4.5 percentage points. During the same period, average real SSDI benefits per recipient increased 43 percent. Our estimates of behavioral response imply that this increase in benefit generosity would induce a decrease in the labor force participation rate of, at most, 1.81 percentage points.[16] Hence much of the observed decrease must be attributed to factors other than the increased generosity of disability benefits.[17]

We address one final question with our preferred estimates from the extended model: which groups are most responsive to changes in expected disability income? In table 5 we present the elasticities of labor market participation for people with a variety of characteristics. (Recall that when results from the extended equation are used, the elasticities

16. Over the ten-year period from 1968 to 1978, the mean increase of transfers per recipient was 42.9 percent for SSDI (the weighted average payment for males and females adjusted by the CPI). Our simulated change from the 80 percent level to the 120 percent level equals 93 percent of the actual mean increase in SSDI benefits over the period. This simulated change accounts for a 1.68 percentage point change in the labor force participation rate.

17. This simulation presumes that benefit increases from 1968 to 1978 were uniform across population groups. If benefits rose faster for low-wage than for high-wage workers, a larger decline in the simulated change in the labor force participation rate would result.

on both of the expected income terms fall substantially.) The role of current disability status is clearly important. Those who are impaired are much more responsive to changes in expected income flows than are the nondisabled. This response presumably reflects eligibility perceptions and program practices as well as stigma costs. The responsiveness of older people is somewhat larger than that for younger people. The level of expected earnings also plays an important role. People with earnings expectations one standard deviation below the mean are much more responsive to changes in transfer income flows than people at or above the average. People with disability transfer expectations one standard deviation above the mean are much more responsive to changes in transfer income than people with below-average expectations. These differences are much larger than those based on any other characteristic and suggest that disability transfer flows are targeted primarily on the older disadvantaged worker population with some health problem. This finding implies that the disability transfer programs are "target efficient." It also implies that these programs have a smaller effect on national output than is suggested by the associated reduction in work hours and participation rates. To the extent that such induced early retirement permits increased employment opportunities for youths and other potential workers, this productivity effect is still smaller.

The Effect of Reducing SSDI Rolls

Our conclusion in the second section—that those people who have been attracted to SSDI by increased benefits are those with the lowest earnings prospects—does not mean that all current recipients would experience large income losses if eliminated from the rolls. Indeed, given the appeal and review process and the uneven application of eligibility requirements by state agencies, some individuals currently receiving SSDI benefits might well secure satisfactory replacements to terminated benefits. In this section we analyze the effect of removing some of the disabled from the disability insurance rolls. In an evaluation of the effect of this policy on the economic well-being of a particular population, the ideal process would be to observe the economic status of the affected population with and without the policy change. The proposed nature of the policy action in question here obviously makes this method impossible. Consequently, we base our prediction of the economic losses experienced by those removed from the rolls on the earnings and income experiences of persons who voluntarily applied for SSDI benefits but who were denied benefits.

We use data from the 1978 Disability Survey, which contains a sample of recent applicants to SSDI as well as a sample from the Health Interview Survey. Our analysis sample consists of 1,391 people (men and women) who applied for disability benefits during the period 1976–78. Subsequent to application, 1,079 of these people were awarded benefits. In simulating the effects of alternative policy actions, we examine the economic status of members of subgroups of this recipient population both when they are SSDI recipients and if they were removed from the SSDI rolls. The economic position of the remaining 312 people, who were denied benefits, serves as the basis for our prediction of the economic position that would be achieved by recipients eliminated from the rolls.

To obtain a measure of probable income in the event of loss of eligibility, we regress total family income on the characteristics of the population of individuals denied benefits. (A Tobit specification is used for this purpose.) The estimated regression is shown in table 6. The explanatory variables include demographic characteristics (race, sex, age, education, headship and marital status, geographical region of residence, and household size), the labor force status of spouse, and subjective health status variables indicating the severity of disability, general health condition, and mobility. Also included as an explanatory variable is the appropriate inverse Mill's ratio to adjust for potential selection bias.[18] The probit regression used in the calculation of the ratio is presented in appendix B. That regression is designed to explain the accepted-denied status of individuals who applied for SSDI benefits in the 1976–78 period. The explanatory variables are specific health conditions, job requirements interfering with work after the onset of disability, and demographic variables.

The estimated coefficients shown in table 6 are used in combination with the observed characteristics of current beneficiaries to predict levels of family income for these persons in the event they had been denied benefits. This process, of course, assumes (1) that the opportunities open to those denied benefits (who may have withdrawn from the labor force for only six months) are similar to the opportunities of those

18. The use of the inverse Mill's ratio in a Tobit regression would appear a natural extension of the Heckman technique. However, the extent of bias contained in the implied correction for selectivity is unknown.

Table 6. Tobit Regression for Predicting Total Family Income for Those Eliminated from Disability Rolls[a]

Explanatory variables	Regression coefficient	Asymptotic t-statistic	Mean
Race (white = 1)	3,313.0	2.82*	0.7266
South (0,1)	−2,053.0	−2.06*	0.4532
Age	45.59	0.13	47.46
Education	197.7	1.22	9.655
Urban (0,1)	75.04	0.07	0.7453
Married (0,1)	−3,564	−1.03	0.6292
Never married (0,1)	2,689	1.36	0.0749
Severely disabled (0,1)	−2,328	−1.16	0.7678
Occupational disability (0,1)	−3,675	−1.68	0.1685
Family receives railroad retirement or civil service benefits (0,1)	1,831	1.47	0.2135
Family receives SSI, AFDC, or public assistance (0,1)[b]	−341.5	−0.27	0.2547
Family receives veterans', workers' compensation, or unemployment benefits (0,1)	2,098	1.96*	0.3296
Spouse work (0,1)	4,707	3.42*	0.4045
Excellent, good health (0,1)	5,297	3.59*	0.1648
Fair health (0,1)	2,375	2.17*	0.3333
Household size	988.6	3.45*	3.225
Nonmobile (0,1)	40.92	0.03	0.0936
Sex (male = 1)	1,454.0	0.73	1.569
Age squared	0.0954	0.02	2,374
Married male	3,415.0	1.67	0.9588
Selectivity correction variable	527.7	0.41	0.7970
Constant	−5,442	−0.60	. . .
Number of observations	267	. . .	. . .

Source: Authors' calculations.
* Significant at 5 percent level.
a. Sample: applicants denied SSDI benefits, 1976–77; dependent variable is total family income. Mean of dependent variable is $10,244.
b. SSI: supplementary security income; AFDC: aid to families with dependent children.

removed from the rolls and (2) that all the relevant differences between these two groups are captured by the probit equation on denial.

We now examine the effects of seven policy changes: (1) eliminating current SSDI beneficiaries suffering only from back ailments; (2) eliminating current SSDI beneficiaries who claim only to be limited in type of work (not severely disabled); (3) eliminating those current SSDI beneficiaries suffering only from alcoholism or mental illness; (4) eliminating current SSDI beneficiaries who are less than 50 years of age; (5) eliminating current SSDI beneficiaries who have more than twelve years of education; (6) eliminating current SSDI beneficiaries who applied more than once before receiving benefits; and (7) eliminating current SSDI beneficiaries who attained beneficiary status through the appeals process.

The primary individual outcome measure is the difference between observed total family income (reflecting the receipt of SSDI benefits) and predicted total family income were people eliminated from the rolls, expressed as a percentage of observed income. This difference is interpreted as the percentage change in income attributable to the elimination from SSDI rolls. The primary program impact measures are the percentage reduction in SSDI caseload and benefits.[19]

The simulated effects of the seven retrenchment policies are shown in table 7. These results are based on a 9 percent sample of the total SSDI beneficiary population in 1978. We assume this sample is a random and therefore a representative one.

These policy actions are directed at groups who share the characteristics of that portion of the SSDI recipient population who are awarded benefits only when vocational factors as well as medical factors are taken into account.[20] Hence we simulate the elimination of recipients who are of prime working age, those who are well educated, and those who claim

19. Additional simulations could have been undertaken. In particular, two options have been suggested. In the first, each individual would be assigned a probability of acceptance for SSDI benefits, given application. The assigned value would be the predicted value from the probit regression of appendix B, plus or minus a random shock related to the implicit truncated distribution of the normal error term in the regression. Then, those N percent of recipients with the lowest assigned probability of acceptance would be eliminated from the rolls. This procedure presumes that program officials make decisions on some implied function relating acceptability to individual characteristics, and that our equation resembles this function. A second option would be to develop a measure of disability status using a variety of variables related to this unobserved variable in a latent variable estimation model, such as LISREL. Each recipient would be assigned a "true disability" value from the estimated model, and it would be used to simulate the elimination from the rolls of the N percent of recipients with the lowest assigned value. This procedure presumes that program officials possess true disability information on individuals, coincident with that forthcoming from the imputation. In addition to the difficulty of interpreting the results from such simulations, little evidence suggests that program officials have the additional information implied by these approaches or that they would base decisions on it even if they did.

20. Age, education, and work experience are the vocational factors of primary importance to disability determination. It is stated in the *Social Security Handbook*, 6th ed. (GPO, 1979), p. 104, that "a younger or better educated worker, or one who has been trained in another line of work that could be performed despite the disability, might not be considered disabled."

Table 7. Predicted Effects of Retrenchment Policies on SSDI Caseloads and Costs and on Beneficiary Family Income and Earnings
Income in dollars

Categorical characteristics of eliminated beneficiaries	Percent reduction of caseload	Percent reduction in total benefits	Total family income		
			Mean		Percent change
			Before	After	
1. Has back ailments	9.0	9.2	13,452	8,708	− 35.3
2. Has occupational disability	5.0	4.3	13,141	8,704	− 33.8
3. Suffers from alcoholism or mental illness	3.2	2.8	8,595	8,296	− 3.5
4. Is less than 50 years old	31.8	35.4	12,315	8,089	− 34.3
5. Has more than 12 years of education	13.2	14.8	16,437	9,031	− 45.1
6. Has applied more than once	24.7	24.8	10,842	6,923	− 36.1
7. Won benefits on appeal	9.4	8.1	10,972	7,358	− 32.9

Source: Authors' calculations.

to be occupationally, but not severely, disabled. We also selected two diagnostic categories for which a large proportion of determinations involve vocational factors: back ailments and alcoholism. Although it is unlikely that actual retrenchment policy openly targets any of these groups for elimination from the rolls, few of those current recipients who are eliminated are likely to have initially qualified on medical grounds alone. To the extent that beneficiaries who qualified only after vocational factors were considered are at a higher risk of being removed from the rolls, our results are suggestive of the impact of actual retrenchment policy.

One of these groups accounts for a large and significant proportion of the disabled: those of prime working age. Cutting the entire group of people below age 50 from the SSDI rolls would reduce the caseload by 31.8 percent and reduce total benefits by slightly over 35 percent. Undoubtedly, some of these people would be unable to find employment, would be too disabled to be retrained for alternative employment, and would need other government support such as food stamps, medicaid, and general assistance. Hence the total savings in government transfers would be significantly less than the 35 percent reduction in SSDI benefits implies.

The next largest subgroup is those with more than a high school education (simulation 5). Since members of this group might be more receptive to training or be able to perform more jobs than those with less education, they might be singled out for removal from the rolls. Excluding this group would reduce the rolls by slightly over 13 percent and reduce benefits by nearly 15 percent. Again, individual factors, including age and severity of disability, might well mean that many would require some form of transfer if denied SSDI benefits.

The next largest group whose removal is simulated is comprised of those whose only ailment is back problems, defined to include back stiffness and arthritis. Excluding this group would remove 9 percent of the beneficiaries from the SSDI rolls and reduce benefit payments by 9.2 percent.

Next, if the group that claims to be only occupationally disabled— that is, those who claim that their disability limits the type of work they can do but that their disability is not severe—was eliminated from the rolls, the caseload would be reduced by 5 percent, but total benefits would be reduced somewhat less—by 4.3 percent. And finally, if those whose only disability is alcoholism or general mental disorder were eliminated from the rolls, the rolls would be reduced by only 3.2 percent and total benefits by 2.8 percent.

All these groups report receiving benefits that diverge little from the overall reported average annual benefit of $4,165—thus the percent reduction in benefits is quite similar to the percent reduction in caseload for each of the groups. The few differences suggest that eliminating from the rolls the prime-age beneficiary, the well-educated beneficiary, and those with only back ailments would save more dollars than eliminating people included in the other policy simulations.

The second set of policy actions (6 and 7) involves removal from the rolls of those recipients not granted benefits upon first application. Those in both these groups must have appeared, at least to the first examiner, as persons whose disability did not prevent them from "substantial gainful activity." Nearly a quarter of current beneficiaries applied more than once to receive benefits. Eliminating them from the rolls would reduce benefit payments by an equivalent percentage. A much smaller percentage won benefits on appeal: 9.4 percent. The typical recipient in this group receives lower than average SSDI benefits, so that eliminating this group from the rolls would reduce payments by only 8.1 percent.

These comparisons ignore a primary question: will economic hardship result if these subgroups of beneficiaries are eliminated from the SSDI rolls? To answer this question, we compare our income estimates (based on the income equation of the applicants who were denied as reported in table 6) with the actual 1977 reported family incomes of these individuals. These comparisons are also reported in table 7. The percentage change in total family income is substantial for all the groups except those who suffer only from alcoholism or mental illness. Income losses range from 33 percent to 45 percent of total family incomes.

The simulated reductions in economic status are substantial. These economic hardships can be ranked (from smallest to largest adverse impact) by two criteria: the percentage reduction in family income[21] and the absolute level of total family income after elimination from the SSDI rolls. In terms of the percentage reduction criterion, the ranking is

1. those whose only medically validated ailment is alcoholism or mental problems (simulation 3);
2. those who won benefits on appeal (simulation 7);
3. those who are occupationally not severely disabled (simulation 2);
4. those below age 50 (simulation 4);
5. those who have only back problems (simulation 1);
6. those who applied for benefits more than once (simulation 6); and
7. those who have more than a high school education (simulation 5).

If, instead, we use the ranking based on the absolute level of expected family income without SSDI, the ranking is quite different: the order of the simulations is 5, 1, 2, 3, 4, 7, and 6.

Summary

In this paper we have examined the SSDI program, a program currently under pressure to reduce its growth and to reduce both its number of beneficiaries and its total benefit payments. This pressure is tied to two criticisms of the program: its very large growth during the early 1970s and its detrimental effect on labor force participation. Those fearing such cutbacks suggest that economic hardship will result. They also question the link between SSDI and labor force participation.

21. It should be emphasized that the change discussed here is that from current beneficiary to nonrecipient status. The analysis does not consider the hardship incurred by disabled individuals at the onset of disablement.

We have focused on two questions within this debate: what is the responsiveness to SSDI in terms of decreasing labor force participation among older (aged 45–62) men? And to what extent will there be economic hardship if current beneficiaries are eliminated from the rolls? In answering this last question, we go one step further and investigate the potential hardship to particular groups who have been singled out as potential "debeneficiaries."

The difference between these results and those of other researchers is large. With respect to the work of Parsons,[22] we conclude that our results differ from his because of differences in (1) the basic index function model used, (2) the extent of selection bias in the samples employed, (3) the comprehensiveness of the income flows used to characterize income expectations in the two options, and (4) the implicit assumptions regarding the probability of successfully securing income in the options. We judge that Parsons' very large elasticity estimates overstate the response of people to transfer benefits and are due to misspecification in all four of these dimensions.[23]

The response to increased transfer benefits, we find, is concentrated among older disabled men with low expected earnings. Therefore, a policy of reducing disability transfers, with the objective of increasing labor supply and total output, is unlikely to have marked success. Moreover, those persons most likely to be hurt have low earnings capacities and few alternative sources of income support. Hence retrenchment can be expected to reduce equity without a substantial gain in efficiency.

Our estimates suggest that the increasing relative generosity, leniency, or both of disability income transfer programs do have a statistically significant, though quantitatively small, effect on the work effort choices of older workers. They also partially explain the growth in these programs, and suggest that older, low-income earners with serious health impairments are most responsive to changes in expected transfer income. Nevertheless, many questions remain unanswered. Our results shed little light on the contribution of other variables to the observed decrease in labor force participation rates. While disability benefit generosity has accounted for a relatively modest amount of the reduction, the contri-

22. Parsons, "Decline in Male Labor Force Participation," and "Racial Trends in Male Labor Force Participation."

23. Robert H. Haveman and Barbara L. Wolfe, "The Decline in Male Labor Force Participation: Comment," *Journal of Political Economy* (forthcoming).

bution of changes in tastes for work, changes in social expectations regarding early retirement, changes in the physical demands of occupations, changes in the incidence of impairments, and changes in income from spouses and other sources remains unexplained.

To test the robustness of our results, we undertook a variety of alternative specifications. From them, we are confident that the response to increases in transfer program generosity or leniency is a statistically significant factor in the work status choice. However, it is quantitatively small.

In analyzing the economic hardship that would be imposed if particular subgroups were removed from the rolls, we undertook seven simulations. These include subgroups with particular ailments, socioeconomic characteristics, or means of gaining access to benefits: those with only back problems, alcoholics, prime-age workers, those with more than a high school education, those occupationally (as opposed to severely) disabled, those who applied more than once, and those who appealed to secure SSDI benefits. All groups (except perhaps those with alcohol problems) would suffer substantial economic hardship, with a reduction in family income of 33 to 45 percent.

Overall, then, our findings suggest that (1) reducing benefits is not likely to lead to significant changes in work effort and productivity; (2) SSDI cutbacks, if they do take place, should be targeted at specific groups to minimize economic hardship; and (3) microeconomic simulations can contribute to the identification of these groups.

Appendix A: Two-Stage Probit Model of Work Status Choices

Our estimates of the effect of disability transfers on the labor force participation decision of older workers are based on a reduced form, two-stage probit model. This model assumes that people choose between labor force participation and disability transfer recipiency on the basis of expectations regarding the level of economic well-being that would be afforded by each option. The income flows associated with each option determine the well-being experienced in each option, together with other sources of utility such as the utility of time spent in leisure and the stigma cost associated with public transfer recipiency.

Utility in the labor market option is

(2) $U_L = U_L(LE + N, \bar{H}),$

where LE is the income flow in the labor market option, N is nontransfer, nonwage income, and $\bar{H}$ is the hours of market work. In analogous fashion,

(3) $U_D = U_D(DT + N, 0)$

is the utility in the disability transfer option, where DT is the income flow in the disability transfer option, and $\bar{H} = 0$. The partial derivatives of both functions with respect to $\bar{H}$ are negative and with respect to income are positive.

We approximate the utility functions by assuming that they are linear in their arguments. Hence the utility-maximizing individual follows the decision function

(4) $I^* = U_L(LE + N, \bar{H}) - U_D(DT + N, 0)$
            $\cong \alpha(LE + N) - \gamma(DT + N) + \underline{\omega}'\underline{X} + V,$

where $\underline{X}$ is a vector of parameters of the utility function and V is a random error term with a zero mean measuring tastes and other unobserved variables. Given this rule,

$$I = \begin{cases} 1 & \text{if } I^* > 0 \\ 0 & \text{if } I^* \le 0, \end{cases}$$

where 1 represents the labor market option and 0 represents the disability transfer option.

Equation 4 could be estimated if all of the right-hand-side variables were observed. The expected coefficient signs are positive for LE and negative for DT if leisure is a normal good. But a difficulty is raised by the fact that the income flows (LE, DT) are observed only if the respective choice were made. Hence, we need to determine LE explicitly or implicitly for those with $I = 0$ and DT for those with $I = 1$. Equations 5 and 6 describe the determination of LE and DT as a function of variables $\underline{Z}$, including exogenous permanent characteristics of individuals expected to influence labor market and disability transfer income flows, and the characteristics of labor and disability transfer markets describing the terms on which the respective flows are available. In this representation we simplify and let LE represent $LE + N$ and DT represent $DT + N$:

(5) $LE_j = \underline{\beta}_1'\underline{Z}_j + \epsilon_{1j}$

(6) $DT_j = \underline{\beta}_2'\underline{Z}_j + \epsilon_{2j}.$

Since $\underline{Z}_j$ is assumed to be exogenous, $E(\epsilon_{ij} \mid \underline{Z}) = 0$ for $i = 1, 2$.

From this, we can write the model as a simultaneous equation system:

(7) $$LE_j = \underline{\beta}_1' \underline{Z}_j + \epsilon_{ij} \quad \text{iff } I_j^* > 0$$

(8) $$DT_j = \underline{\beta}_2' \underline{Z}_j + \epsilon_{2j} \quad \text{iff } I_j^* \leq 0$$

(9) $$I_j^* = (\alpha\underline{\beta}_1 - \gamma\underline{\beta}_2)' \underline{Z}_j + (\alpha\epsilon_{ij} - \gamma\epsilon_{2j}) + \underline{\omega}' \underline{X}_j + v_j$$
$$= \underline{\beta}_3' \underline{Z}_j + \underline{\omega}' \underline{X}_j + \epsilon_{3j},$$

where $\underline{\beta}_3 = (\alpha\underline{\beta}_1 - \gamma\underline{\beta}_2)$

$$\epsilon_{3j} = \frac{1}{\sigma^{*2}} (V_j - \alpha\epsilon_{1j} - \gamma\epsilon_{2j})$$

$$\sigma^{*2} = E(V_j - \alpha\epsilon_{1j} - \gamma\epsilon_{2j})^2.$$

The selection rule presumes that people know the outcome should either option be chosen, implying that they have engaged in search activity in both options and have achieved a long-run equilibrium. The selection equation, however, recognizes that for some people the search may be incomplete so that the realized income flow in an option may fall short of or exceed the ex ante estimate of expected income. The equation also reflects the cost of application and the discretionary role of employers and administrators to the extent that they depend on observed characteristics $\underline{Z}$.

Since LE_j and DT_j are involved in the decision process but our observation of them depends on the final choice, the observed values are truncated (limited-dependent or censored). Hence, ordinary least squares estimates of these variables will yield biased estimates. However, given sample separation, we observe the final choice. Hence, $\underline{\beta}_1$, $\underline{\beta}_2$, ϵ_1^2, and ϵ_2^2 are identified and can be consistently estimated by a two-stage method involving modified least squares and probit maximum likelihood.

This, then, is an example of a "switching regression" that has been discussed by Heckman and Lee.[24] Indeed, our model is precisely that of Lee, to whom the reader is referred. We have chosen to derive estimates from the two-stage probit procedure because the estimates from full maximum-likelihood procedures rest on the availability of good initial estimates in highly nonlinear models. Our two-stage probit procedure utilizes modified least squares in the first stage and probit maximum likelihood in the second.

24. Heckman, "Sample Selection Bias as a Specification Error"; and Lee, "Identification and Estimation in Binary Choice Models."

For this model to be identified:

—not all variables in the LE and DT equation can be in the final stage decision function; and

—either there exists no covariance between the residuals of the income flows, that is, $\text{cov}(\epsilon_1, \epsilon_2) = 0$ or there exists no covariance between the error term of the decision function and the error terms of LE and DT, that is, $\text{cov}(\epsilon_1, V)$, $\text{cov}(\epsilon_2, V) = 0$.

With this formulation, the estimates from the two-stage probit analysis will be strongly consistent, and the error terms can be shown to be asymptotically normally distributed.[25]

Estimation of expected flows is not straightforward because, as stated above, people are observed to have only labor earnings or disability transfers as a result of their decisions. Given the self-selection of these groups, direct estimation of equations 7 and 8 will not yield consistent estimates of β_1 and β_2. Following Heckman we assume that $\epsilon_j = (\epsilon_{1j}, \epsilon_{2j})$ has a bivariate normal distribution and that ϵ_j is independent of ϵ_j' for $j \neq j'$.[26] Given the selection rule and the normality assumption, the appropriate regression functions for equations 7 and 8 are

$$(10) \qquad E(LE_j \mid \underline{Z}_j, I^* > 0) = \underline{\beta}_1' \underline{Z}_j + E(\epsilon_{1j} \mid \underline{Z}_j, I^* > 0)$$
$$= \underline{\beta}_1' \underline{Z}_j + E(\epsilon_{1j} \mid \epsilon_{3j} > -\underline{\beta}_3' \underline{Z}_j)$$
$$= \underline{\beta}_1' \underline{Z}_j + \frac{\sigma_{13}}{\sigma_{33}^{1/2}} \lambda_{1j}(-\underline{\beta}_3' \underline{Z}_j / \sigma_{33}^{1/2})$$

$$(11) \qquad E(DT_j \mid \underline{Z}_j, I^* \leq 0) = \underline{\beta}_2' \underline{Z}_j + E(\epsilon_{2j} \mid \underline{Z}_j, I^* < 0)$$
$$= \underline{\beta}_2' \underline{Z}_j + E(\epsilon_{2j} \mid \epsilon_{3j} < -\underline{\beta}_3' \underline{Z}_j)$$
$$= \underline{\beta}_2' \underline{Z}_j + \frac{\sigma_{23}}{\sigma_{33}^{1/2}} \lambda_{2j}(-\underline{\beta}_3' \underline{Z}_j / \sigma_{33}^{1/2}),$$

where $\lambda_1(s) = \phi(s)/1 - \Phi(s)$ and $\lambda_2(s) = -\phi(s)/\Phi(s)$. The final equality in equations 10 and 11 is based on the formula for the mean of a truncated normal random variable.

The parameters in equations 10 and 11 are estimated in three steps. Let $D_j = 1$ if $I^* > 0$ and $D_j = 0$ if $I^* \leq 0$. With equation 9,

$$(12) \quad P(D_j = 1 \mid \underline{Z}_j) = P(\epsilon_{3j} > -\underline{\beta}_3' \underline{Z}_j \mid \underline{Z}_j) = 1 - P\left(\frac{\epsilon_{3j}}{\sigma_{33}^{1/2}} < \frac{-\underline{\beta}_3' \underline{Z}_j}{\sigma_{33}^{1/2}}\right).$$

25. Lee, "Identification and Estimation in Binary Choice Models."
26. Heckman, "Shadow Prices, Market Wages, and Labor Supply," and "Sample Selection Bias as a Specification Error."

Performing the probit regression implied by equation 12, we obtain consistent estimates of $\beta_3/\sigma_{33}^{1/2}$, denoted $\widehat{\beta_3/\sigma_{33}^{1/2}}$. With $\widehat{\beta_3/\sigma_{33}^{1/2}}$, we next construct estimates of $\lambda_{ij}(\cdot)$ (the inverse Mill's ratio), which we label $\hat{\lambda}_{1j}(\cdot)$ and $\hat{\lambda}_{2j}(\cdot)$. Finally, with the $\hat{\lambda}(\cdot)$ variables, the ordinary least squares regressions of LE_j on $\underline{Z}_j$, $\hat{\lambda}_{1j}(\cdot)$ and DT_j on $\underline{Z}_j$, $\hat{\lambda}_{2j}(\cdot)$ are estimated over the appropriate subsamples. This procedure provides consistent estimates of β_1, β_2, $\sigma_{13}/\sigma_{33}^{1/2}$, and $\sigma_{23}/\sigma_{33}^{1/2}$.

In this model disability transfer programs are viewed as influencing participation decisions through their impact on expected income flows. From equations 10 and 11 we obtain estimates of LE_j and DT_j—designated as $\widehat{LE}_j$ and $\widehat{DT}_j$—which are expected income flows in the labor market and disability transfer options. These can be used in a nonlinear probit equation to estimate the elasticity of labor force participation with respect to disability program generosity as follows:

$$(13) \qquad P(D_j = 1 \mid LE_j, DT_j) = \Phi(\delta\widehat{LE}_j + \eta\widehat{DT}_j) + \epsilon_{4j}.$$

In estimating this model, several alternative measures of $\widehat{LE}_j$ and $\widehat{DT}_j$ can be specified as proxies of LE_j and DT_j. Each represents a different assumption regarding how individuals form their expectations of outcomes contingent on choices. In one formulation consistent with equation 7 through equation 9, LE_j can be represented by $\hat{E}(LE_j \mid \underline{Z}_j, I^* > 0)$. (An analogous representation exists for DT_j.) In an estimation using the selectivity term in predicting income flows, a person's expectation is based on the outcomes of those with identical observed characteristics who have chosen the labor market option. It reflects the selection process, such that some people with given characteristics are, and others are not, successful in that option. This is the procedure we use in this paper. An alternative estimation would not use the selectivity term for prediction. In this case a person's expected outcome in an option is based on the observed income flows of those with like characteristics who are in each of the two options. This procedure neglects the fact that some people participate in an option while others do not and implicitly assumes that everyone can successfully participate in that option at some level.

92   Robert H. Haveman, Barbara L. Wolfe, and Jennifer L. Warlick

Appendix B: Statistical Table

Table 8. Probit Regression of Probability of Denial Given Application in 1976–78

Variable	Estimated coefficient	Asymptotic t-statistic	Mean
Constant	−0.32	−0.73	. . .
Bed- or chair-ridden (0,1)	1.07	2.25	0.032
Male, not presently married (0,1)	0.036	0.24	0.234
Severely disabled (0,1)	−0.785	−3.67*	0.887
Occupationally disabled (0,1)	0.107	0.43	0.075
Race (white = 1)	−0.179	−1.38	0.827
Missing spouse works (0,1)	0.045	0.30	0.329
Female, not presently working (0,1)	1.578	8.07*	0.084
Female, married (0,1)	−1.921	−10.99*	0.098
South (0,1)	0.148	1.43	0.393
Age at application	−0.009	−1.57	43.4
Time to last application	0.011	1.43	3.55
Education	−0.021	−1.31	9.63
Last applied 1978 (0,1)	1.268	8.35*	0.106
Last applied 1977 (0,1)	0.804	6.95*	0.318
Year applied missing (0,1)	−0.291	−0.92	0.113
Respiratory (0,1)	0.102	0.82	0.234
Hardening arteries (0,1)	−0.076	−0.47	0.155
High blood pressure (0,1)	0.191	1.70	0.347
Coronary disease, stroke (0,1)	−0.338	−2.56*	0.253
Tumor (0,1)	0.043	0.20	0.055
Cancer (0,1)	−0.218	−0.86	0.049
Stomach, liver trouble (0,1)	0.205	1.86	0.285
Kidney (0,1)	−0.087	−0.46	0.084
Arthritis (0,1)	0.223	2.06*	0.408
Mental illness (0,1)	−0.189	−1.70	0.326
Diabetes (0,1)	−0.083	−0.49	0.103
Epileptic (0,1)	−0.208	−0.77	0.041
Alcoholism, drug abuse (0,1)	0.494	1.82	0.022
Deaf (0,1)	−0.350	−1.94*	0.117
Blind (0,1)	0.078	0.54	0.142
No legs (0,1)	0.215	0.45	0.014
No arms (0,1)	0.046	0.14	0.028
Bone stiffness, deformity (0,1)	0.013	0.11	0.262
Paralysis, other back (0,1)	0.067	0.64	0.378
Severe allergy (0,1)	0.219	1.08	0.058
Number of applications (0,1)	0.057	1.70	1.57
Spouse in labor force (0,1)	0.048	0.04	0.309
Walk, climb stairs (0,1)	−0.422	−2.16*	0.308
Stand (0,1)	0.028	0.15	0.275
Sit (0,1)	0.184	1.01	0.092

Table 8 (*continued*)

Variable	Estimated coefficient	Asymptotic t-statistic	Mean
Stoop or kneel (0,1)	0.008	0.04	0.249
Hands or fingers (0,1)	−0.129	−0.76	0.240
Sight problems (0,1)	−0.112	−0.57	0.102
Lift ten pounds (0,1)	−0.156	−0.75	0.309
Lift twenty-five pounds (0,1)	−0.025	−0.14	0.245
Veteran (0,1) (0,1)	0.324	2.59*	0.420
Appended (0,1)	0.356	2.55*	0.121
Missing data (0,1)	−0.548	−2.60*	0.599
Number of observations	1,391	. . .	. . .
Awards (0)	1,079	. . .	. . .
Denials (1)	3,312	. . .	. . .

Source: Authors' calculations.
* Significant at the 5 percent level.

Comment by Joseph P. Newhouse

The authors of this paper address two questions. First, they explore how much of the decline in participation in the labor force by older males can be explained by the increased generosity of disability insurance throughout the 1970s. Some studies of this question, and in particular those by Donald Parsons of Ohio State University, have shown that the effect of disability transfers has been quite substantial. But the authors' estimates of the responsiveness of labor force participation to disability transfers are considerably lower than the earlier estimates.

Second, the authors estimate how successful current or proposed reforms in the program aimed at reducing the size of the disability rolls might be. This section of the paper provides estimates of the effect of the reforms on family incomes and the size of the population receiving disability insurance. The authors assess the degree to which families cut from the rolls have alternative sources of income to replace their lost insurance and thus how well they could adjust. These are interesting issues, and they are usually not adequately treated when reforms of this type are proposed. But the issues surrounding the effects of reform are quite distinct from those considered in the first part of the paper. I will consider each set of issues in turn.

In the first section of the paper the authors write as though they were quite confident of their conclusions. They report *t*-statistics on the effect of disability insurance on participation that range around six or seven, depending on the exact specification used. In my view, the actual confidence that we can place in the estimates is not as high as suggested by these t-statistics, because the t-statistics are conditional on the specification adopted by the authors, which may be right or wrong.

In particular, the estimates depend heavily on the functional form assumptions in the Heckman correction procedure for self-selection bias. For example, it is necessary for the authors to estimate the potential disability income of persons who do not now collect such income. Almost all full-time workers are not disabled and do not have disability income. So to predict a level of potential disability income for full-time workers the authors extrapolate the effect of "extent of disabilities" on disability income into a range of observations where one has either no or very few actual observations of disability income. The authors use a quadratic specification in the two disability variables to make this extrapolation. While I have no objection to this particular specification, the resulting estimates, of necessity, reflect a heavy reliance on functional form because we have little evidence to guide us.

Similarly, the authors assume that the disturbances in their earnings functions are distributed as a random normal variable. It seems to me more plausible to assume log normality here. Moreover, their procedure requires two steps to estimate expected earnings and expected disability income. In predicting labor force participation, the first step, the authors include six variables that they exclude when they come to the second step, predicting income flows. I do not find any compelling theoretical reasons for their exclusion, yet those variables are potentially important to the authors' quantitative estimates. I conclude that the (assumed) restrictions on which variables enter the second stage, as well as functional form assumptions, are carrying much of the weight in correcting for the obvious selectivity problems in their model. As a result, the true uncertainty surrounding the estimates is greater than may seem apparent.

The authors have provided some tests for their model's validity, but their tests tell us little about the reliability of a key number, the estimated coefficient on expected disability income. They report that their model can distinguish between people who are in the labor force and people who are not. But the basis for their accurate prediction of this matter is the set of diseases or handicaps contained in table 1; it is not the assumed restrictions and functional form. The authors also state that the overall labor force participation rate is accurately predicted by their model, but this would be the case for any model where the probit program is applied properly.

Although the major interest in the first section of the paper is empirical, the economic theory lying behind the estimates is a bit peculiar. The theoretical model rests on the assumption that people maximize income. However, it seems more plausible to assume that people maximize utility, taking account of the disutility, if any, arising out of work.

Finally, in interpreting the effect of a 20 percent increase in the value of disability transfers, it is important to recognize that the authors' estimates are conditional on the design of the current system. Changes in marginal tax rates or administrative rules cannot be properly treated in their current model. It presumably matters how the 20 percent change in benefits comes about. In sum, the new findings certainly cast doubt on the earlier estimates obtained by Parsons, but they cannot be considered definitive.

In the second part of the paper the authors' strategy is to select a personal or family characteristic and then to simulate the effect of denying benefits to individuals or families with that characteristic. The most compelling aspect of the findings is that most of the simulated policy actions seem to induce the same percentage reduction in affected families' incomes. However, the policy actions selected for simulation are not very plausible. For example, one reform would eliminate from the rolls all families with the top 10 percent or 20 percent of expected family income. If adopted, this policy would obviously represent an extraordinary tax on income.

Another question is whether the selected characteristics really identify the people to whom society would most wish to deny disability benefits. These characteristics in practice would probably yield a number of false positives, that is, people to whom society would not wish to deny disability benefits but who nonetheless would be denied them. The simulations accurately show us the average effect of denying benefits to people with a given characteristic but do not reveal what is of greater interest, namely, the marginal effect of denying benefits. For example, the average person with back pain who is denied benefits may lose 60 percent of his income, taking account of his probable wage earnings. But the person with back pain who is marginally eligible for benefits under current regulation and administrative practice may be able to replace 100 percent of his lost disability transfers with new wage earnings.

In summary, the findings reported in this paper are sufficiently strong to cast serious doubt on some earlier estimates of the effect of disability insurance on labor force participation, but I differ with the authors in assessing the reliability of their new findings. The results are conditional on some assumptions that are not testable and that do not emerge from standard economic theory. The resulting predictions may, of course, be right. But the amount of uncertainty is greater than the authors imply.

Peter A. Diamond and Jerry A. Hausman

The Retirement and Unemployment Behavior of Older Men

Simple life-cycle models of labor supply and savings generally omit uncertainty. Yet people experience considerable uncertainty about wealth accumulation, financial needs, health, and job opportunities. These uncertainties imply that people are continuously reconsidering their plans for retirement and wealth accumulation as their economic and health positions develop. The starting point of our research is to recognize the central place of these uncertainties and to explore the potential of longitudinal data for estimating labor supply in this setting.

In this paper we focus on two sources of uncertainty for aged workers: physical health and involuntary unemployment. Both sources of uncertainty have a large potential effect on the timing of retirement. Unexpected bad health may sharply reduce the kind and amount of work that an older worker can perform. Similarly, older workers who are permanently discharged from their lifetime jobs may find it difficult if not impossible to find equivalent employment. Because these unexpected events can seriously disrupt the retirement plans of even farsighted workers, it is unreasonable to assume that a simple life-cycle model will explain lifetime labor supply and savings generally or retirement behavior in particular.

The principal contribution of the present paper is to construct and estimate careful statistical models of the effects of bad health, unemployment, and permanent income on retirement. The paper has two main sections. In the first we explain and estimate a hazard-rate model of retirement. This model provides an exact mathematical representation of the relation between a worker's age and his rate of entry into

The authors are grateful to Lynn Paquette for research assistance and to Henry Farber for his helpful comments.

retirement, which is the "hazard" of interest. This model is a natural one for working with longitudinal data, especially if uncertainty is an important determinant of individual behavior. In part, this fit between technique and approach comes because the hazard model provides a logical method for handling censoring of observations, which is an inevitable occurrence in longitudinal data. (Censorship occurs for members of the sample where the dependent variable of interest is not observed. In our case, censorship occurs when retirement does not take place by the time a worker has completed his last interview. Consequently, no retirement age is observed.) In addition, as we show below, the hazard model is capable of taking account of variables that change over time, such as pension wealth. This capability is obviously crucial when an important set of factors affecting retirement is subject to either random or predictable change.

In the second main section, we evaluate the effect of involuntary unemployment on retirement and subsequent labor market behavior. To accomplish this task, we consider a particular subset of older workers, namely, those who have been permanently discharged from their jobs. Because these fired workers may be particularly affected by a delay in the normal retirement age under social security, their response to permanent separation is of special interest for policymakers. In particular, it is important to establish whether discharged workers will retire or succeed in finding alternative employment. Those who retire may face a serious loss in retirement income if the normal retirement age is significantly pushed back. To assess the effect of involuntary unemployment, we fit two types of statistical models. The first is a simple probit model in which the dependent variable indicates the outcome of the older worker's spell of unemployment (either retirement or reemployment). The second is a competing-risks model, which not only takes account of the outcome of a spell of unemployment, but also accounts for the length of the spell of unemployment leading up either to retirement or to reemployment. In both the probit and the competing-risks models, we consider the effect of age, poor health, private pensions, and social security benefits on the labor force decision of the discharged workers. Our paper concludes with a brief summary of major findings.

A Model of Retirement Behavior

The main focus of our empirical work in this section is the determination of factors that affect the actual retirement decision. Two definitional problems require brief discussion before we describe our statistical model, however. First, the definition of retirement is not straightforward because multiple definitions are possible. We identified three possible definitions of the retirement age: the age at which a person stopped working full time, at which he declared himself retired or unable to work, or at which he declared himself retired, irrespective of his health status. The correlation among the definitions is high, and since the first definition is based upon measurable behavior in the labor market, it seemed the best definition for our formal statistical models.[1]

Another definitional problem is caused by the possibility of multiple transitions. Some workers reenter the labor market after retirement. Full statistical treatment of the decision would require a considerably more elaborate model, which we leave to future research. Instead, our analysis focuses on the first retirement. Nonetheless, it is worthwhile considering the frequency of transition from retirement back to full-time work.

To see the importance of the phenomenon, we report labor market reentry hazards in table 1. We show the fraction of retired workers recorded on one survey who are not retired in the subsequent survey.

Some consecutive surveys are separated by a single year while others are separated by two years. Rather than merging these in some way, we separately report one-year and two-year reentry hazards. The reentry probabilities are high, suggesting the value of modifying or extending our present analysis of first retirement. The probability of reentry into the labor market decreases with age, as one would expect. Note that the probability of reentry is lower under the self-described definition of retirement than under the full-time work measure. This difference suggests that movement between part-time and full-time work may be more important than movement between full retirement and part-time work. One puzzling aspect of the table is the fact that the two-year reentry hazards are similar in magnitude to the one-year hazards. Formally, this finding suggests high frequency of "re-retirement" after retirees reenter the labor market. Possibly, it reflects problems with the

1. The age at which the worker stopped working full time usually occurred at the same time or somewhat earlier than the events described by the other two definitions. In a previous paper we estimated a retirement model with the three different definitions of retirement to assess the sensitivity of the results. Overall, the estimated coefficients were quite similar although the coefficient of the health variable was sensitive to the definition of retirement used. Peter Diamond and Jerry A. Hausman, "Individual Retirement and Savings Behavior," paper presented at a National Bureau of Economic Research–Social Science Research Center conference, Oxford, England, July 1982.

Table 1. Labor Market Reentry Rates[a]

Percent

	One-year reentry rates		Two-year reentry rates	
Age	Self-described retired or unable to work	Not full-time worker	Self-described retired or unable to work	Not full-time worker
45–49	18.54	52.55	4.00	53.76
	(151)	(314)	(25)	(93)
50–54	16.23	46.93	17.68	41.03
	(228)	(473)	(181)	(446)
55–59	15.94	31.85	10.31	25.23
	(552)	(741)	(524)	(769)
60–64	13.37	15.45	9.57	7.15
	(501)	(466)	(993)	(1,147)
65–69	11.74	5.02	9.04	2.94
	(426)	(438)	(686)	(715)
Total	14.53	29.48	10.13	16.72
	(1,858)	(2,432)	(2,409)	(3,170)

Source: Authors' calculations using the National Longitudinal Survey of Older Men.
a. Number of observations is given in parentheses.

measures employed to describe behavior rather than actual behavioral changes.[2]

To some extent we expect that those people who decide to reenter the labor force after retiring have made a mistake in their planning. That is, their actual experience during retirement did not conform to their expectations. In this paper we focus on an individual's initial retirement since we assume it provides the best reflection of the life-cycle decision. A change in health might also cause a transitory retirement; we attempt to control for this possibility in our analysis. A more difficult problem is presented by the possibility of a *planned* "crossover." For instance, because of the earnings test in the social security law, it is possible that a person may plan to return to the work force after his initial retirement. Our model does not allow for this possibility. It seems unlikely that an

2. In 1978, individuals were asked to compare their health with that in 1976. We have cross tabulated these answers with retirement status in the same pair of years, using the full-time work definition of retirement. Of the four possible pairs of retirement statuses, those reentering work are most likely to report improving health. Yet almost as many of those reentrants report worsening health. The other three groups have a much higher ratio of persons reporting worsening health to those reporting improving health. Thus, health improvement is an important correlate with reentry into the labor market but must be viewed as only a partial explanation of this phenomenon.

important fraction of the population is in circumstances or has preferences that would lead to such planned behavior.

We now consider the model that lies behind our specification though we do not develop an explicit economic choice model for our specification.[3] At any time a person can choose to retire. The probability of retiring at a particular age is the product of the probability that he was not previously retired and the conditional probability of his decision to retire at the current age. The probability that a worker has not previously retired depends on past values of the conditional probability of retirement. Those past conditional probabilities in turn depend on the factors that made past retirement more or less attractive than continuing to work. The factors affecting the conditional probability of retirement at a particular age include both current variables and expectations about future variables. Among current variables are wealth, financial needs, earnings opportunities, job satisfaction, taste for work, health, and retirement opportunities (which may be affected by family mobility considerations such as employment of a spouse). Among future expectations variables are the rate of return on current wealth, future financial needs, the real value of future pension benefits, and the real value of future social security benefits. Inflation and possible legislative action cause major uncertainties about the latter two variables. Continuation of work also affects the value of future private pension and social security entitlements, and this, too, affects the relative attractiveness of work. An additional future expectation variable is the availability and attractiveness of future earnings opportunities and the relationship of future opportunities to the current work decision. For many employed people, retirement implies a sizable diminution of future earnings prospects. It is this fact that makes the retirement question an empirically different one from the standard hours of work decision more commonly treated in the labor supply literature. By ignoring the possibility of postretirement reentry to the labor force, we implicitly assume that retirement eliminates later full-time work opportunities.[4]

Before turning to our formal statistical model of the retirement age, we should consider the actual retirement patterns observed in our data

3. For a formal presentation and analysis of a model covering some aspects of this informal model, see Peter Diamond and James Mirrlees, "Social Insurance with Variable Retirement and Private Savings" (Massachusetts Institute of Technology, 1982).

4. People who return to full-time employment after retirement usually do so at a considerably lower wage than they received on their preretirement job.

set, the National Longitudinal Survey (NLS) of Older Men. Because it
is so central to the economic choice aspect of retirement, we consider in
particular the relationship between the ages of retirement and the ages
at which retirement income starts. Analysts who use cross-sectional
methods to investigate the impact of retirement income on retirement
behavior are frequently led astray by the correlation at a particular time
between retirement status and pension or social security income. If a
person is receiving retirement benefits and is not working, cross-sectional
analysis attributes both a substitution effect and an income effect to the
retirement benefit. If the person retired several years before the start of
retirement income, however, then the substitution effect may not have
been present at the time of retirement. (Strictly speaking, the possible
link of labor supplies across years prevents us from saying that the
substitution effect was completely absent.) We document the importance
of this phenomenon.

In each NLS survey, men were asked about their labor force status
in the survey week. People out of the labor force could describe
themselves as retired, unable to work, or out of the labor force for other
reasons. For each survey, we coded a person as retired if he described
himself as retired or unable to work.[5] A second way to define retirement
was based on behavior in the year before the survey. People were coded
as full-time workers if they were in the labor force at least forty of the
fifty-two previous weeks and did not answer no to the question of
whether they normally worked at least thirty-five hours per week.
Anyone who was not a full-time worker was considered retired. To pick
an age of (first) retirement under either definition, we first examined the
string of retirement codes recorded for each of the survey years and
located the first survey (if any) when a man was retired and a previous
last survey (if any) when a man was not retired. The date of retirement
was located midway between the two surveys (or in 1966, the date of the
first survey, if retired at the start) unless there was information permitting
an alternative date.[6]

For each survey year we then looked to see whether the worker was

5. Movement between retired and unable to work seemed to make self-declared
retirement status alone an unsatisfactory definition.
6. This information sometimes came from the answer to the question about the date
last worked, provided this was between the two surveys. Weeks out of the labor force
between surveys were sometimes used to determine the date, assuming work preceded
time out of the labor force. (With a two-year gap between some surveys, this measure
was not available.) We refer to the two measures as self-defined retirement and work-
defined retirement.

receiving retirement or disability income. The variable "age first began receiving retirement income" is set equal to the respondent's age during the year he first indicated having received retirement or disability income from social security or private or government pensions. In the case of surveys that are two years apart, if the respondent reported receiving retirement income during the year before the later survey and had not reported receiving retirement income two years earlier, the age at start of retirement is set equal to the respondent's age at the midpoint between the two years.[7]

In table 2 we report the difference between the age of retirement and the age of first receipt of retirement income. The first six columns of the table, based on the full-time work definition of retirement, provide a cross tabulation by permanent income and show the number retiring in each income category with and without retirement income. Columns 7 through 10 permit a comparison between the full-time work and self-defined definitions of retirement. They show the relation between retirement income, retirement age, and health status under the two definitions. Note that our tabulations are affected by the truncation of the observation period; some men who retired shortly before the last survey may eventually receive pensions.[8]

Nevertheless, the table makes clear the sizable presence of long delays between retirement and the onset of retirement income.[9] Dispro-portionately, those retiring well before the start of retirement income

7. The 1966, 1967, and 1969 survey questionnaires did not ask the respondent if he received nondisability pension income. However, if he was receiving a private pension at the time of the 1976 survey, he was asked to report his age at the time he began receiving it. In this case, the age variable is set equal to the lesser of this age and the age at which he first reported receiving any other retirement income. The 1978 survey did not distinguish between social security received by the respondent and that received by his wife. To determine if the social security reported for the year 1977 is the wife's rather than the respondent's, the social security nondisability income reported for the wife for 1975 is inflated by the ratio of the consumer price index in 1977 to the CPI in 1975. If the amount of social security reported in 1977 is within 20 percent of the wife's inflated 1975 social security, then the respondent is assumed not to have begun receiving social security in 1977.

8. To offset the race-weighted sampling of the National Longitudinal Survey, we counted whites three times and nonwhites once in doing the tabulations. Hence, sample sizes are overstated in the table.

9. This analysis complements that of Eric Kingson, who examined young retirees and found that the group who described themselves as unhealthy but ineligible for social security disability benefits appeared to contain a sizable group likely to be suffering economic distress. See Eric Kingson, "The Early Retirement Myth: Why Men Retire Before Age 62," A Report by the House Select Committee on Aging, 97 Cong. 1 sess. (Government Printing Office, 1981).

Table 2. Age of Retirement Minus Age at Start of Retirement Income Related to Permanent Income and Health Limitations[a]

	Percent with permanent income (1966 dollars)					Full-time-work definition of retirement			Self-description definition of retirement	
Item	Less than $4,200 (1)	$4,200–$5,599 (2)	$5,600–$6,799 (3)	$6,800–$8,699 (4)	$8,700 and over (5)	Number of observations[b] (6)	Percent reporting work limitations (7)	Number of observations (8)	Percent reporting work limitations (9)	Number of observations (10)
Beginning of retirement income										
5 or more years after retirement	41	18	16	14	10	478	41	871	75	171
2–4 years after retirement	32	19	23	13	13	435	46	727	64	264
Within year of retirement	22	23	17	22	17	1,813	42	2,392	45	2,522
2–4 years before retirement	27	26	14	19	14	745	48	773	57	893
5 or more years before retirement	14	29	17	22	17	276	46	271	54	420
Retired, no retirement income	36	21	14	14	15	923	33	1,741	55	552
Not retired, no retirement income	19	22	17	21	21	2,251	28	1,719	30	2,349
Not retired, retirement income	15	21	20	19	25	652	35	672	46	1,245

Source: Same as table 1.
a. Race weighted.
b. Sum of observations used in columns 1–5.

have low permanent incomes.[10] The same is true for those with a retirement but no retirement income in the sample period. (This latter group is likely to include some who died or were otherwise lost to the sample after retirement but before retirement income commenced.) The results are qualitatively similar when the definition of retirement is based on a self-description of retirement or inability to work. In other analysis, not reported here, we have found that a disproportionate number of those with low ratios of wealth (before retirement) to permanent income retire well before the start of retirement income.

The last four columns of table 2 provide an illustration of the relation between poor health, income, and retirement. Using the self-described definition of retirement, we find a correlation between health problems, on the one hand, and the delay between retirement and retirement income, on the other. For the full-time work definition we do not find this correlation. Thus the definition of retirement appears to be important in assessing the effect of health.

We now consider a statistical model of retirement that more formally treats these issues. To determine the effect of variables such as pensions and health on the age of retirement, a natural approach would be to estimate a regression model with age of retirement as the left-hand-side variable. The coefficient of a particular right-hand-side variable could then be interpreted in a straightforward way as the effect of the variable on the expected age of retirement. However, a regression model is inappropriate to use on most longitudinal data sets because a large proportion of people will have no recorded age of retirement, as they have not yet retired. This statistical problem of censorship leaves the regression model without a left-hand-side variable for the people who are not retired.[11] An alternative approach, which we use here, is to develop an explicit conditional probability distribution for the age of retirement. By assuming a particular mathematical form of the probability distribution, we can correctly treat the information provided by censored (nonretired) persons. Essentially, our mathematical assumption permits us to calculate the expected age of retirement for the

10. Permanent income is the average of real earnings (in 1966 dollars), plus unemployment compensation adjusted for taxes, over preretirement years, provided there are at least three such observations.

11. The statistical and econometrics literature has demonstrated the large biases in estimated coefficients that can result if the regression is fit on only the noncensored (retired) individuals.

nonretired individuals and hence implicitly gives us a value for the dependent variable (age of retirement).

Our statistical model takes full advantage of the longitudinal aspect of the data. In considering the conditional probability that retirement will take place at a particular age, we can use information about all members of the sample, even those who have still not retired by that age. The observed conditional probability of retirement at that age can then be used, together with our assumption about the mathematical shape of the probability distribution function, to obtain estimates of the actual probability function that generates retirement behavior. (Of course, information on the probabilities of retirement at *all* ages is used in forming our estimates.) Therefore, the censorship problem is correctly treated, and all available information contained in the longitudinal data is utilized.

The statistical specification that we use for analysis is the regression type of hazard model, which has undergone rapid development in the biometrics literature since the paper by Cox.[12] The continuous time-hazards model that we estimate eliminates three possible problems that may arise in other statistical models of retirement. First, as we have discussed, a censoring problem will exist in most longitudinal data on retirement. Ordinary regression-type specifications are not well adapted to take account of the censoring problem, and the Tobit specification, which otherwise might be appropriate, does not make use of the fact that all people in a sample must eventually retire. This aspect of the retirement process is captured by our hazards specification. Second, the fact that the regressor variables change over time is also handled more naturally within our framework than it can be in a regression specification, even if there is no censoring problem.[13] This problem could, in principle, be

12. D. R. Cox, "Regression Models and Life-Tables," *Journal of the Royal Statistical Society,* vol. 34-B, no. 2 (1972), pp. 187–201. To the best of our knowledge it was used first in the econometrics literature by Lancaster, who analyzed reemployment probabilities for a sample of unemployed workers. Other recent applications are by Lancaster and Lancaster and Nickell. Tony Lancaster, "Econometric Methods for the Duration of Unemployment," *Econometrica,* vol. 47 (July 1979), pp. 939–56; and Tony Lancaster and Stephen Nickell, "The Analysis of Re-Employment Probabilities for the Unemployed," *Journal of the Royal Statistical Society,* vol. 143-A, pt. 2 (1980), pp. 141–65. These papers concentrate much more on the particular shape of the hazard function than we do. Our interest is primarily in the regression part of the problem.

13. Some type of averaging might be used for these changing regressors. However, an averaging procedure seems inappropriate for variables that change in discontinuous moves such as health status or pension eligibility.

avoided by use of logit or probit statistical models. Using this procedure, the analyst would arrange the retirement history data into a series of year-by-year cross sections, where the dependent variable would reflect whether people chose to be retired at a particular age. But then a third problem is introduced: "dynamic self-selection." Note that the sample at risk for retirement in each year is determined by past history. That history is not likely to be repeated if, for example, policy were to change. Thus the sample of nonretirees in a given year is not representative of the population at risk under different historical values of the policy variables, since the people who have elected to retire or to remain employed at particular ages would change. By implication, the coefficients obtained in a logit or probit model could be highly sensitive to the past history of the policy variables and virtually useless in evaluating the long-term effect of changes in those variables. We present empirical evidence on the magnitude of this problem later in the section. However, our hazard model does lack a formal choice model basis that can often be given to probit models. Additional research to determine an explicit choice basis for the specifications would be a useful addition to the literature.

At any time, say t, we assume that the instantaneous hazard rate of retirement for a given person who has not yet retired is shown by the mathematical function $\theta(t)$. Therefore, over a short time the probability of retirement is $\theta(t)\,dt$. Now $\theta(t)$ corresponds to an ordinary probability density function and has an associated distribution function determined by

$$(1) \qquad 1 - G(t) = \exp\left[-\int_0^t \theta(u)\,du\right].^{14}$$

In our sample we assume that time starts at age 44 since the youngest age is 45 years and no sample member has retired by that age. At any point in time the individual is presumed to have solved the choice problem that arises from the complicated stochastic dynamic problem of whether to retire. Formulation and formal solution of this complicated choice is well beyond the scope of the current research; instead we use current values of variables without attempting to model explicitly

---

14. Equation 1 follows from integration of the fundamental relationship $\theta(t)dt = g(t)$ $dt/[1 - G(t)]$. Note that the denominator in this expression reflects the conditioning event of "not yet retired."

expectations of future events except for future social security and private pension benefits.

We specify our hazard rate in the form

(2) $$\theta(t) = \psi_1(x_1)\psi_2[x_2(t), t],$$

where x_1 is a vector of variables that remain constant for each person over the sample period, $x_2(t)$ is a vector function that describes the path of exogenous variables that vary for each individual over the sample period, and t is time that we specify as age minus 44. Since we do not observe the instantaneous paths of the variables that change in value, $x_2(t)$, some approximation is required that presumably has only a minor effect on the estimates.[15] Following Lancaster, we assume the mathematical form of $\psi_1(x_1)$ to be

(3) $$\psi_1(x_1) = \eta \exp(z_1 \cdot \beta_1),$$

where unobserved individual factors are given by the random variable η.[16] This variable is assumed to be distributed independently across individuals as well as independently of the vectors z_1 and $x_2(t)$ for each individual.[17]

Next, we assume that η follows a gamma distribution with mean equal to one and variance equal to δ^2. The choice of a gamma density function is mainly for computational convenience since it integrates out to a closed form expression. Taking equations 1, 2, and 3 and performing the required integration yields:

(4) $$1 - G[t \mid z_1, X_2(t)] = \int_0^\infty \left(1 - G[t \mid \eta, z_1, X_2(t)]\right)$$
$$\times \eta^{(1-\sigma^2)/\sigma^2} \exp(-\eta/\sigma^2)\, d\eta$$
$$= \left(1 + \sigma^2 \exp(z_1\beta_1) \int_0^t \psi_2[x_2(u)\, du]\right)^{-1/\sigma^2},$$

where $x_2(u)$ refers to the sample path from time 0 to time t.

15. The problems that arise here have been studied thoroughly in the context of simultaneous equation and regression models. See the collection of papers in Albert R. Bergstrom, ed., *Statistical Inference in Continuous Time Economic Analysis* (Amsterdam: North Holland, 1976).

16 Lancaster, "Econometric Methods for the Duration of Unemployment."

17. This assumption of independence of η from z_1 and $x_2(t)$ corresponds to the usual regression assumption of the independence of regressors and the stochastic disturbance. With wealth as one of the x_2 variables, this assumption is less satisfactory given the simultaneous determination of savings and labor supply.

To complete our statistical specification, we must describe the final term in the hazard function of equation 4, $\psi_2[x_2(t), t]$, so that the required integration $\int_o^t \psi_2[x_2(u), u] \, du$ can be performed. We discuss the specifications of the ψ_2 function in appendix B, where an averaging procedure for the $x_2(t)$ variables is formally specified. The time-varying variables fall roughly into two categories, and we use an appropriate averaging procedure for each category.

1. *Discretely changing variables*. Some variables such as health and the number of dependents change in discrete jumps. For these variables we take $\bar{x}_2(p)$, the average during period p, to be the value observed at time $t_f(p)$, which is the end of period p. To some extent this procedure corresponds to the use of the variables in lagged form. An important implication of this procedure is that the discretely changing variables are assumed constant between age 44 and the age of the initial observation (that is, first interview). Given that the data set contains no retrospective information, some technique of extrapolation is required.

2. *Continuously changing variables*. For this category of variables, which includes such variables as wealth and social security, we used a linear interpolation technique. We constructed a time path for a particular variable by connecting all observed values of that variable with linear segments. Values of the variable were observed or predicted at each interview date, with interview dates separated by one or two years. We assume that the unobserved time path of these variables can be approximated by linear interpolation between the observed sample points.

The sample paths of those two categories of variables are then used to form the function ψ_2 as we discuss in appendix B. To obtain estimates of the value of $x_2(t)$ for the period after age 44 and before the first interview date the values at the time of first and second interviews were extrapolated backwards with a linear extrapolation since no sample points are available. The average values $\bar{z}_2(p)$ are then taken as equal to the average in each period.

To give a notion of the role of the regressor variables in a hazard model, we consider the effect of changes in these variables on the probability that retirement will be chosen by a particular age. We first consider the effect of a variable that does not change over time, say, husband's permanent income. The exact formula is given as equation 11 in appendix B. The result indicates that the elasticity of the probability of retirement in a given year with respect to a change in permanent income is proportional to the estimated coefficient (β_{1j}) in the hazard

Figure 1. Effect of Permanent Income and Health on Retirement

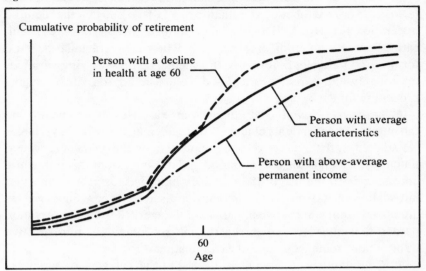

model times permanent income times the probability that the individual has not yet retired. In figure 1, we provide a graphical interpretation of this result. The solid line in that graph corresponds to the probability at each age that a person with, say, average permanent income will have already retired. The dashed line reflects the probability of retirement for a person with higher-than-average permanent income. Note that the dashed line lies everywhere below the solid line, since, as we estimate below, higher permanent income causes a reduction in the probability of retirement.

The other type of regressor variable that enters the hazard model is a variable that changes over time, for example, health status. The formula for the change in the retirement probability given a change in this type of variable is provided in equation 12 of appendix B. Because it is more difficult to interpret than equation 11, we will once again try to illuminate the relation with a graphical illustration. The figure shows the change in the retirement probability distribution that would occur for a change from good to bad health at age 60. The probability distribution shifts upward and remains higher in subsequent years.

Our estimation sample consists of three groups of men, two of which have censored dependent variables.

1. *Men who retired before the beginning of the sample period.* The

only information we have about this group is that retirement occurred sometime before the first observation took place. This case corresponds to "left censorship." The probability that retirement would occur before the date of the first interview (call it $t_0[1]$) is given by the cumulative probability $G[t_0(1)]$.

2. *Men who do not retire during the sample period.* For these men the probability of an observation is given by the cumulative distribution function $1 - G(t_m)$, where t_m is the last date at which the man was observed. This situation corresponds to "right censorship." The majority of the sample is observed for twelve years, but sample attrition also might lead to right censorship.[18]

3. *Men who retire during the sample period.* For this group we do not observe the exact age of retirement since interviews were separated by up to two years. Since we know the dates of the two sample points before and after retirement (say t_1 and t_2), the appropriate probability for this type of observation is $G(t_2) - G(t_1)$. For the three sets of men we construct the likelihood function,[19]

(5) $$L(\beta_1, \beta_2, \sigma^2) = \prod_{i=1}^{N_1} G_i[t_0(1)] \times \prod_{i=1}^{N_2} [1 - G_i(t_m)]$$
$$\times \prod_{i=1}^{N_3} [G_i(t_2) - G_i(t_1)];$$

$$N_1 + N_2 + N_3 = 1,356.$$

Our primary set of results for the retirement model is given in table 3. Exact definitions of the variable are given in the data appendix. First, note that the estimates in the first column of table 3 are quite precise. Both pension and social security have the expected strong positive effects on the probability of retirement. We interact social security with age variables to account for the age-related provisions of the social security law. That is, before age 62 there is an income effect arising from social security because the program raises lifetime expected income.

18. Sample attrition here is taken to be independent of the causes of retirement. A model of nonindependent attrition like that used by Hausman and Wise could be specified in the current context with a competing-risks model, such as that used in the next section of the paper. Jerry A. Hausman and David A. Wise, "Attrition Bias in Experimental and Panel Data: The Gary Income Maintenance Experiment," *Econometrica*, vol. 47 (March 1979), pp. 457–73

19. The log likelihood function was maximized by use of the Berndt-Hall-Hall-Hausman algorithm. See E. K. Berndt and others, "Estimation and Inference in Nonlinear Structural Models," *Annals of Economic and Social Measurement*, vol. 3 (October 1974), pp. 653–65.

Table 3. Retirement Model Results[a]

Variable	Full sample (1)	Ages 45–49 (2)	Alternative health (3)	Truncated 1973–78 sample (4)
	Parameter estimates			
Predicted pension (thousands)	0.14	0.08	0.13	0.26
	(0.03)	(0.04)	(0.03)	(0.08)
Permanent income, husband	−6.23	−8.31	−6.03	−3.93
(PYH)	(−1.25)	(−2.12)	(−1.30)	(−3.62)
PYH times middle one-third	6.08	6.49	6.56	8.57
	(1.17)	(2.31)	(1.63)	(4.01)
PYH times top one-third	1.16	2.49	1.68	−3.75
	(1.12)	(1.63)	(1.16)	(−2.65)
Permanent income, wife	1.06	0.63	1.36	1.77
	(0.53)	(0.76)	(0.54)	(1.07)
Bad health	0.92	0.82	0.82	2.18
	(0.15)	(0.22)	(0.17)	(0.55)
Social security times age 62	2.17	. . .	2.13	5.17
	(0.65)	. . .	(0.66)	(1.73)
Social security times ages 63, 64	4.39	. . .	4.78	11.62
	(0.84)	. . .	(0.92)	(3.38)
Social security times age 65	10.70	. . .	12.04	33.70
	(1.99)	. . .	(2.32)	(10.1)
Social security times age over 65	17.96	. . .	19.62	58.6
	(3.22)	. . .	(3.63)	(17.3)
Pension times reduced dummy	−0.05	−0.03	−0.04	−0.04
	(−0.06)	(−0.08)	(−0.06)	(−0.12)
Pension times partial reduction	−0.03	−0.04	−0.03	−0.01
	(−0.05)	(−0.06)	(−0.05)	(−0.12)
Full pension	0.08	0.07	0.09	0.16
	(0.04)	(0.06)	(0.04)	(0.10)
Beyond full pension	0.06	0.13	0.07	0.25
	(0.05)	(0.06)	(0.05)	(0.13)
Education	−0.61	0.02	−0.05	−0.21
	(−0.029)	(0.04)	(−0.03)	(−0.07)
Marital status[b]	−3.56	−1.95	−3.80	−10.6
	(−0.583)	(−0.81)	(−0.60)	(−2.86)
Dependents	0.02	−0.04	0.04	−0.16
	(0.05)	(−0.07)	(0.05)	(−0.17)
Wealth (instrumental variable)	−0.25	−0.11	−0.28	−0.58
	(−0.09)	(−0.23)	(−0.09)	(−0.35)
Time	0.14	0.08	0.20	1.13
	(0.04)	(0.05)	(0.04)	(0.30)
α (from equation 10)	1.89	1.77	1.92	1.56
	(0.17)	(0.32)	(0.17)	(0.61)
γ (from equation 10)	2.77	. . .	2.94	2.23
	(0.29)	. . .	(0.30)	(0.83)
σ (from equation 8)	1.95	1.68	2.09	3.68
	(0.18)	(0.34)	(0.19)	(0.53)
Number of observations	1,356	573	1,411	977
Log likelihood function	. . .	. . .	. . .	−1162.8

Source: Same as table 1.
a. Retirement = 1 for left-hand-side variables. The numbers in parentheses are asymptotic standard errors.
b. Married = 1.

Beyond age 62 there is also a substitution effect because workers who postpone retirement beyond that age may be forgoing social security benefits. The social security variable in any year is the benefit anticipated in that year. It is a real benefit measured in constant dollars based on 1976 law and derived from an algorithm for the social security formula that is based on a worker's permanent income. We find the expected pattern of coefficients that rise monotonically with age. An interesting finding is that while an increase in the probability of retirement occurs at age 62 when a person becomes eligible to receive social security benefits, the increase in the hazard ratio is only about one-fifth as large as the increase at age 65. This finding of no "blip" in retirement at age 62 is also present in our raw data on retirement age. However, the possibility that some retirements at age 62 are attributed to ages 61 or 63 by our classification must be considered. Reductions in pension caused by early retirement have only a small effect.

People with larger permanent incomes, however, are less likely to retire. We entered permanent income in piecewise linear form with breakpoints corresponding to one-third and two-thirds in our sample. Note that the marginal effect of permanent income decreases as permanent income increases but that it remains negative throughout. The effect of wealth on retirement is quite small although its sign is contrary to what might be expected from most economic theories that do not include a bequest motive for wealth accumulation. Because wealth is really a jointly endogenous variable, however, we attribute little significance to this finding.

The demographic variable that has by far the largest effect is health. A shift from good to bad health causes the same percentage rise in the probability of retirement as an increase in a pension equal to about $6,500 a year. Single males are much more likely to retire early, while the effect of education and number of dependents is small. Even apart from all these influences, we still find quite a strong secular trend leading to earlier retirement over our period, 1966–78. (This secular trend is reflected by the coefficient on time.) Previous analysts have attributed the decline in the typical age at retirement to more generous social security retirement benefits. Our model attempts to control for this factor by the use of current social security regulations, but we still find a significant and large pure time effect. Finally, note that the estimated age coefficients α and γ indicate that the probability of retirement increases considerably more quickly after the age of 55 than before.

These coefficients determine the exogenous effect of age on retirement. (See equation 10 in appendix B, where the exact specification of the retirement model is given.) Additional experimentation with the time function might be useful further research.

A similar model has been estimated by us on the same sample of men but using only the first ten years of data rather than all twelve years of data.[20] A check on the similarity of the coefficient estimates indicates the validity of the specification in view of the significantly higher rates of retirement in the last two years of the survey in comparison to the ten years covered by the earlier study. Overall, the coefficients obtained in the two studies are quite similar: the social security coefficients reported in table 3 are 2.2, 4.4, 10.7, and 17.9 while for the earlier study they are, after normalization, 2.2, 4.8, 11.7, and 14.4. The bad health coefficient is 0.92 in table 3; in the earlier study it is 0.86. Therefore, the inferences about the effect of the economic and health variables seem quite stable. However, a Hausman type of specification test rejects the hypothesis that the estimates are not statistically different, suggesting that further experimentation might be called for.[21]

The second column of estimates in table 3 is based on behavior of men in the original sample who were aged 45–49 in the initial sample. Because of their age these men do not qualify for social security retirement benefits during any part of the period under study. Nevertheless, 228 out of 573, or about 40 percent of men, retired, which is a significant proportion. In comparison, 256 out of 296, or 86.5 percent of the men aged 55–59 at the beginning of the longitudinal survey, retired by 1978. The results in column 2 are roughly similar to those for the full sample although some significant differences do occur. After normalization, bad health has an estimated coefficient of 0.95 compared with 0.92 for the entire sample.[22] The pension coefficients are also quite close. However, coefficients on both permanent income and marital status differ significantly. From a policy perspective it is important to note the prevalence of early retirement as well as the effect of health on retirement. According to the coefficient in the second column, bad health has an

20. Diamond and Hausman, "Individual Retirement and Savings Behavior."
21. J. A. Hausman, "Specification Tests in Econometrics," *Econometrica,* vol. 46 (November 1978), pp. 1251–71.
22. We normalize by the estimated standard deviation to allow for the comparison of the coefficients. This procedure corresponds to the implicit normalization procedure of probit models.

Table 4. U.S. Male Labor Force Participation Rates, Selected Years, 1965–75
Percent

Age	1965	1967	1969	1971	1973	1975
60–64	78.4	78.2	75.8	74.0	68.9	65.4
65 and older	28.9	28.5	27.4	26.3	23.4	21.9

Sources: *Employment and Earnings,* various issues.

impact equivalent to a $10,000 per year pension. Given our findings, changes in the age requirement for social security benefits could have an important effect on the welfare of these early retirees if health is the main cause of their early retirement. The probability of early retirement might be nearly unaffected by a change in the normal retirement age for these individuals.

Because of the importance of the health variable in our results, we made additional runs with alternative definitions of health status. In the first two columns of table 3 bad health corresponds to the answer of the NLS question on whether health limits work. In column 3 we replace this definition with the response to the question, "Are you in poor health compared to other men your age?" The correlation between the responses to these two questions is surprisingly low although both are self-reported measures.[23] The statistical results are nonetheless virtually identical in the first and third columns of table 3. The coefficients of the health, pension status, and social security variables are all very close. Thus, we conclude that our results are not sensitive to the precise definition of health status, a variable that appears to be crucial in determining the probability of retirement.

Using results from our model of retirement behavior, we attempted to isolate the effect of social security on early retirement in 1975. Labor force participation fell significantly over the period of our sample. As table 4 demonstrates, the drop in the participation rate is largest during the 1971–75 period after social security benefits increased by about 20 percent in real terms in 1971. We use simulated results from our model to see what effect changes in social security benefits have on retirement of men aged 61–64. We use the estimates in the first column of table 3

23. For an investigation of problems that arise because of the self-reported nature of the health variable, see Thomas N. Chirikos and Gilbert Nestel, "Impairment and Labor Market Outcomes: A Cross-Sectional and Longitudinal Analysis," in Herbert S. Parnes, ed., *Work and Retirement: A Longitudinal Study of Men* (MIT Press, 1981), pp. 93–131.

Table 5. Estimated Effect of Delayed Retirement Age

Age in 1975	Fraction retired in 1976	Fraction retired or lost in 1976	Estimated fraction retired in 1976	Estimated fraction retired in 1976 with zero early retirement coefficients
61	0.24	0.24	0.17	0.09
62	0.20	0.24	0.22	0.09
63	0.36	0.45	0.13	0.09

Source: Same as table 1.

for our calculations. To perform our simulation, we use men in our sample who were aged 61–63 and not yet retired in 1975. (Since the sample sizes at these years range from 20 to 46 there is considerable uncertainty associated with our simulation results.) In table 5 we report the fractions actually retiring in the next year (1976), retiring or lost to the sample in that year, the estimated fractions retiring in the next year, and the estimated fractions retiring in the next year if we set all the coefficients on social security interacted with ages below 65 equal to zero. Our estimates show that about half of all retirements of men aged 62–64 are due to the availability of reduced benefits.

Delaying the normal retirement age is a much-discussed policy proposal that involves two elements—a drop in the size of benefits and a change in the age-specific incentives to work. To obtain some feeling for the effects of the latter, we have simulated (up to 1978) the work histories of those who were 58 and 59 (and not retired) in 1966 using the coefficients in the first column of table 3 and again assuming the coefficients of the ages 62 to 64 (interacted with social security) were zero, while those of 65 to 68 (interacted with social security) were equal to the 62 to 64 coefficients. We did not change the coefficient for social security (not interacted). Under current law, nonretired 58-year-olds could be expected to average 2.97 years of additional work while 59-year-olds would average 2.77 additional years. Under our simulated reform, the average years of additional work are 3.62 and 3.33, for 58- and 59-year-olds, respectively. Thus we estimate that a three-year delay in the normal retirement age (with benefits adjusted to have no income effect) would increase the average working life by about 0.6 years.

The availability of social security benefits before age 65 does have a significant effect on retirement, and the size of the benefits also matters. However, it is important to note that social security benefits are less than half the story in explaining early retirement. It is likely that we have not captured the effect of the growth of social security disability benefits on early retirement. This task would require an interaction of social security benefits with bad health. More generally, it would have been desirable to have interactions between social security benefits and several other variables. Nevertheless, while altering the initial age of eligibility or reducing benefits for early retirement will affect individual behavior, the secular trend to earlier retirement seems likely to continue.[24]

We now consider the problem of dynamic self-selection. Many previous empirical studies of retirement estimate a model on a cross section of people who have not yet retired.[25] People who have retired previously are excluded from the studies. A potentially important self-selection problem is created by this procedure, which can lead to important biases in the estimated coefficients. The problem arises from the stochastic term of equation 3. People with high ηs are more likely to retire early, other things equal. Since other right-hand-side variables also influence retirement, correlation between η and these variables will result from the sample selection procedure; for example, a negative correlation will arise for those variables that lead to a higher probability of retirement when they increase. A hazard model is not sensitive to this problem since it follows individuals throughout the sample period by using the panel nature of the data.

To compare our results with those that could be obtained with earlier cross-sectional methods, we artificially truncated the sample. We reestimated our hazard model but restricted the sample to the 977 self-selected men who had *not* retired as of 1973. We estimated the model

24. The closest study to ours in terms of measuring the effect of social security on retirement is Michael D. Hurd and Michael J. Boskin, "The Effect of Social Security on Retirement in the Early 1970s," National Bureau of Economic Research Working Paper 659 (Cambridge, Mass.: NBER, 1981). They use the Retirement History Survey and similarly find an important effect of social security on retirement. Their results are in contrast to those of Gordon and Blinder, who find that the social security system has no effect on retirement. Roger H. Gordon and Alan S. Blinder, "Market Wages, Reservation Wages, and Retirement," NBER Working Paper 513 (Cambridge, Mass.: NBER, 1980). The magnitude of the Hurd-Boskin results cannot be compared directly to ours since they use a different model of retirement. Their use of a sequence of logit models leads to a problem of dynamic self-selection so that it is not clear that policy analysis can be done properly with their model. Nevertheless, our results on the importance of social security to retirement do agree qualitatively with the Hurd-Boskin findings although our finding on the magnitude of the effect of social security on retirement seems smaller than what they found.

25. See, for example, Hurd and Boskin, "Effect of Social Security on Retirement."

over the 1973–78 period. The coefficient estimates for this self-selected sample are given in the last column of table 3. After normalization, the coefficient of the pension variable is 0.08, compared with 0.14 in column 1. The coefficient on husband's permanent income is -2.08, compared with -6.23 in column 1. However, the effects of bad health and social security are all estimated to be larger on the self-selected sample. For instance, the four social security variables (suitably normalized) are 2.74, 6.16, 17.8, and 31.1, compared with 2.17, 4.39, 10.70, and 17.96 in column 1. A Hausman specification test leads to the conclusion that the coefficients are significantly different and thus that dynamic self-selection is a potentially serious problem.[26] However, it does not seem possible to give the direction of the bias in general due to the intercorrelation of the right-hand-side variables. Nevertheless, the artificially truncated sample seems to assign more importance to social security benefits than does estimation using the full sample. These results are in accord with the difference between our full sample results and those obtained by Hurd and Boskin. We might well conclude that an important reason for the different results lies in the problem of dynamic self-selection in the Hurd-Boskin samples. This finding is quite important for policy reasons. In a simulation of the effect of policy changes such as an increase in the minimum age for receipt of social security benefits, the samples "at risk" for retirement will change depending on the policies in effect in each year of the past. If dynamic self-selection is not taken into account, very biased forecasts of the effects of changes in existing legislation are likely to result.

Labor Force Behavior after Workers Are Fired

In the present section we move from considering the general question of when workers retire to the much more specific problem of the effect of involuntary unemployment on that decision. Most models of retirement behavior are based implicitly on a life-cycle model in which workers decide to retire based on a classical economic trade-off between leisure and forgone labor earnings. However, job market reality may not allow workers to alter their labor supply at a constant wage approximated by past earning levels. In particular a worker may be fired from his job and then face limited job opportunities. The effect of bad health on oppor-

26. Hausman, "Specification Tests in Econometrics."

Table 6. Experience of Workers after Being Fired, by Age Group, 1966–78

Age	Number of cases	Percent retired	Average period before another job (months)
45–49	57	1.8	3.0
50–54	132	2.0	3.3
55–59	152	10.5	4.7
60–64	75	36.0	3.9
65–71	12	41.7	8.0
All ages	428	12.1	3.9

Source: Same as table 1.

tunities is represented in our work by the bad health variable. Insurance for inability to work due to serious health problems is provided, to some extent, by the social security disability program. Loss of job is much less well insured. Only unemployment benefits, private pension benefits, and (generally small or nonexistent) severance pay provide income after a job separation. Unemployment insurance and severance pay typically last for less than a year. In this section we investigate individual labor market experience after involuntary separation.[27] If a significant proportion of older men who are fired do not take another job, changes in the minimum age of receipt for social security benefits may have an important adverse effect on their welfare. Currently, the minimum benefit age is 62. If this minimum age were raised to, say, 65 as some proposed legislation calls for, then the option to retire and to begin collecting social security benefits disappears for workers aged 62–64.

In the NLS data for 1966–78 we found 428 men aged 45–71 who were fired and for whom we had other needed information to fit an econometric model. Of the 428 men, 12 percent retired after being fired. Most other men found another job, while a small proportion remained unemployed through the end of our sample period. However, the labor market experience differs considerably across age groups. As figures in table 6 show, only about 2 percent of the men who were fired at the age of 45–54 retired. But for those aged 60–64, 36 percent of discharged men failed to find another job but retired instead. Presumably, it is this older group that would be most affected by the change in the minimum age for receipt of social security benefits.

Table 6 also shows the length of time required for people to find other

27. We considered only firings, not layoffs or quits, because of the difficulty in interpreting the behavior underlying the latter events.

Table 7. Probit and Competing-Risks Model Results, 1966–78[a]

Variable	Probit model ($y_i = 1$ is retired) (1)	Competing risks model[b] Y_1^* (new job) (2)	Y_2^* (retirement) (3)	Implied retirement coefficient (4)
Intercept	−7.80	−0.492	2.09	−9.58
	(−1.97)	(−0.765)	(0.698)	(−0.770)
Pension	0.128	. . .	−0.038	0.141
	(0.061)	. . .	(−0.011)	(0.041)
Education	−0.067	−0.013	0.011	−0.089
	(−0.045)	(−0.181)	(0.133)	(−0.014)
Married	−0.598	−1.53	−1.37	−0.594
	(−1.24)	(−0.359)	(−0.592)	(−0.491)
Permanent income, husband	−0.427	−0.063	0.127	−0.705
	(−0.219)	(−0.021)	(0.025)	(−0.285)
Permanent income, wife	1.03	−0.192	−0.630	1.62
	(0.597)	(−0.436)	(−0.285)	(0.255)
Bad health	0.154	0.477	−0.052	1.96
	(0.028)	(0.125)	(−0.006)	(0.096)
Dependents	−0.016	0.00002	0.008	−0.029
	(−0.091)	(0.039)	(0.020)	(−0.024)
Wealth	0.121	. . .	−0.063	0.234
	(0.034)	. . .	(−0.037)	(0.137)
Time	0.200	0.127	0.052	0.278
	(0.048)	(0.022)	(0.010)	(0.017)
Age	0.111	0.035	0.032	0.249
	(0.032)	(0.013)	(0.006)	(0.095)
Social security benefits, ages 62–64	0.961	. . .	−0.167	0.620
	(0.565)	. . .	(−0.026)	(0.097)
Social security benefits, ages 65 and over	0.446	. . .	−0.236	0.876
	(1.72)	. . .	(−0.034)	(0.126)
Pension, reduced	−0.019	. . .	−0.013	0.048
	(−0.113)	. . .	(−0.030)	(0.111)
Pension, full	0.185	. . .	−0.158	0.586
	(0.099)	. . .	(−0.026)	(0.096)
σ_1[c]	. . .	0.817	. . .	. . .
σ_2[c]	. . .	. . .	0.863	. . .
ρ[c]	. . .	0.953	0.953	. . .
Number of observations	414	414	. . .	414
Likelihood function	−99.49	−491.4	. . .	. . .

Source: Same as table 1.
a. Numbers in parentheses are asymptotic standard errors.
b. Dependent variable measured in log months.
c. σ_i are the standard deviations and ρ is the correlation coefficient of the error terms.

jobs. (Since we do not know the exact length of the period of unemployment, these results indicate our best estimate of the unemployment period.) Note that the average length of the unemployment spell rises with age at firing. The distribution of length of unemployment spells is highly skewed. For example, the percentage of men who do find another job but remain unemployed for more than six months more than doubles as we go from the age group 50–54 to the age group 55–59. For the 50–54-year-olds, 9 percent are unemployed for longer than six months while for the 55–59-year-olds, the percentage of long-term unemployed rises to over 22 percent. This skewness in the distribution of unemployment spells and its relationship to age must be accounted for in an econometric model of people's labor force experience.

The first econometric model we estimate is a simple probit model of workers who were discharged. The left-hand-side variable indicates whether the discharged worker found another job ($y_i = 0$) or retired ($y_i = 1$). This model is not quite complete since it ignores the 4 percent of the sample who were still unemployed at the end of our sample period. Furthermore, it takes no account of the length of time an individual remained unemployed. (These problems will be treated below.) Nevertheless, the probit model is quite familiar and allows for a good initial look at the data.

The probit results are presented in the first column of table 7. The results indicate the importance of economic variables. The amounts of pension and social security benefits available are important determinants of retirement behavior. Permanent incomes of both husband and wife also play important roles in the retirement decision. Finally, wealth has the expected role since an extra $1,000 of wealth has a positive effect on the worker's probability of choosing retirement. Sociodemographic variables are also important. Both advancing age and bad health lead to a significant increase in the probability of retirement after being fired. Also note that the positive secular trend in retirement probabilities that we found in the hazard model is present here. Over the period 1966–78 it appears that a growing proportion of men retired after being fired, even controlling for other economic and sociodemographic variables. This trend may be caused by secular increases in unemployment, a variable that is omitted from our equation.

We now estimate a more general model, of which the probit model is a special case. It is called the competing-risks model and was proposed

by David and Moeschberger.[28] The competing-risks model is more
general than the probit model because it takes account of individuals
who remain unemployed and unretired at the end of the sample period.
Also, the model makes use of the length of time before another job begins
or before retirement begins. The competing-risks model is also in some
respects a generalization of the hazard model for retirement that we
estimated in the last section. In this model, however, there are two
possible events—retirement and finding another job—rather than only
one—retirement—as is the case in the hazard model.

We now describe briefly the setup of the competing-risks model
(a more technical description is given in appendix C). Upon being fired,
a worker faces two possible outcomes: he finds a new job or he retires.
Consider a latent (unobservable) variable specification, where the left-
hand-side variable is the logarithm of time until the event occurs:

(6) $$y_1^* = X_1\beta_1 + \epsilon_1$$

$$y_2^* = X_2\beta_2 + \epsilon_2,$$

where y_1^* is the length of time until a new job is found and y_2^* is the length
of time until retirement. Since the two events are mutually exclusive,
only one can be observed and directly measured; the other remains
unobserved. In this case, only the minimum of y_1^*, y_2^* will be observed
for each person. If we observed the outcome of both events, we could
simply use regression methods to estimate β_1 and β_2 of equation 6. But
since only the smaller of y_1^*, y_2^*, say y_2^* in a particular case, is observed,
we use this information as well as the fact that y_1^* is greater than y_2^* to
estimate the unknown parameters. (The model is similar to the well-
known Tobit model to the extent that we have censored observations on
the events not observed.)

Now an interesting feature of this setup is that the probit model can
be interpreted as the outcome of a competing-risks model. To see this,
note from equation 6 that the probability that individual i retires is given
by

(7) $$pr(y_i = 1) = pr(Y_{2i} < Y_{1i}^*)$$

$$= pr(X_{1i}\beta_1 - X_{2i}\beta_2 > \epsilon_{1i} - \epsilon_{2i})$$

$$= pr(Z_i\delta > \eta_i),$$

28. Herbert A. David and M. L. Moeschberger, *The Theory of Competing Risks*
(London: Griffen, 1978).

where η is distributed normally and Z is the combination of variables in X_1 and X_2. The probit model uses only the inequality information on the left-hand-side variables in equation 6 to form estimates of δ while the competing-risks model also uses information on the actual amount of time until the observed event occurs to form the estimates of the βs.

The results for the competing-risks model are given in the second and third columns in table 7. The second column contains estimates of β_1 in equation 6, where $X_1\beta_1$ predicts the latent variable that determines time until a new job is begun. The third column gives estimates of β_2 where $X_2\beta_2$ determines the latent variable for time until retirement. Both left-hand-side variables are measured in the log of months passed until the event. The individual coefficients can thus be interpreted as the effect of a unit change in the independent variable on the number of log months in the spell of unemployment leading up to the indicated event.

Although we do not present a formal model, the two equations can be given "reduced form" interpretations within a search model framework. Suppose that a person is fired. He searches for a new job using a reservation wage policy. His reservation wage is a function of his education, age, permanent income, and the socioeconomic variables. However, to determine his exact reservation wage, he must gather information on the distribution of wage offers. Presumably, he has considerable uncertainty about the distribution of wage offers because it is unlikely that he has been actively searching before his discharge. Now if the distribution of wage offers is not encouraging, he may choose retirement over the alternative of returning to work. The attractiveness of retirement depends on his pension, wealth, social security, age, and other personal characteristics. We might think of a type of sequential decision process in which the individual partly resolves the uncertainty over the wage distribution as he learns about ϵ_1 in equation 6. The two stochastic terms ϵ_1 and ϵ_2 should then be positively correlated; our results indicate a high positive correlation. At some point the uncertainty is sufficiently resolved, and the individual decides to return to work or to retire.[29]

From column 2 we see that among those who find new jobs both increasing age and bad health increase the amount of time before a new job is begun. For instance, bad health increases the period of unemploy-

29. A formal model of this process is quite difficult to specify except under implausible assumptions about the stochastic processes for wage offers and the learning process. We therefore present the results as a first look at the problem. Further research is certainly in order.

ment by 48 percent for otherwise observationally equivalent individuals. Of course, since bad health also increases Y_1^*, this difference in health status also tends to increase the probability of retirement, an interpretation we will consider subsequently when we adjust for the fact that Y_2^* is also affected. The other variable that has a large influence is husband's permanent income. The cost of unemployment increases with permanent income, and this cost should lead to shorter periods of unemployment. The effect we find is that a person with $5,000 higher permanent income would on average be unemployed for about 31 percent less time, given the values of the other right-hand-side variables.

We now turn to the estimates of coefficients on variables affecting Y_2^* reported in column 3 of table 7. Here we focus on variables that reduce Y_2^* because they increase the probability of retirement after being fired. The actual size of Y_2^* is the log of the number of months before the retirement actually takes place. First, note that both the pension and the social security variables have a pronounced effect on retirement behavior. The effect of the social security variables is stronger than the pension variables, but an extra $1,000 of either reduces Y_2^* by about 15 percent or more. Again, bad health and advancing age also have significant effects. Bad health reduces Y_2^* by over 5 percent. Thus, an image emerges that people whose health restricts their work have a considerably higher probability of retirement after being fired. Likewise, an extra five years of age reduces Y_2^* by 15 percent. Finally, the amount of wealth also affects the retirement probability although its effect is not very precisely estimated. Permanent income of the husband is the most important variable that decreases the probability of retirement. This effect is to be expected, especially once the amount of wealth is controlled for.

In the last column of table 7 we combine the two latent variables of equation 6 and use equation 7 to calculate the probability that the individual retires after being fired, $pr(Y_2^* < Y_1^*)$.[30] Note the high correlation, $\rho = 0.95$, between the stochastic terms, which is an implication of the search model framework sketched out above.

Comparison of $\hat{\delta}$ with the probit coefficients in the first column of table 7 lends some support to the competing-risks model. The competing-

---

30. To scale δ equivalently to the earlier probit run, we calculate the variance of η, $\sigma_\eta^2 = \sigma_1^2 + \sigma_2^2 - 2\rho\sigma_1\sigma_2 = 0.073$ so that the standard deviation is $\sigma_\eta = 0.269$. We then calculate $(\beta_1 - \beta_2)/\sigma_\eta$ as our estimate of δ. Asymptotic standard errors are calculated from the usual first-order formulas. See, for example, C. Radhakrishna Rao, *Linear Statistical Inference and Its Applications* (Wiley, 1965).

risks model is based on unobserved latent variables, with the time to an event providing the left-hand-side variable. When we compare it to the probit results that are based solely on which event occurred, we find quite close agreement in the rescaled coefficient estimates. The effects of the pension, social security, and permanent income variables on the probability of retirement are reasonably similar and certainly within sampling error in the two models. Likewise, the estimated effects of education, marital status, and dependents are quite close. The only two variables whose estimates differ significantly across the two models are bad health and age. The effect of age on the probability of retirement in the competing-risks model is about double its effect in the probit model. The difference in the estimated effect of the bad health variable is much more dramatic, with the effect in the competing-risks model over ten times as large as in the probit model.

In this section we have estimated two different models of job market experience after a worker is fired. The probit model explains the probability of either a new job or retirement. The competing-risks model considers the amount of time until the event occurs as well as whether the outcome is a new job or retirement. As expected, both the probit results and the competing-risks results indicate that pensions and social security eligibility have an important effect on the probability of retirement. Both permanent income and wealth also have significant effects in both models. Among sociodemographic variables, marital status, bad health, and advancing age have the largest effects in both models. But additionally, the competing-risks model yields the result that, among those individuals who do take new jobs, both bad health and advances in age increase the expected period of unemployment significantly. These results might well be important in consideration of proposed changes in social insurance programs.

Conclusions

In this paper we have considered several statistical models of retirement among older men and labor market experience of involuntarily unemployed older workers. We reported the results of fitting a hazard or time-to-failure statistical model of the age of retirement. According to our results, both private pensions and social security have strong positive effects on the probability of retirement. In the case of social security, the effect is especially strong at age 62 when benefits first become available and rises considerably for workers over 62. However, there is a significant addition to the numbers of retirees at all ages as a consequence of bad health, irrespective of the financial incentives provided by pensions and social security. Because many of these retirees stop work well before they receive retirement or disability benefits, a substantial fraction of older men are only incompletely insured against income loss arising out of bad health or partial disability.

Aside from their policy interest, these results also have important implications for statistical modeling of the retirement process. For example, when we compare those results to findings in our earlier study, which used only ten years' rather than all twelve years' data from the NLS, the coefficients appear quite similar. Given the large change in the population of retirees as a consequence of the additional two years of observation, the correspondence of coefficients appears to provide some assurance that the hazard model is describing the retirement process well. (However, we should note that a Hausman specification test rejects the hypothesis that the two sets of estimates are not statistically different.) To provide an even more stringent test of our model, we restrict the estimation sample to men aged 45–49 at the time of the initial NLS. While the results are generally similar to our full-sample results, coefficients showing the impact of marital status and permanent income differ quite significantly. Nonetheless, these results once again strongly confirm the importance of health as a determinant of early retirement.

In contrast to these generally reassuring statistical results, we also report findings based on a narrowly self-selected sample—namely, men in the NLS sample who have not yet retired by 1973. The importance of this restriction is that it corresponds to that often used in past research on retirement, for example, in the study by Hurd and Boskin. When we fit our hazard model to this self-selected sample over the period 1973–78, we find a much more pronounced effect of social security. This effect appears to correspond to the Hurd-Boskin conclusions, which thus may be attributable to bias arising out of dynamic self-selection. This result underlines the importance of adjusting for the effects of past policies on the composition of the "population at risk," both in estimating and in simulating the impact of future policy changes. This analysis treats the timing of retirement quite generally and does not identify unexpected changes in labor market opportunities except insofar as they arise from changes in health status.

Later, we consider the effect of permanent discharge from a job, an unanticipated event that may seriously disrupt retirement plans. In our statistical analysis of this problem, we restrict our sample to older men who are involuntarily discharged from their jobs and then analyze the outcome of their unemployment spells using both the probit and the competing-risks models. Our findings show that poor health, advances in age, and greater potential benefits from pensions and social security all tend to increase the probability that a discharged worker will retire rather than take a new job. Poor health, advances in age, and lower levels of permanent income are all associated with longer spells of unemployment for those workers who do succeed in obtaining a job.

Our results point up the importance of caution in reforming public programs aimed at the aged and disabled. First, the tabulations reported near the beginning of our paper show that many older workers already experience a considerable delay between the onset of retirement or a disability and the start of a retirement income stream. Many suggested reforms only prolong this already lengthy delay. Second, our statistical results suggest that a high fraction of early retirees are motivated to retire by poor health rather than by incentives provided by social security or pensions. Consequently, any modification in those incentives—such as an advance in the early retirement age—may seriously reduce and delay retirement incomes without substantially affecting retirement behavior of many present early retirees. And third, our study of unemployment experiences of older workers suggests that workers with the lowest levels of permanent income face the longest spells of unemployment if they choose to continue working rather than to retire. Thus although reductions in early retirement benefits and increases in the stringency of requirements for disability benefits will indeed reduce present incentives to retire, many workers with poor health prospects will simply face longer spells of involuntary unemployment. An important component of any major social security reform should be to maintain present income protection for these discharged workers.

Appendix A: Data Definitions

Pension: As reported in Diamond and Hausman, "Individual Retirement and Savings Behavior," we estimated pension receipts in 1975 as a function of permanent income, marital status, occupation, union status,

length of job tenure, age at retirement, age eligible for full benefit, time
since retirement (separate for government and private pensions), and a
Mill's ratio for sample selection bias. This equation was used to assign a
pension benefit at age eligible for full retirement for each person saying
in 1966 that he would be eligible for a pension on retirement.

Permanent income: Average over preretirement years of net real
earnings in 1966 dollars, subtracting income and FICA tax liabilities and
adding in unemployment insurance benefits. The variable was assumed
to be missing if there were fewer than three observations from the NLS.

Permanent income of wife: Average of spouse's net real earnings (in
1966 dollars) after tax, based on family's permanent income. Spouse's
earnings were set at zero if there were two or fewer positive observations.

Bad health: Response to questions whether health limits amount or
type of work.

Age: Age first eligible for reduced pension and age eligible for full
pension were taken from answers in 1966.

Social security benefits: A lifetime profile of nominal earnings was
constructed on the basis of our estimate of permanent income. Taking
account of the taxable maximum earnings for each year, each man and
wife was given an earnings record up to age 65. Average monthly
earnings (AME) were then calculated for each observation using the
appropriate number of averaging years. The 1976 benefit table (in 1966
dollars) was then applied to compute the primary insurance amount
(PIA). The family's benefit is the maximum of 1.5 times the husband's
benefit or the sum of husband's and wife's benefits. Perceived benefits
were smaller than this. Real perceived benefits were unchanged in any
year without legislation. They rose by the average real increase since
previous law in the year of any law change.

Appendix B: The Retirement Model

The probability of "not yet retired" is repeated from equation 4:

$$(8) \quad 1 - G[t \mid z_1, X_2(t)] = \int_0^\infty \left(1 - G[t \mid \eta, z_1, X_2(t)]\right)$$
$$\times \eta^{(1-\sigma^2)/\sigma^2} \exp[-\eta/\sigma^2] \, d\eta$$
$$= \left(1 + \sigma^2 \exp(z_1\beta_1) \int_0^t \Psi_2[x_2(u) \, du]\right)^{-1/\sigma^2},$$

where $X_2(u)$ refers to the sample path from time 0 to time t. We now discuss the specification of time-varying variables, the term $\Psi_2[X_2(t), t]$. Since we have only point sampling, an approximation is needed. We chose the approximation

$$(9) \qquad \int_0^t \Psi_2[x_2(u), u] \, du = \sum_{p=0}^N \bar{x}_2(p)\beta_2 \int_{t_0(p)}^{t_f(p)} \phi(u) \, du,$$

where p denotes the period. The time period between the sample points is not constant. We use average values of the changing variables $\bar{z}_2(p)$ during the length of period p. Then $t_0(p)$ and $t_f(p)$ are the initial age and final age of a particular individual during the period p. For our time function we chose a more general function than Lancaster, "Econometric Methods for the Duration of Unemployment," to allow for increased flexibility. The time function is assumed to take the form $\phi(t) = t^{\alpha-1}/\alpha + [\max(0, t - 11)]^{\gamma-1}/\gamma$ for $\gamma > 1$ so that upon integration

$$(10) \qquad \int_{t_1}^{t_2} \phi(u) \, du = t_2^\alpha - t_1^\alpha + [\max(0, t_2 - 11)]^\gamma$$

$$- [\max(0, t_1 - 11)]^\gamma.$$

Thus we have separated the time function into two parts, where the second piece becomes operable at age 55.[31] The parameters α and γ allow for different shapes of the time paths between ages 44 and 55 and ages 55 and beyond.

Interpretation of the results is aided by the elasticities

$$(11) \qquad \frac{\partial \log \theta_1(t)}{\partial z_{1j}} = \beta_{1j}[1 - G(t)]^{\sigma^2}$$

$$(12) \qquad \frac{\partial \log \theta(t)}{\partial z_{2j}} = \beta_{2j}\left([\partial \sum \bar{z}(p)/\partial z_2] \right.$$

$$\left. \times \, [1 - \sigma^2 \exp(z_1\beta_1)] \int \phi(u)/[1 - G(t)]\sigma^2 \right).$$

The first result indicates that the influence of the z_1 variables diminish

---

31. In the specification we also allow for a shift of the entire hazard function at ages 62 and 65 for eligibility for social security. While Lancaster considered reemployment, we might well expect some use of this type of specification at the point where individual unemployment benefits expire. Whether events such as these are better entered through the multiplicative z variables or through the time function is often problematical.

over time as the probability of retirement increases. Changes in the z_2 variables are more difficult to interpret, but equation 12 gives the change in the average of z_2 multiplied by a variable that is positive and decreasing over time.

Appendix C: The Competing-Risks Model

The competing-risks model can be cast into a latent variable framework very similar to the probit model. Let n_k for $k = 1, \ldots, K$ denote K competing risks. Introduce the latent random variable $Y_k^* \geq 0$ for $k = 1, \ldots, K$, which would be the length of period if the particular risk were the only risk present. Denote the distribution function of Y_k^* by $F_k(x) = pr(Y_k^* \leq x)$. However, Y_k^* is a latent variable in general since it cannot necessarily be observed. Instead, only the minimum Y_k^* of the theoretical lifetimes is observed:

(13) $$Y = \min(Y_1^*, \ldots, Y_k^*) = \min_k Y_k^*.$$

The information we have here, including the actual outcomes, includes the fact that if Y is greater than x, then the survivor distribution function, $\overline{F}_y(x) = 1 - F_y(x)$, along with the survivor function, $r_y(x) = f_y(x)/\overline{F}_y(x)$, gives the conditional failure rate function for the observable variable Y. If $g_k(x)$ denotes the probability of failure from n_k in the interval $(x, x + dx)$, then in the presence of all k risks we find

(14) $$r_y(x) = \sum_{k=1}^{K} g_k(x),$$

so long as the probability of more than one simultaneous failure is negligible.

The competing-risks model bears a close relationship to the sample selection models in econometrics. Here we know the value of the left-hand-side variables in both cases (for $K = 2$) while in the sample selection models, we only know the value of the left-hand-side variables for one of the equations since the other equation is a probit model. Nonetheless, the competing-risks model has had a somewhat dubious reputation, since both Cox and Tsiatis questioned whether the model was identified.[32] We will not discuss these issues at length here. However, we will claim that our competing-risks model is identified so long as at least one right-hand-side variable differs across the two equations, a result that again is similar to the sample selection model.

For our current application we have $K = 2$ with a new job and retirement being the two causes of "failure." The amount of time until one of these events occurs is min Y_k^* with only the smaller of Y_1^* and Y_2^* being observed. We assume that Y_1^* and Y_2^* are distributed as bivariate log normal so that correlation can be allowed for.[33] Above we claimed that the competing-risks model generalizes the probit model. Write the models for the latent variables as

$$(15) \qquad Y_1^* = X_1\beta_1 + \epsilon_1$$

$$Y_2^* = X_2\beta_2 + \epsilon_2.$$

If Y_1^* is length of time to a new job, then the probability of retirement that corresponds to the probit model of table 7 is

$$(16) \qquad pr(Y_2^* < Y_1^*) = pr(X_1\beta_1 - X_2\beta_2 > \epsilon_1 - \epsilon_2)$$
$$= pr(Z\delta > \eta),$$

where η is distributed normally and Z is the union of variables in X_1 and X_2. Thus, our probit model can be seen as the outcome of a competing-risks model.

The complication accounted for in the competing-risks model that the probit model cannot account for was sample censoring: $Y_1^* > \tau$ and $Y_2^* > \tau$. That is, at the end of our survey, say time t, a small proportion of men remained unemployed, and for these men it is unknown whether Y_1^* exceeds Y_2^* or vice versa. But hazard models are designed to account for censoring, as we explained before. Therefore, our model is a bivariate Tobit model with censoring above for one of the two latent variables with the possibility of censorship for both latent variables.

The other econometric problem we must account for is that we do not

32. D. R. Cox, "The Analysis of Exponentially Distributed Lifetimes with Two Types of Failure," *Journal of the Royal Statistical Society*, vol. 2-B, no. 2 (1959), pp. 411–21; and Anastasios Tsiatis, "A Nonidentifiability Aspect of the Problem of Competing Risks," *Proceedings of the National Academy of Sciences*, vol. 72 (January 1975), pp. 20–22.

33. The hazard rate first increases and then decreases for the distribution. This qualitative property seems appropriate for our application.

actually observe the exact value of Y in equation 6. Instead, we only observe an interval that includes Y. Hence we do not allow for continuously changing variables but keep all right-hand-side variables constant at the value when the individual was first fired. Our sample consists of three groups of men:

1. *Men who find a new job during an interval* (t_1, t_2). Therefore, we know that $t_1 \leq Y_1^* \leq t_2$ and that $Y_1^* \leq Y_2^*$. The probability density is formed from the expression

$$(17) \qquad f_1(Z) = \frac{1}{\pi_1 \sigma_1} \phi \left(\frac{Z - X_1 \beta_1}{\sigma_1} \right) \left[1 - \Phi \left(\frac{Z - \tilde{\mu}_1}{\tilde{\sigma}_1} \right) \right],$$

where ϕ, Φ are the standard normal density and distribution, $\pi_1 = pr(Y_2^* > Y_1^*)$, and $\tilde{\mu}_1 = \alpha_1 X_2 \beta_2 + (1 - \alpha_1) X_1 \beta_2$, $\tilde{\sigma}_1 = \alpha_1 \sigma_2 (1 - \rho^2)^{1/2}$ for $\alpha_1 = 1/(1 - \rho \sigma_2 / \sigma_1)$. We determine $f_2(z)$ similarly.

2. *Men who retire during an interval* $(\tilde{t}_1, \tilde{t}_2)$. For these men we know that $\tilde{t}_1 \leq Y_2^* \leq \tilde{t}_2$ and $Y_2^* < Y_1^*$. The probability densities are calculated similarly to case 1 with Y_1^* and Y_2^* reversed.

3. *Men who do neither during the sample period and are censored at time* τ. The survivor function for them is $\bar{F}(\tau, \tau) = 1 - F(\tau, \tau)$.

For these three sets of men the appropriate likelihood function is

$$(18) \qquad L \left(\beta_1, \beta_2, \sum \right) = \prod_{i=1}^{N_1} G_{1i}(t_1, t_2) \prod_{i=1}^{N_2} G_{2i}(t_1, t_2) \prod_{i=1}^{N_3} G_{3i}(\tau, \tau);$$

$$N_1 + N_2 + N_3 = 414,$$

where the $G(\cdot)$ functions are formed from the appropriate survivor probabilities.

Comment by Martin Neil Baily

This is a strong paper that applies careful econometric techniques to a labor market decision of considerable importance. The modeling is based upon hazard functions. This technique fits best for something like death. Everyone dies, and, apart from some notable exceptions, nobody returns from the dead. The advantage of the hazard function approach is that it really uses the longitudinal character of the data set. In this paper retirement is modeled as if it were like death. People decide to stop working full time and never return to full-time work. That is not literally true, as the authors note. Some people retire and then unretire. Moreover, as I learned from Tom Gustafson's dissertation, for many people there is a gradual scaling down of labor force participation rather than an abrupt retirement.[34] So there are gains and losses from using the hazard function approach.

The National Longitudinal Survey data set used by the authors is not an easy one to work with, and they handle several technical problems well. They also get good results. Social security does have a clear impact in encouraging retirement. For example, in 1975 the probability of retirement of a 62-year-old is 0.089. Without social security this probability would drop to 0.056, a 46 percent change. For 63- and 64-year-olds the impact is even greater. Their probability of retirement would drop even more, from 0.088 to 0.028.

Diamond and Hausman are able to demonstrate the importance of using the longitudinal character of the data and hence show the value of their statistical approach. They argue that studies that focus only on those who have not retired will suffer from sample selection bias. And by truncating their own sample in a similar way, they reveal the potential bias. This is good stuff.

Their results were interesting in other ways. They found that the generosity of private pensions affects retirement and that a high permanent income lowers the probability of retirement. Reported health problems are also a major factor in the retirement decision.

A problem I had with the paper is that the statistical modeling has driven out the economic modeling. The economic framework in which decisions are made is not well articulated, and that failing makes it hard to evaluate some of the variables and coefficients. A few examples will illustrate the problem.

First, permanent income is one variable used. Presumably the idea is that people compare their permanent incomes if they do or do not retire. But if a worker's current wage happens to be well above his permanent wage, he may choose not to retire in order to take advantage of this fact.

Second, how do we evaluate the coefficients? Do the estimates predict plausible behavior for someone with, say, no social security or pension income but with large wealth? Is that behavior consistent with the prediction for someone with no wealth but with a large private pension?

34. Thomas A. Gustafson, "The Retirement Decision of Older Men: An Empirical Analysis" (Ph.D. dissertation, Yale University, 1982).

Third, there are important issues in specifying the retirement decision that are left implicit. For example, are people constrained by liquidity or not? In a world of perfect capital markets the actual timing of pension or social security benefits may be irrelevant to the retirement decision. This is part of a more general point. Certain variables should not affect the retirement decision. If they in fact enter an equation with significant coefficients, then the model is suspect.

Fourth, the paper starts out by stressing the importance of uncertainty. But this area is not really explored. Certainly, as time progresses variables change, or expected values become realized values. But the authors do not consider the effect of uncertainty on behavior—the response to risk, for example.

As well as the specific concerns, I have a more general point about methodology. For many years the number of young children a woman had was taken as an exogenous determinant of the probability of labor force participation. The new home-economics literature has pointed out that for most women the decisions about number of children and labor force participation are made jointly. The neglect of this fact could bias the coefficient on, say, the wage rate as a determinant of participation. A rise in the wage rate could increase participation not only directly, but also indirectly through its effect on the desired number of children.

In an ideal experimental setting one would estimate the effects of changing the social security system by comparing different groups of people who faced different social security *systems*. Creating such an experimental approach was the idea behind the income-maintenance experiments. However, the NLS data cover a sample of U.S. males of similar ages, all of whom faced basically the same social security system. The observed differences in behavior must be due to individual differences and not to social security.

Stated in this way, the problem is exaggerated. After all, if other variables are different, the people in the sample will end up with different social security wealth as they approach retirement. And this fact gives identifying power to the data. Nevertheless, to the extent that people with a taste for retirement make occupational or other choices that result in large pension and social security benefits available to them upon retirement, then the variables used in this study are not exogenous, and the effect of social security on retirement is overstated.

Gary Burtless and Robert A. Moffitt

The Effect of Social Security Benefits
on the Labor Supply of the Aged

The social security system has had a profound effect
on the well-being of America's elderly, making it by far the most popular
legacy of the New Deal. In recent years, however, the system has come
under increasing attack because of its mounting cost and the growing
suspicion that it has depressed economic growth by discouraging private
saving and encouraging early retirement. In this paper we examine the
impact of social security benefits on labor supply of the aged. The payroll
tax used to finance social security also influences labor supply decisions
of the nonaged, but we will not address this effect here. We are
particularly concerned with social security's effect on two aspects of
labor supply among the elderly: the age at retirement and the level of
work effort after retirement.

The question of whether social security affects decisions regarding
retirement age and postretirement labor supply and the extent of that
effect is an important issue in current discussions of the program. The
system was designed to provide retirement income to the aged population
of the United States and to maintain consumption levels for the aged
after retirement. If the provision of such benefits causes substantial
disincentive effects either on labor supply or on saving for retirement,
the goal of the program is to some degree frustrated because reductions
in labor supply or saving result in reductions in private resources
available to finance retirement that may offset the gains represented by
social security benefits. In addition, any disincentive effects on labor
supply of the aged will increase the budgetary cost of the program, raise

We gratefully acknowledge the computational assistance of Paul E. Morawski, Diane
Levin, and Karen Hanovice and the comments of Alan Fox, Cordelia Reimers, and
Sherwin Rosen.

135

tax burdens on the nonelderly, and reduce aggregate labor supply and, hence, national output. It should also be mentioned, however, that one of the original goals of the program in the 1930s was to encourage older workers to retire, thus opening up employment opportunities for the involuntarily unemployed. Because unemployment levels prevailing since World War II have been substantially lower than those in the Depression, this goal appears to have been largely forgotten.

Considerations of labor supply response are also important in assessing the changes in social security retirement benefits currently under public discussion. Advancing the age at which full retirement benefits can be received, changing the actuarial increase in benefits with delayed retirement, reducing the stringency of the retirement earnings test, and other proposed reforms might all have significant effects on retirement ages and retirement hours of work. In the short run, with retirement ages and hours to some extent fixed, changes in program cost would result from these reforms. But in the long run, as people alter their retirement ages and work effort, these cost effects could rise or decline. Here we are interested in assessing the longer-term effects of social security reform.

The effect of social security on labor supply has already received considerable attention from economists. Several studies have treated the retirement decision alone,[1] examined the postretirement work effort decision alone,[2] and attempted to study implicitly or explicitly both

1. Michael J. Boskin, "Social Security and Retirement Decisions," *Economic Inquiry,* vol. 15 (January 1977), pp. 1–25; Richard V. Burkhauser, "The Early Acceptance of Social Security: An Asset Maximization Approach," *Industrial and Labor Relations Review,* vol. 33 (July 1980), pp. 484–92; P. Diamond and J. Hausman, "Retirement and Savings Behavior" (MIT, 1981); Laurence J. Kotlikoff, "Testing the Theory of Social Security and Life Cycle Accumulation," *American Economic Review,* vol. 69 (June 1979), pp. 396–410; Joseph F. Quinn, "Microeconomic Determinants of Early Retirement: A Cross-Sectional View of White Married Men," *Journal of Human Resources,* vol. 12 (Summer 1977), pp. 329–46; Cordelia K. W. Reimers, "The Timing of Retirement of American Men" (Ph.D. dissertation, Columbia University, 1977); and others.

2. Michael J. Boskin and Michael D. Hurd. "The Effect of Social Security on Early Retirement," *Journal of Public Economics,* vol. 10 (December 1978), pp. 361–77; Alan L. Gustman and Thomas L. Steinmeier, "Partial Retirement and the Analysis of Retirement Behavior," National Bureau of Economic Research Working Paper 763 (Cambridge, Mass.: NBER, September 1981); Anthony J. Pellechio, "Estimation of Labor Supply over Kinked Budget Constraints: Some New Econometric Methodology," NBER Working Paper 387 (NBER, August 1979); A. Zabalza, C. Pissarides, and M. Barton, "Social Security and the Choice between Full-Time Work, Part-Time Work, and Retirement," *Journal of Public Economics,* vol. 14 (October 1980), pp. 245–76.

decisions together.[3] These studies have generally found disincentive effects of social security on labor supply, although the magnitudes of the estimated effects have differed greatly. But none of these studies has specified the combined effect of social security on retirement age and postretirement hours with the detail we attempt in this paper. Nor have any of the previous studies specified the individual elements of the benefit formula in a structural model of combined labor supply response as we try to do here.

The estimates reported in this paper show that social security has some important effects on the exact timing of retirement and amount of labor supplied after retirement. Nonetheless, we should emphasize at the outset that many proposed changes in the social security benefit formula will cause only modest changes in work effort among the elderly. For example, social security causes a large number of men to retire exactly at ages 62 and 65, and the retirement test strongly discourages elderly workers from having earnings above the social security exempt amount. However, a 20 percent reduction in social security retirement benefits would cause men with average characteristics to delay their retirements by only about two or three months. Similarly, the complete elimination of the retirement test would affect the weekly work effort of only a limited number of retirees, since only about one retiree in five is a worker. Our estimates are especially useful in predicting the impact of detailed changes of this type on the work decisions of the elderly.

In the second section of this paper, we provide a simple discussion of the economic theory of retirement and social security as it relates to labor supply decisions. That section contains a less technical summary of a model whose full details are reported elsewhere.[4] In the following section we present our estimation model and the results of our empirical estimation of that model. The fourth section contains estimates of the impact of reforming the social security formula in several specific ways. The paper concludes with a brief summary.

3. Alan S. Blinder, Roger H. Gordon, and Donald E. Wise, "Reconsidering the Work Disincentive Effects of Social Security," *National Tax Journal,* vol. 33 (December 1980), pp. 431–42; Anthony J. Pellechio, "Social Security and the Decision to Retire," NBER Working Paper 734 (NBER, August 1981); and, to some degree, references cited in notes 1 and 2.

4. Gary Burtless and Robert A. Moffitt, "The Joint Choice of Retirement Age and Post-Retirement Hours of Work" (Brookings Institution, 1983).

Retirement Labor Supply and Social Security

Throughout this paper we focus on two aspects of individual labor supply: the age at retirement and the amount of postretirement work effort. Of these, the former has the greater effect on aggregate labor supply. In the sample we study, for example, four-fifths of retiring men do not work at all in the first year or two after their retirements, and most of the remainder work only a small amount. Hence the exact timing of retirement has the more significant impact on the total amount of labor supplied over the lifetime. As is well known, the timing of retirement has changed substantially in recent years. If we use labor force participation rates as an approximate indicator of retirements, the average age at retirement can be seen to have declined significantly since World War II. For men over the age of 65, the labor force participation rate has fallen by more than half, from 46 percent in 1950 to 20 percent in 1979. For men aged 55 to 64, the rate has fallen from 87 percent to 73 percent in the same period, with all of the decline occurring after 1961 when early old age insurance benefits were first extended to men between 62 and 65.[5]

A variety of definitions of retirement have appeared in the literature. Some analysts have used labor force participation or self-defined retirement status to identify retirees, and others have used the onset of pensions or social security payments to date the beginning of retirement. In this study we concentrate on observable aspects of labor supply and define the retirement age as the point in life at which a person has a *discontinuous drop in labor supply*. We exclude reductions caused by spells of involuntary unemployment that end with reemployment in a full-time job. Our definition does not imply that hours of work fall to zero upon retirement; some retirees may continue to work. But our definition does imply that anyone continuing to work the same number of hours per week, even if he defines himself as "retired," has not yet commenced retirement. We recognize that some individuals define themselves as retired in such a circumstance, but we prefer our definition because it is based more squarely upon the notion of retirement as intrinsically related to an increase in leisure. We should also note that

5. U.S. Department of Labor, *Employment and Training Report of the President* (Government Printing Office, 1980), p. 224.

we define retirement as a reduction in work effort that is discontinuous rather than continuous. For whatever reason, whether it be the preferences of the older population or simply the institutional constraints on part-time work, very few people reduce their hours gradually with age.

Given this definition, one may ask: why do workers retire? There is no single answer to this question; for in truth there are a variety of reasons for retirement. To say that individuals retire *because* they are tired of working is misleading, for the natural subsequent question is why the desire to stop working becomes strong enough to induce retirement at one point rather than at another. In this paper we take it as given that workers prefer to arrange consumption of leisure over the lifetime so that its consumption is concentrated near the end of life. The fundamental economic determinant affecting retirement decisions is then the choice between accepting more leisure but less goods consumption in the short term or less leisure but more goods consumption over the remainder of the life span. More concretely, in deciding whether to retire now or at some later date, the aged worker must choose between the attractions of stopping full-time work immediately or accumulating additional savings to provide for a more affluent—but briefer—retirement in the future.

The goal behind retirement savings is, of course, to increase consumption during retirement. The basic economic theory of retirement posits that retirement occurs when the disutility of working another year just begins to outweigh the extra utility obtained by the additional consumption provided by another year of preretirement savings. These economic considerations can be summarized in a simple graph. Suppose that a person is given an asset endowment A at the beginning of his worklife, that the length of lifetime T is known with certainty, and that the person's preretirement hours of work H_P and consumption level C_P are fixed (see figure 1). Under these assumptions the individual would be saving a constant amount per year out of earnings, $W_P H_P - C_P$, where W_P is the preretirement wage rate. (We assume that savings are positive.) To simplify the exposition, assume that the interest rate on savings is zero. Let R be the age at retirement, or the number of years spent working before retirement, so the number of years spent in retirement is $T - R$. For the person who ceases work entirely upon retirement, lifetime savings during his work life will permit him to consume a total of $A + R(W_P H_P - C_P)$ during retirement. The relationship between the retirement age R and total retirement consumption $(T - R)C_R$ under

Figure 1. Lifetime Budget Constraint

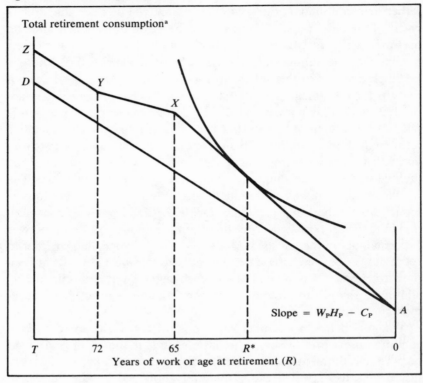

Total retirement consumption[a]

Slope $= W_P H_P - C_P$

Years of work or age at retirement (R)

a. $(T - R)C_R$.

these simplifying assumptions is represented as the straight line AD in figure 1. AD can be interpreted in the usual manner as a budget constraint, with the person choosing the combination of R and $(T - R)$ C_R along that constraint that maximizes his utility. Maximization occurs at the tangency point of the budget constraint and an indifference curve representing preferences for retirement and retirement consumption.

Social security affects the timing of retirement through its effect on the trade-off between retirement age and retirement consumption just described. We assume here that social security has no effect on tastes for retirement and retirement consumption, or, in other words, that the indifference map in figure 1 is unchanged by the program.[6] Social security

6. This may not be the case, for it is possible that by establishing standard retirement ages at 62 and 65, social security may create societal norms for retiring at those ages quite apart from providing economic inducements to do so. We ignore this possibility because it is obviously very difficult to measure and impossible to prove.

has strong effects on both the level of nonwage income during retirement and the rate at which that income changes as the retirement date is postponed. Both these effects can be analyzed by reference to figure 1.

Ignoring for a moment the payroll tax used to finance social security and all complications inherent in the actual benefit formula, assume that social security offers a retiree a fixed benefit per year $\overline{B}$, starting at age 62 if he retires on or before his sixty-second birthday. For one retiring at a later age, the annual benefit, which cannot commence until retirement, is adjusted in an actuarially fair manner so that total benefits over retirement remain equal to $(T - 62)\overline{B}$.[7] Assuming that preretirement consumption and hours remain unchanged, the effect of this benefit formula on the budget constraint drawn in figure 1 would be to shift the constraint upward from AD in parallel fashion, exactly as though the individual's initial assets were increased. If time spent in retirement is a normal good, this budget line shift will cause retirement to occur at a younger age (that is, a pure income effect will occur). Although, as discussed below, the payroll tax and various features of the benefit formula complicate this picture, the simple case just described is nonetheless relevant: all beneficiary cohorts since the inception of social security, including the ones studied here, have received benefits, the discounted values of which have far exceeded contributions.

In addition to providing such windfalls that substantially raise consumption during retirement and tend to lower retirement ages, social security alters the rate at which retirement income and consumption can be raised as retirement is postponed an additional year. In contrast to the simple benefit formula mentioned above, the total lifetime benefit depends on lifetime average earnings and the age at retirement. The higher the lifetime earnings, the higher the benefit; the later the retirement age, the higher the benefit. The relation between average earnings and benefits is generally redistributive, with low-earnings workers receiving proportionately more from the system than high-earnings workers. The age at retirement affects benefits in two ways. First, it affects average monthly earnings over the lifetime, which is the basis for the primary insurance amount calculation in social security. Because annual earnings close to the age of retirement are generally much higher than earnings in earlier working years, the addition of one more year of preretirement earnings can have a significant effect on the primary insurance amount.[8]

7. The benefit per year is thus $(T - 62)\overline{B}/(T - R)$, where R is the age at retirement.
8. For a fuller discussion, see Blinder, Gordon, and Wise, "Reconsidering the Work Disincentive Effects of Social Security."

Second, if people postpone benefits beyond age 62, the earliest age at which benefits can be received, an actuarial adjustment factor is applied against the primary insurance amount to compensate in whole or in part for the delay in benefit receipt. Holding constant the primary insurance amount, this adjustment factor causes benefits to rise by about 8 percent per year for postponing retirement between ages 62 and 65 and to rise by a much smaller percentage thereafter.[9] Delayed retirement past the age of 62 also raises the primary insurance amount just as it does before 62. To reflect the combined retirement age impact on social security benefits, we represent annual benefits as $B = B(R)$, where $dB/dR > 0$.

Returning now to our graphical exposition, we may summarize social security's effects quite briefly. The historical generosity of benefits in relation to contributions implies that the program has substantially raised consumption levels of recent retiree cohorts. This relationship is reflected in figure 1 by a social security budget constraint $AXYZ$, which is above the constraint AD, which represents a person's position in the absence of social security. The vertical distance between the two lines is $[T - \max(R, 62)] B(R)$, equivalent to the total benefits received from social security.[10] Note that before age 65 the social security constraint rises more sharply with retirement age than does the non-social-security constraint. This rise reflects the generous benefit payoffs historically provided by our system.[11] After age 65, however, the social security constraint turns markedly less generous because further postponements in retirement after that age are not fairly compensated by increases in the annual benefit. Consequently, lifetime benefits decline as retirement is postponed from age 65 to 72. Because at the latter age people can begin receiving benefits regardless of whether they have stopped working, lifetime benefits remain constant for all retirement ages past 72.[12]

Maximization of utility occurs at some tangency point such as that

9. Between ages 62 and 65 the actuarial adjustment factor is close to actuarially fair; after 65 the adjustment is unfair, and a person will lose lifetime benefits by postponing retirement beyond that age. In the period under study in this paper (1969–77), the actuarial adjustment factor after 65 was 1 percent per year; since that time it has been raised to 3 percent per year.

10. We continue to ignore social security tax contributions; taking these into account would lower the social security constraint.

11. The budget segment between A and X is probably concave because of the redistributive nature of the benefit formula alluded to earlier.

12. The age at which benefits can be received irrespective of current earnings was lowered in 1983 to 70.

shown on the figure, corresponding to the marginal condition mentioned earlier. Changes in the constraint have the usual effects. An increase in social security benefits that does not affect the rate at which benefits grow with changes in R will shift the constraint out in parallel fashion and will lead to reductions in the age at retirement if retirement is a normal good. An increase in the rate at which benefits grow with changes in R will rotate the constraint in a clockwise direction and will increase retirement ages if substitution effects are greater than income effects. Note that the kink in the lifetime constraint at age 65 will induce a "piling up" of retirements at exactly that age. A variety of sets of preferences regarding the relative attractiveness of work and consumption is consistent with optimization at point X, so a variety of types of people would choose to retire at that age. This theoretical inference is consistent with census information about work behavior as well as data discussed below from the Retirement History Survey. The overall effect of social security benefits on the age at retirement is predictable only past the age of 65, when income and substitution effects unambiguously combine to reduce retirement ages. Before 65 the effect of benefits is unknown, because while income effects probably reduce the retirement age, substitution effects may push retirement in the opposite direction.

Another aspect of our model touching on social security's impact is our hypothesis that program benefits may be viewed quite differently from the way income from other sources and liquid assets are viewed, especially by people under 62 who are not yet eligible to receive benefits. On the one hand, benefits are reasonably secure, having been indexed since 1972 and effectively indexed before then by legislated adjustments. Hence they differ significantly from other types of income, which are subject to the vagaries of price inflation, the stock market, or the economy in general. The greater certainty of social security benefits should give them a greater effect on retirement behavior than an equivalent amount of income from private sources. On the other hand, benefits are completely illiquid before retirement, for by law one cannot borrow against them in providing for consumption prior to retirement. As we have shown elsewhere, this latter effect provides a plausible explanation for the clustering of retirements at age 62—the earliest age at which social security retirement benefits can be received and hence used for consumption.[13] To account for these effects in our model, we assume that

13. See Burtless and Moffitt, "Social Security and the Retirement Decision: A Graphical Analysis" (Brookings Institution, 1981).

"effective" social security benefits at a particular retirement age are equal to $g_R B(R)$, where g_R is understood to be the relative effect of social security in comparison to other forms of income. If $g_R = 0$ over some age ranges, benefits have no effect on retirement behavior at those ages; if $g_R = 1$, benefits are interchangeable with income from private sources and have identical effects on behavior; and if $g_R > 1$, benefits have a greater effect on behavior than an equivalent amount of private income. Because the illiquidity of benefits should cause the relative benefit effect to vary with age, in our empirical model we treat g_R as a function of R.

Thus far we have assumed that retirees do not work and that retirement consumption is financed only with social security and income from preretirement savings. Many retirees do in fact work, though much less after retirement than before. To simplify our analysis we assume that, whatever the level of postretirement work effort, it is maintained at a constant level throughout retirement. Although this assumption is unlikely to be true for all retirees who decide to work, it is a close enough approximation during early retirement years to permit us to evaluate the trade-off between postretirement work and the age of retirement. The factors affecting a retiree's labor supply are much the same as those typically assumed to affect preretirement hours of work: the net wage rate, available nonwage income, and sociodemographic variables such as race, education, and marital status. In addition, retirees over 62 who are eligible to receive social security benefits are subject to the retirement test. Under this provision, earnings above a certain exempt amount cause benefits to be reduced by 50 cents for each dollar of excess earnings.[14]

The effect of wages, nonwage income, and the retirement test on postretirement work can be analyzed in terms of a conventional labor-leisure diagram. In figure 2 we show the trade-off between labor supply and goods consumption for a retiree past the age of 62. The straight line AG represents the retiree's situation in the absence of social security. The intercept A indicates the level of nonwage income per period

14. The actual test is somewhat more complicated. Before 1972, earnings above a second, higher amount were subject to a 100 percent benefit reduction rate. In recent years, pensioners younger than 65 have been subject to a different and lower exempt amount than pensioners over 65. Also, retirees who suffer benefit reductions before 65 have their benefits actuarially adjusted at that age to compensate them for the lost benefits. In this paper we ignore the last complication because retirees seem to be generally unaware of its existence. The retirement test will also be modified in the future under the social security legislation passed by Congress in 1983.

Figure 2. Single-Period Budget Constraint during Retirement

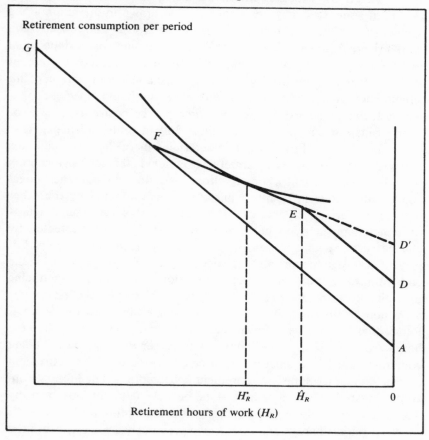

Retirement consumption per period

G

F

E

D'

D

A

H_R^* $\hat{H}_R$ 0

Retirement hours of work (H_R)

received by the retiree, presumably derived from his own savings; the slope of AG is W, the postretirement wage rate. (In this figure we assume no income or payroll taxes, an assumption we relax in our empirical work.) A person retiring between ages 62 and 72 faces the kinked budget constraint DEF, indicating that for work at less than a critical level $\hat{H}_R$—the hour level where the exempt amount is attained—the retiree faces no loss in benefits and simply receives his basic grant $B(R)$. Beyond that point the retirement test applies and the retiree can earn a net wage of only $0.5W$. For the same reasons mentioned above in our discussion of the kinks in the lifetime constraint, we expect that there should be a clustering of retirement hours at the convex kink point E. As seen below, this expectation is strongly confirmed in the data. Maximization of utility occurs at some tangency point such as that drawn in the graph along segment EF. Note that the same optimum point would be chosen if the worker were facing a strictly linear budget constraint with a slope equal to $0.5W$ and unearned income indicated by point D', the income intercept of the budget segment EF. Since the net wage and income intercept are simultaneously determined along with observed hours, special econometric techniques must be used in estimating the postretirement labor supply function, a point we discuss more fully in our technical paper.

Having discussed the economic determinants of the retirement age and postretirement hours separately, we conclude this section by noting how these two variables are simultaneously determined. The budget constraints drawn in figures 1 and 2 are each affected by the other dependent variable of interest. For example, the retirement hours–retirement consumption constraint drawn in figure 2 is affected by changes in the age at retirement. As R is advanced, both the level of private nonwage income and the social security grant rise, causing the constraint to shift upward in parallel fashion and presumably inducing the retiree to work fewer hours. Similarly, a different level of postretirement hours causes a shift in the lifetime constraint drawn in figure 1. Recall that figure 1 was drawn under the assumption that retirement hours are zero. If retirement hours are greater than zero, the budget constraint must rise since postretirement work provides retirement income and hence supports retirement consumption. The lifetime constraint must also have a smaller slope because delay in retirement by one year would only increase retirement consumption by $W_P H_P - C_P - WH_R$, rather than $W_P H_P - C_P$ as we previously assumed. Since the lifetime constraint with $H_R > 0$ both lies above and has a smaller slope than the constraint with $H_R = 0$, retirements should occur earlier in this case.

Against this background, how does the retirement test affect the retirement decision? Assume for a moment that all retirement earnings after age 62 are taxed at rate t by the test. Clearly, by reducing social security benefits, this tax reduces retirement income from what it would be in the absence of the test and hence lowers the lifetime constraint. Furthermore, it increases the slope of the lifetime constraint, at least after age 62, from $W_P H_P - C_P - WH_R$ to $W_P H_P - C_P - WH_R + tWH_R$.[15]

15. For simplicity, we ignore here the fact that the basic social security grant is also affected by R. This makes no difference to our argument, however.

Thus, in contrast to the no-retirement-test constraint, the retirement test will provide unambiguous incentives to *postpone* retirement. The intuition behind this result is relatively simple: by taxing postretirement earnings, the test reduces the increment in retirement consumption that the social security formula would otherwise make possible.

In this discussion of the simultaneity of R and H_R, we have concentrated on the simultaneous determination of the two budget lines of interest. We should also note that people can work a given number of hours in different ways: by retiring early and working a lot afterward, or by retiring late and working a little or not at all afterward. We have not attempted to illustrate this substitutability in our graphical analysis because it takes the form of a complex interaction between the indifference maps in the two diagrams. In our empirical model below, we allow for such substitutability. The strength of the individual response to social security and the way in which the response is divided between date of retirement and postretirement work will then depend on this critical relationship.

Estimation Model, Data, and Results

The description of behavior just sketched is highly general. To estimate empirically the effects of social security on retirement and labor supply, we must specify equations with a particular mathematical form.[16]

To make the estimation problem tractable, we maintain a number of simplifying assumptions, several of which we have already noted informally. First, preretirement hours and consumption are assumed fixed and are therefore not considered further here. By implication, preretirement savings rates are also fixed. Second, we are interested in the relationship between the age at retirement and the level of *average* consumption throughout retirement, or, more technically, the annuitized income flow from assets as of the date of retirement. To estimate our model, we assume that consumption is constant over the retirement period and that private assets are exhausted as of the expected end of retirement. Retirement hours are similarly assumed constant. Third, we assume as well that receipt of social security benefits begins at age 62 or

16. For a fuller discussion, see Burtless and Moffitt, "Joint Choice of Retirement Age."

at the age of retirement, whichever is later. We thus ignore complications arising for people who do not apply for benefits as soon as they retire. And fourth, we assume that the real after-tax interest rate is 2 percent and that the expected life probabilities around 1970 are appropriate to our person's decision. The assumed interest rate is probably close to the average rate over the late 1960s and early 1970s, the period considered here, but is obviously only an approximation. We doubt that our results would significantly change if an interest rate a point or two above or below 2 percent were used instead.

The formal maximization problem is described in our technical paper, where we write down the utility function and the budget constraint of the problem. Here we present only the solution equations for the two choice variables in the model: postretirement hours of work (H_R) and the age at retirement (R). We must estimate one equation for each of these variables. The H_R equation is simpler and will be described first. We assume a conventional linear labor supply function:

$$(1) \qquad\qquad H_R = \alpha X + \beta W_i + \delta Y_{Ri} + \epsilon_1,$$

where X is a set of sociodemographic variables affecting taste for work, W_i is the retirement net wage on segment i, Y_{Ri} is the "virtual" annuitized flow of nonwage income for an individual retiring at age R and on segment i, ϵ_1 is an error term, and α, β, and δ are unknown parameters. The net wage and amount of nonwage income differ depending upon which segment the individual is on (see figure 2). On the upper segment, for example, the net wage is reduced by 50 percent and the virtual nonwage income term is the linearized, or extended, intercept of the upper segment to the right-hand axis. Estimation of labor supply in the presence of this type of kinked constraint is a straightforward extension of previous work by Burtless and Hausman, Hausman, and Moffitt and Nicholson, to which the interested reader is referred.[17]

The net wage and nonwage incomes both have social security as well

17. See Gary Burtless and Jerry A. Hausman, "The Effect of Taxation on Labor Supply: Evaluating the Gary Negative Income Tax Experiment," *Journal of Political Economy*, vol. 86 (December 1978), pp. 1103–30; Jerry A. Hausman, "Labor Supply," in Henry J. Aaron and Joseph A. Pechman, eds., *How Taxes Affect Economic Behavior* (Brookings Institution, 1981), pp. 27–72; and Robert Moffitt and Walter Nicholson, "The Effect of Unemployment Insurance on Unemployment: The Case of Federal Supplemental Benefits," *Review of Economics and Statistics*, vol. 64 (February 1982), pp. 1–11. For a summary of these techniques see Robert A. Moffitt, "The Econometrics of Piecewise-Linear Budget Constraints: An Exposition" (Rutgers University, 1982).

as non-social-security components. As noted in the previous section, these two components probably have different effects on behavior. We incorporate this hypothesis by specifying W_i and Y_{Ri} as follows:

(2) $$W_i = W(1 - p - g_R t_i),$$

(3) $$Y_{Ri} = N_R + g_R M_R,$$

(4) $$g_R = \max\{0, [\theta_1 + \theta_2 R + \theta_3 \max(0, R - 62)]\}.$$

Here p is the positive tax rate (federal and FICA), t_i is the social security benefit reduction rate on segment i (either 0.0 or 0.5), N_R is the flow of nonwage income during retirement from private savings, M_{Ri} is the discounted flow of income from social security, and g_R is the relative impact of social security benefits. As equation 4 indicates, we allow this relative impact to vary with age and to vary differently before and after age 62.

The retirement equation we estimate is based upon the rather formidable equation:

(5) $$MU(R) = \frac{s_R}{(1 + \rho)^{R-1}} [U^P(\bar{H}_P, \bar{C}_P) - U^R(H_R, C_R)]$$

$$+ \sum_{t=R+1}^{T} \frac{s_t}{(1 + \rho)^t} \left[\frac{\partial U^R(\cdot)}{\partial C_R} \frac{\partial C_R}{\partial R} \right] = 0,$$

where $MU(R)$ is the marginal utility of increasing R (that is, delaying retirement), U^P and U^R are the utility levels during preretirement and postretirement, respectively, C_R is the level of consumption during retirement for an individual who retires at age R, s_t is the probability of survival to age t, and ρ is the subjective rate of time discount. Although the equation may appear complex, it follows from simple lifetime utility maximization because it shows that the utility of delaying retirement is determined by the discounted value of two terms: (1) the difference between the utility of working and retiring holding C_R constant in year R, $U^P(\cdot) - U^R(\cdot)$, and (2) the increase in utility that comes from the rise in retirement consumption ($\partial U^R/\partial C_R$) resulting from the delayed retirement ($\partial C_R/\partial R$), summed over the remainder of the lifetime. For nonretirees the negative effect of the first term is outweighed by the positive effect of the second; but as people age, the utility of continuing to work falls until the negative effect of the first term outweighs the positive effect of the second. The chosen retirement age is that age at which $MU(R) = 0$. At that point the marginal disutility of continuing to work is just counterbalanced by the marginal utility of the extra consumption made possible by the extra work. We provide the specific mathematical forms of the functions in equation 5 in the appendix.

The estimation method appropriate to this problem is nonlinear maximum likelihood. There are several reasons for this. First, the nonlinearity of the budget constraints means our two choice equations of interest—1 and 5—are highly nonlinear. Second, we do not observe retirement ages for all workers in our sample because many were not retired at the time of their last interviews. Consequently, the estimation method must be modified to account for the truncation of retirement age in the sample. And third, the dependent variable R in the retirement equation cannot be obtained in closed form, as just noted above. The full likelihood function is presented in our longer technical paper, cited earlier.

Data

We use the Retirement History Survey (RHS) to estimate our model. The survey provides a longitudinal panel of approximately 11,000 families headed by a person aged between 58 and 63 when the survey began in 1969. Each family head was interviewed at two-year intervals through 1979, though information from this last survey was only recently released and is not used here. Individuals were asked a wide variety of detailed questions concerning their assets, income, health, pension entitlements, work status, and employment history.[18] In addition, the RHS file contains earnings history records covering annual social-security-covered wages up through 1974. In this paper we use data on the 8,131 aged men who were originally sampled; the behavior of women is not studied.

We have obtained measures of the retirement age and postretirement hours of work for men in our sample. Our determination of the retirement age follows the definition given earlier (that is, a discontinuous drop in labor supply). For most men there is a clear point at which hours suddenly and discontinuously drop below thirty hours per week. For men who are involuntarily unemployed or who work an indeterminate

18. For more complete details, see Lola M. Irelan, "Retirement History Study: Introduction," in U.S. Department of Health, Education, and Welfare, Social Security Administration, Office of Research and Statistics, *Almost 65: Baseline Data from the Retirement History Study* (GPO, 1976).

number of hours during a particular survey, we use information on the immediately preceding and succeeding interviews to resolve the ambiguity about retirement status. In a very small percentage of cases, we use self-reported retirement status and information about receipt of social security to resolve ambiguous labor force status determinations based on hours worked. In cases where the retiree later returned to full-time work, we use the *first* drop in labor supply as our best indicator of planned retirement age. According to our definition, 6,378 out of the 8,131 male RHS respondents were retired by their last completed interview. To obtain an exact age at retirement between interviews, we use information about the date a respondent left his last full-time job.[19]

Retirement hours of work are obtained from the interview immediately following the retirement date. Our analysis of postretirement hours should consequently be considered an analysis of the hours chosen immediately upon retirement. Hours of work probably fall with increasing age, but it is beyond the scope of this paper (and the capability of any simple model) to account for these reductions in hours.

The independent variables of greatest interest are the asset levels (private and social security) available upon retirement and the *changes* in asset levels an individual would experience if retirement were postponed one year. Social security benefits at retirement were calculated using the earnings history records available in the RHS file. The potential change in social security benefits from delayed retirement was derived by computing the effect on benefits of an added year of preretirement earnings.[20] The average monthly benefit in our sample was $206 in 1967 dollars and would have risen by 5.2 percent to $217 if retirements had been postponed one year. A measure of private retirement assets was constructed that included the value of home equity, other real estate holdings, bonds, stocks, savings, checking accounts, and equity in one's own business. This asset value was annuitized at the observed retirement age to obtain our measure of N_R, the retirement income flow from private sources (see equation 3 above). Private pensions and contributions from

19. In the small number of cases where the job-leaving date was not supplied, we used data about the pattern of annual earnings after the last preretirement survey to date the age at retirement.

20. We assumed that earnings covered by social security—in the absence of retirement—would continue to grow or decline at the same rate observed over the five-to-seven-year period before retirement. For full details, see Burtless and Moffitt, "Joint Choice of Retirement Age."

Gary Burtless and Robert A. Moffitt

Table 1. Average Characteristics of Men in the Sample
1967 dollars

Variable	Entire sample	Retirees			Nonretirees
		R < 62	R > 62	All	
Age at retirement (R)	. . .	59.51	64.40	63.60	. . .
Age at last completed interview	. . .	. . .	. . .	. . .	64.06
Postretirement hours per week	. . .	4.06	3.23	3.37	. . .
Fraction working	. . .	0.223	0.176	0.184	. . .
Private nonwage retirement income (dollars per week)					
N_{R-1}	66.92	58.67	70.05	68.18	62.75
N_R	70.93	61.79	74.49	72.40	66.05
N_{R+1}	75.44	65.29	79.51	77.17	69.71
Social security grant (dollars per week)					
G_{R-1}	41.60	29.59	44.08	41.70	41.29
G_R	45.87	30.20	49.06	45.96	45.68
G_{R+1}	48.40	30.80	52.02	48.53	47.97
W: postretirement wage (dollars per hour)	2.35	2.24	2.36	2.34	2.36
W_P: preretirement wage (dollars per hour)	3.17	2.92	3.24	3.19	3.11
H_R: weekly hours at exempt amount	18.38	19.20	18.33	18.48	18.06
Eligible for private pension at retirement	0.21	0.10	0.24	0.21	0.19
Eligible for delayed pension at retirement	0.13	0.17	0.08	0.10	0.23
Marital status (0 = single; 1 = married)	0.82	0.74	0.84	0.82	0.80
Health "worse than average" in 1969	0.13	0.24	0.12	0.14	0.10
Nonwhite	0.09	0.13	0.09	0.09	0.08
Eight or fewer years of schooling	0.41	0.44	0.43	0.43	0.35
Received some college	0.15	0.12	0.13	0.13	0.22
Number of observations	4,612	582	2,959	3,541	1,071

Source: Authors' calculations using the Retirement History Survey file.

family members outside the household were also included in N_R. To compute the change in private income flows that would have resulted from postponing retirement, we exploited the panel nature of the RHS data to compute a preretirement net savings rate for each household. Because the rate of change in preretirement assets could be directly observed for only half the sample—the half that had at least two preretirement interviews—we relied on a modified instrumental variable procedure to impute savings rates to the remainder.[21] Finally, to estimate our model, we needed a measure of the attainable wage rate after retirement. A value of the hourly wage is directly observed for all working retirees. For nonretirees and nonemployed retirees we constructed a retirement wage prediction using modified instrumental variable procedures.

The sample used in our analysis consists of 4,612 out of the 8,131 men originally interviewed in the 1969 RHS survey. Individuals were excluded from the final estimation for a number of reasons: (1) severe handicaps—men who reported they had been too disabled to work for at least a year in the 1969 survey; (2) farmers—men who reported their main occupation as farming in their preretirement jobs; (3) very early retirement—men who retired at age 54 or younger; (4) very great wealth—men who reported that either their home or their other financial assets were worth more than $100,000 in 1967 dollars (or over $270,000 in 1981 dollars); (5) recipients of public assistance, railroad retirement, or federal civil service pensions; and (6) men with missing data or inconsistent survey responses. Recipients of public assistance, railroad retirement, and federal pensions were excluded because the RHS does not contain enough information to predict their main sources of retirement income. We are not interested here in explaining the determinants of retirement among the other excluded groups, except the very small group of men (under 2 percent of the entire sample) who simply have unusable data.

Table 1 contains descriptive information about the men in our analysis sample. The average retirement age is 63.6. (This average applies, of course, to the retiree subsample only.) Average work effort among retirees is 3.4 hours per week, although because only one-fifth of retirees work, the average work week among employed retirees is over sixteen hours per week. Thus the employment rate in the sample is relatively

---

21. Separate rates were derived for housing wealth and other forms of wealth, and the estimates explicitly controlled for the possibility of selection bias. See ibid.

Figure 3. Frequency Distribution of Retirement Ages

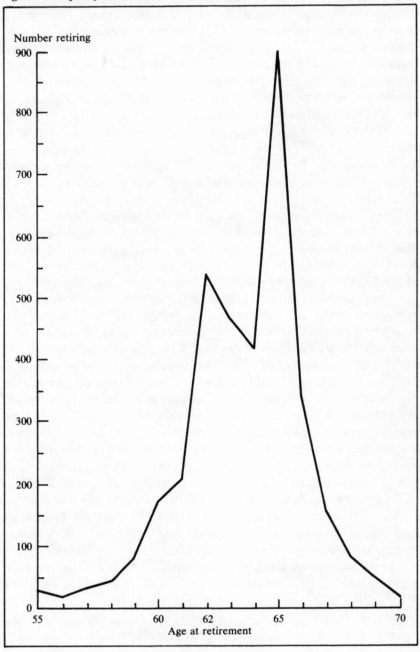

low.[22] The retirement test can explain why people work few hours, but not why they do not work at all. As can be seen in figure 2, the retirement test affects only the decision of how much to work at or above $\hat{H}_R$, the hours level at the exempt amount. In our model, eliminating the retirement test would not alter the decision to work zero versus some small number of hours. If we took account of fixed costs of working and the limited availability of part-time jobs, the retirement test might appear to have larger effects.

The average annuitized value of income from private sources at the retirement age N_R is \$3,765 per year for retirees in our sample (1967 dollars are used throughout). Not surprisingly, this figure is higher for men with later retirement ages since late retirees have had longer to save and have fewer retirement years in which to spend their accumulated assets. The value of N_R rose by an average of \$220 from $R - 1$ to R and by \$248 from R to $R + 1$, indicating significant increases in income associated with delayed retirement. Social security benefits at the point of retirement average \$2,389 per year. The available benefit also rises with delayed retirement, but by considerably smaller amounts than does income from private sources.

Figures 3 and 4 show the frequency distributions of the two variables we are attempting to explain—the age at retirement and postretirement hours of work. Casual observation indicates that the social security system has a powerful effect on both distributions. Note that the age distribution of retirements has two peaks, a lower one at age 62 and a very sharp one at age 65. The possible reasons for clustering of retirements at these two ages have already been mentioned: at 65 there is a convex kink in the lifetime budget constraint (see figure 1), and at 62 relaxation of liquidity constraints induces a surge of retirements.

Figure 4 shows the relation between observed retiree hours and hours at the earnings-test exempt amount, for persons who retired at age 62 or after. This frequency distribution provides strong evidence that retired workers are highly sensitive to the incentives provided by the retirement test. (We should note, on the one hand, the possibility that retirees

22. This low rate is partially dependent on our stringent definition of retirement and the way we measure postretirement hours. Presumably, a larger fraction of retirees work at one point or another after retirement has occurred, but we consider only retirement work effort reported in the interview subsequent to retirement. We are grateful to Alan Fox of the Social Security Administration for drawing this point to our attention.

Figure 4. Distribution of Retirement Earnings among Working Retirees

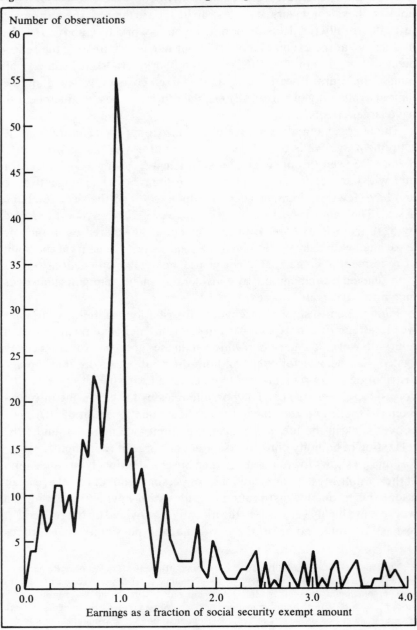

Number of observations

Earnings as a fraction of social security exempt amount

Figure 5. Convexity of the Social Security Budget Constraint, by Age at Retirement

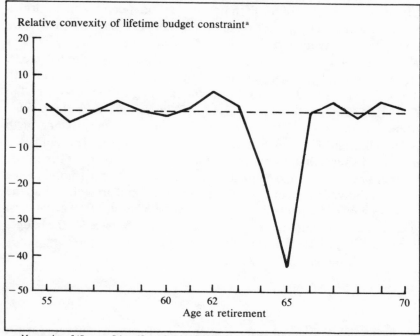

a. Mean value of $(S_{R+1} - S_R) - (S_R - S_{R-1})$, where S_R is the asset value of future social security benefits at age R. Values above 0 reflect nonconvex points, and values less than 0 reflect convex points on the lifetime constraint.

underreport their true earnings to avoid the high implicit tax on earnings above the exempt amount. On the other hand, data in figure 3 are based on interviews conducted by census interviewers, not on information supplied to the Social Security Administration.) There is a very pronounced peak in the distribution at exactly the earnings exempt amount, precisely the result one would predict from consideration of figure 2. Moreover, there is a very sharp decline in the frequency distribution for earnings in excess of the exempt amount, where earnings are subject to a reduction of 50 percent in the benefit rate. Whether social security's impact on the distribution of retirement hours has a feedback effect on the distribution of retirement age remains to be seen.

Figure 5 provides evidence about the incentives caused by the social security benefit structure. As noted in figure 1, consideration of the benefit formula suggests a convex kink in the relationship between benefits and retirement age at age 65 because the value of the annual benefit does not rise sufficiently after that age to compensate for the delay in benefit receipt. To illustrate this point, we computed the "relative convexity" of the lifetime social security constraint at various retirement ages. To measure relative convexity at a particular age R, we computed the average asset value of social security, say S_t, at ages $R - 1, R$, and $R + 1$ for all retirees in our sample who retired at age R. Relative convexity is then determined by subtracting the rate of growth in assets in the year $R - 1$ to R from the rate of growth in the year R to $R + 1$: $(S_{R+1} - S_R) - (S_R - S_{R-1})$. If this value is zero, no change occurs in the rate of growth of assets; if it is negative, the rate of growth is declining; and if it is positive, the rate of growth is rising. The tabulation in figure 5 shows that, as expected, the relative convexity of benefits is far more negative at age 65 than at any other age. Furthermore, at age 62 the relative convexity is of the opposite sign, implying that the clustering of retirements at that age must be a result of other factors, such as liquidity constraints.[23] Before age 62 and after age 65, the budget constraint is relatively linear, for while the relative convexity varies somewhat it centers around zero.

Results

Our model consists of two equations, one for the age at retirement, equation 5, and one for hours of work after retirement, equation 1. Results of our maximum-likelihood estimation are presented in table 2. The upper panel contains parameter estimates associated with retirement age; the middle panel, estimates associated with retirement hours; and the bottom panel, estimates of the social security relative impact parameters. Variables were selected for inclusion in the retirement age and retirement hours equations after exploratory specification search using ordinary least squares. All estimates are statistically significant at no less than the 10 percent level.

Consider first parameters associated with the retirement age decision. Because these are difficult to interpret directly, we have translated them into an effect on the average age at retirement. Not surprisingly, poor health status reported on the 1969 survey is associated with significantly earlier retirement. For men who otherwise have average characteristics, those who describe themselves as having poorer health than average

23. At a sufficiently high interest rate, the sign of the relative convexity at age 62 will be reversed.

Table 2. Maximum Likelihood Estimates of Retirement Age–Retirement Hours Model[a]

Parameter or variable	Parameter estimate	Asymptotic standard error
Age at retirement		
γ_1: constant term	139.310	14.026
poor health in 1969	−3.436	0.520
nonwhite	−0.782	0.442
educated less than eight years	−0.943	0.306
vested in pension plan	2.634	0.406
γ_2: W_P, preretirement wage	−0.179	0.089
γ_3: age	−2.132	0.213
$1/(1 + \rho)$: time preference factor	0.763	0.009
σ_2: standard deviation of ϵ_2	6.663	0.686
Weekly hours of work during retirement		
α: constant term	9.541	1.956
college education	19.692	1.736
married	19.100	1.791
β: W, net retirement age wage rate	0.729	0.074
δ: Y_R, weekly retirement income flow	−0.177	0.001
σ_1: standard deviation of ϵ_1	38.929	0.941
Relative impact of social security		
g_R: θ_1, constant	−50.160	0.159
θ_2, age	0.870	0.003
θ_3, max(0, age − 62)	−0.468	0.021

Source: Same as table 1.
a. Value of likelihood function = −12,824.
   Number of observations = 4,603; retirees = 3,535; working retirees = 594; nonworking retirees = 2,801; retirees with missing hours = 140; nonretirees = 1,068.

retire approximately 1.1 years earlier than those reporting normal or above-average health.[24] Nonwhites and those who failed to complete eight years of schooling also retire at younger ages, probably because of

24. The translation of this coefficient into an effect on R is obtained by simulation of the age distribution of "average" men using two different levels of the health variable. The effect cannot be read off table 2 directly. The translations of other coefficients mentioned below were similarly obtained. The simulations are based on an "average" case, though it is difficult for us to define such a case because men in our sample had their social security benefits computed under a variety of different benefit formulas. The social security law changed significantly over the period 1965–77, when retirements in our sample were taking place. Unless otherwise indicated, we have therefore used the 1978 benefit formula for a person born in 1909 to compute the lifetime constraint of our "average" case. His potential earnings at each age are simply the average earnings of all workers in our sample at that age. Like most men in our sample, he is married and his spouse has some previous earnings of her own.

systematic taste differences or because their work years were spent in more physically demanding occupations. Workers vested in employer pension plans tend to retire later than unvested workers. For men who otherwise have average characteristics, vested workers retire about ten months later than unvested workers. This might seem surprising, but it is at least partially offset by the fact that vested workers also have higher retirement incomes than unvested workers and, as we shall see below, the higher the level of potential retirement income, the earlier a worker retires. Surprisingly, workers with high preretirement wages are found to retire slightly earlier than those with low wages. For example, persons with twice the average wage retire approximately 2.2 months earlier than workers earning exactly the average wage. We should point out that the full effect of the preretirement wage is considerably more complex than this direct effect because of its impact on savings and postretirement wage rates, both of which also affect the retirement age. Our estimate of γ_3 shows, not surprisingly, that advances in age are associated with sharp declines in taste for full-time work. Finally, our results show a fairly high estimate of ρ, the subjective rate of time preference. The estimate of $1/(1 + \rho)$, which is very precisely estimated, implies a value of ρ of about 31 percent a year. This finding suggests that when people consider the net utility of an added year of full-time work, they tend to discount fairly heavily the future consumption gains arising from that extra work. For example, the utility weight ten years in the future is only about 0.10.

The next set of parameters is associated with the retirement hours equation. These show that college education and marriage significantly increase postretirement hours, that increases in the net retirement wage have a small but significant positive effect on weekly hours (β is 0.729), and that rises in net nonwage income have a significant negative effect on hours (δ is -0.177). To understand the implications of these effects on actual postretirement hours, we should note that the hours equation being estimated contains 80 percent zero observations. Our maximum-likelihood technique incorporates a Tobit specification into the likelihood function, implying that the coefficients in the hours-of-work equation must be interpreted as those on a latent (unobserved) "taste-for-work" index. This index is negative for approximately 80 percent of the sample—namely, those who do not work after retirement. In this circumstance the parameters have their stated effects on hours for only a small portion of the sample. The implied changes in total hours of work, including the zero hours observations, can be approximated by multiplying the parameters by 0.20.[25] Consequently, the effect of college education, for example, on average retirement work effort is approximately four hours per week. The effect of a $1.00 rise in the net retirement wage is to raise average hours by about 0.15 per week, while the effect of a $10.00 rise in weekly nonwage income is to reduce average hours by about one-third of an hour per week. We should also note that the retirement hours parameters have an important impact on retirement age because of their implicit inclusion in the retirement equation. (See equations 5 above and 6 in the appendix.) Not surprisingly, variables associated with higher work effort after retirement are also associated with later retirement. Thus, men with some college education retire about one year later than those with less schooling, and men who are married retire 1.2 years later than otherwise identical men who are single.

As we turn next to the parameters measuring the relative social security impact g_R, we find strong evidence that the relative impact rises with age, though the rate of increase falls off sharply after age 62. As expected, because of borrowing constraints on social security benefits, benefits have no effect or only negligible effects on the behavior of younger men, but these effects grow as men become older. Using the formula for g_R (given in equation 4), note that the relative social security impact is 0.0 before about age 57 and rises to 1.0 by about age 59, to 3.8 by age 62, and, more slowly, to 5.0 by age 65. Thus after about age 59 our estimates imply that a dollar of social security benefits has a larger impact on hours and retirement than does a dollar of non-social-security income. At age 64, which is around the mean retirement age in our sample, the estimate of g_R implies that a dollar of social security benefits has 4.6 times the impact on behavior of a dollar of other unearned income. For example, the coefficient β measures the effect of a one-dollar change in the net wage in the absence of the retirement test. As just noted, this effect is extremely small—less than three-quarters of an hour per week for working retirees. But the effect of an equivalent change in Wt—the retirement test impact on the net wage—is 3.34 hours per week. Likewise, the income effect for social security benefits at age

25. See John McDonald and Robert A. Moffitt, "The Uses of Tobit Analysis," *Review of Economics and Statistics*, vol. 62 (May 1980), pp. 318–21.

64 is -0.811, considerably larger than for non-social-security income. Hence a \$10 per week increase in the basic benefit lowers weekly hours among all 64-year-old retirees by 1.62 hours per week.

The effect of social security on postretirement hours is complicated by the nonlinearities implicit in the retirement test. As discussed earlier, the structure of that test will produce a tendency for a "piling up" in the earnings distribution at exactly the exempt amount. The estimated wage and income parameters in the hours equation generate a distribution of hours along the piecewise linear constraint (figure 2) that approximates the data. While it is difficult to describe a "typical" retiree's response to the retirement test because the variation in g_R affects responses at different ages, for illustrative purposes we shall describe the responses of men who retire at age 62 and receive the mean nonwage income and social security benefit reported in our sample for men retiring at that age. Of this group, our parameters imply that only 20 percent will work, and among workers fully one-half will choose to earn less than the exempt amount. Of the remaining workers, two-thirds will choose to earn about the exempt amount, and only one-third will earn more than the exempt amount. By implication only 10 percent of retirees at age 62 are affected by the retirement test; the remainder would be unaffected by its elimination. Evaluating the hours along each segment and the probabilities of locating along each shows that expected hours are about 3.2 per week (sixteen hours among those who work). In the absence of the retirement test this number would rise to 4.2 hours per week assuming that the age of retirement remains unchanged. Thus, the elimination of the test is predicted to raise the hours of 62-year-old retirees by only about one hour. Of those who respond at all—about 10 percent of the retirees—the increase is on average about 10.6 hours per week, however. Note that the effect of the earnings test must decline with advances in the retirement age beyond 62 because (1) social security benefits and private nonwage income rise with delays in retirement, implying that fewer retirees would choose to work even without the earnings test, and (2) the relative effect of social security g_R also rises with age, leading to a decline in the proportion of working retirees for a given level of benefits.

Before turning to a more general consideration of financial determinants of the retirement age, we should mention the impact of the retirement test on retirement age. We simulated this impact by considering the effect of eliminating the test on males with "average" work histories. We assume that, before allowing retirement benefits to begin, the Social Security Administration will require proof of retirement according to our definition—that is, will require a discontinuous drop in hours. This reform has only a very slight impact on the average age at retirement because only a small proportion of retirees expect to have high enough retirement earnings to be affected by the retirement test. For an "average" male who would otherwise earn at or above the earnings exempt amount, elimination of the test would cause retirement to occur about three weeks *earlier*. Since only 9.5 percent of retirees aged 62 and older are affected by the retirement test, the effect on the overall retirement distribution would be virtually undetectable.

The implications of our results for the choice of retirement age require some explication of the nature of the retirement equation. Note in equation 5 that the level and rate of change of retirement income, from both private and social security sources, enter the retirement equation through the terms containing C_R. If C_R is raised by a constant amount, say \$10 per week, at every potential retirement age, $\partial C_R/\partial R$ would be left unaffected and the probability of retirement at earlier ages should rise; if C_R at a particular age is held constant but $\partial C_R/\partial R$ is raised, the probability of retirement at that age should decline. For our "average" case, we have computed that raising N_R at every age by \$10 per week (about 14 percent of the mean N_R) would cause the average retirement age to decline by 0.106 years; raising the social security grant at every age by \$10 per week (about 22 percent of the mean G_R) would cause the average retirement age to decline by 0.234 years. If work life begins at age 20 and extends to age 64—close to the average retirement age in our sample—then these declines in the retirement age represent changes in the average work life of only 0.24 percent and 0.53 percent, respectively. Thus, rather sizable percentage increases in retirement income are associated with only small reductions in the length of work life.

To determine the impact of the rate of change of retirement income on the date of retirement, we conceived the following experiment. Holding N_R constant at all ages prior to and including age 62, we increased the rate of change of weekly N_R by \$1.00 per year at all ages after age 62. Since for the "average" case weekly N_R rises by about \$3.00 for each year of delay in retirement, this amount represents a one-third rise in the rate of increment in N_R. However, this experiment affected retirements at age 62 only very slightly. The proportion of all men who would retire at age 62 declined from 13.9 percent to 13.6 percent; thus, only about 2 percent of men who would otherwise retire at age 62 were induced to postpone retirement to 63 or later. In a similar experiment, we simulated the impact of raising the rate of growth of weekly social security benefits by $1.00 per year beginning at age 62. Here the impact was somewhat larger. The proportion of men who would retire at age 62 declined from 13.9 percent to 12.6 percent; about 9 percent of men who would otherwise retire at 62 were induced to retire at age 63 or later.

In summary, our results suggest that variations in the social security benefit formula will have significant but relatively small effects on the timing of retirement. This finding is confirmed in the next section in which we consider the effect of some changes in the benefit formula currently under public discussion. However, our findings show that benefits have a very important effect on work effort after retirement. This impact is not due solely to the social security retirement test, although that provision does substantially reduce hours among the small proportion of retirees who would otherwise earn above the exempt amount. Social security benefits have an important income effect that significantly reduces both the level of hours among working retirees and the fraction of retirees who work. Note that in table 1 the average retiree over the age of 62 qualifies for about $49.00 per week in social security benefits and works an average of 3.2 hours per week. At the mean retirement age for this group (64.4) the relative impact of social security (g_R) is 4.7. Thus if the mean benefit were reduced by 10 percent, or $4.90, working retirees would raise weekly work effort by $(0.177)(4.7)(4.90) =$ 4.08 hours. Averaged across all retirees, working and nonworking, this change in hours translates into an average rise of 0.82 hours per week or slightly more than 25 percent. Although this response is proportionally quite large, recall that it amounts to only about one week a year of average preretirement work effort.

Reform of the Benefit Formula

A variety of social security reforms have been suggested to deal with the short- and long-run problems in social security financing. In this section, we briefly examine three reforms in the benefit formula and predict their effects on representative men in our sample. To measure the effect of a proposed change, we must first define a baseline case. For comparative purposes we selected the 1978 benefit formula, which is similar to the social security formula in effect for current retirees. Using this formula, we computed potential benefits that representative workers could obtain if they retired at ages 54 through 72.[26]

Three reforms in the benefit formula are considered: (1) delay the normal retirement age from 65 to 68 but continue to permit early retirement at age 62. The actuarial reduction factor at age 62 is reduced from 0.80 to 0.60; at 65 from 1.00 to 0.80; and at 68 from 1.09 to 1.00; (2) reduce the primary insurance amount by 20 percent at every retirement age; (3) make the actuarial reduction factor actuarially fair for single men using 1970 life tables. This last approach involves a very slight reduction in benefits between ages 62 and 64, where at our assumed interest rate the present actuarial reduction factor is slightly more than fair. However, the main effect is to increase substantially the rate of rise of benefits after age 65 by increasing the payoff to delayed retirement.[27]

The effects of the reforms are summarized in table 3 for three representative males in our sample. The top part contains estimated responses for a married male whose spouse is a low-wage worker; the middle part gives responses of a married male with a spouse who does not qualify for benefits under her own earnings records; and the bottom part gives responses of an unmarried male. All three males have identical wage histories and wage rates and are assumed to differ only with regard to marital status or labor force status of their wives. Because of the variance of ϵ_2 there will be a dispersion of retirement ages, even for otherwise identical men. The first column in the table shows the average retirement age under each of the three reformed benefit formulas; the second column shows the change in average retirement age resulting from the formula reform. The third column gives the average weekly social security benefit taking account of the dispersion of retirement ages under each of the benefit formulas. The fourth and fifth columns show

26. As mentioned earlier, we assumed that the workers could earn the average reported wages at each of those ages 54–72. Shortly after we completed research for this paper, the social security benefit formula was significantly altered for future retirees. Under legislation passed early in 1983, Congress modified the retirement test, advanced the normal retirement age to 66 in 2009 and to 67 in 2027, and increased the actuarial adjustment factor for retirees who postpone their initial benefit receipts past the normal retirement age. As a result of these reforms, workers retiring between 62 and 65 can expect to receive smaller social security benefits in the next century than similar retirees at present.

27. For example, at 66 the actuarial reduction factor would rise from 1.03 under current law to 1.10; at age 68 the actuarial reduction factor would rise from 1.09 to 1.33; and at age 72 the actuarial reduction factor would rise from 1.21 to 2.05.

Table 3. Effect on Retirement Age and Benefits of Three Reforms in Social Security[a]

Reform	Average retirement age (1)	Change in retirement age (in years) (2)	Average annual benefit[b] (3)	Change in benefit with no retirement response[b] (4)	Change in benefit due to retirement response[b] (5)	Percent total change in annual benefit (6)	Percent total change in net lifetime benefit[c] (7)
Married male, working spouse							
Normal retirement age 68	64.75	0.38	7,774	−1,619	325	−14.3	−15.7
20 percent reduction in primary insurance amount	64.58	0.21	7,362	−1,813	103	−18.8	−19.8
Actuarially fair actuarial reduction factor	64.74	0.37	10,212	625	520	12.6	11.5
Married male, nonworking spouse							
Normal retirement age 68	64.94	0.34	7,154	−1,391	299	−13.3	−15.0
20 percent reduction in primary insurance amount	64.79	0.18	6,700	−1,649	104	−18.8	−19.6
Actuarially fair actuarial reduction factor	65.00	0.39	9,606	760	598	16.5	13.9
Unmarried male							
Normal retirement age 68	63.84	0.20	4,394	−934	125	−15.6	−17.0
20 percent reduction in primary insurance amount	63.71	0.08	4,197	−1,040	35	−19.4	−19.8
Actuarially fair actuarial reduction factor	64.00	0.37	5,947	401	342	14.3	11.1

Source: Same as table 1.

a. Predictions are based on parameter estimates reported in table 2. The male is assumed to have average characteristics in our sample and potential earnings at ages 42 through 72 equal to those reported for our sample in the Social Security Administration's earnings histories. The 1978 benefit formula is used to compute base case benefit levels and retirement ages. Details of social security reforms are provided in the text.

b. Measured in 1982 dollars.

c. Change in family lifetime benefits taking account of retirement age response and added social security tax contributions paid before the new retirement age.

why average benefits under a particular reform formula differ from those provided under the baseline formula. Thus column 4 shows how much benefits would be raised or lowered by the reform *if the retirement distribution remained unchanged*; column 5 shows how much the average benefit rises as a result of the fact that retirements are postponed.

Column 6 gives the resulting percentage change in annual social security grants, after taking account of the retirement age delay. The last column shows the percentage change in net discounted lifetime social security benefits from the original age of retirement (that is, the average age at which males retire under the 1978 formula). In computing this net change, we took account of the fact that workers would pay additional FICA taxes because of their delayed retirements. Note that this column essentially shows the net discounted savings to the social security system of instituting the indicated reform.

The first two reforms cause sizable reductions in social security benefits. Delaying the normal retirement age to 68 effectively reduces weekly benefits by 16 percent to 18 percent, holding the retirement distribution constant. Reducing the primary insurance amount by 20 percent is obviously equivalent to reducing benefits by 20 percent. But because men would postpone their retirements by a few months, the net reduction in weekly benefits is somewhat smaller. For example, the behavioral response to delaying the normal retirement age causes social security benefits to rise slightly so that the net drop in weekly benefits is only about 13 percent to 16 percent.

Since men receive benefits for a reduced period, however, the cut in lifetime benefits is still quite substantial. Thus, advancing the normal retirement age reduces lifetime benefits by 15 percent to 17 percent. Our results provide clear evidence that either of the first two reforms would substantially reduce social security outlays in the long term, even taking account of the likely adjustments in retirement ages. As mentioned in the previous section, substantial reductions in retirement benefits have only a modest impact on lengthening the work life. If the average worker began his work career at age 20 and survived until age 80, a delay in retirement of 4.5 months lengthens the work life by less than 1 percent and shortens retirement by less than 2.5 percent. For this reason, our estimates lead us to predict that even major reforms in the social security formula will lead to no revolution in retirement trends.

The third reform we consider substantially *raises* social security benefits for workers who postpone retirement past age 65. Reforms of this type are sometimes proposed to encourage later retirement, although by definition an actuarially fair formula to compensate late retirees for delayed benefit receipt cannot reduce program outlays; it can only postpone them. And indeed, our estimates show that this reform delays the typical retirement by about four and a half months. This goal is achieved, however, at considerable budgetary cost, for average annual benefits rise by 12 percent to 17 percent after taking account of the induced delay in retirement and by 11 percent to 14 percent over a worker's lifetime. Since retirement is shortened by only about 4.5 months (or 2.5 percent), it is obvious that substantially higher lifetime benefits will be paid under the reform than under the 1978 law. Hence, while this reform may be regarded as "fairer" than current law and will undoubtedly reduce the incentive to retire at age 65, our results strongly suggest that its implementation would greatly exacerbate the financing problems facing social security.

Summary

In this paper we analyzed the retirement behavior of approximately 4,600 men interviewed in the Retirement History Survey in an attempt to infer the effect of social security benefits on their age at retirement and work effort after retirement. The structure of social security benefits affects both these aspects of labor supply because it provides incentives for workers to retire at one age rather than another and because it imposes a high implicit tax on postretirement earnings in excess of an exempt amount. We have described the basic benefit formula with some care in an attempt to show its likely impact on the fraction of life that individuals will choose to devote to retirement.

Our empirical model of retirement age is based on an extension of the economic model ordinarily applied to consumer choice. We show that social security benefits affect the level and rate of growth of retirement consumption, with consequent effects on the retirement age analogous to the income and substitution effects in ordinary demand analysis. Our empirical specification of postretirement work effort is a straightforward application of past econometric models of labor supply in the presence of piecewise linear budget constraints. A unique feature of the present work is its integration of the two labor supply decisions—retirement age and level of retirement work effort—into a single, jointly estimated model. Of course, as with any econometric study, our estimation is based upon certain assumptions that to some degree limit the applicability of our findings. For example, since we examine only work effort decisions immediately after retirement, the results cannot be used to predict hours of work throughout retirement. Also, since we take savings rates and asset holdings in our sample as given, our parameter estimates and predictions have limited generalizability if savings rates or private pensions respond strongly to modifications in the social security benefit formula.

With these caveats in mind, our results provide strong confirmation of some important social security effects. For example, the distributions of retirement ages and postretirement hours in our sample conform to a striking degree to our theoretical predictions: retirements cluster at age 62 and later at 65, and postretirement hours concentrate at the level where retirement earnings are just equal to the social security exempt amount. This clustering of retirement ages and hours is captured in our specification of the behavioral response function.

Next, our estimation of the model confirms the existence of statistically significant social security impacts on both retirement ages and retirement hours. But the estimates do not imply that the average age at retirement is highly responsive to changes in benefit levels. For example, our simulation of the effect of a 20 percent reduction in social security benefits indicates that married men with average earnings histories would delay their retirements by only about two or two and a half months in response to the benefit cut. Single men with identical earnings histories would delay retirement by less than half that, or about one month. This change in the retirement age represents only a very small reduction in the length of a typical retirement and represents an even smaller percentage increase in the length of an average working career. Our estimate of the retirement hours equation shows that social security has a larger proportional effect on work effort after retirement. For example, elimination of the social security retirement test is estimated to raise the work effort of average retirees over age 62 by 30 percent to 40 percent. In absolute terms, however, even this response is quite small—about 1 to 1.5 hours per week—since only about 20 percent of retirees in our sample work.

A major implication of our findings is that the average retirement age is rather insensitive to variations in the social security benefit formula, at least within the range of reforms currently under public discussion. A delay in the normal retirement age to 68, a 20 percent reduction in benefits, and a substantial increase in the reward for delaying retirement past 65 each have only modest effects on the retirement age distribution of men with average earnings histories.[28] These findings imply that a cutback in social security benefits will do more to reduce retirement consumption levels than to delay retirement. The consequences for retirement consumption are considerable. Social security accounts for 40 percent of potential retirement income among retirees in our sample over age 62, assuming that they are willing to liquidate all their private assets over the course of their retirements. (If they do not plan to do so, the percentage of income provided by social security is even higher.) Thus, a 20 percent cut in social security benefits, even taking account of the induced delay in retirement, will essentially reduce retirement consumption by 7 percent or 8 percent, since workers do not delay their retirements enough to maintain postretirement consumption levels. For workers with few assets aside from social security, the cut in benefits may therefore involve a considerable rise in hardship.

Appendix: Functions of the Retirement Equation

The forms of the various functions in equation 5 are as follows:

(6) $\quad U^R(H_R, C_R) = -\ln(\beta - \delta H_R) - \dfrac{\delta(H_R - \alpha X - \epsilon_1 - \delta C_R)}{\beta - \delta H_R},$

(7) $\qquad\qquad\qquad \dfrac{\partial U^R(\cdot)}{\partial C_R} = \dfrac{\delta^2}{\beta - \delta H_R},$

(8) $\qquad\qquad U^P(\overline{H}_P, \overline{C}_P) = \gamma_1 Z + \gamma_2 W_P + \gamma_3 \text{age} + \epsilon_2,$

(9) $\qquad\qquad\qquad \dfrac{\partial C_R}{\partial R} = N_{R+1} - N_R + g_{R+1} M_{R+1} - g_R M_R.$

Equation 6 is the utility function for consumption and hours during

---

28. However, our estimates do suggest that elimination of early retirement benefits might have a major effect in reducing retirements between ages 62 and 64. The reported estimates of the relative social security impact g_R imply that benefits do not have a measurable impact on retirement behavior until about four years before they can commence. By delaying the year of initial benefit receipt from 62 to 65, a large portion of retirements between those two ages would be eliminated.

retirement, and it is implied by the assumed labor supply function in equation 1. It is therefore not an extra assumption, but just a consequence of the functional form assumed in 1. Equation 7 is implied by equation 6. We assume that the preretirement utility function, $U^P(\cdot)$, differs considerably from preferences for work and consumption during retirement. Since we have no interest in examining preretirement hours of work explicitly, however, we have not specified a formal preretirement utility function. Instead, we have just approximated it in equation 8 by a function of the variables we know affect the preretirement level of well-being, namely, a vector of socioeconomic variables (Z), the preretirement wage rate (W_P), age, and an error term (ϵ_2). Equation 9 shows that the increase in retirement consumption arising from an increase in R (holding H_R constant) equals the net increase in private nonwage income (resulting from added savings) plus the increase in M_R (social security income). Note that the benefit terms are allowed to have relative effects different from private income.

The complete retirement equation estimated in this paper can be obtained by substituting equations 6 through 9 into equation 5. Our dependent variable R is not obtainable in explicit and closed form on the left-hand side of the equation. For this reason, among others, we use a nonlinear estimation procedure.

Comment by Sherwin Rosen

This paper presents an interesting and novel approach to the analysis of retirement. Life-cycle utility is approximated by dual-state dependent preferences, one component referring to consumption and leisure decisions before retirement and the other to postretirement choices concerning consumption and leisure. This approach allows the retirement decision to be analyzed as an optimal stopping problem, not unlike the old problem of when to cut the tree or drink the wine. It also clarifies the relationship between postretirement work decisions and choice of retirement date (stopping time). The retirement date is determined in part by the difference in utility between pre- and postretirement intervals, but postretirement utility itself depends on labor supply decisions after regular work activities have ceased. Therefore a simultaneous equation model is required to analyze these choices consistently.

This model departs in significant ways from the standard treatment.

State-dependent differences in preferences are the driving force behind the retirement decision. Retirement would never occur in this model as currently formulated if preferences were independent of age. Little in the way of economic argument is offered to explain why age-dependent preferences are a plausible specification. The available alternative model focuses on a much different form of age dependence to explain retirement, namely on life-cycle wage prospects and human capital considerations. Retirement occurs when market wage rates fall to sufficiently low levels with advancing age, even if the utility function is independent of age.

These approaches are not mutually exclusive, and it would be of some value to know how they differ, and if they do, how the estimates and their interpretations are affected. It may even be true that a model containing elements of both would be superior to either one. An obvious difference is that the wage-dependence view brings productivity and demand factors into the picture and introduces another kind of simultaneity in terms of investment decisions about human capital. Retirement decisions obviously interact with decisions to maintain labor market skills and may also be affected by provisions of the Social Security Act. It seems difficult to rationalize many of the institutional features of retirement behavior and labor contracts containing mandatory retirement clauses without recourse to age-related productivity factors.

If we consider the model on its own merits, the empirical work goes only part way toward the life-cycle framework discussed in the theoretical section. The main reason is that data are available near the time of retirement only and not before. Nonetheless, consumption, savings, and work decisions prior to retirement are expected to interact with retirement and postretirement work decisions. The empirical specification apparently ignores all those things and assumes that preretirement utility is a declining function of retirement age along with a fixed effect. At minimum, the interactions between the two regimes suggest that the rate of decline in u^P should differ across persons and be functionally related to such available indicators as family circumstances, health status, and wealth. By maintaining the assumption that the rate of decline in u^P is the same for all persons, the authors seem to compromise their own model.

Yet another general point of specification that seems worthy of attention is the opportunity set for retirees. The authors follow conventional practice in assuming that a person can work as much or as little as desired at the going wage. Yet it seems obvious that many jobs available to retirees do not meet these conditions. Rather, working hours are specified in advance and are not subject to choice on any given job because productivity depends on the timing of work effort in most jobs. Choices, then, are better described as all-or-nothing wage-hours pairs, one pair for each job available. To make a long story short, this fact makes the budget constraint nonlinear, even in the absence of the work test. Some short-hours jobs may not even appear on the market at all. Similar indivisibilities arise if labor force participation involves fixed time or money costs. Factors such as this may well explain why so few retirees report any work at all in this sample, in addition to the retirement test. While the frequency distributions in the data compellingly support the proposition that the work test affects labor supply decisions of the elderly, one must keep in mind that only a small number of retirees work at all. Perhaps many retirees do not work because jobs with desired hours and working conditions are not available. If so, the estimates of the labor supply of the elderly from this model are biased and overstate the effects of the work test.

A few other procedural questions are raised by the paper. First, the case for a linear hours-supply specification would be more convincing were the budget set linear. Even in that case it leads to a complicated nonlinear expression for the stopping time. Because nonlinearities due to the retirement test make the supply equation difficult to estimate anyway, perhaps a little more complexity in the hours equation would lead to a simpler retirement equation and make the model easier to estimate overall. Second, the role of health has been shown to be important in retirement decisions in other studies and ultimately finds its way into the empirical work, but its effect on the structural model should be discussed with more care. In this same vein, medical subsidies to the aged and availability of disability insurance also affect retirement decisions but are not discussed. Third, some of the imputations for financial wealth and housing add random numbers to the instrumental estimates, adding undesirable noise and measurement error to these variables. This situation needs more explanation. In the housing impu- tations the authors are also vague about the symmetrical effects of housing inflation on both capital gains and imputed rental user costs to owner-occupiers. And fourth, there has been a remarkable increase in longevity of the aged population over this period, which, if anticipated, would have affected retirement decisions. The use of cross-sectional mortality tables gives biased estimates of life expectancy for people in this sample.

In sum, this very sophisticated paper is at the frontier of econometric methods in this field and addresses certain conceptual dimensions of the problem in a very innovative way. But it is deficient in other dimensions. It ultimately is an empirical question whether the model as it now stands captures most of the interesting variation in the data and requires no additional modifications to render it adequate for policy simulation and prediction. I hope the authors will use their estimates to help explain the remarkable time-series changes that have occurred in the labor market activities of the elderly in the last two decades. If their estimates do explain the changes this should resolve whether the points raised here are just quibbles or serious issues worth addressing.

Sheldon Danziger, Jacques van der Gaag,
Eugene Smolensky, and Michael K. Taussig

Implications of the Relative
Economic Status of the Elderly
for Transfer Policy

What is the economic status of the elderly? It is easy to measure their current money income, but it is harder to measure the standard of living that the elderly can achieve with their income. Their needs are different from those of other age groups. They are more likely to own durable goods, including homes unencumbered by mortgages. For these and other reasons, it is unlikely that the elderly require the same amount of current income as the nonelderly to achieve a given standard of living.

We presume that comparisons of the economic status of the elderly and of other demographic groups are relevant for public policy. For example, how high should social security retirement benefits be? By clarifying several measurement issues in this paper, we seek to make such comparisons more meaningful than those found elsewhere in the literature. Toward that end, the first section briefly reviews the census data on the relative money income of the elderly. The next section shows how we adjust the money income data and correct for some of their deficiencies. The third section discusses the implications of the relative economic status of the elderly for income transfer policy by analyzing the equity effects of current tax transfer programs and two social security reform options. A brief summary concludes our discussion.

Frank Levy and John Menefee provided helpful comments on an earlier version of the paper; Daniel Feaster gave valuable computational assistance.

175

Census Data

We classify people by the age of the head of their household. People living in households where the head is 65 years of age or older are counted among the elderly; those in households where the head is younger than 65, among the nonelderly.[1] U.S. Census Bureau data on money income for all families and unrelated individuals (census units) and for those in which the head is over 65 provide the conventional starting point for appraising the relative economic status of the elderly.[2] The mean money income of all families and unrelated individuals in 1980 was $19,500. The corresponding figure for the elderly was $12,226, or about 63 percent of the all-census-unit average. For census units with nonelderly female household heads it was $11,351, or 58 percent of the average, and for nonelderly nonwhite households it was $15,117, or 78 percent of the average. These estimates show the relatively low money incomes of the elderly, but they also point to the similarly low relative incomes of female-headed and nonwhite households.

Table 1 provides a time series of the published Census Bureau money income data for the past fifteen years. It shows evidence of substantial improvement in the median income and poverty incidence of the elderly relative to those of all families and persons.[3] This improvement occurred despite the considerable decrease in the retirement age and hence a corresponding decline in labor force participation over the same period. The most remarkable feature of these data is that by 1981 the incidence of poverty for the white elderly was less than for the population as a

1. Until 1980 the U.S. Bureau of the Census designated the "head" to be the person regarded by the members of the household or family as the head. The head of a husband-wife unit was always the husband if the couple were living together. In 1980 the Census Bureau switched to the concept of the householder, defined as the person in whose name the home is owned or rented. If owned or rented jointly, the householder may be either the husband or the wife. In the March 1980 Current Population Survey, only about 3 percent of married couple units designated the wife as the householder. In the next section we classify persons by their own age rather than by the age of the head of the consumer unit and examine the empirical implications.

2. Data in this paragraph are our computations from the March 1981 Current Population Survey computer tapes. Census units are defined to include families and unrelated individuals.

3. The Census Bureau publishes separate median income data for families and unrelated individuals. Although unrelated individuals are not counted in column 1 of the table, they are included in the poverty data in the remaining columns.

Table 1. The Relative Economic Status of the Elderly, 1966–81[a]

Year	Ratio of median incomes of families with elderly head to all families	Ratio of poverty incidence				
		All elderly to all persons	White elderly to all persons	Black elderly to all persons	Female elderly to all persons	All females to all persons
1966	0.49	1.94	1.80	3.75	3.01	2.79
1967	0.49	2.08	1.95	3.75	3.33	2.86
1968	0.53	1.95	1.81	3.73	3.21	3.04
1969	0.51	2.09	1.93	4.15	3.40	3.17
1970	0.51	1.94	1.79	3.81	3.26	3.03
1971	0.53	1.73	1.59	3.14	3.07	3.04
1972	0.54	1.56	1.41	3.35	2.56	3.14
1973	0.53	1.47	1.30	3.34	2.56	3.14
1974	0.57	1.30	1.14	3.06	2.35	3.00
1975	0.59	1.24	1.09	2.95	2.15	2.81
1976	0.58	1.27	1.12	2.95	2.21	2.92
1977	0.57	1.22	1.03	3.13	2.08	2.83
1978	0.57	1.23	1.06	2.97	2.10	2.83
1979	0.58	1.30	1.14	3.06	2.23	2.75
1980	0.61	1.21	1.05	2.93	2.14	2.60
1981	0.64	1.09	0.94	2.79	1.96	2.51
Addendum						
Ratio of 1981 value to 1966 value	1.31	0.56	0.52	0.74	0.65	0.90

Source: U.S. Bureau of the Census, *Current Population Reports,* series P-60, no. 134, "Money Income and Poverty Status of Families and Persons in the United States, 1981" (Government Printing Office, 1982), and earlier reports in the P-60 series.

a. Elderly are those census units in which the head is 65 years of age or more.

whole. The ratios in the addendum show that the relative poverty incidence of black and female elderly has improved much more slowly than that of their white and male counterparts.[4]

Much recent research has been directed at improving the measurement of economic status by correcting the deficiencies in the money income concept.[5] Quantifying all these sources of bias is a formidable research

4. See F. T. Juster, "Current and Prospective Financial Status of the Elderly Population," Institute for Social Research Working Paper (University of Michigan, Survey Research Center, 1981).

5. The research is summarized in Marilyn Moon and Eugene Smolensky, eds., *Improving Measures of Economic Well-Being* (Academic Press, 1977); Moon and Smolensky, "Income, Economic Status, and Policy toward the Aged," in G. Tolley and R. Burkhauser, eds., *Income Support Policies for the Aged* (Ballinger, 1977), pp. 45–60; and Sheldon Danziger and Michael K. Taussig, *Conference on the Trend in*

agenda, made even more difficult by the lack of appropriate data. In the next section of this paper, we attempt to correct for the following biases in the census money data that understate the true relative economic status of the elderly:[6] first, the elderly pay less in personal taxes than the nonelderly at the same money income level; second, the elderly own more assets than the nonelderly at the same money income level, including a disproportionate share of assets such as equity in their own homes and consumer durables that yield nonmoney income flows; third, the elderly generally live in smaller income-pooling units than do the nonelderly and usually have no childrearing expenses; and fourth, some low-income elderly persons can save on housing and other expenses by living with their children or in other nonelderly households.

In addition, other biases occur in the data, which we do not attempt to correct in this study. Some of these further understate the true relative economic status of the elderly: the elderly receive a disproportionate share of government in-kind benefits that are not included in the census money income measure; the retired elderly have more time available for consumption or for nonmarket production of services; the retired elderly do not have work expenses such as commuting costs; and the elderly may share resources with their nonelderly children even if they live in separate households.

We can add to this list the finding by Daniel Radner that the elderly understate their money income in response to census surveys much more than the nonelderly.[7] The elderly, however, are more likely to have serious health problems that increase their consumption of medical services and limit their consumption of other goods, and, after retirement, they no longer enjoy a number of fringe benefits of employment. We speculate that, even after the corrections we have made, our results still understate the true relative economic status of the elderly.

Economic Inequality in the U.S., Special Report 11 (University of Wisconsin–Madison, Institute for Research on Poverty, 1977). Marilyn Moon, *The Measurement of Economic Welfare: Its Application to the Aged Poor* (Academic Press, 1977), concentrates on comparisons of the economic status of the elderly and nonelderly.

6. For a similar, more complete list, see *Emerging Options for Work and Retirement Policy*, Senate Special Committee on Aging, 96 Cong. 2 sess. (Government Printing Office, 1980).

7. Daniel B. Radner, "Adjusted Estimates of the Size Distribution of Family Money Income for 1972," Office of Research and Statistics Working Paper 24 (Social Security Administration, October 1981).

Table 2. Effects of Adjustments to Money Income on the Relative Economic Status of the Elderly, 1973

Incremental adjustments to income	Relative economic status of elderly (percent)[a]	Change in relative status due to adjustment (percent of total change)
Household weights[b]		
1. Reported cash income	48.6	. . .
2. For durables	52.2	8.7
3. For direct taxes	56.2	9.7
4. For family size and composition	85.3	70.3
Person weights[b]		
5. For household units	88.0	6.5
6. For age of each household member	90.0	4.8
7. Total	90.0	100.0

Source: Authors' calculations from 1973 Consumer Expenditure Survey data.
a. Defined as the mean value of the income concept for the elderly divided by the mean for the nonelderly.
b. See text for explanation of weights.

Some Adjustments to the Data

The empirical work reported here is based on data from the 1973 observations of the 1972–73 Consumer Expenditure Survey (CEX).[8] Table 2 summarizes the effects of our adjustments on the relative economic status of the elderly. Down the stub we list six concepts of economic status. Then we show the progression of relative mean economic status of the elderly from 48.6 percent of that of the nonelderly (cash income as reported in the CEX) to 90.0 percent (cash income adjusted for durable flows, direct taxes, family size and composition, person weighting, and the age of each household member). That in 1973 the elderly were on average 90 percent as well off as the nonelderly is our most policy-relevant finding, since much of the current policy debate about poverty and about social security presumes that the elderly, as a group, are economically disadvantaged.

8. This section draws on two previous papers. See Sheldon Danziger and others, "The Life Cycle Hypothesis and the Consumption Behavior of the Elderly," *Journal of Post Keynesian Economics*, vol. 5 (Winter 1982–83), pp. 208–27; and Danziger and others, "Transfers and the Economic Status of the Elderly," in Marilyn Moon, ed., *Social Accounting for Transfers* (University of Chicago Press, forthcoming).

From Consumer Expenditures to Consumption

The elderly are more likely than the nonelderly to enjoy service flows from houses they own and live in and from other durables than are the nonelderly at given money income levels. Any measure of money income that omits the dollar value of these service flows understates the relative status of the elderly. Our adjustment for this bias is to use the CEX data to estimate the value of these service flows net of the expenditures to purchase durables and to add the new value as an adjustment to each consumer unit's money income. We deal with the problem of durables by combining data on owned durables from the Inventory of Consumer Durables with the data from the CEX. By matching information on the inventory tape with expenditure data on the CEX tape, we obtain a measure of household consumption that excludes expenditures on durables made during the year of the survey but includes service flows from all durables owned by the household.[9]

Income before taxes changes considerably, both for the elderly and the nonelderly, after we include the service flows. For example, for elderly households in the first quintile of the size distribution of income for the whole sample, the change is as large as 40 percent; for the nonelderly in the same quintile, it is 24 percent. On average, the adjusted income measure is 13 percent higher than reported money income for the nonelderly and 22 percent higher for the elderly. A comparison of the first two rows of table 2 shows that this adjustment raises the mean before-tax income of the elderly from 48.6 to 52.2 percent of that of the nonelderly.

From Income before Taxes to Income after Taxes

Because of the favorable income tax treatment of the elderly, any before-tax measure of income is likely to bias comparisons of the elderly

9. For a complete description, see Jacques van der Gaag and Eugene Smolensky, "True Household Equivalence Scales and Characteristics of the Poor in the United States," *Review of Income and Wealth*, vol. 28 (March 1982), pp. 17–28; and Danziger and others, "Transfers and the Economic Status of the Elderly." We included service flows only from major durables and vehicles. Rental values of residential units were either as reported or as estimated from a hedonic regression. In a letter to us, James Morgan objects that the elderly are "mostly overhoused" so that our adjustment is biased upward. We agree, but we do not know how to take account of this criticism empirically.

and the nonelderly. According to Joseph Pechman, "the federal income tax has been particularly solicitous of the special circumstances of the aged."[10] Special provisions include an additional personal exemption, exclusion of social security from taxation, and the retirement income credit. After we deduct federal and state taxes from before-tax income, elderly household mean income increases from 52.2 to 56.2 percent of that of the nonelderly (table 2, rows 2 and 3).

Household Size and Composition of Equivalence Scales

Average household size varies greatly by age of the head. For example, households in the 35–54 age group are twice as big on average as elderly households. This difference suggests that the mean income comparisons of the elderly and the nonelderly, such as the ones just presented, are too crude for purposes of transfer policy. Two distinct kinds of adjustments for household size differences are needed. First, if one goal of transfer policy is to meet the insufficiency of incomes relative to needs, then one can adopt some welfare ratio, defined as the ratio of income to an estimated index of need that depends on family size and composition. Second, however the income concept is adjusted for differences in need, one has to decide how to weight the incomes of large recipient units relative to small recipient units in calculating the average economic status of any group. We take up these two issues in turn.

Two extreme possibilities bound the range of choice of an appropriate index of need for households that differ in size and composition. The first makes no adjustment for differences in the number of persons in the household on the presumption that people voluntarily choose the form and size of their households.[11] The other defines economic status as income per capita. The per capita measure is easy to understand and mathematically convenient but has little else to recommend it.[12] Its use

10. Joseph A. Pechman, *Federal Tax Policy*, 3d ed. (Brookings Institution, 1977), p. 97.

11. For the case against the use of any equivalence scale, see Stanley Lebergott, *The American Economy: Income, Wealth, and Want* (Princeton University Press, 1976); and Robert A. Pollak and Terence J. Wales, "Welfare Comparisons and Equivalence Scales," *American Economic Review*, vol 69 (May 1979, *Papers and Proceedings, 1978*), pp. 216–21.

12. But see Gautam Datta and Jacob Meerman, "Household Income or Household Income Per Capita in Welfare Comparisons," *Review of Income and Wealth*, vol. 26 (December 1981), pp. 401–18; and Michael Hurd and John B. Shoven, "Real Income and Wealth of the Elderly," *American Economic Review*, vol. 72 (May 1982, *Papers and Proceedings, 1981*), pp. 314–18.

implies, for example, that people who marry spouses with no income or earning potential are cutting their economic well-being in half. The per capita income measure also ignores all economies of scale and special-ization within households and is especially inappropriate for households that derive a large share of their full income in the form of leisure or production of home services.

Between these two extremes are a number of possible adjustments. The index of household need required in the denominator of any welfare ratio is, in principle, a function of its size, composition, health status, age and sex of the head, and other relevant circumstances. An equiva-lence scale is a full set of such indexes for all household types. In principle, equivalence scales should also vary by income level, for there is no reason to think that the same equivalence scale would hold at incomes of $10,000 and $40,000. One widely used equivalence scale is implicit in the Orshansky (official U.S.) set of poverty lines. The Orshansky scale is deficient, however, because it is based solely on food consumption needs. We use instead a constant utility scale (table 3) that is estimated on the basis of expenditures on all consumption categories.[13]

The empirical importance of using an equivalence scale to adjust for differences in household size and composition can be illustrated by a few simple comparisons from the 1973 CEX. Row 3 in table 2 shows that the ratio of mean after-tax income of elderly households to the mean of the nonelderly is 0.562. As shown in row 4, it is 0.853 on a welfare ratio basis. (On a per capita basis, the corresponding ratio is 0.92.) Thus the relative economic status of the elderly is much more sensitive to the treatment of the income unit (household or per capita or welfare ratio) than to the treatment of the income concept (income before or after taxes, or income adjusted for durables).

Given our intention to use the relative economic status of the elderly as a basis for analyzing the equity effects of tax transfer policies, we believe that the estimated welfare ratios based on our equivalence scale provide the most appropriate adjustment for differences in household size and composition. We reject the per capita income alternative

13. Because our scale is stable over a large range of incomes, we use it to calculate welfare ratios for all households. Although the Orshansky and constant utility equivalence scales and the corresponding welfare ratios derived from them are quite different, the choice between them is not important for this study because they lead to quite similar results for the relative economic status of the elderly. We therefore report only our findings on welfare ratios based on the constant utility scale.

Table 3. Constant Utility Equivalence Scale[a]

	Age of head			
Consumer unit composition	35	35–54	54–64	65 and over
One person				
Male	60	63	56	47
Female	50	53	46	37
Two persons				
Husband and wife	77	80	73	64
Female head, child 6–11	56	60	53	. . .
Three persons (couple, child)				
Age of child				
Under 6	76	80	73	64
6–11	88	91	84	75
12–17	90	93	86	77
18 and over	94	98	90	82
Four persons (couple, two children)				
Age of children				
Under 6	83	87	80	71
6–11, under 6	85	89	82	73
6–11	95	98	91	82
12–17, 6–11	97	100	93	84
12–17	97	100	93	84
18 and over, 6–17	110	113	106	98
18 and over	101	105	97	89
Five persons (couple, three children)[b]				
Age of children				
6–11	91	94	87	. . .
12–17, 6–11	102	105	98	. . .
18 and over, 6–17	115	119	112	. . .

Source: Sheldon Danziger and others, "Transfers and the Economic Status of the Elderly," in Marilyn Moon, ed., *Social Accounting for Transfers* (University of Chicago Press, forthcoming).

a. A consumer unit consisting of a husband and wife with two children, aged 12–17 and 6–11, is 100.

b. Adding more children to the consumer unit adds 4 or 5 percentage points to the scale up to family size eight. After that only 2 to 3 percentage points should be added.

because it ignores all economies of scale and the unadjusted household income alternative because the household status of the poor may not be a matter of rational free choice.

Households versus Persons as Weights for Recipient Units

Up to this point we have followed the common practice of entering the incomes of all households in our sample into an array ordered by size of income and then calculating the mean of the resulting size distribution of household incomes. Implicit in this procedure is the assumption that each household's economic status is equally important in the social welfare function. The implicit weight of each person's economic status is thus inversely related to his or her household size.[14] A single individual household's economic status is given five times more weight than that of a person in a five-member household. To address this problem, we adopt a social welfare function that gives equal weight to each person.

We calculate size distributions that give equal weight to all persons. We assign each person the economic status measure of his or her household and enter this amount into a size distribution of personal economic status. To illustrate, let us suppose that a household consisting of two nonelderly adults, with the head aged 45 and with one child under 6 years old, has a 1973 income of $10,000. Its economic status is $10,000 on an unadjusted basis, $3,333 on a per capita basis, and $12,500 on a welfare ratio basis.[15] We have the choice of taking any of these measures of the household's economic status and including it once in the household size distribution or three times in the personal size distribution. Only the latter procedure measures the distribution of economic welfare among all persons.

Rows 4 and 5 of table 2 show that when we apply person weights to our preferred income concept of the welfare ratio (adjusted income after taxes deflated by our equivalence scales), the relative economic status of the elderly is raised from 85.3 to 88.0 percent of that of the nonelderly. We attribute this rather modest difference to the combined effects of two factors: first, the mean unit size for the elderly is less than two persons, as compared with an average of about three persons for all units; and second, the relationship between income and household size differs sharply between the elderly and the nonelderly.

14. The empirical importance of this distinction is suggested by the fact that household money incomes in the United States are strongly positively correlated with household size. Sheldon Danziger and Michael K. Taussig, "Income Unit and the Anatomy of Income Distribution," *Review of Income and Wealth,* vol. 25 (April 1979), pp. 365–75, show that the top decile of the census money income distribution for families and unrelated individuals includes twice as many persons as the bottom decile. However, the bottom decile of the corresponding per capita money income distribution includes twice as many persons as the top decile.

15. The welfare ratio value in this example is calculated as $10,000 ÷ 0.80 = $12,500, where 0.80 is the appropriate index of need for this category of household (as shown in table 3).

Classification by Age of Head versus Age of Person

The issue of weighting by household versus weighting by person raises a related issue. We have followed thus far the common practice of identifying the elderly by the age of the household head and implicitly assumed that every person in a household shares household resources equally. We know, however, that some elderly persons live in households headed by the nonelderly and vice versa. To deal with this issue, we maintain our assumption of equal sharing of resources within all households but classify each person as elderly or nonelderly according to his or her age. For example, consider a couple with a head over 65, but with a spouse under 65; the ratio of adjusted income after taxes to the equivalence scale is 2.01. Under our person-weighting procedure, we assign both the head and the spouse a welfare ratio of 2.01 in the elderly personal size distribution. Now, however, we assign by the age of the person, counting one person as elderly and one as nonelderly. This change raises the relative economic status of the elderly from 88 percent to 90 percent of that of the nonelderly (rows 5 and 6).[16]

A Summing Up

The last column of table 2 distributes the entire change between lines 1 and 6 among our adjustments. The adjustment for family size and

16. This small change can be explained by the fact that over 96 percent of all persons are correctly classified as elderly or nonelderly by the age of the household head. Elderly persons living in households headed by nonelderly persons are only 1.3 percent of the whole population and 13.1 percent of the elderly. The nonelderly who live in households with an elderly head are about 2.47 percent of the whole population and 2.75 percent of the nonelderly. The former group of elderly lives in households with a mean income almost identical to that of households including only nonelderly persons. The latter group of nonelderly persons lives in households with a mean income equal to only 82 percent of that of households including only nonelderly persons but 144 percent of that of households including only elderly persons. Thus when we classify all persons by their own age but assign them the economic status of their households, our estimates of the relative economic status of the elderly increase.

This result depends crucially, of course, on our maintained hypothesis that all persons share equally in the income and consumption of their household. Moon, *Measurement of Economic Welfare*, pp. 57–59, discusses the alternatives to the equal-sharing assumption. Our view is that as long as we assume equal sharing for households with either all elderly persons or all nonelderly persons, we should follow the same assumption for households with persons in both age groups. Also, we assume that personal welfare is not affected one way or the other by living in an extended family.

composition accounts for 70 percent of the substantial rise in relative status conferred on the elderly by our accounting adjustments. If it is for some reason inappropriate to take family size into account when formulating income transfer policy, then our policy conclusions will not hold. However, policymakers take family size and composition into account in setting nearly all taxes and transfers, and we assume in our policy discussion that it is appropriate for them to do so.

Before we turn to policy issues, two important points should be made explicit. First, the bottom-line result of 90 percent is based on a comparison of the mean economic status of the elderly and the nonelderly. The variance or inequality of the elderly distribution is, however, substantially larger than that of the nonelderly distribution. If we had measured instead the relative status of the elderly in the bottom quintile of the distribution, the result would have been less than 90 percent and vice versa, of course, for a similar comparison for the top quintile. Second, we used 1973 data. Table 1 shows that the ratio of median unadjusted money income of the elderly to the nonelderly rose from 0.53 in 1973 to 0.64 in 1980, an increase of about 17 percent. Furthermore, Timothy Smeeding showed that the elderly have benefited disproportionately from the growth of in-kind benefits in recent years.[17] Thus the elderly are today certainly at least as well off on average as the nonelderly.

Policy Implications

Our approach to the policy implications of our research is to ask whether it is possible to reduce future social security expenditures without sacrificing equity. Our basic premise is that comparisons of the economic status of the elderly and of other needy groups are of major significance for transfer policy. We observe that both the defenders of the maintenance of social security benefit levels and their opponents cite selected evidence about the relative economic status of the elderly in support of their positions. We compare current transfers to the elderly with those to the nonelderly and find that the elderly disproportionately

17. Timothy M. Smeeding, *Alternative Methods for Valuing Selected Transfer Benefits and Measuring Their Effect on Poverty*, U.S. Bureau of the Census Technical Paper 50 (GPO, 1982).

Table 4. Taxes and Transfers and Economic Status by Demographic Group[a]

Consumer unit head	Pretransfer income (Y)	Taxes (T)	Transfers (R)	Net transfer ratio [(R − T)/Y]	Income after taxes and transfers (YAT)
White male					
65 and over	2.32	0.33	0.06	− 0.12	2.05
64 and under	1.47	0.15	0.47	0.22	1.79
Nonwhite male					
65 and over	1.64	0.18	0.10	− 0.05	1.56
64 and under	0.56	0.03	0.33	0.54	0.86
White female					
65 and over	1.40	0.17	0.22	0.04	1.45
64 and under	1.24	0.12	0.58	0.37	1.70
Nonwhite female					
65 and over	0.58	0.06	0.33	0.47	0.85
64 and under	0.65	0.08	0.37	0.46	0.94
All consumer units	2.03	0.27	0.13	− 0.07	1.88

Source: Authors' calculations from 1973 Consumer Expenditure Survey data.
a. Pretransfer income Y is defined as income before taxes less transfers R. The "earned" component of social security benefits is included in pretransfer income; the remainder is treated as a transfer. The measure of income or taxes or transfers for each household is divided by the constant utility equivalence scale given in table 3 and weighted by the number of persons.

benefit. Finally, we simulate two social security reform options and examine their equity effects.

The Equity Effects of Current Tax and Transfer Policies

Table 4 presents data on pretransfer income, Y; transfers, R; taxes, T; the net transfer ratio, defined as $(R − T)/Y$; and income after taxes and transfers, YAT.[18] Both pretransfer income and income after tax are

18. To obtain the estimates in table 4, we begin by calculating pretransfer income, defined as measured income net of all transfers received. We then use the results of Burkhauser and Warlick to estimate the annuity value of each individual's total (employer plus employee shares) social security tax contributions and denote the difference between current benefits and the estimated annuity value as the "transfer component." Richard V. Burkhauser and Jennifer L. Warlick, "Disentangling the Annuity from the Redistribution Aspects of Social Security in the United States," *Review of Income and Wealth*, vol. 27 (December 1981), pp. 401–21. They estimate that in 1972 the transfer component was, on average, 73 percent of the current benefit. Using their data, we construct a matrix of the ratios of the transfer component to the total benefit in which all social security recipients are classified by five age categories, their race, sex, and marital status, and seven social security benefit classes. The current social security benefit of each recipient is multiplied by the appropriate ratio to calculate the transfer

expressed as welfare ratios and are based on the equivalence scale shown in table 3. We set the equivalence scale for a family of four, consisting of a working husband and a nonworking wife with two children, at 100. The dollar value assigned to this household is approximately the average consumption expenditure for the bottom third of these households. This level, which was about $8,800, is similar to the lower workers' budget of the Bureau of Labor Statistics. Thus the value of 1.88 for all consumer units means that *YAT* for the average unit is 88 percent higher than the lower budget level for families of that size.

Our results, presented for eight mutually exclusive age-race-sex groups, reveal that the elderly groups have higher net transfer ratios than their nonelderly counterparts (with the exception that the ratios are similar for nonwhite females). A negative net transfer ratio means that the group pays more in taxes than it receives in transfers. These ratios are negative only for units headed by nonelderly males.

We consider the net transfer ratio to be a crude measure of equity for making comparisons among groups with similar levels of pretransfer income. To hold income approximately constant, we calculate net transfer ratios within each quintile of pretransfer income for the whole sample. The results (not shown) strongly confirm the positive relationship between age and the net transfer ratio. Within any quintile, the elderly enjoy a higher net transfer ratio than their race-sex counterparts and their quintile as a whole. For example, nonelderly males are net taxpayers by the second quintile, but the elderly become net taxpayers only in the top quintile. The tax transfer system clearly treats the elderly more favorably than the nonelderly.

The Equity Effects of Two Social Security Reforms

We simulate two widely discussed proposals for social security reform. First, we subject one-half of social security benefits to the federal income tax, a proposal similar to the one put forward in 1979 by the Social Security Advisory Council. Second, we simulate an across-the-board reduction in social security benefits that raises the same revenue. This second proposal has the same equity effects as proposals to cap the

---

component. The earned annuity component is treated as if it were private pension income, that is, as a part of pretransfer income.

After netting out transfers, we order all consumer units by size of pretransfer income, divide by the appropriate equivalence scale, and weight equally for each person. We do not reclassify persons according to their own age for the estimates in this section.

Table 5. Simulated Effects of Taxing Social Security Benefits and Reducing Benefits across the Board, All Consumer Units Receiving Social Security Benefits[a]

Upper limit of income class (1973 dollars)[b] (1)	Upper limit of income class (1983 dollars) (2)	Percent of units in class (3)	Tax as percent of		Reduction as percent of	
			Social security (4)	Total income (5)	Social security (6)	Total income (7)
1,000	2,280	19.8	0.0	0.0	5.2	4.6
2,000	4,560	12.9	0.0	0.0	5.2	3.2
3,000	6,840	10.6	0.6	0.3	5.2	2.7
4,000	9,120	8.3	3.1	1.4	5.2	2.4
5,000	11,400	6.4	5.9	2.2	5.2	2.0
6,000	13,680	5.0	7.0	2.4	5.2	1.8
7,000	15,960	4.3	8.1	2.4	5.2	1.5
8,000	18,240	4.5	8.7	2.4	5.2	1.4
9,000	20,520	3.3	9.3	2.3	5.2	1.3
10,000	22,800	3.2	9.8	2.1	5.2	1.1
12,500	28,500	5.2	10.3	2.1	5.2	1.0
15,000	34,200	4.6	10.6	1.7	5.2	0.8
17,500	39,900	3.5	11.3	1.5	5.2	0.7
20,000	45,600	1.8	12.4	1.4	5.2	0.6
25,000	57,000	2.8	13.0	1.0	5.2	0.4
Over 25,000	Over 57,000	3.9	16.7	1.1	5.2	0.3
All units	All units	100.0	5.2	1.4	5.2	1.4

Source: Same as table 4.
a. Social security income was received by 26.3 percent of all consumer units.
b. Income classes are based on income before taxes less social security transfers.

annual cost-of-living adjustment. We assume that the tax revenues and the reduced benefits are used to reduce the government deficit.[19]

Table 5 shows our simulation results. The first three columns show the distribution of social security recipients by income class in 1973 and 1983 dollars (income is defined as income before taxes less social security benefits). In the lowest three income classes, containing about 40 percent of recipients, more than half of total income is derived from social security. Columns 4 and 5 show the effects of taxing one-half of social security benefits in the federal income tax. Because the aged receive double personal exemptions, the tax is paid by only about one-half of all

19. After this study was completed, the Social Security Amendments of 1983 included a provision requiring that, beginning in 1984, OASI beneficiaries include half their benefits in taxable income if doing so raises their adjusted gross income to more than $25,000 (for individuals) or $32,000 (for married couples filing jointly). Another provision in the 1983 law postponed the cost-of-living adjustment of OASI benefits for six months. Our simulations in this paper remain relevant for future transfer policy decisions, especially in the event of future OASI deficits.

consumer units receiving social security.[20] For recipients, income before social security in 1973 averaged $6,704, benefits averaged $2,566, and the new tax averaged $134. The new tax raised $2.4 billion, which was 5.2 percent of all benefits.[21] Because social security represented about a third of recipients' incomes, the tax was only 1.4 percent of their total income. Column 4 shows that the tax is progressive with respect to social security benefits, rising from zero for the poorest units to 16.7 percent for the wealthiest. However, because social security as a percentage of total income declines monotonically with income, the tax is regressive with respect to incomes over $7,000.

The last two columns present our simulation of an across-the-board reduction in benefits. This simulation has the same distributional effects as capping the annual cost-of-living adjustment. Since the taxation of benefits raises $2.4 billion, we reduce all benefits by 5.2 percent. Obviously, the difference in these two equal revenue-raising simulations is that the first taxes benefits progressively and the second, proportionately. Comparing columns 6 and 7 with columns 4 and 5 shows that the poorest 40 percent of recipient units are harmed the most by the shift from the taxation of benefits to across-the-board reductions.[22] Although these units pay only 1.4 percent of the taxes, they are the source of 40 percent of the savings from the across-the-board reductions. Similarly,

20. We assume that the consumer and the taxpaying units are identical. We then estimate a marginal tax rate for all social security recipients and multiply this tax rate by one-half the social security benefit. We estimate the marginal tax rate by assuming that taxable income was defined as income less all income transfers less a standard deduction less $750 times the number of personal exemptions, or as zero, whichever is greater. Our procedure overstates the marginal tax rates, and hence the revenue raised, because it does not take into account the retirement credit or itemized deductions that would further reduce taxable income.

21. Our results for taxing one-half of benefits are similar to those derived by others. Richard Dye presents estimates from the U.S. Treasury Department's Office of Tax Analysis that show that 44 percent of units receiving social security would have paid taxes totaling $3.7 billion in 1978. Richard F. Dye, "Analysis of the Advisory Council's Proposal to Tax One-Half of Social Security Benefits," ORS Working Paper 25 (Social Security Administration, October 1981), p. 7. M. D. Levy, *The Tax Treatment of Social Security* (American Enterprise Institute for Public Policy Research, 1980), estimates that total benefits would have been reduced by 3.6 percent in fiscal year 1979. The rise in the minimum standard deduction by 1978 probably explains the lower estimates for the later years.

22. The introduction of supplementary security income in 1974 partially offsets the effects of across-the-board social security reductions on the poor. For participants, a one-dollar reduction in social security benefits would be exactly offset by a one-dollar increase in supplementary security income. However, not all the elderly poor receive supplementary security income.

Table 6. Effects of the Current Tax-Transfer System and Simulated Reforms on the Relative Economic Status of the Elderly

Income concept[a]	Gini coefficient[b]	Ratio of mean incomes (elderly to nonelderly)	Percent of elderly units with an income/ equivalence scale of less than 1
1. Income after transfers and direct taxes	0.312	0.88	33.4
2. Income before transfers and direct taxes[c]	0.367	0.62	57.1
3. Same as 1, but one-half of social security benefits are subject to federal income tax	0.311	0.87	33.6
4. Same as 1, but social security benefits are reduced by 5.2 percent across-the-board	0.313	0.86	34.4

Source: Same as table 4.
a. Incomes are divided by equivalence scale values and weighted by the number of persons in each unit.
b. For all consumer units. Persons are not reclassified by their own age in these estimates.
c. The earned annuity component of social security is treated as pretransfer income; the remaining portion is treated as a transfer.

the top three income classes, which contain 8.5 percent of recipients, would pay 21.3 percent of the taxes but account for only 7.5 percent of the benefit reductions.

As a basis for comparing the equity effects of our simulations, lines 1 and 2 of table 6 show the effects of the current tax-transfer system on the relative economic status of the elderly. The Gini coefficient of inequality of our preferred measure of economic status—income after taxes and all transfers adjusted for differences in family size and composition and weighted by persons—is shown in row 1. Also shown are the ratio of the mean income of the elderly to that of the nonelderly and the percentage of the elderly whose welfare ratio is less than 1.0. Row 2 shows what would have been the case had there been no transfers (we assume that the earned component of social security is included in pretransfer income and that there are no labor supply responses) and no direct taxes. The current system reduces the Gini coefficient for all units from 0.367 to 0.312, raises the economic status of the elderly from 62 percent to 88 percent of that of the nonelderly, and reduces the percentage of elderly units with incomes below their equivalence scale index of need from 57.1 percent to 33.4 percent.

Rows 3 and 4 present the same estimates from our simulations. Taxation of benefits reduces inequality, while across-the-board reductions increase inequality. However, the magnitudes of the effects are trivial, primarily because the $2.4 billion dollars raised is only 1.4 percent of the income of social security recipients and only 0.4 percent of the total income of all consumer units. As a result, the decline in the relative status of the elderly is quite small. Either change in the social security program would move the net transfer ratios of the elderly closer to those of the nonelderly (data not shown), but only the taxation of benefits would also promote vertical equity. But given the small equity gains and the political popularity of the existing system, it is perhaps not surprising that politicians have avoided making these changes.

This analysis, however, is a static one. We compare the effects in the first year of the simulations, and because of our interest in the equity effects of the two alternatives, we hold revenues constant. In practice each of these changes would inevitably raise different amounts of revenues over time and would have different cumulative effects. As a result, while the equity effects are similar in the single year, actual reductions in the cost-of-living adjustment have cumulative effects because each subsequent year's cost-of-living adjustment is applied to a permanently lower base. The Congressional Budget Office shows that the "compound-interest effect" of capping the cost-of-living adjustment produces escalating savings relative to taxing benefits.[23] There are also large differences in the cumulative equity effects of these proposals on households in various income classes.[24]

For equity considerations, the critical factor is that capping the cost-of-living adjustment is a proportional tax on benefits and is therefore clearly regressive with respect to income, while the taxation of benefits is progressive with respect to benefits and regressive with respect to total income only beyond the midpoint of the distribution.

Summary

We began by showing that a series of theoretically preferred adjustments to conventional money income measures of economic well-being

23. U.S. Congressional Budget Office, *Financing Social Security: Issues and Options for the Long Run* (CBO, November 1982), pp. 107–10.

24. We perform a rough simulation of the cumulative effect of capping the cost-of-living adjustments using data from the March 1979 Current Population Survey. If social security benefits had grown only as fast as pretransfer income over the 1965–78 period, the incidence of poverty, as officially measured among the elderly, would have been 23 percent rather than the actual value of 14 percent in 1978. (We multiply all social security benefits by the ratio of the growth rate in pretransfer incomes divided by the growth rate in social security benefits.) We find that taxation of benefits would have had only a small effect on poverty in 1978.

increased the relative economic status of the elderly in 1973 from 48.6 to 90.0 percent of that of the nonelderly. The largest single factor accounting for this increase was the adjustment for differences in the size and composition of households. Since the elderly and nonelderly are about equally well-off, we considered alternative ways to limit the growth of social security benefits. Before undertaking such a change, we demonstrated that in the absence of the current tax transfer system the relative economic status of the elderly would have been only 62 percent of that of the nonelderly. We showed also that two widely discussed social security reforms could have quite different revenue and equity effects over time, even though their effects in the year they are implemented would be small and similar. Finally, we pointed out that since our data are for 1973, the relative economic status of the elderly must be even higher now.

Comment by Frank Levy

This paper is divided into two main parts. In the first part the authors briefly review standard census income statistics to show trends in the relative economic status of elderly families according to official numbers. They then cite a series of reasons why these official numbers may yield misleading implications for economic welfare: (1) the elderly pay less personal taxes than the nonelderly with comparable incomes; (2) the elderly derive greater service flows from durables—in particular, wholly owned houses—than the nonelderly; (3) the elderly typically live in smaller families than the nonelderly, so that a given dollar income is divided among fewer people; (4) the elderly do not have the work expenses and commuting costs of the nonelderly; and (5) the elderly receive a relatively large portion of their incomes in in-kind benefits.

The authors then perform a series of adjustments for some, but not all, of these problems to obtain more accurate estimates of the relative economic welfare of the elderly. In these comparisons they make extensive use of the 1973 Consumer Expenditure Survey. In one instance, the CEX helps them to estimate net service flow income for certain consumer durables. The CEX also provides the basis for estimating constant utility equivalence scales, which allow the authors to correct income for differences in household size. These constant utility corrections are more refined than either the Orshansky ratio or simple per capita computations.

The magnitude, though not the direction, of these corrections may surprise many people. In 1973 a comparison of standard CPS median family income statistics suggested that the income of elderly families averaged about 49 percent of the income of all families. The use of the adjusted figures raised this rate to 90 percent. Although some might quarrel with one or another aspect of the authors' adjustments, it should be noted that about three-fourths of the 40 percentage point increase comes from adjustments for differences in household size between the elderly and nonelderly. Size adjustments other than those made by the authors—the Orshansky ratio or calculations on a per capita basis— would produce similar results.

In the second part of the paper, the authors address the issue of horizontal equity as it relates to the current transfer system. They interpret horizontal equity—the idea that like persons should be treated alike—to mean that demographic groups with high probabilities of poverty should receive equal treatment from the government transfer system. Given this definition, they present data to show that the elderly receive a far greater share of their income from transfers than do nonaged black male-headed households and nonaged black and white female-headed households—all groups with high probabilities of being poor. These inequalities hold even within income quintiles.

The authors then examine two social security reforms—the taxation of one-half of all social security benefits and an across-the-board reduction in social security benefits—to see what effect the reforms would have on the horizontal inequality they have defined. They find that in the short run either reform would move closer to horizontal equity (though they do not present numbers on this point) but only the taxation of benefits would move toward horizontal equity while also promoting vertical equity among the elderly.

I believe that the authors failed to develop sufficiently one important theme. In concluding the section on income adjustments, they make the following statement: "That in 1973 the elderly were on average 90 percent as well off as the nonelderly is our most policy-relevant finding, since much of the current debate about poverty and about social security presumes that the elderly, as a group, are economically disadvantaged." That finding is, in fact, striking, particularly since the authors used no controversial techniques to derive it, such as counting the insurance value equivalent of medicare as income. And they are also constrained to use the year 1973 by academic rigor because many of their adjustments were derived from the 1973 Consumer Expenditure Survey. But much has happened since then. In particular, census income figures show that median incomes for all families declined by 6 percent between 1973 and 1980 (in real terms) while median incomes for elderly families rose by 13.5 percent over the same period, a fact implicit in the authors' historical table 1. The indexation of social security benefits saved the elderly from many of the ravages of 1980, when, based on the consumer price index, median family income fell by 5.8 percent in one year alone. Given the extent of the post-1973 divergence between the elderly and other families, no one would have faulted the authors if they had done back-of-the envelope extrapolations of their 1973 estimates into 1980 or 1981. These results would surely have been more remarkable than the 0.90 ratio now in the paper.

Having brought their income adjustments up to the present (even by such rough-and-ready means), I would then have made some additional future projections of these results and used those projections rather than horizontal equity as the basis for the paper's second part.

The authors' definition of horizontal equity will raise objections from many people, including those far more liberal than I. As I noted before, the authors interpret horizontal equity to mean that families with equal incomes (corrected perhaps for family size) should have equal access to transfers, regardless of other family characteristics. To say that a family headed by a disabled 68-year-old black man and one headed by a healthy 35-year-old black man are "alike" because they have equal incomes is a proposition that few people would accept. Even the authors do not seem fond of the idea, for, having used the issue of horizontal equity to motivate simulations of social security reforms, they never explore in any detail the effect of the reforms on improving horizontal equity.

But, as I suggested, I would have taken a different tack. Using a combination of envelope backs and macroeconomic models, I would have continued projections of the ratio of adjusted elderly family incomes to adjusted incomes for all families four or five years into the future, assuming social security law remains unchanged. Suppose, for example, that the economy experiences a slow-to-moderate recovery, but that CPI inflation remains in the 6 percent range. What would happen (roughly) to the authors' 0.90 ratio? I expect that it would increase dramatically and add to the perception that social security regulations are unsustainable.

If they had made such projections, the authors would have had a much stronger motivation for the simulations that appear in the present paper. If my expectations are correct, their projections would have shown that adjusted median incomes of the elderly, pushed by indexed social security benefits, will be very high relative to the income of all families, but that certain groups of elderly below the median will still need substantial assistance. This mean-versus-variance situation is an obvious candidate for the kinds of disaggregated analyses that the authors' simulations produce. A discussion of these results would have provided an ending to the paper of even greater interest to policymakers than the one they have presented.

Sally R. Merrill

Home Equity and the Elderly

As the long-term financing problems of social security have become more serious, increasing attention has been directed to assessing alternative sources of retirement income. In particular, the decumulation of personal wealth could make a larger contribution to providing for consumption after retirement. In the economic literature total wealth is considered in the context of the life-cycle theory of savings. Less attention has been paid to the composition of the asset portfolio or to the behavior of home equity in the context of the life-cycle model.[1]

Housing is the major asset of most elderly households. Approximately 70 percent of elderly householders currently own their home, and a

1. The life-cycle theory of savings has received extensive theoretical development and empirical testing. See, for example, Franco Modigliani and Richard Brumberg, "Utility Analysis and the Consumption Function: An Interpretation of Cross-Section Data," in Kenneth K. Kurihara, ed., *Post Keynesian Economics* (Rutgers University Press, 1954), pp. 388–436; Milton Friedman, *A Theory of the Consumption Function* (Princeton University Press, 1957); Menahem E. Yaari, "Uncertain Lifetime, Life Insurance, and the Theory of the Consumer," *Review of Economic Studies*, vol. 32 (April 1965), pp. 137–49; Martin Feldstein, "Social Security, Induced Retirement, and Aggregate Capital Accumulation," *Journal of Political Economy*, vol. 82 (September–October 1974), pp. 905–25; Feldstein, "The Effect of Social Security on Saving," National Bureau of Economic Research Working Paper 334 (Cambridge, Mass.: NBER, April 1979); Feldstein, "Social Security Benefits and the Accumulation of Preretirement Wealth," NBER Working Paper 477 (NBER, May 1980); Martin Feldstein and Anthony Pellechio, "The Determinants of Exchange Rate Flexibility: An Empirical Investigation," *Review of Economics and Statistics*, vol. 61 (August 1979), pp. 361–67; and Peter Diamond and Jerry A. Hausman, "Individual Savings Behavior," a paper prepared for the National Commission on Social Security, May 1980. In its simplest form, the theory assumes a hump-shaped curve for total wealth across the life cycle with the maximum being reached at the point of retirement. The primary motivation for accumulating wealth is synchronization of consumption and income during the life cycle of work and retirement periods. The theory can also accommodate other savings motives, such as bequests, and other humps in the curve, such as financing of children's education.

substantial portion have no outstanding mortgage debt. On average, home equity accounts for over 70 percent of total wealth (aside from social security wealth), and the median percentage is even higher, over 76 percent. Yet very little is known about the accumulation and decumulation of home equity by the elderly or about what factors, including retirement, influence these decisions. Most analyses of savings behavior and wealth have focused on total wealth, although assets differ greatly in their liquidity, fungibility, and provision of consumption services. Housing is unique in many respects. It is both an investment and a consumption good. Furthermore, households generally have to move in order to change appreciably the quantity or type of housing services they are consuming.

This paper addresses three principal issues: first, whether, on balance, elderly households accumulate or dissave home equity; second, the extent to which the change in home equity takes place through trading down or switching tenure; and third, whether home equity declines as the time since retirement rises, specifically, whether decumulation accelerates as time since retirement increases.[2]

Elderly homeowners can increase home equity by decreasing debt or by increasing the quantity of housing services via rehabilitation or tenure change. Market appreciation, of course, may also increase home equity. Alternatively, homeowners may reduce home equity by increasing mortgage debt, trading down, changing tenure status from homeownership to renting, deferring home maintenance and repair, or using equity conversion schemes such as reverse annuity mortgages, tax deferrals, or sale-leasebacks.

To examine these patterns, I have used data from the Retirement History Study (RHS), which provides panel data on a large representative sample of elderly households. The first survey wave was conducted in 1969, when respondents were 58 to 63 years old, and the interviews were repeated every second year until 1979. The RHS contains extensive information on income, assets, participation in the labor force, and health. Mobility data are also available, but information on housing characteristics, neighborhood, and maintenance are not. Thus decumulation of home equity through trading down or changing tenure is the major focus of this analysis; consumption of home equity by under-

2. A parallel analysis of the relationship between total wealth, nonhome equity assets, and time since retirement was prepared by Joseph Friedman, "Asset Accumulation and Depletion" (Cambridge, Mass.: Abt Associates, 1982).

maintenance or through relatively greater depreciation of the home value of the elderly because of declining neighborhood surroundings, for example, cannot be studied with these data. Both homeowner maintenance and equity conversion are of policy interest with regard to the elderly, and these issues have been addressed in recent research.[3] Thus, although these issues are certainly of concern, dissaving through trading down and switching tenure is potentially of much greater magnitude and is the main focus here.

As indicated above, the life-cycle theory hypothesizes that the accumulation and decumulation of total assets follow a hump-shaped pattern that peaks at retirement. Nothing, however, suggests that the components of assets will follow the same pattern. In fact, to the extent that housing is perceived differently from other assets, the conventional life-cycle model could hold with less relevance or not at all. And on balance, ample evidence indicates that such might be the case.

Housing provides a flow of services as well as a store of value. The decision to dissave by trading down (or undermaintenance) is likely to be more complicated than the decision to liquidate other assets, particularly liquid assets. The demand for home equity involves a joint decision concerning purchase of housing services and an investment. Thus, just as traditional demand models have generally ignored the investment aspects of the homeownership decision, the life-cycle theory has not considered the special characteristics of the elderly that make them immobile. Mobility among elderly homeowners is very low. The same stimuli that might produce a housing-adjustment response among younger households may produce only a very limited housing consumption response among the elderly. The real and psychological costs of leaving familiar surroundings are high for the elderly. Thus declines in income

3. See Bruce Jacobs, "An Overview of the National Potential for Home Equity Conversion into Income for the Elderly" (Rochester, N.Y.: The Home Equity Commission Project, March 1982); Jack M. Guttentag, "Creating New Financial Instruments for the Aged," *Bulletin,* New York University Graduate School of Business Administration, Center for the Study of Financial Institutions, no. 1975-5, pp. 5–51; Guttentag, "Reverse Annuities: A Progress Report," in C. B. Meeks and R. Bilderback, eds., *Alternative Mortgage Instruments* (Cornell University Press, 1978); Raymond J. Struyk and Beth Soldo, *Improving the Elderly's Housing* (Ballinger, 1980); and Howard Hammerman, "Estimating the Housing Impact of Reverse Annuity Mortgages" (Department of Housing and Urban Development, May 1979). Equity conversion schemes have been very infrequently used to date. In theory, some schemes would be reflected in the RHS data through an increase in home debt. Tax deferral schemes would be reflected only in lower shelter costs; reported equity would probably be unchanged.

or household size, changes in family composition, or breaks in the traditional locational attachment to the workplace may not have the predicted results of a model based on preferences of younger house-holders.

In addition, the relative performance of housing as an investment was very good during the RHS survey years. Interest rates rose throughout the period and long-term homeowners experienced capital gains on their mortgages. The implicit subsidization of housing by the tax system has been analyzed by many researchers. One conclusion is that the subsidy rises as housing debt is amortized, and this rise tends to favor older homeowners.[4] Finally, the light taxation of capital gains can be expected to affect the decumulation decision. Because the laws for elderly homeowners were less liberal during the period of analysis than now, a financial barrier to mobility might have been present. These factors may dictate a shift out of other assets into housing rather than the reverse. At the very least, consumption of other assets is likely to occur before liquidation of home equity.

On balance, then, the expectation is that little or no decumulation of home equity will occur for elderly households. Furthermore, since mobility declines as a function of age, increasing the time since retirement may do little to accelerate the pace of decumulation.

Many elderly householders have adequate income or liquid assets, or both, and for these households home equity accumulation or decumu-lation is primarily a matter of personal preference. Others, however, have inadequate income and comparatively few assets other than their home equity. Without liquid assets to supplement retirement income, remaining in the home (and providing proper maintenance) may be difficult. The desire of these people to age in place, however, may forestall adjustment by means of dissaving their home equity.[5] Thus the

4. See David Kiefer, "The Interaction of Inflation and the U.S. Income Tax Subsidies of Housing," *National Tax Journal,* vol. 34 (December 1981), pp. 433–43; Henry J. Aaron, "Income Taxes and Housing," *American Economic Review,* vol. 60 (December 1970), pp. 789–805; Aaron, *Shelter and Subsidies: Who Benefits from Federal Housing Policies?* (Brookings Institution, 1972); Aaron, "Inflation and the Income Tax," *American Economic Review,* vol. 66 (May 1976, *Papers and Proceedings, 1975*), pp. 193–99; and Michelle J. White and Lawrence J. White, "The Tax Subsidy to Owner-Occupied Housing: Who Benefits?" *Journal of Public Economics,* vol. 7 (February 1977), pp. 111–26.

5. In addition, gerontologists have been concerned over the poor effects on health of unfamiliar surroundings. See M. Powell Lawton, Morton H. Kleban, and Diane A.

paper ends with a comment on the potential for equity consumption schemes, such as reverse annuity mortgages.

Summary of Findings

During the eight-year period under review, elderly householders on average increased their home equity. A few elderly homeowners traded down or became renters. Others, however, traded up or switched from renting to owning. The net effect (for households that owned homes in 1969 or 1977, or both) was an increase in home equity of about $3,600 (all figures are in 1980 dollars). This increase is roughly 12 percent of average home equity in 1969.

As would be expected, home equity increased for households that did not move, as mortgage balances were reduced and housing prices appreciated. Home equity also increased for movers, however; the average increase was $1,780, compared with $4,470 for homeowners who never moved. Thus, on balance, movers did not trade down, in part because owners who moved and bought again increased their equity position: the value of their homes was greater in 1977 than in 1969 and mortgage debt had fallen. Of course, owners who became renters decumulated substantial home equity. However, trading up outweighed trading down: there was a greater propensity to switch from renting to owning than the reverse. Thus housing clearly remained a popular investment during this period.

During the 1969–77 period, the RHS households experienced many changes. For example, most family heads retired by 1977, income fell by roughly one-third, and household size fell. Mobility, however, was low for these households: 1969 owners moved at an annual rate of only about 3 percent. Thus in addition to a high rate of return on homeownership, the desire to consume *familiar* housing services apparently

Carlson, "The Inner City Resident: To Move or Not to Move?" *The Gerontologist,* vol. 13 (Winter 1973), pp. 443–48; and Burton D. Dunlop, "Expanded Home-Based Care for the Impaired Elderly: Solution or Pipe Dream?" *American Journal of Public Health,* vol. 70 (May 1980), pp. 514–18. The current interest in reverse annuity mortgages, tax deferrals, sale-leasebacks, and other equity consumption schemes stems largely from their ability to let the elderly remain in the homes and maintain a sense of continuity and self-reliance.

dampens consumption adjustment to changes in income and household circumstances.

The life-cycle theory was tested by looking at the relationships among the time since retirement, moving, and the change in home equity for three groups of householders: homeowners who purchased another home, homeowners who became renters, and renters who switched to owning. Support for the theory was found for only one of these groups: homeowners who moved and purchased another home. For these elderly householders, the probability of moving increased with the time since retirement. Furthermore, although home equity accumulated for these movers (on average), it accumulated at a slower rate as time since retirement increased. Thus these homeowners were more likely to trade down the longer they had been retired. The estimates suggest that home equity increased by $45 a month prior to retirement and decreased by about that amount after retirement.

These life-cycle findings do not hold, however, for homeowners who became renters (about 16 percent of the 1969 homeowners that moved). Neither the propensity to move nor the size of the drop in home equity for this group was influenced by the time since retirement. Rather, homeowners who switched tenure status tended to be small households responding to a need for increased liquidity.

Finally, the life-cycle approach must definitely be rejected for the group of renters who became homeowners (310 households did so, nearly one-fourth of the 1969 renter sample, compared with 172 homeowners who became renters). The probability of buying a home *increased* after retirement. In many ways, these households reflect the homeowner population they have joined rather than the renter group they have left. Apparently, the appeal of housing as an investment (as well as the consumption value of having a retirement home) prevailed against a decrease in liquidity after the purchase.

Retirement History Survey Data and the Analytical Samples

Before presenting any estimates, we should consider both the source and nature of the information analyzed below. This study is based on data from the Retirement History Survey.

I examine the tenure patterns of householders who remained in the

RHS sample through 1977 and who either owned their homes or rented in 1969 and 1977. The sample excludes householders living with others or living in circumstances where all shelter costs have been assumed by relatives or friends. The goal of the study was to assess the role of home equity as a possible source of income during an independent period of retirement, before institutionalization or dependence on others. Ultimately, of course, home equity and all other assets will be transferred through bequests or inheritance. By excluding dependent households from the analysis, however, the focus can more easily remain on decumulation of home equity by means of trading down or switching to renter status while the household is making fairly independent tenure and mobility decisions.[6]

In 1977 just over 70 percent of the RHS householders were homeowners and 22 percent were renters; about 7.9 percent were categorized as "other tenure" and were thus excluded from the analysis.[7] Thus, the sample includes roughly 4,200 homeowners and 1,300 renters; the sample available for analysis includes all homeowners and renters having valid 1969 and 1977 data on income, home equity, assets, and so forth, subject to the restriction described above.[8]

Several types of variables have been derived for use in the analysis. Home equity is defined as the value of the home less any outstanding mortgage or other debt secured by the home. Liquid assets include savings and checking accounts, stocks, bonds, and mutual funds. Illiquid assets are equities in businesses, professional practices, and real estate. All financial data were updated to 1980 dollars using the consumer price

6. Because only households that remained in the sample during 1969–77 are included, the issue of home equity consumption just before death or during institutionalization is not addressed. The RHS data do not allow a direct assessment of inheritance. Also, transfers of home equity wealth before becoming dependent cannot easily be distinguished from trading down; no attempt was made to analyze individual shifts in portfolio composition.

7. See the paper by Saul Schwartz, Sheldon Danziger, and Eugene Smolensky in this volume for an analysis of the choice of living arrangements by the elderly. There is, of course, no single definition of dependence, but living with others or not being responsible for shelter costs (including utility costs, taxes, and so on, in addition to mortgage payments) is one approach. The authors note that there is a strong relationship between dependence and living with others when the respondent is not the head of household.

8. Missing data reduce the samples used for multivariate analysis to about 4,300 cases: roughly 3,250 owners in 1969 and 850 renters. Data for 1969 are more likely to be missing than for 1977.

index.[9] One of the major dependent variables used in the analysis is the *change* in home equity between 1969 and 1977 (in 1980 dollars).[10]

Retirement status is measured by a continuous variable, time since retirement. Time since retirement is defined for the entire sample and is measured in months. It is negative for respondents still working, zero at the month of retirement, and positive after retirement.[11] All six waves of the RHS were used to ascertain whether and when a respondent retired. For respondents not yet retired, time since retirement was computed from self-reported expected age of retirement. For those few respondents saying they did not expect to retire, a maximum of two years before retirement was established (in 1977 these householders were aged 66–71).

Demographic variables used in the analysis include household size, age, marital status, education, and household composition. In addition, the RHS provides respondents' opinions concerning their health compared with others', their health compared with that two years ago, various disabilities, and limitations on their ability to work. Similar information was provided for the spouse if present. A number of health and disability variables were derived and tested in the analysis. Because these variables tend to be collinear, only three variables were used in final estimation: dummy variables for respondent work limitations, respondent health status, and disabled spouse. Data on eligibility for or receipt of a private pension are also available for the RHS sample. The actual amount received if the individual is already retired is available; however, since the amount for those not retired is not known, a dummy variable is used simply to represent existence of a private pension.[12]

9. The distributions of assets and income are quite skewed, and the means are generally much higher than the medians. Thus a handful of extremely wealthy households were excluded from the estimates. Respondents with assets over $750,000 were excluded. In addition, annual income, home equity, liquid assets, and illiquid assets were all limited to $250,000.

10. The value of the home is the respondent's assessment. Whether or not any bias is introduced as a function of length of tenure, age, or other variables is not known. The RHS cannot easily be used to assess this bias, since housing characteristics (such as might be used in hedonic estimates) are not included. For 1969 owners who sold their homes to become renters, the respondent's latest available assessment was used to measure the change.

11. Respondents are defined as retired if they state that they are completely retired; if they state that they are partially retired but are not working or not looking for work, they are also considered to be retired.

12. A desirable extension of this analysis would be to construct a pension wealth variable. Social security wealth is calculated for a subset of the sample for which the

Table 1. Mobility and Tenure among Homeowners and Renters, 1969 and 1977

Item	Number	Percent of total
Total[a]	**5,566**	**100**
All homeowners in 1969	4,251	76
Renters in 1977	172	. . .
Homeowners in 1977	4,079	. . .
Stayed in same home	3,180	. . .
Moved	899	. . .
All renters in 1969	1,315	24
Homeowners in 1977	310	. . .
Renters in 1977	1,005	. . .
Stayed in same place	446	. . .
Moved	559	. . .
All homeowners in 1977	4,389	79
All renters in 1977	1,177	21

Source: Author's calculations using the Retirement History Survey.
a. Total excludes those living with others or living in units owned or paid for by others. In both 1969 and 1977, 7.9 percent of the people in the full sample were neither renters nor owners.

Because the decision to move, trade up or down, or switch tenure status was likely to be influenced by a *change* in household or health circumstances, variables were also derived describing the changes in income, assets, household size, and the decline or improvement in health or disability status between 1969 and 1977.

Tenure Choice and Mobility

Mobility and tenure choices for elderly householders are the keys to understanding how home equity will change. Table 1 provides an overview of tenure status and moving behavior of RHS householders

principal insurance amount is available. The principal insurance amount derives from the Social Security Administration's computations for respondents at age 62, based on actual earnings records. The principal insurance amount is available for about 3,000 households but includes only male-headed households. As a consequence, this sample tends to be much wealthier than the full sample. A parallel analysis was carried out for the social security sample and, when appropriate, comments are included in footnotes. Because of possible bias, however, only the results for the full sample are reported. The value of social security wealth for this analysis is computed as the actuarial present value assuming a real interest rate of 3 percent. Ideally, social security wealth should be calculated for all respondents. See, for example, the paper by Gary Burtless and Robert A. Moffitt in this volume.

between 1969 and 1977.[13] In 1969, 76 percent of the householders were homeowners. The great majority of these homeowners remained home-owners: only 4 percent had become renters by 1977. Furthermore, most 1969 homeowners stayed in the same unit; just 21 percent moved and purchased another home between 1969 and 1977, an annual mobility rate of 2.65 percent. Overall, all 1969 homeowners moved at an annual rate of 3.16 percent.

Renters, on the other hand, were much more mobile: 66.1 percent of the 1969 renters had moved by 1977, an annual rate of 8.26 percent. And, interestingly, 24 percent of the renters had become homeowners by 1977. As a result, the share of the sample represented by homeowners grew to 79 percent in 1977. The rate of tenure switching is much higher for renters than for homeowners; this difference suggests that overall, home equity may increase rather than decrease for elderly households.

Table 2 confirms this trend. As will be discussed in the following section, home equity increased by nearly $3,600 (in constant 1980 dollars) for the sample of householders that were homeowners in either or both 1969 and 1977. Table 2 provides descriptive information for the home-owners, renters, and tenure switchers that will be the subject of three subsequent analyses: assessments of the characteristics of renters, homeowners, and movers; estimates of the probability of moving; and estimates of the change in home equity—all as a function of household characteristics in 1969, the change in characteristics, and time since retirement (in 1977).

Several important differences between renters and homeowners are apparent from table 2. Homeowners have both higher incomes and substantially more assets than renters. Homeowners are likely to have larger households, and the head of household is more likely to be married.[14] In other respects the two groups are similar. About 90 percent

13. Recall that the "other tenure" (dependent) households, about 8 percent of the total sample, are excluded from the analysis.

14. The ratio of shelter cost to income was higher for renters, a consequence of both lower income and higher costs, since many of the homeowners live in mortgage-free situations. The shelter cost ratio was 0.325 for renters in 1977 and 0.228 for homeowners. It is not clear, however, how these relationships might shift if imputed rent for homeowners and a tenure discount adjustment for long-term renters were included in the calculations. The U.S. income tax includes significant subsidies for homeownership; partly, this special treatment stems from the tax-exempt status of income imputed to the ownership of housing equity. See Kiefer, "Interaction of Inflation and the U.S. Income Tax Subsidies of Housing." Unless interest rates are changing,

of both groups had retired by 1977; the ratio of 1976 income (mostly retirement income) to 1968 income (when only about 20 percent had retired) is roughly two-thirds to three-fourths for most of the households. Note also that illiquid assets declined for all groups while liquid assets rose (with the exception of renters who purchased homes). As would be expected, household size fell, and the percentage of unmarried men and women rose dramatically. Finally, while work limitations increased between 1969 and 1977, the respondents' perception of their health did not change as much.

Households that switch tenure appeared to share characteristics of both renters and homeowners. For example, renters who became owners had income, household size, and marital status profiles more similar to owners than to the renter group they left. On the other hand, they had somewhat fewer assets, were more likely to be black, and were much more likely to be illiquid (see below) than the homeowners they were joining in 1977. Homeowners who became renters were similar to renters in household size and holdings of illiquid assets in 1977; in other respects, they appeared to be representative of homeowners.

From a policy perspective, renters are an important group because many of them are relatively poor and have a limited asset cushion to draw upon during retirement. However, many homeowners are not particularly wealthy either. For most homeowners, home equity represents a substantial share of total wealth. To the extent that assets are or could be used to finance consumption during retirement, home equity must at least be considered as a candidate source of funds.[15]

The distributions of liquid and illiquid assets are extremely skewed; the medians are much lower than the means, and many households have few assets. A combination of limited (nonhome equity) assets and limited income could plausibly lead to an increase in moving in order to trade down. To assess this possibility, I identified 1969 homeowners with this combination of factors. Illiquid 1969 households (see table 2) had less than median income in 1969 ($17,850 in 1980 dollars), less than median

---

an estimate of the flow value is the interest rate times asset value. Interest rates probably were changing, however. Also, a hedonic approach can be used to estimate implicit rental value. Finally, the hedonic estimates for renters would yield the estimated tenure discount.

15. In many cases, however, the amount of home equity is moderate; as an annuity, for example, it would provide only a small supplement to retirement income. This issue is addressed later.

Table 2. Descriptor Variables by Tenure and Mobility Status, 1969 and 1977
1980 dollars unless otherwise specified

Variable	All, 1969 or 1977	Homeowners, 1969 and/or 1977						Renters, 1969
		All, 1969	All nonmovers	Movers				
				All	Own, 1969, own, 1977	Tenure switchers		
						Own, 1969, rent, 1977	Rent, 1969, own, 1977	
Mean change in home equity	3,584	2,663	4,472	1,778	1,250	−31,610	23,993	⋯
Home equity, 1969	31,036	33,351	33,098	26,372[a]	33,744	31,610	0	⋯
Home equity, 1977	35,208	35,825	37,671	29,891[a]	37,505	0	23,993	⋯
Liquid assets, 1969	15,999	16,065	15,663	16,815	17,004	18,960	15,093	10,276
Liquid assets, 1977	20,520	21,139	20,069	21,641	22,825	27,089	15,024	11,493
Illiquid assets, 1969	10,474	10,726	10,068	11,492	13,762	7,124	7,315	2,706
Illiquid assets, 1977	5,387	5,696	5,564	5,017	6,155	2,985	2,440	1,228
Income 1968	20,836	21,031	20,402	21,886	23,104	21,028	19,027	14,704
Income 1976	13,804	13,989	13,839	13,755	14,306	13,389	12,356	10,007
Time since retirement (1977, months)	51.70	51.70	50.30	55.10	55.50	59.10	51.40	54.50
Household size, 1969	2.44	2.44	2.46	2.40	2.40	2.25	2.25	2.10
Household size, 1977	2.04	2.03	2.05	2.04	2.06	1.65	2.20	1.76

Age, 1977	68.20	68.20	68.20	68.10	68.10	68.40	68.00	68.20
Percent black	7.80	7.30	7.90	7.60	5.80	4.10	14.80	17.50
Percent college education	20.50	20.40	19.40	23.10	21.80	30.80	22.50	16.20
Percent high school education	44.50	44.90	43.90	46.00	49.70	41.30	37.80	40.80
Percent unmarried female, 1969	2.60	2.50	2.70	2.40	1.30	3.60	4.80	8.20
Percent unmarried female, 1977	21.20	20.90	21.60	20.20	16.20	28.50	27.40	45.80
Percent unmarried male, 1969	1.60	1.60	1.70	1.30	1.10	2.10	1.60	3.10
Percent unmarried male, 1977	7.80	8.10	8.00	7.30	6.40	16.20	4.80	13.90
Percent good health, 1969	39.70	39.70	39.10	41.80	43.60	32.10	39.90	37.80
Percent good health, 1977	36.50	36.50	36.50	36.90	37.60	34.90	36.10	35.00
Percent work limitations, 1969	27.40	27.90	27.90	26.20	28.00	28.50	19.60	30.20
Percent work limitations, 1977	42.40	42.40	42.40	42.20	42.20	42.40	42.30	43.30
Percent disabled spouse, 1969	0.90	1.00	1.10	0.80	0.40	2.60	0.60	0.50
Percent disabled spouse, 1977	2.20	2.10	2.20	2.10	2.20	1.20	2.60	1.80
Percent retired, 1969	17.00	17.40	17.60	15.50	15.30	22.30	11.90	21.10
Percent retired, 1977	90.40	90.20	89.20	93.20	93.60	91.90	92.90	90.60
Percent illiquid, 1969	33.90	36.30	37.20	…	32.10	36.40	…	…
Percent illiquid, 1977	32.00	32.80	34.10	…	27.70	…	41.10	…
Sample size	4,583[b]	4,287	3,180	1,383	899	172	310	1,334

Source: Same as table 1.
a. The mean includes households having no home equity during this period.
b. The total slightly exceeds movers and nonmovers because of missing data on movers.

liquid assets ($2,260), and less than the mean level of illiquid assets ($10,495; because the median is zero, the mean was used instead).[16] These criteria are, of course, completely arbitrary; poverty-level income or other cutoffs are equally relevant. The goal is simply to identify a group with a relatively higher chance of having financial incentives to move and consume home equity. Similar households were identified in 1977. In that year median income was $10,811, median liquid assets were $5,550, and mean illiquid assets were $5,478.

To assess better the factors that distinguish homeowners and renters, I estimated a logit regression predicting homeowners in 1977 among the RHS sample. The results are presented in table 3.[17] As indicated above, 1969 owners generally remained homeowners in 1977. Income and increases in income are important predictors of ownership; illiquid assets are also higher for those who remain or become homeowners. Interestingly, the level of liquid assets in 1969 was not a significant factor, once income and other variables are controlled for; however, the more that liquid assets had decreased, the higher the likelihood of being a homeowner (suggesting some amount of portfolio redistribution). Larger households were more likely to be homeowners and also households whose size has increased. Many previous studies have found that black households are much less likely than white households to be homeowners, but no such tendency is found in this sample after controlling for income, assets, and other relevant factors.[18] In addition, as seen in the descriptive statistics, unmarried men and women were less likely than their married counterparts to have purchased homes. These variables are not significant here, however, probably because homeownership in 1969 was already included.[19]

---

16. No limits were placed on home equity; the mean 1969 value was $25,350 for these illiquid households, compared with $35,360 for households that are not illiquid.

17. In most cases, of course, the decision to become a homeowner was made years before the RHS interview as a function of the relative price of housing, credit terms, tax benefits, and so on, as well as income and household characteristics. Thus the equation includes a variable representing homeownership in 1969.

18. See, for example, John F. Kain and John M. Quigley, *Housing Markets and Racial Discrimination: A Microeconomic Analysis* (NBER, 1975); and Kain and Quigley, "Housing Market Discrimination, Homeownership, and Savings Behavior," *American Economic Review*, vol. 62 (May 1972, *Papers and Proceedings, 1971*), pp. 263–76.

19. The results for the social security sample indicate that male householders with greater social security wealth are also more likely to be homeowners; no doubt this is a function of permanent income.

The Probability of Moving: Owners and Renters

A number of factors influence mobility among elderly householders. Very elderly householders may be less likely to move because of the increased psychological and real costs associated with moving. Householders with disabilities or work limitations may be more likely to move, either in response to reduced income or to find more suitable living quarters. The effect of income and assets is hard to predict. While low-income, low-asset households might move to reduce living costs or make their asset holding more liquid, wealthier households may move in response to changed preferences (for example, desire for better climate or higher quality of housing). Thus, although owners may be less likely to move than renters, the effect that the *level* of home equity will have on mobility is unclear.[20] Finally, retirement should be positively associated with mobility because retired homeowners are free to break the locational link with their former workplace. Also, if income declines during retirement, shelter costs may need to be reduced.

To clarify some of the major influences on the mobility of elderly households, I estimated a straightforward logit equation predicting whether renters and homeowners in the RHS sample moved between 1969 and 1977. The dependent variable indicates whether a household moved between the two years; the independent variables are the same as those for the homeownership equation. The results are given in the third column of table 3.

As expected, homeowners are much less likely to move than renters. Interestingly, income and illiquid assets do not have strong effects on moving.[21] If we control for other influences, mobility declines with age. In addition, households in which the respondent's health is good are more likely to move. More educated householders appear to be much more mobile. Finally, unmarried women (and to a lesser extent unmarried men) are much less likely to move. Retirement has an important effect on mobility: mobility increases with the time since retirement, but at a decreasing rate. (Several functional forms were tested for this variable;

20. The income tax subsidy that accrues to housing is greater for homeowners in high tax brackets and for those who have amortized more of their housing debt. Kiefer, "Interaction of Inflation and the U.S. Income Tax Subsidies of Housing." Also, in 1977 capital gains laws posed a greater barrier to tenure switching than does current law. All this suggests that level of home equity is negatively related to the probability of moving.

21. I also estimated an equation for the subsample with social security data; this equation indicates that the likelihood of moving falls as social security wealth increases.

Table 3. Logistic Model Results for Probability of Homeownership and Probability of Moving[a]

Independent variables	Probability of being homeowner in 1977		Probability of ever moving, 1969–77	
	Parameter estimate (1)	Asymptotic t-statistic (2)	Parameter estimate (3)	Asymptotic t-statistic (4)
Income, 1968/10,000	0.288**	3.20	0.021	0.43
Liquid assets, 1969/10,000	−0.048	−1.55	−0.005	−0.28
Illiquid assets, 1969/10,000	0.196**	2.56	−0.002	−0.05
Household size, 1969	0.463**	7.10	−0.053	−1.38
Age, 1969	−0.048	−1.36	−0.041	−1.89
Unmarried male, 1969 (0, 1)	−0.149	−0.43	−0.346	−1.41
Unmarried female, 1969 (0, 1)	−0.274	−1.07	−0.689**	−3.74
Black (0, 1)	0.030	0.16	−0.124	−1.00
College education (0, 1)	−0.115	−0.63	0.302**	2.70
High school education (0, 1)	0.013	0.10	0.195**	2.41
Good health, 1969 (0, 1)	0.113	0.69	0.202*	2.03
Work limitation, 1969 (0, 1)	−0.095	−0.55	0.156	1.49
Disabled spouse, 1969 (0, 1)	−0.583	−0.88	0.143	0.35
Pension, 1969 (0, 1)	0.042	0.33	−0.091	−1.20
Income change, 1969–77	0.172	1.91	−0.066	−1.34
Liquid assets change, 1969–77	−0.102**	−3.36	0.021	1.24
Illiquid assets change, 1969–77	0.075	1.01	−0.022	−0.68
Household size change, 1969–77	0.550**	7.14	−0.044	−0.94
Good health change, 1969–77	0.072	0.56	−0.036	−0.44
Work limitation change, 1969–77	0.106	0.82	0.053	0.67
Disabled spouse change, 1969–77	0.213	0.53	0.214	0.92
Owner, 1969 (0, 1)	4.159**	30.58	−1.701**	−18.96
Illiquid, 1969	0.132	0.69	−0.138	−1.30
Time since retirement, 1977	0.004	1.06	0.011**	4.70
(Time since retirement)^2	−0.00003	1.00	−0.00005**	−2.59
Intercept	0.389	0.18	2.566*	1.97
Model chi-square	2349.27**		572.77**	
−2 log L	2,235		4,948	
−2 log L intercept only	4,585		5,521	
Mean of dependent variable	0.78		0.34	
N	4,302		4,302	

Source: Same as table 1.
*. Statistically significant at the 5 percent level using a two-tailed test.
** Statistically significant at the 1 percent level using a two-tailed test.
a. Sample is 1969 homeowners and renters.

the quadratic was the most satisfactory.) Recall that time since retirement is negative-valued for households not yet retired in 1977; these households are less likely to move, other factors being equal. Because both age and time since retirement have independent effects on mobility, age at retirement must be considered an important underlying factor.

To focus on three unique types of moves, I estimated separate equations for homeowner-movers and tenure-switchers. This technique permits us to consider three distinct phenomena: (1) the probability of moving to another owned home, (2) the probability of homeowners becoming renters, and (3) the probability of renters purchasing homes. I consider each of these in turn.

Retirement status has a very strong influence on the probability that homeowners will purchase another home (see the first column in table 4). The maximum effect of time since retirement is reached after about twelve years. Note again, however, that because moving decreases as a function of age, these factors should be considered together. Income and nonhome equity assets have no influence on the probability of purchasing another home. As expected, however, the higher the level of home equity, the lower the probability of moving. Other significant influences are higher education, which makes a move more likely; good health or a work limitation, which both have a positive effect; and being an unmarried woman, which makes repurchasing less likely. Note that, contrary to hypothesis, the effect of being illiquid is not significant for this group of homeowners.

Next consider the factors that cause a homeowning household to sell its residence and become a renter (see the third column in table 4). While time since retirement appears to have no influence on the decision to become a renter, householders with lower incomes in 1969, greater decreases in income, and less illiquid assets were much more likely to sell. A general profile suggests that, relative to other homeowners, well-educated householders from smaller households, who had less equity to begin with and whose household size fell (a substantial portion of these households became single), traded down for increased liquidity and, perhaps, more suitable living arrangements. Not surprisingly, liquid assets of these tenure-switching households increased between 1969 and 1977.

Renters who became homeowners reflected yet another type of behavior. Relative to renters who remained renters, the home buyers were more educated, had higher incomes, larger households, and greater

Table 4. Logistic Model Results for Probability of Moving to Repurchase and Probability of Tenure Switching

Independent variable	Probability of moving to purchase another home[a]		Probability of homeowners becoming renters[a]		Probability of renters becoming owners[b]	
	Parameter estimate	Asymptotic t-statistic	Parameter estimate	Asymptotic t-statistic	Parameter estimate	Asymptotic t-statistic
Income, 1968/10,000	0.091	1.58	-0.269	-1.76	0.243*	2.06
Liquid assets, 1969/10,000	-0.008	-0.37	0.096*	2.34	-0.008	-0.07
Illiquid assets, 1969/10,000	0.035	1.11	-0.194	-1.84	0.151	1.18
Household size, 1969	0.010	0.24	-0.563**	-3.81	0.454**	6.02
Age, 1969	-0.065**	-2.35	0.037	0.69	-0.066	-1.35
Unmarried male, 1969 (0, 1)	-0.207	-0.58	-0.302	-0.49	-0.657	-1.15
Unmarried female, 1969 (0, 1)	-0.588	-1.70	0.042	0.09	-0.417	-1.28
Black (0, 1)	-0.116	-0.60	-0.649	-1.47	-0.125	-0.54
College education (0, 1)	0.307*	2.15	0.849**	3.42	0.434	1.79
High school education (0, 1)	0.277**	2.64	0.231	1.08	0.074	0.40
Good health, 1969 (0, 1)	0.348**	2.77	-0.209	-0.85	-0.074	-0.21
Work limitation, 1969 (0, 1)	-0.233	-1.75	-0.093	-0.36	-0.367	-1.48
Disabled spouse, 1969 (0, 1)	-0.553	-0.94	0.422	0.48	0.785	0.62
Pension, 1969 (0, 1)	0.066	0.67	-0.008	-0.04	0.064	0.36
Income change, 1969–77/10,000	-0.033	-0.56	-0.291	-1.87	0.085	0.78

Liquid assets change, 1969–77/10,000	0.011	0.52	0.134**	3.27	−0.045	−0.91
Illiquid assets change, 1969–77/10,000	0.002	0.06	−0.139	−1.30	−0.027	−0.22
Household size change, 1969–77	0.090	1.48	−0.775**	−4.78	0.462**	5.12
Good health change, 1969–77	−0.015	−0.15	0.074	0.37	0.108	0.62
Work limitation change, 1969–77	−0.008	−0.08	0.138	0.71	0.242	1.37
Disabled spouse change, 1969–1977	0.265	0.93	−0.451	−0.61	0.301	0.65
Home equity, 1969/10,000	−0.046**	−2.09	−0.094	−1.93	n.a.	n.a.
Illiquid, 1969	−0.183	−1.50	0.207	0.97	n.a.	n.a.
Time since retirement, 1977	0.013**	4.18	0.007	0.97	0.012*	2.09
(Time since retirement)^2	−0.00009***	−2.87	−0.00003	−0.51	−0.00009	−1.67
Intercept	1.849	1.10	−4.408	−1.34	1.332	0.45
Model chi-square	94.79**		85.39**		112.99**	
−2 log L	3,198		1,106		1,019	
−2 log L intercept only	3,293		1,191		1,132	
Mean of dependent variable	0.20		0.04		0.23	
N	3,248		3,248		1,052	

Source: Same as table 1.
n.a. Not available.
* Statistically significant at the 5 percent level using a two-tailed test.
** Statistically significant at the 1 percent level using a two-tailed test.
a. Sample consists of 1969 homeowners.
b. Sample consists of 1969 renters.

increases in their household size. The probability of purchase increased with time since retirement; thus, for this group, home equity was clearly being accumulated rather than decumulated as a function of time since retirement.

In summary, the probability of moving is affected by different factors for the three different types of households. In particular, time since retirement increased the likelihood that homeowners would move and purchase another home. It did not appreciably affect the decisions of those homeowners who become renters, however. In contrast, renters were more likely to purchase homes as time since retirement increased. In addition, income, changes in income, and changes in the need for space all appeared to have important effects on tenure-switchers.

Life-Cycle Theory and Changes in Home Equity

Simply interpreted, the life-cycle model suggests that people will accumulate assets before retirement and decumulate after retirement, so that wealth holdings will follow a hump-shaped curve over the lifetime. Ordinary assets include liquid and illiquid assets as well as home equity. In addition, Feldstein suggests that the present values of both social security and pension benefits should be included as a component of family assets.[22] Social security and pension assets are only imperfect substitutes for ordinary assets, however, because they are nontradable and cannot be used as collateral. They should therefore be discounted when added to total assets. Thus

(1) $$V = HE + L + I + \lambda_1 SSW + \lambda_2 P ,$$

where V = total assets
    HE = home equity
      L = liquid assets
      I = illiquid assets
  SSW = social security wealth
     P = pension wealth
 λ_1, λ_2 = discount factors.

With regard to home equity, the major problem with the life-cycle

22. Feldstein, "Social Security, Induced Retirement, and Aggregate Capital Accumulation."

model is that it provides no guidance concerning the behavior of this component of assets. In fact, there is no reason to believe that any of the components (except social security and pensions) necessarily behave as expected for the total: that is, that they peak at retirement and decline thereafter. Indeed, casual empiricism suggests that retired households either do not wish to decumulate home equity or find it difficult to become more liquid by moving.

An empirical approach has been adopted here to test the manner in which home equity changes as a function of time since retirement. The independent variables are generally the same as those included in the mobility functions: that is, household characteristics in 1969, the change in those characteristics between 1969 and 1977, and the time since retirement. Thus the general model to be estimated is

$$(2) \qquad \Delta HE = \alpha + \sum_i \beta_i X_i + \sum_i \delta_i \Delta X_i + \lambda TSR ,$$

where ΔHE = change in home equity, 1969–77
  X = household characteristics, 1969
  ΔX = change in household characteristics, 1969–77
  TSR = time since retirement.

No prior expectations exist with regard to the signs of the parameters estimated for liquid and illiquid assets. Home equity, liquid assets, and illiquid assets should be positively related because of their direct relation to permanent income. For any person at a given time, however, an increase in one type of asset (from the previous period) may or may not imply a decrease in another: shifts in portfolio, bequests, windfalls, capital gains and losses, and changes in preferences for liquidity may all be occurring.[23]

I considered but rejected one alternative empirical specification for testing the effects of time since retirement on home equity: using the *level* rather than the *change* in home equity to assess the life-cycle hypothesis. A cross-sectional approach is inappropriate, however, because the time since retirement is likely to be correlated with many other factors that determine the level of home equity in the 1977 cross-sectional sample.[24]

23. As discussed above, social security information (the PIA) was available only for a subset of male-headed households and thus has not been included.

24. In fact, much of the controversy surrounding the various tests of the life-cycle model have involved cross-sectional versus time-series data. See, for example, Thad

As discussed above, elderly homeowners accumulated home equity during the period 1969–77. (The relevant data on home equity values are presented in table 2.) Householders who did not move experienced the largest accumulation ($4,472).[25] Householders who moved also increased their home equity ($1,778). However, as a result of trading up, trading down, and tenure switching, homeowners who moved accumulated significantly less home equity, on average, than those who did not move during this period. Homeowners in 1969 who purchased another home by 1977 increased their equity by a small amount ($1,250); value rose and mortgage debt fell. Homeowners who became renters gave up considerably more equity, on average, than that gained by renters who purchased homes. However, the fact that the latter outnumber the former contributes to the overall gains for movers.[26]

Regression results reported in table 5 reveal the relationship between home equity changes and important economic and demographic factors. Equations were estimated for all 1969 homeowners and renters and for 1969 homeowners only. Since tenure switchers and repurchasers responded differently to time since retirement, my specification included separate shift and interaction variables for each group. (The final specification included only those move and time-since-retirement variables for which the t-statistic for the estimated parameter exceeded one.)

The results indicate that, overall, movers accumulate somewhat less home equity than nonmovers. Time since retirement has different effects on the probability of moving for different subgroups, and specifying separate terms for each type of mover avoids the possibility that opposite effects will simply cancel out. Indeed, the most significant aspect of the

---

W. Mirer, "The Wealth-Age Relation among the Aged," *American Economic Review,* vol. 69 (June 1979), pp. 435–42; and Alicia H. Munnell, "Social Security, Private Pensions, and Saving," in Phillip Cagan, ed., *Saving for Retirement* (American Council of Life Insurance and Columbia University Graduate School of Business, 1981). Given the longitudinal sample design, a procedure for time series–cross section regression could also be used. This has the advantage of controlling for unobserved, individual-specific effects. The data base is not now arrayed in a way that permits use of this approach.

25. Housing rose in value and mortgage debt fell (by $3,394, on average); average mortgage debt was only $1,581 in 1977, since most stayers had no remaining debt.

26. Regression estimates (not presented here) for the level of home equity indicate that renters purchased $11,685 less equity than otherwise similar homeowners. In part, this finding reflects the purchase of mobile homes. In 1977, 15 percent of the renters who became homeowners purchased mobile homes or trailers; equity in these averaged only $10,424.

Table 5. The Change in Home Equity, 1969–77

Independent variable	Change in home equity, 1969 owners and renters		Change in home equity, 1969 owners	
	Parameter estimate	Asymptotic t-statistic	Parameter estimate	Asymptotic t-statistic
Income, 1968	0.272**	4.88	0.265**	3.84
Liquid assets, 1969	−0.044*	−2.15	−0.064**	−2.56
Illiquid assets, 1969	0.077*	2.25	0.071	1.78
Household size, 1969	628.200	1.41	803.700	1.36
Age, 1969	−345.200	−1.40	−561.900	−1.78
Unmarried male, 1969 (0, 1)	817.700	0.29	n.a.	n.a.
Unmarried female, 1969 (0, 1)	2,589.000	1.21	2,500.700	0.63
Black (0, 1)	−4,087.100**	−2.82	−4,917.800*	−2.33
College education (0, 1)	1,217.000	0.91	887.900	0.52
High school education (0, 1)	2,193.400*	2.29	2,781.500*	2.26
Good health, 1969 (0, 1)	1,539.200	1.30	2,294.200	1.51
Work limitation, 1969 (0, 1)	−423.300	−0.35	−55.300	−0.04
Disabled spouse, 1969 (0, 1)	−9,791.800*	−1.97	−10,706.000	−1.79
Pension, 1969 (0, 1)	163.000	0.18	−416.300	−0.36
Income change, 1969–77	0.318**	5.72	0.373**	5.45
Liquid assets change, 1969–77	−0.041*	−2.00	−0.054*	−2.14
Illiquid assets change, 1969–77	0.046	1.25	0.041	0.96
Household size change, 1969–77	573.100	1.05	616.200	0.86
Good health change, 1969–77	352.400	0.37	606.300	0.49
Work limitation change, 1969–77	−147.800	−0.16	102.700	0.80
Disabled spouse change, 1969–77	−2,565.900	−0.91	−2,810.600	−0.80
Illiquid, 1969	1,513.700	1.34	−170.500	−0.12
Repurchase · TSR	−36.330*	−2.08	−45.150*	−2.28
Owner to renter (0, 1)	−35,442,500**	−7.77	−36,317.000**	7.14
Owner to renter · TSR	68.950	1.04	75.850	1.03
Renter to owner	20,318.300**	11.09	n.a.	n.a.
Intercept	19,396.000	1.29	33,697.000*	1.75
R^2	0.09		0.07	
F	15.92**		9.19**	
Mean of dependent variable	3,824		3,291	
N	4,288		3,236	

Source: Same as table 1.
n.a. Not available.
* Statistically significant at the 5 percent level using a two-tailed test.
** Statistically significant at the 1 percent level using a two-tailed test.

findings is that time since retirement does affect the amount of equity accumulation among homeowners who purchase another home. These households decrease their equity holdings, since retirement rises. At the sample average time since retirement, roughly four years for this sample, the change in home equity for households that repurchase does not differ significantly from that for homeowners who do not move.[27] However,

27. The "move to repurchase" shift term did not meet the inclusion criteria for the moving and time-since-retirement variables ($t = 1.0$) and was therefore excluded.

eventually, retired homeowners who purchase another home accumulate home equity at a slower rate than homeowners who do not move. (The estimated rate of accumulation is about $45 dollars per month.) This observation indicates that older homeowners who move, but remain homeowners, effectively trade down, at least in relation to nonmovers.

The story for households that switch tenure is quite different. Our earlier results showed that time since retirement had no effect on the probability of homeowners becoming renters. Results in table 5 indicate that it does not affect the magnitude of the decrease in equity holdings either. With regard to renters who purchase homes, while time since retirement had a positive effect on the probability of purchase, it had no effect on the amount of the purchase (about $20,000, as shown in table 5). Thus, in summary, the life-cycle hypothesis "applies" to home equity for only one group of elderly movers: homeowners who move and repurchase. These households do, in fact, eventually trade down as a function of time since retirement. For example, equity falls by about $540 for homeowners who move and repurchase ten years after retirement. Thus, although the effect is not large, trading down does eventually take place.

Many other factors, in addition to time since retirement, have an impact on the change in home equity. These include income, liquid and illiquid assets, household size, race, education, the health of the respondent or a disabled spouse, and the changes in income, liquid assets, and household size.

As would be expected, the change in home equity is positively related to income in 1969 and to the 1969–77 change in income. Indeed, as noted in the probability equations, higher income induces renters to become owners and dissuades homeowners from tenure switching. A similar relationship holds for illiquid assets. The expected outcome with regard to liquid assets is not found, however. Households with lower liquid assets in 1969, for example, might be expected to decrease home equity to enhance liquidity. Instead, the lower the initial level of liquid assets, the more positive the change in home equity.[28] In contrast, the *change* in liquid assets is negatively related to the change in home equity; to the extent that this change reflects a portfolio adjustment, this outcome is the expected one.

28. In fact, homeowners who became renters had high levels of liquid assets in 1969 (as well as 1977), which suggests a very high preference for liquidity by this group.

Several other variables also deserve mention. As might be expected, large households and households that had grown had greater increases in home equity (recall that the probability of a renter becoming a homeowner increases with size while the probability of switching to renting decreases). Other households tended to accumulate less equity. To see the implication of this tendency, note that the average age of the 1969 homeowner is 68.4; the estimated coefficient for this sample is − $561.90. Thus home equity decumulation would begin to occur sooner after retirement for homeowners (who repurchase) who are older than average. If the head of household were 70.4 years old, for example, decumulation would begin 2.5 rather than 4.5 years after retirement.

Home equity fell for black households relative to white. Two explanations may be relevant to this finding. First, black households were much more likely to be renters than owners. Also, black homeowners tended to have significantly less home equity than whites, other things equal.

Household heads with a high school education experienced greater increases in home equity than those without. It is not entirely clear why the college education variable was not also significant. College-educated homeowners were more likely to become renters, while college-educated renters were likely to become owners; the effects may simply cancel. Finally, household heads enjoying good health accumulated home equity (recall that they were more likely to move and repurchase), while households with a disabled spouse experienced substantial declines in home equity.

Conclusions and Policy Implications

The life-cycle theory predicts that total wealth will peak at retirement and decrease thereafter. There is no reason to conclude that the components of wealth will behave as the aggregate, however. Indeed, households in the Retirement History Survey as a group increased their home equity during the eight-year period 1969–77, though by the latter year 90 percent of the household heads had retired. Equity accumulation occurred for households that did not move because of the appreciation of their homes and, in addition, for some renting households that switched tenure status to become homeowners. Some homeowners traded down or switched to renting. Nevertheless, the net effect of housing appreciation and tenure switching was to increase the home equity holdings of families in the RHS survey.

Mobility among elderly homeowners is extremely low. The real and psychological costs of moving are apparently strong disincentives to changing residence. In addition, during this period homeowners were experiencing substantial capital gains on their mortgages as well as increases in unit prices. Even households that moved chose, on average, to increase their home equity. Homeowners who purchased new homes tended to trade up; also, many more renters purchased homes than the reverse switch in tenure: nearly one-fourth of the 1969 renter sample purchased homes, whereas only 4 percent of homeowners became renters.

Thus, for homeowners overall, the life-cycle hypothesis that total assets peak at retirement and decline thereafter is not borne out for the major component of assets, home equity. For homeowners who move and purchase another house, however, retirement does appear to bring about a decline in home equity. The magnitude of the effect is not particularly large. Nevertheless, the longer a homeowner has been retired, the more likely he or she is to trade down at the time of repurchase. This group constitutes 21 percent of 1969 homeowners. Thus the implications of trading down as a function of time since retirement should not be ignored, especially at older ages. However, renters who purchase homes are *more* likely to do so as time since retirement increases. This propensity clearly contradicts the life-cycle notion of decumulation after retirement.

What policy implications, if any, follow from these findings? Many elderly homeowners are simply following the consumption preferences and investment portfolio decisions best for them. Presumably they are not constrained by having a substantial share of their total wealth in home equity. What about those homeowners who are presumed to have some financial incentive to trade down; so-called illiquid households, having relatively low incomes and low nonhome equity resources? Illiquid homeowners were no more likely to move and trade down than were other homeowners. This limited mobility suggests that in the absence of policies such as equity consumption schemes, home equity will not be used in a major way to supplement retirement income.

Even so, from a policy perspective, it might be useful to know how many households might be able to benefit from home equity consumption if an appropriate means were available. Again, the (arbitrary) concept

Table 6. Comparison of Illiquid and Other Households of 1977 Homeowners

Item	Illiquid households[a]	Households not illiquid
Home equity, 1977 (1980 dollars)	22,233	42,305
Percent with home equity of less than $30,000	70	38
Liquid assets, 1977 (1980 dollars)	912	30,823
Illiquid assets, 1977 (1980 dollars)	84.3	8,218.0
Income, 1977 (1980 dollars)	5,937	17,592
Change in home equity, 1969–77	−837	3,786
Ratio of shelter costs to income, 1977	0.32	0.20
Persons per room	0.39	0.37
Percent mobility, 1969–77	22.7	26.7
Percent with private pension (eligible for or receiving)	18.6	44.7
Percent illiquid in 1969	61.3	22.9
Number in sample	1,387	2,853
Percent of sample	33	67

Source: Same as table 1.

a. Illiquid households have median or less than median income in 1977 ($10,811 in 1980 dollars); median or less than median liquid assets ($5,550); median or less than median illiquid assets ($5,478). No limits are placed on home equity.

of an illiquid household is used to help address this issue, defined this time for 1977.[29] Several questions are relevant. What proportion of the sample was relatively illiquid in 1977? How do these households compare with households not categorized as illiquid? To what extent was their home equity sufficient to provide more than a minimal supplement?

Table 6 provides a comparison of illiquid households with those not considered illiquid. One-third of the sample of homeowners was illiquid in 1977. By definition, illiquid households had lower income and nonhome equity assets; their home equity was also lower. Although crowding was not a problem for either group, shelter costs were a heavier burden for the illiquid homeowners. Very little trading down occurred for this group, however. In fact, illiquid households were slightly less likely to have moved than other households.

How many elderly homeowners might benefit from home equity conversion schemes? Some, but not all. Seventy percent of the illiquid households had home equity of less than $30,000 (and 78 percent had less than $40,000). Thus, while a few of these households could benefit

29. The 1977 definition is the same as that used for 1969 except 1977 limits are used (in 1980 dollars). Illiquid households in 1977 are homeowners who had median income or less ($10,811); median liquid assets or less ($5,550); and average or less-than-average illiquid assets ($5,478).

from annuity-type schemes, those with very low home equity would require an alternative policy (for example, tax deferrals, home maintenance loans) to help them age in place. In contrast, over 60 percent of the relatively more affluent homeowners had $30,000 or more in home equity. For this group, the feasibility of various types of reverse annuity mortgages depends on relationships among the annuity rate, the mortgage rate, housing price appreciation, and the household's age and composition (which determine joint or survivor life expectancy, or both).

Bruce Jacobs's report to the Home Equity Conversion Project provides a useful overview of the national potential for home equity conversion.[30] Using 1977 data from the Annual Housing Survey, Jacobs has assessed the benefits of equity conversion schemes for different types of elderly households. In 1977 a fairly large number of "candidate" households were present in urban areas. Depending on geographic region, one-fourth to one-half of the elderly homeowners (those aged 65 and over) had incomes less than 150 percent of the official poverty line but had at least $30,000 in home equity (1977 prices).

According to Jacobs, only about a fifth of all elderly homeowners in 1977 could have received as much as $50 a month or 10 percent of their incomes from a reverse annuity mortgage. Nevertheless, benefits would accrue particularly to the older elderly (those aged 75 and over) and to single persons. As would be expected, poverty-level homeowners also get larger relative boosts in income. This effect suggests that home equity conversion schemes could be helpful to an important fraction of poor elderly households.

This study represents only a first step in exploring changes in home equity for elderly households. A number of issues should be addressed in further research. Use of a cross-sectional, time-series statistical

30. Jacobs, "An Overview of the National Potential for Home Equity Conversion"; Jack M. Guttentag, "Creating New Financial Instruments for the Aged"; Guttentag, "How to Sell Your House (and Keep It Too)," *Wharton Magazine*, vol. 1 (Fall 1976), pp. 36–40; Guttentag, "Reverse Annuity Mortgages: How S and L's Can Write Them," *Federal Home Loan Bank Board Journal*, vol. 10 (July 1977), pp. 18–23; Guttentag, "Reverse Annuities: A Progress Report," in C. B. Meeks and R. Bilderback, eds., *Alternative Mortgage Instruments* (Cornell University Press, 1978); D. Edwards, "Reverse Annuity Mortgages," in D. M. Kaplan, ed., *Alternative Mortgage Instruments Research Study* (Federal Home Loan Bank Board, 1977); and T. Neubig, "Reverse Annuity Mortgages—A Dissaving Mechanism for Older Home Owners," in James N. Morgan and others, *Five Thousand American Families—Patterns of Economic Progress*, vol. 8: *Analyses of the First Eleven Years of the Panel Study of Income Dynamics* (University of Michigan, Institute for Social Research, 1980), pp. 315–37.

estimation approach may be desirable. Also, including an economic model of portfolio choice would introduce a more realistic level of complexity. Thus the interdependence of decisions by elderly householders concerning home equity and other assets, housing consumption, and retirement remains to be explored more fully.

Comment by Raymond J. Struyk

Sally Merrill's paper addresses three principal issues: (1) whether, on balance, elderly households accumulate or reduce home equity; (2) the extent to which decumulation takes place through trading down from more expensive to less expensive homes and through changing tenure status from homeownership to rental housing; and (3) whether decumulation of home equity is related to the timing of retirement and specifically whether it accelerates in the years after retirement.

To examine these issues, the author uses the Retirement History Survey, a body of data rich in information on households' economic positions. Unfortunately, the RHS does not include information on the quality of dwelling units, on the characteristics of neighborhoods, or on the amount of maintenance. Consequently, the accumulation of equity is measured primarily by owner assessments of home values. Such assessments change when owners trade down or change tenure status, although it is also possible that the change in the value of dwellings may reflect unattributed depreciation resulting from undermaintenance.

The paper recognizes that the decision on home equity holdings is a complex one, inasmuch as equity changes stem from decisions about housing consumption, investment portfolio decisions, and relocations— sometimes to different markets where rates of return may be different. Decisions about home equity are hypothesized to be part of the larger savings decisions flowing from the life-cycle model of wealth accumulation. Based on her empirical analysis of these decisions, Merrill draws the following conclusions about the three issues addressed in the paper. First, on balance, elderly households do increase their home equity holdings. Second, decumulation, to the extent that it is occurring, is associated with trading down and a switch to rental status. But even for households that moved, home equity increases moderately. The third point, in contrast, is that the probability of moving increases with the time since retirement, so that home equity is tentatively found to decline eventually sometime after retirement. The net increase in equity found for this sample, therefore, appears to be attributable to the dominance of recently retired households in the RHS.

Before considering the broader significance of the paper, I should note that it deals with a particularly difficult problem. Indeed, earlier work on mobility of elderly households and on their changes in tenure has produced only a limited number of clear findings. One of the few clear findings is that the decisions under analysis are indeed complex. In addition, addressing home equity accumulation requires the analyst to deal with families' portfolio composition decisions.

An analysis of the housing adjustments of the elderly usually begins with three observations. First, the housing consumption and the housing investments of many elderly families are quite far from their strict equilibrium positions. This situation holds true for the near elderly as well. Speedy adjustment among the elderly seems to be impeded by deeply ingrained habits and an inability to find new dwelling units with certain cherished characteristics.

Second, the various elements of the housing consumption decision— including unit size, tenure, and amount of home equity—are jointly and simultaneously determined. Third, housing economists observe that the extent of investment in home equity depends on the rate of return on housing in comparison to other investments. This relationship is certainly fundamental to the tenure choice and down-payment decisions of those who choose to become homeowners and also to the refinancing decisions of those homeowners who choose not to move.

The present paper devotes too little energy to considering these fundamental propositions now current in the housing literature. In addition, not enough is made of the dynamic aspects of the home equity decisions of the elderly. It seems likely that the model estimated would have been substantially altered by considering these basic propositions more thoroughly.

The empirical specification of the estimated model is also extremely puzzling to me. In some of the reported estimations, stationary and relocating homeowners are pooled for the regression analysis. I would like to point out, however, that the mechanisms leading to equity change are so radically different for these two groups that this pooling may yield estimates of only limited usefulness. For stationary households the principal source of change in home equity is probably simple apprecia-tion, which depends predominantly on a home's location. Because no location variables are included in the model, some bias in the coefficients is likely, given the correlation between appreciation and income, for

example. (I say that home appreciation is "probably" the main source
of change because the paper does not inform us about changes in
mortgage debt and house values of stationary homeowners over the
period.) In contrast, among relocating households, families are compelled to make decisions about tenure status and about trading up or
down. This situation is obviously very different from that of stationary
households. Under these circumstances, interpretation of some of the
estimated equations is very difficult. They provide a general summary
of information via reduced-form estimates, and these are of some value
in giving an impression about the association between change in home
equity and the included variables.

At the descriptive level these associations are fairly exciting. For
example, low-income, low-asset homeowners experience much lower
home equity gains than do other types of homeowners. Are they
refinancing their homes to obtain income? Or when they move, do they
always shift to rented dwellings? Are some living in areas where housing
is actually declining in value?

Some question also must be raised about the RHS sample used for
this analysis. In particular, I am surprised by the tabulation showing that
60 percent of the sample households that changed tenure status switched
from being renters to being homeowners. Other data sources show a
different pattern. The Annual Housing Survey for 1979, for example,
shows that three out of four of elderly households that change tenure
status shift from homeownership to rental status. These data are not
necessarily in conflict with Merrill's findings because the RHS covers
only a limited fraction of the elderly, namely, those aged 66 to 71 in 1977.
But the different pattern of shifting out of homeownership for this group
does demonstrate the need to qualify findings reported in this paper.

Another qualification might also be worth noting. The period covered
by this paper was one in which homeownership was an exceptionally
good investment, especially during the latter part of the period considered. If relative rates of return on homeownership are going to be lower
in the years ahead, as seems likely, home equity holdings among the
elderly may decline rather than rise. In addition, provisions of the 1978
tax legislation greatly increased the amount of capital gains on home
equity excluded from capital gains taxation. This change should give
rise to somewhat higher mobility and some additional shifting from
homeownership to rental status. A fundamental question for future
research is whether these shifts will induce significant changes in the
position of housing in the wealth portfolios of elderly households.

*Saul Schwartz, Sheldon Danziger,
and Eugene Smolensky*

The Choice of Living Arrangements
by the Elderly

Three reasons highlight the importance of under-
standing the determinants of living arrangements of the elderly: recent
changes in living arrangements have perversely affected measures of
income inequality; living alone or with others affects eligibility for public
transfer programs and the extent of benefits from these programs; and
the degree to which the noninstitutionalized elderly live alone may be
some measure of their economic well-being.

We discuss only the third of these observations, and even then only
briefly, because we are primarily concerned in this paper with the
determinants of the choice of living arrangements. In particular, we are
interested in two of those determinants—income and health. It may be
helpful, however, to expand on the consequences that stem from the
decision to live alone rather than to live with others.

Income distribution studies start by defining the recipient income
unit. Frequently that unit is defined by residence: people who live in the
same dwelling are assumed to pool their incomes in some unknown way.
If, over time, the elderly come increasingly to live apart from their
children (because the incomes of the elderly are rising), then, paradoxically, there will be greater measured inequality. That is, there are now
more recipient units—these elderly households—and the new units have
incomes that are relatively low when compared with other recipient
units in the same year. If these elderly had continued living with others,
measured inequality would have been less than it is. Increasingly, the
trend has been, of course, for the elderly to live alone. Presumably, this

We thank Douglas A. Wolf for his comments on an early version of this paper.

229

tendency reflects a preference made possible (in part) by rising income; yet this improved well-being for the elderly may be showing up in our income distribution measures as increased inequality. For that reason we hold that recent changes in living arrangements affect our measures of income inequality perversely.

Eligibility and benefit levels of at least two programs are affected by the choice of living arrangements—food stamps and supplemental security income (SSI). Food stamps take those persons sharing the same cooking facilities as the recipient unit. Upon setting up separate quarters, an elderly low-income couple could, therefore, become eligible for food stamps when they were previously ineligible. SSI assumes income sharing in setting benefit levels among all members of a residential unit.

Finally, if the elderly do want to live alone, then the extent to which they can do so is a measure of their economic well-being.

These conclusions rest on the premise that the elderly will live alone if they can. The previous literature on living arrangements suggests that this is the case.[1] There are two sorts of evidence for this supposition. One arises from surveys in which the elderly are asked which living arrangement they prefer.[2] Unconstrained by income or health, they seem to prefer living alone but in close proximity to their families. The other evidence derives from the data on living arrangements, which also suggest that living alone is the preferred arrangement. A positive simple correlation exists between income and living alone; and, over time, as incomes have risen, so has the proportion of the elderly who live alone.

In this paper we explore this question: what is the relationship between income and health and the choice by the elderly to live with their adult children (or with others) or by themselves? Our empirical work basically involves translating this question into a testable hypothesis. This question is important because if the elderly would like to live alone, and we

1. See, for example, Frances E. Kobrin, "The Fall in Household Size and the Rise of the Primary Individual in the United States," *Demography*, vol. 13 (February 1976), pp. 127–38; Kobrin, "The Primary Individual and the Family: Changes in Living Arrangements in the United States since 1940," *Journal of Marriage and the Family*, vol. 8 (1976), pp. 233–38; Robert T. Michael, Victor R. Fuchs, and Sharon R. Scott, "Changes in the Propensity to Live Alone, 1950–1976," *Demography*, vol. 17 (February 1980), pp. 39–56; Beth Soldo and G. C. Meyers, "The Effects of Life-Time Fertility on the Living Arrangements of Older Women," paper presented at the annual meeting of the Gerontological Society, New York, 1976; and Thomas Tissue and John L. McCoy, "Income and Living Arrangements among Poor Aged Singles," *Social Security Bulletin*, vol. 44 (April 1981), pp. 3–13.

2. James N. Morgan and others, *Income and Welfare in the United States* (McGraw-Hill, 1962), pp. 158–78.

think they do, then public transfers to the elderly can be judged in part by the extent to which they facilitate independent living.

Living arrangements, then, affect the economic well-being of the elderly. (They also affect the economic well-being of the nonelderly, but we do not consider that issue here.) Furthermore, by choosing among living arrangements, the elderly affect our measures of inequality. We concentrate, however, on the way the choice among living arrangements is made, not on the consequences that flow from any particular choice.

Under our null hypothesis, the elderly are more likely to live alone the higher their income is and the better their health, when other variables are held constant. Lack of income may force an elderly person (or couple) to live with others, as might a health condition that limits one's ability to carry on the activities of daily life. In fact, only the income and health of the elderly themselves are relevant. For example, two elderly persons who differ only in that one has wealthy children and the other does not will both have the same probability of living alone. Only their own income (after intrafamily transfers) is relevant.

Some of the findings to be presented later suggest an alternative hypothesis. Consider an elderly couple whose (adult) children are poor. This couple may have the income and health to live alone but may feel an obligation to allow their children to live with them if their children cannot maintain their own households. Under this hypothesis, the incomes of all living children will affect the probability that the elderly live alone. Elderly couples who have poor children will be less likely to live alone than will elderly couples, with identical incomes, who have children who are not poor.

In our analysis, we define as living alone a household unit that contains a couple (or elderly individual, if there is no spouse present) and any children under the age of 21. This unit is the smallest group of people for whom we assume that the preferred arrangement is living together and sharing income. We hypothesize that the bonds of love and the obligation to both spouse and children under 21 (but not to those over 21) outweigh the desire of the head of the household to live alone. All other units are classified as living with others, including units in which the elderly are household heads and have persons other than minor children living with them (who may or may not be related). Also classified as living with others are units in which the elderly live in households headed by others.[3]

3. An alternative classification would be "household head" and "not household head," combining those who live alone and those who are household heads and have others living with them.

In the following section, we describe the sample and define the relevant variables. We next present simple descriptive results concerning living arrangements and their correlates. The econometric model we use is then briefly described, followed by a discussion of results. Last is a brief summary that draws some tentative policy implications from what has gone before.

Data Description

In 1969 information was collected in the longitudinal Retirement History Survey (RHS) on 11,153 married men, unmarried men, and unmarried women who were 58 to 63 years old in that year.[4] Every two years until 1979, these original respondents were reinterviewed. We analyzed the data for the years 1971 (when the respondents were 60–65 years of age) and 1977 (when the respondents were 66–71). Thus we are dealing with the "young" among the elderly. A respondent who was no longer in the sample by 1977 or who did not provide data in both years was excluded. We also excluded respondents who had faulty or incomplete data on the income and health variables.[5] These exclusions reduced the sample size to 7,653. A small set of additional exclusions, discussed in note 5, reduced our final sample to 7,502.

Definition of Living Arrangements Variable

We classified these 7,502 respondents into three mutually exclusive types of living arrangements. Respondents either stayed in the same living arrangement (stayers); moved from living alone in 1971 to living

4. Douglas A. Wolf of the Urban Institute was kind enough to allow us to use his extracts.
5. The two main reasons for being excluded from the sample were attrition and incorrect income data. The first exclusion is straightforward. For the second, we examined the completion codes attached to each income variable. We excluded all respondents for whom the value of the income variable was defective, was reported as a lump sum, or was a loss. These exclusions brought the sample size down to 7,653. A small number of respondents did not answer the question about their health status, and they were excluded. Sixteen couples were excluded because the difference in their 1971 and 1977 incomes was greater than $50,000. Finally, the exclusion, because of their small number, of respondents who were single persons in 1971 but had a spouse present in 1977 brought the final sample size to 7,502.

Table 1. Classification of Respondents by Presence of Spouse and Change in Living Arrangements[a]

Type of respondent	Single people in both years (1)	Couples in both years (2)	Couples who become single people (3)	All respondents (4)
Stayers	2,127	3,467	808	6,402
	(81.6)	(88.6)	(82.0)	(85.3)
Movers	479	444	177	1,100
	(18.4)	(11.4)	(18.0)	(14.7)
Dependents	225	126	97	448
	(8.6)	(3.2)	(9.8)	(6.0)
Independents	254	318	80	652
	(9.7)	(8.1)	(8.1)	(8.7)
All respondents	2,606	3,911	985	7,502
	(100.0)	(100.0)	(100.0)	(100.0)

Source: Authors' tabulations of data from the Retirement History Survey.
a. The numbers in parentheses are the percentages for each column. Figures are rounded.

with others in 1977 (dependents); or moved from living with others in 1971 to living alone in 1977 (independents).

In our empirical work, we grouped together respondents who moved from living alone to living with others and respondents who moved from living alone to having others live with them. For example, a widow who lived alone in 1971 and who later moved in with her adult son (who is the head of a household) then lives with others and is classified as a dependent. Another widow who previously lived alone and who, as head of household, was joined by her elderly sister has others living with her. Since we referred to those whose living arrangement changed from living alone to living with others as dependents, she is also a dependent. Those who moved from living with others to living alone are independents.

In addition to these distinctions among living arrangements, we distinguished between those who were couples and those who were single people in 1971. Among the couples, we made a further distinction between those who were still couples in 1977 and those who had become single, usually because of the death of a spouse.

Table 1 shows the number of cases for each of the three subgroups and divides the respondents into stayers and movers. Movers are further divided into those who become dependent and those who become independent. Most of the RHS respondents stayed in the same living arrangement (6,402, or 85 percent). For the whole sample, independents outnumber dependents primarily because only 3 percent of couples who remained couples became dependent.[6]

Variables Associated with Choice of Living Arrangements

Many variables in the RHS data describe these respondents and might be included in our analysis. For example, the number and economic status of living children, parents, and siblings are important determinants of living arrangements. However, for econometric reasons discussed below, only variables that are observed and that change over time are relevant to our search for estimates of the impact of income and health on the choice of living arrangements.

Income and health, both of which directly affect the respondents' ability to live alone, are the focus of our analyses. Income is the sum of the respondent's income and the spouse's income (if the spouse was present). The income of other household members, if present, is not included. This exclusion results from our null hypothesis—the elderly will live alone if they themselves can afford to.

Our health variable is actually a measure of disability. Respondents were asked if they were forced to stay in bed all or most of the time and if they were unable to leave their houses or use public transportation without help. If they answered yes to any of these questions, they were classified as disabled.

Two additional variables relate to retirement status and poverty. First, retirement status was indicated directly by the respondent. Second, the income of each respondent (plus the income of a spouse, if present) was classified above or below the official Social Security Administration poverty lines.[7]

6. Had we classified by headship status (as suggested in note 3), only those who moved from household head to living in a household headed by others would have been classified as movers. This classification would have greatly decreased the number of movers. For example, for couples, there would have been only 40 dependents and 13 independents, rather than the 126 and 318 shown in table 1.

7. Actually, we define retirement for RHS respondents as answering "retired," "unable to work," or "other" to the question about employment status. The poverty lines that we used were taken from U.S. Bureau of the Census, *Current Population Reports*, series P-60, no. 81, "Characteristics of the Low-Income Population" (Government Printing Office, 1971), p. 20; and Bureau of the Census, *Current Population Reports*, series P-60, no. 115, "Characteristics of the Population below the Poverty Level, 1976" (GPO, 1978), p. 207. For couples, the poverty lines were $2,328 and $3,417 (for two-person households with the head over sixty-five years old). For single people, the lines are $1,852 and $2,720 while for couples who become widows or widowers, we used $2,328 and $2,720.

The Choice of Living Arrangements

In this section we describe each of the subgroups in terms of how these independent variables changed between 1971 and 1977.

Single People

There are 2,606 people who were single in both years (34 percent of the full sample). These include widows and widowers, people who were never married, and people who were divorced. Table 2 shows that 82 percent (or 2,127) of them maintained the same living arrangement. Of the 479 movers, people who moved from living with others to living alone (independents) outnumbered (254 to 225) people who moved from living alone to living with others (dependents).

The total nominal income of both movers and stayers was about 1.6 times higher in 1977 than in 1971, but among the movers the income of independents rose more than that of dependents (1.7 times higher for the former and 1.4 times higher for the latter). A similar result holds for absolute differences in income.[8] The income of stayers rose by more than that of movers, while among the movers, the income of dependents rose by much less than that of independents. All these results are as expected.

Changes in disability and retirement status are also reported in table 2. About one-fifth of the singles reported becoming disabled, and about one-third retired. We expected that people who became disabled would tend to become dependents. In fact, no relationship was revealed between disability (as measured here) and changes in living arrangements.[9] Whereas disability status might affect living arrangements

8. For the econometric analysis, discussed below, income differences are relevant. If each additional dollar has the same effect on the probability of living alone, the absolute difference is relevant. If, however, the effect of an additional dollar declines as income rises, then the probability of living alone can be expressed as a function of the logarithm of the ratio of income. We use income ratios rather than the logarithm of the ratio since the two are monotonically related. The absolute difference will be mentioned when the evidence on a particular point varies according to which measure is used.

9. We also used two other definitions of becoming disabled or retired. Respondents were asked directly if they had a disability. If they answered yes in 1977 but no in 1971, they were classified as becoming disabled by our second definition. The other definition of retirement was having positive income in 1971 and zero earnings in 1977. Neither of these two alternative definitions led to significantly different results.

Table 2. Changes in Income, Disability, and Retirement Status by Change in Living Arrangements, 1971–77

Group	Stayers (1)	Movers (2)	Dependents (3)	Independents (4)	Total (5)
Single people					
Number	2,127	479	225	254	2,606
Income ratio[a]	1.62	1.59	1.42	1.74	1.62
1970 total income (dollars)	4,034	3,821	4,372	3,333	3,995
1976 total income (dollars)	4,895	4,486	4,704	4,293	4,820
Change in total income	861	665	332	960	825
Percent who become disabled (respondent)[b]	19	22	22	21	19
Percent who retire (respondent)[c]	36	34	38	30	36
Couples					
Number	3,647	444	126	318	3,911
Income ratio[a]	1.34	1.29	1.33	1.27	1.33
1970 total income	9,895	9,391	8,410	9,780	9,837
1976 total income	10,743	10,220	9,870	10,359	10,683
Change in total income	848	665	1,460	579	846
Percent who become disabled (respondent)[b]	20	20	20	19	20
Percent who retire (respondent)[c]	53	55	57	53	53
Widow(ers)					
Number	808	177	97	80	985
Income ratio[a]	0.93	1.00	1.06	0.93	0.94
1970 total income	8,603	7,145	7,841	6,728	8,341
1976 total income	5,661	5,441	5,416	5,470	5,621
Change in total income	−2,942	−1,704	−2,073	−1,258	−2,720
Percent who become disabled (respondent)[d]	. . .	. . .	. . .	. . .	. . .
Percent who retire (respondent)[d]	. . .	. . .	. . .	. . .	. . .

Source: Same as table 1.

a. Income ratio is the average of each person's 1976 total income/1970 total income, not the ratio of sample means. The consumer price index increased by 50 percent between the two years, so any ratio below 1.50 represents a decline in real income.

b. Becoming disabled refers to respondents who answered no to the question, "Do you have a disability?" in 1971 and yes to the same question in 1977. See note 9 of the text.

c. Retired refers to respondents who said they were retired in 1977 but not in 1971. See note 9 of the text.

d. Disability and retirement are not defined for couples who became single people (see text).

directly by making it difficult or impossible for the respondent to live alone, retirement status should affect living arrangements only through income. Dependents were more likely to have retired than independents: 38 percent versus 30 percent. We expected that proportionally more of the independents should move from being poor to being not poor and that proportionally more of the dependents should move from being not poor to being poor. This trend holds generally but is not dramatic (data not shown).

Couples Who Remain Couples

There were 3,911 couples who remained couples during the period. Most, 89 percent, were stayers. Of the 444 movers, a majority (72 percent) moved from living with others to living alone.

Table 2 shows that the income ratio was about the same (1.3) for the three groups (stayers, dependents, and independents), and this ratio implies that incomes failed to grow as fast as prices over the period. The pattern of income changes across living arrangements for couples is very different from that of single people. Among couples, the group with the highest income gains contained those who became dependents, while for single people those who became dependents had the smallest income gains. This is the first indication that becoming dependent may not be the appropriate characterization of couples who move from living alone to living with others. Roughly one-fifth of all couples became disabled regardless of change in living arrangements. In contrast with singles, there seems to be little relation between retirement and changes in living arrangements for couples. Finally, crossing the poverty line does not seem to have any effect on changes in living arrangements (data not shown).

Couples Who Become Single People

The last group includes those couples who, usually because of the death of a spouse, became single. There were 985 such couples. About 82 percent were stayers; of the remaining 177 couples 97 moved from living alone to living with others, while 80 moved from living with others to living alone.

In our analysis, if the couple lived alone in 1971 and the surviving person lived alone in 1977, the survivor is a stayer. A move occurs if the couple lived alone in 1971 but the survivor lived with others in 1977 or if the couple had others living with them in 1971 but the survivor lived alone in 1977. A complication arises if the husband died (as was the case for 725 of the 985 couples) because the widow is then the respondent in 1977. This change makes some independent variables ambiguous. For example, in 1971 the husband was asked if he had a disability. If he died before 1977, then his widow was asked if *she* had a disability. Consequently, in table 2, the data referring to disability and retirement are suppressed.

The bottom section of table 2 indicates that movers and stayers experienced about the same change in income. For this group, nominal income actually declined, though the number sharing the income also declined. Among movers, dependents did better than independents based on income ratios but not based on the absolute income differences.

Econometric Models

To begin our construction of a formal econometric model, we assume an index P that summarizes all the relevant variables that the household considers, explicitly or implicitly, in choosing its living arrangement. Both the values of the variables considered and the weight attached to each are unknown to the researcher. That is, even if all variables were measured perfectly, we still would not know how to weight each one in constructing the index. We further assume that the decision about living arrangements is made by comparing the index P to a threshold level T, which is specific to each household. If P is greater than T, the household feels that it can live alone, while if P is less than T, the household feels that it must live with others.

Both the index P and the threshold T are unobserved. What we do observe is the household's choice to live alone or to live with others. Given P and T, our hypothesis about the choice of living arrangements by the elderly is that we will observe a household living alone if and only if P is greater than T.

The probability that a household lives alone is thus related to its characteristics. We classify the relevant characteristics into four distinct groups, two of which can be observed and two of which cannot be observed.

In the first group are observed variables such as income and health that are very likely (although not certain) to change over time. We will refer to these variables as X variables. The second group includes observed variables such as education, race, and sex that we assume do not change over time. We will refer to these variables as Z variables. The third group is composed of unobserved variables related to family structure and interrelationships such as "taste for living alone" and "strength of emotional ties to other family members." These unobserved variables are important to the question at hand, but they are assumed not to change over time for the relevant households. We will refer to these variables as W variables. And the fourth group comprises all unobserved variables that are relevant to the living arrangement decision and that change over time. In the absence of any better information about these variables, we will assume that their distribution among households is random and that this distribution is known. These variables are all included in an error term that we will call ϵ.

Associated with each of the first three sets of characteristics (X, Z, and W) are three sets of coefficients that we denote β, γ, and α, respectively.

Two competing econometric models can be used to analyze our hypothesis. The first, the cross-sectional model, uses information about the characteristics of a group of households at a single point in time. This model has been used to study dichotomous living arrangement choices of female household heads.[10] The second model, the panel model, uses information about a group of households at different points in time. The general form of the panel model appears in Chamberlain,[11] and we apply it here to the problem of living arrangements. Both are described fully in appendix A.

Our primary interest is to obtain the best possible estimates of β, the coefficients associated with the X variables, which include income and health. Knowing, or having estimated, the element of β corresponding to income, we can answer the question, how much would the probability of living alone change if income increased by some amount? This interpretation of that element of β is the same regardless of which model is chosen.

10. For example, see Sheldon Danziger and others, "Work and Welfare as Determinants of Female Poverty and Household Headship," *Quarterly Journal of Economics*, vol. 97 (August 1982), pp. 519–34.

11. Gary Chamberlain, "Analysis of Covariance with Qualitative Data," *Review of Economic Studies*, vol. 47 (April 1980), pp. 225–38.

No matter which of the two models is considered, the W variables—the qualitative variables related to family structure—are unobserved. The single available option is to use only the observed variables X and Z. This constraint makes the estimation of α impossible and jeopardizes the estimation of β and γ. If any of the W variables are correlated with the X and Z variables, then the cross-sectional model will give us biased estimates of the coefficients β and γ. That is, to use the cross-sectional model, we must assume that observed variables such as income, race, sex, and education (Z variables) are independent of unobserved variables such as willingness of kin to live with the elderly and taste for living alone (W variables). This assumption should be avoided where possible. We do so by turning to the panel model.

Our adaptation of the model proposed by Chamberlain is the same as the cross-sectional model in that both are based on the same underlying comparison of the index P and the threshold T. However, the panel model exploits the availability of time-series data to estimate β, the coefficients in which we are most interested, even when the W variables are correlated with the X and Z variables.

The intuition underlying the panel model is that while we observe households changing their living arrangements over time, some of the variables (Z and W) that influence their choice do not change over time and thus are assumed not to have affected the decision to change status. It is the difference between the values of variables that causes households to switch their status, so that any variables whose values do not change are omitted from our analysis.

One disadvantage of the panel model is that no estimates of γ can be made. Also, in estimating the coefficients β using the panel model, we use information only about households who change their living arrangements. In doing so, we are not using most of the sample information, since most of the sample does not change living arrangements over the time period that we consider.

In sum: (1) the cross-sectional model gives unbiased estimates of both β and γ only when W is independent of X and Z; and (2) the panel model gives unbiased estimates of only β but yields those estimates even when W is correlated with X and Z.

If we believe that the W variables are correlated with the X and Z variables, then the panel model is clearly superior since the cross-sectional model will always yield biased estimates of both β and γ. Therefore, the fact that using the panel model forces us to disregard information about a large part of the sample is irrelevant because that information would lead us to biased estimates of the coefficients. We do, however, present estimates from a cross-sectional model in appendix B.

Empirical Results

Our formal model for implementing the comparison of P and T is described in appendix A. It predicts changes in living arrangements from a set of changes in observable variables. For example, the variable representing disability in a given year is a 0–1 variable. The difference between two 0–1 variables can take on three possible values. For the disability variable, +1 implies a disability in 1977 but not in 1971; the value −1 means a disability in 1971 but not in 1977. The value 0 means that no change occurred. A negative coefficient means that having a disability makes the person less likely to live alone (as expected).

Specific definitions of the variables are as follows:

Income difference is the difference between the logarithm of 1971 total income and the logarithm of 1977 total income.

Disability status uses a strict definition of disability (must stay in bed all or most of the time, or unable to leave home without help, or unable to use public transportation without help). It takes the value +1 if the respondent became disabled, 0 if the respondent's disability status did not change, and −1 if the respondent had a disability in 1971 but not in 1977.

Retirement status takes the value +1 if the respondent retired between 1971 and 1977, 0 if employment status did not change, and −1 if the respondent was retired in 1971 but not retired in 1977.

SSI takes the value 0 if the respondent was not on SSI in 1977 and +1 if the respondent had SSI income in 1977.

Poverty status takes the value +1 if the respondent's total income was above the poverty line in 1971 and below it in 1977, 0 if the respondent's poverty status was the same in both years, and −1 if the respondent's income was below the poverty line in 1971 but above it in 1977.

Homeownership takes the value +1 if the respondent owned a home in 1977 but did not own a home in 1971, 0 if the respondent's status did

Table 3. Logistic Coefficient Estimates of the Determinants of Living Arrangements[a]

Variable	Single people (1)	Couples (2)	Couples who become single people (3)
Dependent variable[b]			
Sample size	479	444	177
Mean of dependent variable	0.53	0.72	0.45
−2 log likelihood ratio	21.7	13.8	13.3
Independent variable			
Constant term	0.03	1.10	−0.02
	(0.27)	(6.70)	(−0.14)
Income difference	0.24	−0.49	0.42
	(2.03)	(−3.32)	(1.90)
Disabled[c]	−0.04	0.21	...
	(−0.15)	(0.62)	...
Retired[c]	−0.09	−0.21	...
	(−0.55)	(−0.97)	...
SSI recipient	0.28	0.48	−0.72
	(1.04)	(0.89)	(−0.97)
Income below poverty line	−0.10	−1.28	0.76
	(−0.43)	(−2.86)	(1.77)
Homeowner	0.77	−0.31	1.13
	(2.89)	(−0.94)	(2.69)

Living arrangement spans columns (1)–(3).

Source: Same as table 1.
a. The numbers in parentheses are *t*-statistics.
b. Defined as 0 if the single person or couple lived alone (or with minor children) in 1971 but with others in 1977, and as 1 if the individual or couple lived with others in 1971 but alone in 1977.
c. Disability and retirement are not defined for couples who become single people (see text).

not change between 1971 and 1977, and − 1 if the respondent owned in 1971 but did not own in 1977.

Living arrangement is the 0–1 dependent variable, which takes the value 0 if the individual or couple moved from living alone to living with others and the value 1 if the individual or couple moved from living with others to living alone.

Table 3 shows our logistic estimates of the coefficients for each of the variables for each of the three subsamples.[12] The constant terms capture the effects of all variables that change in the same way for each person, particularly age. But the constant terms also capture the general passage

12. We also estimated three other models for each of the three subsamples. We used the absolute difference between 1971 and 1977 total income in place of the difference in logarithms, and we also used the alternative definitions of disability and retirement.

Table 4. Partial Derivatives of the Probability of Living Alone with Respect to the Independent Variables[a]

Independent variable	Single people[b] (1)	Couples[c] (2)	Couples who become single people[d] (3)
Income difference	0.06	−0.01	0.10
Disabled	−0.01	0.04	...
Retired	−0.02	−0.04	...
SSI recipient	0.08	0.10	−0.18
Income below poverty line	−0.02	−0.26	0.19
Homeowner	0.19	−0.06	0.28

Source: Same as table 1.
a. The effect on the probability of living alone of a one-unit change in the independent variable.
b. Coefficient in table 3, column 1, multiplied by 0.249.
c. Coefficient in table 3, column 2, multiplied by 0.203.
d. Coefficient in table 3, column 3, multiplied by 0.248.

of time—the aging of children and perhaps the death of parents and siblings.

Single People

In the regression for single people, all the signs of the coefficients are as expected. Higher income implies a higher probability of living alone. Being disabled makes it less likely that the respondents live alone, as does being retired or poor. Receiving SSI and owning a home make it more likely that a respondent lives alone.

While the signs are all correct, only two of the coefficients—those on income and homeownership—are significantly different from zero.

To interpret the size of a variable's effect, the coefficients in a logistic regression must be transformed into partial derivatives.[13] The partial derivatives corresponding to the coefficients reported in table 3 are shown in table 4. Consider, for example, a one-unit increase in the logarithm of total income. An increase of $1,000 from the 1971 mean income ($4,000) of this group is associated with an increase in the logarithm of total income from 8.29 to 8.51 (or 0.22), implying an increase

13. The effect of a one-unit change in an independent variable on the probability of living alone—the partial derivative—is the coefficient multiplied by a constant. That constant is the mean of the dependent variable multiplied by the value one minus the mean of the dependent variable.

of 0.013 (or 0.16*0.22) in the probability of living alone. That is, a $1,000 increase in income implies a 1.3 percentage point increase in the probability of living alone. Since the mean probability is 53 percent, the income effect is relatively small.

For the variables other than income, the partial derivatives show their effects directly. For example, becoming disabled would mean a one-unit increase in the variable representing disability status. Since the partial derivative is − 0.01, that one-unit change leads to a decline of 1 percentage point in the probability of living alone. Similarly, retiring would lead to a decline of 2 percentage points, as does becoming poor; receiving SSI implies an increase of 8 percentage points while the sale of a home reduces the probability of living alone by 19 percentage points.

Couples Who Remain Couples

The results for the group of couples who remain couples are not consistent with our basic hypothesis. In fact, they suggest that couples, who are a large part of the elderly population, should be considered part of the supporting rather than the supported population. The only coefficient that is significantly different from zero is that on income. However, the coefficient is negative. That is, having more income does not lead these couples to live alone. Increased income for these couples attracts others to their households, and the coefficient on income indicates the power of this attraction. A 10 percent increase in total income from the 1971 group mean of $9,800 leads to a 3 percent decrease in the probability of living alone.

Couples Who Become Single People

As table 1 shows, in the vast majority of couples in which a spouse died, the survivor continued to live alone. Our estimation concerns the quite small group of movers.

While the descriptive evidence gave us some reason to believe that income may have uncertain effects on the living arrangements of movers, the econometric results suggest that more income implies a greater probability of living alone. The coefficient on income is significant and has the expected sign. A $1,000 increase in income (from the mean of $5,441) increases the probability of living alone by about 4 percent. Of the remaining variables, only homeownership has the expected sign and its coefficient is large and significant. Sale of a home implies a 28 percentage point lower probability of living alone.

Summary and Policy Implications

Almost all those living alone in 1971 were able to maintain that position through 1977. Despite retirement, disability, or death of a spouse, 92 percent of all respondents who lived alone in 1971 continued to live alone in 1977. Only 3 percent of those who lived alone in 1971 became dependents by 1977. Furthermore, of those who did not live alone in 1971 (and who presumably would have preferred to have done so but could not), 19 percent achieved that objective by 1977. Nevertheless, in addition to those who became dependent, 18 percent of all the respondents lived with others throughout the period.

One policy concern is that the population of elderly in nursing homes, drawing benefits from public funds, will grow in coming decades as the population ages. We find that many in this sample of the younger elderly continue to live alone despite some disability. In fact, 30 percent of those who live alone report having a disability. Consequently, a considerable amount of long-term care is already being provided by either the elderly themselves (spouse taking care of spouse) or by relatives (relatives taking care of single individuals). The fact that some of the elderly are able to take in needy adult children, together with the evidence on economic well-being presented in Danziger and others, suggests that the elderly may not prove to be a growing burden on public funds for long-term care.[14]

A second policy conclusion relates to the current concern over social security expenditures. We conclude that proposals to alter the social security system have, on the one hand, the latitude for reducing benefits to couples, but on the other hand, may disrupt a system achieving a desirable goal.

Having painted such a rosy picture, we should close by listing the substantial limitations of this study.

14. That the elderly couples are willing (and able) to take in their children suggests that one reason why the elderly may hold on to homes that are too large for their own needs is that they are a form of insurance for their children. See the paper by Sheldon Danziger and others in this volume.

—The Retirement History Survey excludes people over 75, and we know that dependency increases with age.

—The survey does not follow respondents who enter nursing homes, although for this age group, the number is small.

—Finally, while the panel model provides consistent estimates, very few parameters turn out to be statistically significant. Because of our concentration on obtaining good estimates of the coefficients on income and health, we make no use of information on the 85 percent of respondents who do not change their living arrangements over the period. Less concern about biases due to omitted variables would lead to a broader (though presumably less accurate) view of the problem.[15]

Appendix A: The Econometric Models of Living Arrangements

Let P, an index of a household's ability to live alone, be defined as

$$(1) \qquad P = X'\beta + Z'\gamma + W'\alpha + \epsilon,$$

where X, Z, and W are the vectors of relevant independent variables described in the text, β, γ, and α are the vectors of unknown parameters, and ϵ is an error term whose distribution is known and that is assumed to be independent of X, Z, and W. The index P is a latent variable, so that both the values of the variables and the weights attached to each are unknown to the researcher.

We also assume that each household unit has some unobserved threshold level T above which it is willing to maintain its own household but below which its members live with others. Only the unit's choice to live alone, or to live with others, is observed.

Consider a dichotomous dependent variable, called A, which takes the value 1 if the unit lives alone and 0 if the unit lives with others. The variable A is observed for each unit and indicates whether its ability to live alone exceeds or falls below its threshold. Then,

$$(2) \qquad A = \begin{cases} 1 & \text{if } P \geq T \\ 0 & \text{if } P < T. \end{cases}$$

Both the cross-sectional and panel models (see text on econometric

---

15. Our econometric work provides consistent estimates of the effect of only some variables on living arrangements. Because of this limitation, we are not concerned with the overall explanatory power of the model.

models) can be expressed in the above notation. For any household at a particular point in time,

$$(3) \qquad Pr(A = 1) = F(X'\beta + Z'\gamma + W'\alpha),$$

where $F[\cdot]$ is the cumulative distribution function of the error term ϵ in equation 1.

Given the specification of equation 3, our goal is to derive consistent estimates of β. This interest in β to the exclusion of γ and α is critical in our choice between models.

The Cross-Sectional Model

Since W is unobserved, the only available option is to use just the observed variables X and Z. However, equations 1 and 3 allow the consistent estimation of the vectors of unknown parameters only if X, Z, and W are observed and if ϵ is independent of X, Z, and W. The term ϵ represents all of the unobserved variables used in constructing P. If W is also unobserved, the estimation of α is impossible, and the consistent estimation of β and γ is jeopardized. Consider a new error term, called η, containing all the unmeasured variables now including not only ϵ but also $W'\alpha$. That is, $\eta = W'\alpha + \epsilon$. Suppose that, like ϵ, η is also assumed to have a known distribution function. Then equation 3 becomes

$$(4) \qquad Pr(A = 1) = G(X'\beta + Z'\gamma),$$

where $G[\cdot]$ is the cumulative distribution function of the error term η. Just as ϵ had to be independent of X, Z, and W to allow estimation of the unknown vectors of parameters in equation 3, η must be independent of X and Z to allow the estimation of β and γ. That is, to use the cross-sectional model, we must assume that observed variables are independent of both ϵ and W. If this assumption is false, the coefficient estimates of β and γ will be inconsistent. Since there are many unobserved but relevant variables (such as the willingness of kin to live with elderly relatives), we want to avoid having to assume that these variables are uncorrelated with the observed variables.

The Panel Model

The panel model exploits the availability of time-series data in order to estimate β consistently (the parameters of interest) even when W is correlated with X and Z. We deal here with the case in which there are only two relevant points in time. (In our empirical analysis point 1 is 1971 and point 2 is 1977.) Algebraically, the model is

(5) $Pr[A(1) = 1] = F[X(1)'\beta + Z(1)'\gamma + W(1)'\alpha]$

(6) $Pr[A(2) = 1] = F[X(2)'\beta + Z(2)'\gamma + W(2)'\alpha],$

where $A(i)$ refers to the variable A measured at point i and where $F[\cdot]$ is the cumulative distribution function of $\epsilon(i)$. That is, the probability of any household living alone in 1971 is a function of the 1971 values of X, Z, and W. By assumption, $Z(1) = Z(2)$ and $W(1) = W(2)$, so that their differences are zero.

Chamberlain shows that when ϵ follows the logistic distribution,[16]

(7) $Pr(y = 1) = F\{\beta'[X(1) - X(2)]\},$

where

(8) $y = \begin{cases} 0 & \text{if} \quad A(1) = 1 \quad \text{and} \quad A(2) = 0 \\ 1 & \text{if} \quad A(1) = 0 \quad \text{and} \quad A(2) = 1. \end{cases}$

In words, y takes the value 0 if the unit switched from living alone to living with others and 1 if the unit switched from living with others to living alone. Equations 7 and 8 are the usual form of a standard binary logit problem.

Note that respondents for whom $A(1)$ and $A(2)$ have the same value are ignored in equation 7. However, we could have done our analysis using all respondents, whether they changed status or not. But maximizing the likelihood function associated with that problem would yield the same estimates of β as does maximizing the likelihood function associated with equation 7.

As long as X is uncorrelated with ϵ, the estimates of β will be consistent. Any potential correlation between Z and W and ϵ is irrelevant since Z and X do not appear. This irrelevance is won at the cost of any estimates of γ and α.

Appendix B: Results from a Cross-Sectional Model of Living Arrangements

In this appendix we present the results from a cross-sectional analysis, despite the potential problems mentioned in appendix A. The operational version of the cross-sectional model is

16. "Analysis of Covariance with Qualitative Data."

Table 5. Determinants of Living Arrangements in the Cross-Sectional Analysis of Couples[a]

Variable	Cross-sectional model (1)	Panel model[b] (2)
Dependent variable[c]		
Sample size	3,911	444
Mean of dependent variable	0.843	0.72
−2 log likelihood ratio	39.8	13.8
Independent variable		
Constant	4.29	1.10
	(2.52)	(6.70)
Income	0.09	−0.49
	(1.22)	(−3.32)
Disability	−0.31	0.21
	(−1.71)	(0.62)
Retirement	0.36	−0.21
	(3.08)	(−0.97)
SSI	. . .	0.48
	. . .	(0.89)
Poverty status	−0.05	−1.28
	(−0.25)	(−2.86)
Homeownership	0.17	−0.31
	(1.54)	(−0.94)
Race	−0.40	. . .
	(−2.81)	. . .
Education	0.20	. . .
	(1.56)	. . .
Age	−0.05	. . .
	(−1.80)	. . .
Spouse's age	0.01	. . .
	(2.06)	. . .

Source: Same as table 1.
a. The numbers in parentheses are *t*-statistics
b. Coefficients are the ones from table 3, column 2.
c. Living alone = 1; living with others = 0.

$$(9) \qquad Pr(A = 1) = G(X'\beta + Z'\gamma),$$

where the variables and other notation are defined in the text and in appendix A.

In this section, we compare the estimates from the panel model presented in the text to those from the cross-sectional model above. Since the goal of this appendix is to show the relationship between the cross-sectional and panel models, we show the results only for couples.

We use the entire sample of 3,911 couples who remained couples between 1971 and 1977. The estimates are thus based on both movers and stayers. The analysis is done using values of the variables in 1971. Table 5 shows the results of the cross-sectional model as specified in equation 9.

The coefficients of special interest are the income and disability coefficients. Note that when the entire sample of 3,911 is used, the coefficient on income is positive (although not significant). This finding is in sharp contrast to the negative and significant coefficient obtained in the panel model. Similarly, the coefficients on disability are of opposite sign.

Given this result, we can accept the panel model coefficients on the ground that we thought the cross-sectional coefficient would be inconsistent anyway (see appendix A), or we could conclude that the couples who change status are qualitatively different from the couples who remain in the same status, in contrast to the assumption of our theoretical model. Since our intent here is simply to present a cross-sectional analysis to complement the panel analysis in the text, we do not pursue this question any further.

Comment by Douglas A. Wolf

The paper by Schwartz, Danziger, and Smolensky proceeds from a simple, straightforward, and reasonable testable hypothesis: namely, that older couples and single people prefer to live alone and that income and health status represent constraints on the ability of older people to exercise their preferences. The implication of this hypothesis is that income and good health—more specifically, the absence of disability—will be positively associated with living alone. Since the authors are concerned solely with testing this implication of their hypothesis, they adopt an econometric technique that yields a superior estimator of the income and disability effects, at the cost of ruling out the estimation of several other effects of potential interest. The maintained hypothesis fares rather poorly in the empirical tests reported by the authors. Disability status is unrelated to the choice of living arrangements within the two groups tested, single people and couples. Income, which is positively (and significantly) associated with living alone for single people and survivors (the majority of "couples who became single people"), is significantly negatively related to living alone among couples, which comprise about half the population within the age group considered.

In spite of the somewhat mixed empirical results, I am not inclined to abandon what remains a reasonable hypothesis regarding the preferences and determinants of living alone among older people; nor, I suspect, are the authors so inclined. Their interpretation of the negative income effect for couples—that income "attracts others to their households"— merits further study. In this regard, it should be noted that most other work on the living arrangements of the elderly has been restricted to single people, particularly older unmarried women. The positive income effects for single people found by the authors are in agreement with much of the previous work.

We must also consider additional potential determinants of the choice of living arrangements, excluded from this narrowly focused study. One important such factor, which does receive passing mention, is the existence and characteristics of living relatives. The decision to live alone is not reached in isolation by an older couple or single person; rather, it reflects a decision reached jointly with any living relatives with whom the older person or couple could potentially share a residence. Thus the observed residence patterns of the elderly should reflect not only their own preferences but also the opportunities and constraints represented by the existence and characteristics of living kin as well.

Although the data from the Retirement History Survey used in the study include little information on the characteristics of living kin, they do measure the existence of living kin in several categories. In cross section, RHS respondents exhibit some variation in patterns of kin availability: in 1971, 14 percent of the respondents had one living parent, and 1 percent had two living parents; 80 percent had one or more living children; 89 percent had one or more living siblings. Moreover, during the six-year period studied, there was some longitudinal variation as well: from 1971 to 1977, the percentage with any living parents dropped from 15 to 7 percent.[17] Failure to account for kin availability may distort the estimated income effect if income changes are associated with changes in kin availability. In cross section, at least, income and kin

17. These percentages do not control for household headship, sex, survivorship, or marital status and may not pertain equally to the three sample subgroups analyzed by the authors. The figures cited are based on unpublished tabulations of RHS data performed at the Urban Institute.

availability are strongly related. My own analysis of the RHS data reveals that income is negatively and significantly related to the existence of living parents, of living siblings, and of living children.[18] Whether *changes* in kin availability are correlated with *changes* in income is less certain, although the correlation may exist: the death of relatives reduces potentially important sources of intrafamily financial support but can also convey resources through bequests.

Even if failure to take account of kin availability represents a minor problem for the short-run analysis, the omission is a more serious shortcoming with respect to longer-run analysis of the economic status of the elderly. Changes in patterns of kin availability have been suggested as a possible explanation of changes in the living arrangements of the elderly. In 1940, 13.3 percent of women aged 65 and older were classified as "primary individuals"—persons either living alone, or heading a household containing only nonrelatives—but by 1970 the corresponding figure was 33.4 percent. Aggregate time-series data reveal a downward trend in the ratio of "daughters" (women aged 35 to 44) per "mother" (divorced or widowed women aged 55 and over), which mirrors the increased prevalence of older female primary individuals since 1940.[19]

Future changes in the kinship structures of the elderly, with corresponding implications for living arrangements, can be expected. The Depression-era birth cohort, which will begin to enter the over-65 age group in 1995, will have relatively few living siblings (having been born to mothers with relatively small completed family sizes) and living parents (because of the tendency of their parents to delay childbearing) but relatively many children—children, moreover, who are a relatively short generation younger than their parents. Since the offspring of the Depression-era cohort will be further along in their own life cycles as their parents become potential dependents, the children will be better able to serve as a source of parental care than might otherwise be the case. In contrast, the children of the baby boom, who will begin to cross the age-65 threshold around 2015, will have more living siblings and parents, but fewer children, than the cohorts preceding them if trends observed during the 1970s continue. A recent study that extrapolated

18. Douglas Wolf, "Kinship and the Living Arrangements of Older Americans," Final Report to the National Institute of Child Health and Human Development by the Urban Institute, January 1983.
19. Kobrin, "Fall in Household Size"; and Kobrin, "The Primary Individual and the Family."

first-birth frequency distributions estimated that 29 percent of white women born in 1955 would never bear children, a dramatic increase from the 8 percent of the 1936 birth cohort that remained childless.[20]

If the authors have succeeded in estimating an unbiased income effect, then their findings imply a far lower income elasticity of living alone than do previous studies. When interpreting their findings for single people, they show that a 25 percent increase in income from the sample mean is associated with an increase in the probability of living alone from its sample mean of 0.530 to 0.543. These figures imply an income elasticity of less than 0.01 at the sample mean. In sharp contrast, Michael and others estimate that the income elasticity of the propensity of widows over 65 to live alone is 1.04.[21] There are several reasons to expect differences—Michael and others study only widowed women but include all women aged 65 or more, while the results in the present study include men and women of all marital statuses, in the narrower 66 to 71 age interval. However, I am reluctant to conclude that differences of this order of magnitude reflect only the effects of sample compositions and estimation bias in otherwise comparable studies; instead, I must conclude that the question remains open.

A final comment relates to the policy implication that the authors of this paper derive from their estimated income effects. They conclude that social security benefits to couples might be reduced but that benefit reductions overall may disrupt a system achieving a desirable goal—presumably the goal of assisting single persons in achieving their preferred living arrangement. This conclusion, however, is implicitly based upon a social judgment—or, possibly, a social welfare function—that gives weight solely to the preferences of the elderly. From a wider standpoint, there may be additional desirable goals to be served by distributive policies toward the elderly. These several goals may, however, be in conflict. For example, against the private well-being enjoyed by those who are assisted in living alone must be balanced the forgone economies of scale that would otherwise be achieved through shared living arrangements. It may also be judged socially desirable to change the mix of collectively and privately borne costs of care provided to the elderly.

20. David E. Bloom, "What's Happening to Age at First Birth in the United States? A Study of Recent Cohorts," *Demography*, vol. 19 (August 1982), pp. 351–70.
21. Michael, Fuchs, and Scott, "Changes in the Propensity to Live Alone, 1950–1976."

Alan J. Auerbach and Laurence J. Kotlikoff

Social Security and the Economics
of the Demographic Transition

The remarkable changes in U.S. fertility rates over the last three decades are having increasingly important effects on social institutions and economic performance. Recent elementary school closings, slower wage growth for the young than for the old, and alarming projections of long-term social security deficits are examples of the far-ranging implications of the demographic transition.

Another large swing in fertility occurred earlier in the century. The interwar period witnessed a sizable change in childbearing behavior; but the difference between the postwar peak total fertility rate (the expected number of births over the life span of a woman as she experiences current age-specific birthrates) of 3.7 in 1957 and the trough of 1.7 in 1976 is almost twice the interwar peak-trough difference.[1] More important, the previous birthrate changes were cyclical, with the cycle extending only two decades. In contrast, the current decline in birthrates seems more long lasting. Under the intermediate assumptions of the Social Security Administration's projections, the U.S. fertility rate will remain below 2.2 through 2060.[2]

A two-decade-long baby boom followed by an extended baby bust implies a bulge in the age structure of the population that will pass into older age groups over the next fifty years. The elderly (those over 64) now constitute about one-fifth of all adults; by 2040 they could constitute

We are grateful to Henry J. Aaron, Michael J. Boskin, and other participants in the conference for useful comments, and to Andrew Myers and David Reitman for superb programming assistance.

1. *1982 Annual Report of the Board of Trustees of the Federal Old-Age and Survivors Insurance and Disability Insurance Trust Funds,* transmitted to the House Ways and Means Committee by the Board of Trustees, H. Doc. 97-163 (Government Printing Office, 1982), p. 77.

2. Ibid., p. 35.

as many as two-fifths of all adults.[3] Given social security's pay-as-you-go method of finance, the 60 to 125 percent projected increase in the ratio of beneficiaries to contributors by 2040 portends increases in social security tax rates to levels as high as 25 percent.[4] Such a rise might have important economic effects, but alternative policy choices should be made with a clear understanding of the full economic implications of the demographic transition.

For example, this potential increase in social security taxes need not reduce the living standards of future generations. Fewer children per family means a reduction in the fraction of a family's lifetime resources required for child-raising. Reduced expenditures on child-raising permits parents both to consume more and to save more during their working years. In addition, if an important part of the economy's capital stock is generated by the accumulation of assets for retirement, then the rise in the ratio of old to young that accompanies a decline in population growth may lead to an increase in the economy's capital–labor ratio and hence in the level of wages. Stated differently, the demographic change means fewer young workers with limited asset accumulation relative to elderly persons with sizable retirement savings.

Despite social security's financial requirements, living standards in the next century could also rise because of possible reductions in non–social security government expenditures and taxes. As a fraction of total aggregate output, other government expenditures could decline if much of the expenditures are on programs for the young—for example, schools. The importance of these factors can be evaluated only if one makes explicit assumptions about the response of both private and government behavior to changes in the economic and demographic environment.

This paper simulates the long-term effects of demographic changes by using a general equilibrium model of economic behavior that includes an unfunded social security system, in which the benefits paid out to current retirees are supported by currently collected payroll taxes. The model can analyze many government policies that could be instituted during the demographic transition, including many social security proposals that have recently been suggested to deal with the change in fertility.

3. Ibid., pp. 78–79.
4. Ibid., p. 66; see alternatives II and III.

The model, based on our earlier work,[5] incorporates many new features that are particularly important in the current context. First, the earlier model assumed that all households have a planning horizon that extends over the lifetimes of its members. This model includes households that differ in their motives for saving. Some, as in our previous work, are life-cycle savers, who, while working, accumulate assets strictly to finance consumption during retirement. Other households—called altruistic in this study—have an additional savings motive, namely, the desire to leave a bequest. These households care about the welfare of their children, their children's children, and indeed all future dependents, as well as their own living standards. The distinction between the two types of household may also be characterized in the following way: life-cycle households have a finite (own life) savings horizon, whereas altruistic households have an infinite (own life plus successive heirs) savings horizon. Bequests appear to be an important factor in U.S. capital formation.[6] They are especially important when social security is studied, for an unfunded social security system (which transfers resources from the young to the old) may induce offsetting private intergenerational transfers from the old to the young in the form of bequests or inter vivos gifts.[7]

Both types of household make long-term decisions about consumption and labor supply that are consistent with their long-term budget constraints. These constraints involve current and future interest rates and wage rates. Changes in current or future interest or wage rates induce optimal responses in terms of each household's current consumption and labor supply. To what extent current consumption and work are substituted for future consumption and work depends on the household's

5. Alan J. Auerbach and Laurence J. Kotlikoff, "National Savings, Economic Welfare, and the Structure of Taxation," in Martin Feldstein, ed., *Behavioral Simulation Methods in Tax Policy Analysis* (University of Chicago Press, 1983), pp. 459–93; Auerbach and Kotlikoff, "An Examination of Empirical Tests of Social Security and Savings," in Elhanan Helpman, ed., *Social Policy Evaluation: An Economic Perspective*, Proceedings of the 1981 Pinchas Saphir Conference on Health, Education and Welfare (Academic Press, 1983); and Auerbach and others, "The Efficiency Gains from Dynamic Tax Reform," *International Economic Review*, vol. 24 (February 1983), pp. 81–100.

6. Laurence J. Kotlikoff and Laurence H. Summers, "The Role of Intergenerational Transfers in Aggregate Capital Accumulation," *Journal of Political Economy*, vol. 89 (August 1981), pp. 706–32.

7. Robert J. Barro, "Are Government Bonds Net Wealth?" *Journal of Political Economy*, vol. 82 (November–December 1974), pp. 1106–07.

preferences regarding consumption and leisure. These tastes are modeled explicitly in terms of utility functions, expressing the benefits that
individuals derive from different combinations of consumption and
leisure.

A key element of the model is its equilibrium solution to the complex
and interrelated savings and labor supply decisions of many age cohorts
(seventy-five of these cohorts are alive at any one time). The equilibrium
solution also has the characteristic that announced government policy
is actually sustained in the future; that is, the policy announced by the
government induces the private sector behavior that the government
anticipated in formulating its policy.

A second important element is the explicit modeling of the consumption and labor supply of children. For both life-cycle and altruistic
households, the presence of children can significantly alter patterns of
asset accumulation. A decline in birthrates directly stimulates capital
formation, since some of the resources that would otherwise have been
spent to support children will be saved. An offsetting effect is that a
decline in the projected number of children provides adults with less
reason to save for the future. The net effect of these two forces in the
short run is likely to differ among households, depending on the length
of the households' savings horizons.

A third important element is the variety of social security policy
instruments used in the model to address social security's long-term
funding requirements. These instruments include adjusting tax rates
annually to meet scheduled benefit payments, reducing benefits by
altering the benefit and replacement rate, raising the retirement age for
social security, and generating a social security trust fund, the return on
which could be used to prevent permanently larger social security tax
rates. Additional policies that could easily be incorporated into the model
are general revenue financing of social security's cash flow deficit, taxing
social security benefits under the income tax, and placing earnings tests
on the receipt of benefits.

The chief findings of the paper are as follows.[8]

8. These findings are generally consistent with those of Boskin, Avrin, and Cone,
based on an alternative simulation approach, and are also in line with recent projections
made by the Social Security Administration's actuaries. See Michael J. Boskin, Marcy
Avrin, and Kenneth Cone, "Modeling Alternative Solutions to the Long-Run Social
Security Funding Problem," in Feldstein, ed., *Behavioral Simulation Methods*, pp. 211–
36; and *1982 Annual Report of the Board of Trustees of the Federal Old-Age and
Survivors Insurance and Disability Insurance Trust Funds*.

1. The roughly 50 percent permanent reduction in fertility rates that occurred after the postwar baby boom will mean about a doubling in long-term social security tax rates in the absence of alternative policy responses. Social security's taxable wage base rises with increases in real wages over the demographic transition, but higher real wages also produce higher real benefits because of social security's earnings-based benefit formula. In the long run social security tax rates are essentially determined by demographic factors and the provisions of the benefit formula, such as the replacement rate and retirement age.

2. To avoid increases in social security tax rates above scheduled levels, social security benefits in the long term must be cut by 30 to 40 percent, assuming there are no changes in the retirement age or funding procedures. The benefit cuts in this case are implemented by lowering the benefit replacement rate.

3. The long-term increase in the present retirement age needed to avoid a rise in social security tax rates ranges from three to five years. Since the model assumes a ten-year period of benefit receipts, a three-to-five-year increase in the retirement age is simply another way to produce the same long-term cut in benefits as above.

4. Another way to avoid long-term social security tax rates is by accumulating a larger social security trust fund in the short run. The current trust fund has assets equal to less than three months of benefit payments: the trust fund required to prevent long-term tax rate increases is roughly equal to 6.2 years of benefit payments, or about $1.4 trillion under current circumstances.

5. Despite the possible doubling of long-term social security tax rates, economic welfare, as measured by per capita income or by a combination of per capita consumption and leisure, may rise as a result of the demographic transition. The reduction in the number of nonproductive children per person in the economy means, quite simply, fewer mouths to feed for any given level of national output.

6. Depending on assumptions about government consumption per capita, the demographic transition can involve either small or quite substantial reductions in income tax rates. If the government sought to maintain its consumption per capita constant, as might occur if all government consumption were for national defense, government consumption per adult would fall slightly as the ratio of adults to the total population increased. An alternative, extreme assumption is that government consumption would be targeted primarily toward children—

such as spending on education. Under such an assumption, government consumption per capita and per adult would fall dramatically, permitting reductions in income tax rates by over 30 percent.

The Model and Its Solution

As mentioned, the general equilibrium simulation model used to study the effects of social security is an extension of those discussed in our earlier studies. The current model differs from the previous ones in its explicit treatment of family structure, changes in fertility, and the bequest motive. In addition, our present examination of social security, unlike our previous one, incorporates endogenous labor supply and retirement.[9]

All versions of the model used here include a household sector, a government sector, and a single production sector. Households have perfect foresight and choose paths of consumption and labor supply optimally, given the actual paths of future after-tax wages and interest rates. In some simulations we focus only on steady states that prevail before and after a change in government policy or household behavior; in others we also examine the entire transition path of the economy between such steady states. When modeling transitions, we assume that changes in policy or behavior are not initially anticipated, but that after they occur, individuals accurately foresee the consequences and behave accordingly. The study of such transitions is important for determining the distribution of gains and losses across different cohorts, especially when the bequest motive, which may work to nullify such transfers, is lacking.[10]

Household Behavior

Adults in the model live from ages 21 to 75, with no lifetime uncertainty. Therefore, at any given time, there are fifty-five overlapping generations of adults. In the simplest version of the model, corresponding to that studied in our earlier work, adults have no children and leave no bequests; each family unit consists of a single person living over a fifty-five-year period. We extend this basic life-cycle model by the introduc-

9. Auerbach and Kotlikoff, "National Savings, Economic Welfare, and the Structure of Taxation."
10. Barro, "Are Government Bonds Net Wealth?"

tion of children, whom we assume are born to adults at age 21 and leave the family when they themselves reach this initial adult age. The inclusion of children produces a more realistic pattern of life-cycle consumption behavior and facilitates study of the effects of changes in fertility, either in the number of children per adult or in the age at which adults bear children.

The lifetime utility of each single adult depends on leisure (the difference between total available time and the amount of time spent working) and on consumption of goods and services over time. There is a degree of substitutability between contemporaneous consumption and leisure and between present and future values of these quantities. The utility function that summarizes these preferences is given by equation 5 in the appendix.

In versions of the model where children are explicitly considered, each adult has children at age 21. For families with no bequest motive, the representative individual seeks to maximize the utility of only his immediate family, which consists of himself plus his children until they reach adulthood. The adult chooses his own consumption and leisure and that of his children (according to the utility function described by equation 6), subject to a budget constraint. The constraint, presented in equation 7, states that total lifetime family consumption, in present value, cannot exceed the present value of family earnings (older children may work part-time). In addition to the overall budget constraint, we impose the commonsense requirement that labor supply can never be negative; that is, if the notional demand for leisure in a period exceeds a person's labor endowment, he must "retire" for that period, supplying zero labor.

To model bequests, we assume that one person makes all decisions for his own family as well as all other families present and future, allocating resources optimally subject to the budget constraint that *total* consumption for all families not exceed *total* labor income in present value, plus the individual labor supply constraints. This model produces bequests that reflect a smoothing of consumption across current and future members of this extended family. Increases in bequests could arise, for example, from the introduction of an unfunded social security system in which current retirees receive a windfall gain and their descendants shoulder the corresponding tax burden. Additional bequests from the elderly to the young would undo such intergenerational redistribution by the government.

The model does not allow for general productivity growth; such an extension would be difficult in the presence of the labor-leisure trade-off.[11] But we do allow each person's skill level, and hence wage rate, to increase over time according to the same profile, reflecting the accumulation of human capital over that person's working years.

The social security system alters each family's budget through the payroll tax on wages and through benefits. In our model, people receive benefits starting at a particular age a_R, which we may call the social security retirement age or, more simply, the age of initial benefit receipt. It is important to distinguish between this age and the one at which people choose not to work. As in the real world, these ages can differ among individuals and, on the average, among age groups. Benefits received are based on a worker's average indexed monthly earnings (*AIME*), calculated at age a_R. The *AIME* equals the worker's average annual wages between ages 21 and 65, multiplied by the ratio of the current aggregate wage index to the wage index when the worker was 21. The retired worker annually receives a constant benefit equal to a specified replacement rate times his *AIME* for each year between age a_R and death. The social security tax is a proportional tax on all earnings. We do not impose a ceiling on the amount of labor income subject to the payroll tax; in practice, the ceiling has been rising steadily and is now substantially above median labor income.

In the family's decision problem, we treat social security taxes paid and benefits received as lump-sum quantities, thus ignoring the effects of these taxes and benefits on the marginal return to labor supply. Our treatment reflects not only the lack of professional consensus on the sign and size of such effects but also the difficulty of incorporating such effects into the model. In the same spirit, we ignore the earnings test applied to labor income after the age of payment, a_R. As with the effect of social security taxes on labor supply, the incentive effects of the earnings test are complicated.[12] These conditions reduce to the assumption in this model that a pay-as-you-go social security system with fluctuations in population growth affects behavior because intergenerational transfers occur—in other words, the present value of taxes paid differs in general from the present value of benefits received for each age group. Some cohorts may receive benefits worth more than the taxes they paid, while others receive less.

11. See Auerbach and others, "Efficiency Gains from Dynamic Tax Reform."
12. See the paper by Gary Burtless and Robert A. Moffitt in this volume.

Production Behavior

The economy's single production sector is characterized by the production function in which the logarithm of output at each time t is linear in inputs of capital, K_t, and labor, L_t:[13]

(1) $$\ln y_t = \ln A + \epsilon \ln K_t + (1 - \epsilon) \ln L_t.$$

A is a scaling constant chosen so that the wage of a 21-year-old equals 1.0 in the economy's initial steady state, and ϵ, the capital intensity parameter, which is assumed to be 0.25, approximates the value estimated for the United States based on production functions of this structure. L_t equals the sum of effective units of labor supply of all households; K_t is generated by a recursive equation that dictates that the change in capital stock equals private plus public savings. Competitive behavior by producers and constant returns to scale in production ensure that the gross factor return to capital, r_t, and to labor, w_t, are equated to the marginal products of capital and labor and that factor payments exhaust output. That is,

(2a) $$\frac{w_t}{r_t} = \left(\frac{1 - \epsilon}{\epsilon}\right) \frac{K_t}{L_t}$$

(2b) $$r_t K_t + w_t L_t = Y_t.$$

Government Behavior

The government in this model has two independent fiscal sectors. One sector finances a stream of exogenous government expenditures, G_t, that grows, in the long run, at the same rate as the population. When the population growth rate changes, we consider different assumptions about the change in G per capita. We ignore the effect of these expenditures on individual utility. Aside from an income tax, the government could issue debt to help finance current expenditures, but we simplify matters here by assuming a year-by-year budget balance:

(3) $$R_t = G_t,$$

13. In Auerbach and others, "Efficiency Gains from Dynamic Tax Reform," we allowed the elasticity of substitution in production to differ from unity.

where

(4) $$R_t = \tau_{yt}(w_t L_t + r_t K_t)$$

is the government's tax revenue in year t, from a proportional income tax at rate τ_{yt}.

The second self-financing government sector is the social security system, which pays old-age benefits and collects payroll taxes in each year. In general, we assume the system is financed on a complete pay-as-you-go basis; that is, each year's benefits are paid for by that year's social security taxes. In most simulations, individual retirement benefits begin at age 65. At that age, each person's averaged indexed monthly earnings are calculated as described above. The social security tax is a proportional tax on all earnings and is adjusted annually to meet annual payments.

Solution of the Model

Determining the economy's dynamic equilibrium begins with a characterization of the initial steady state. The next step is to solve for the final steady state based on new government policies or fertility patterns. The final step, not performed in the simulations in the next section, is to solve for the economy's transition to the new steady state that results from adopting the new policy or demographic shift. It is important to remember that the transition described is the one that the economy would actually take if all agents had perfect foresight, after the initial surprise caused by the shock in year 1 of the transition.[14] Moreover, the transition may require many periods, or years, until the new steady state emerges.

The algorithm used to solve for the general equilibrium uses a Gauss-Seidel iteration technique. It begins with guesses of paths of wages and interest rates over time,[15] generates optimal consumption and leisure profiles given these prices, and derives from these profiles paths of the capital stock and aggregate labor supply. These, in turn, give new

14. One can simulate the effects of fully anticipated policy changes by allowing them to begin several years into the transition.
15. In solving for the transition, one must solve all years at once because future years' wages and interest rates influence current behavior under the assumption of perfect foresight.

estimates of the paths of wages and interest rates by way of the production function, which are used to update the previous guesses. Similarly, estimates of the shadow wage parameters (the wages at which retired people would choose to enter the labor force) are generated by the optimal leisure profiles and used to update original guesses. This procedure is repeated until a fixed point is reached, signifying that an equilibrium has been found. There is no guarantee that this solution is unique, although experiments with different initial conditions have produced no cases of multiple equilibria.

In the simulations actually presented, we consider the transition paths of the economy only in certain cases where there is a change in government policy, but not where fertility changes. The latter may also be accommodated by the specification of a pattern of cohort-specific birthrates leading from the old stable population structure to the new one. Procedures to calculate the perfect foresight demographic transition path are currently being developed but were not ready in time for inclusion in this paper.

Simulation Results

In all simulations reported, we assume that the income tax rate in the initial steady state is 30 percent with no exemptions; the level of per capita government consumption is determined by the amount of taxes raised. We also assume an initial fertility rate that yields a 2 percent annual growth in population.

The Effects of Social Security

We begin by analyzing the effects of social security in a model in which half the population consists of selfish life-cycle nuclear families (with children) and the other half is made up of an altruistic infinite horizon family. Experimentation suggests that the results are not sensitive to this ratio. The life-cycle families have a rate of pure time preference of 0.02 (that is, families with constant levels of consumption are equally well off if they receive $1.00 today or $1.02 a year later), while the infinite horizon family has a rate of 0.05. These parameters were chosen to ensure that there is a realistic gross interest rate (since the net-of-tax interest rate must equal the infinite horizon family's discount rate in the steady state) and that life-cycle families in the aggregate have (in the absence of social security) nonnegative total assets. The net-of-tax interest rate must converge to the family's rate of time preference, since the family's annual per capita consumption, which is constant in the steady state, grows at a rate based on the difference between the two rates. A given life-cycle family's assets can be negative in its early years when children are being supported, as borrowing against future earnings occurs. The higher the pure rate of time preference, the less such families will care about future consumption and, hence, the more borrowing they will do. The negative asset position of young life-cycle families could outweigh the positive asset position of older ones, at sufficiently high rates of time preference, generating negative life-cycle assets in the aggregate. In a sense, the lower rate of discount among life-cycle families acts to offset the lower incentive to save associated with their shorter horizon.

The first simulation involves switching from an economy with no social security to one that provides benefits to each person over 65 equal to 60 percent of his *AIME*. In both steady states, the net-of-tax interest rate is 5.0 percent. Hence, with the initial steady state income tax of 30.0 percent, there is a gross interest rate of 7.1 percent.

The characteristics of the initial steady state include realistic consumption and labor supply profiles, as seen in table 1, which also shows the asset accumulation profile for life-cycle families. We measure labor supply by the fraction of full-time hours worked, *full-time* representing roughly 5,000 hours a year. Consumption is measured in the wage units of a 21-year-old, so that annual consumption equal to, say, 0.5 would have a cost equal to the wage of a 21-year-old supplying half his potential labor. (Older workers with higher skill levels would earn such an amount over a shorter work period.) The consumption profiles of both kinds of worker rise steadily before falling off in old age. The reduction in old-age consumption occurs because consumption and leisure are contemporaneous substitutes, and the effective wage rate declines in old age. For members of life-cycle families, consumption rises from 0.11 at age 3 to 0.38 around retirement, and then falls gently to 0.37 near death. The representative altruistic family member's consumption peaks earlier, rising from 0.14 at age 3 to 0.43 at about age 46, and then falling to about 0.33 near death. This earlier peak and sharper decline reflects the altruistic family's higher pure rate of time preference.

Labor supply behavior is also realistic. People do not begin work until

Table 1. Behavior Profiles for Selected Cohorts, with and without Social Security

Age	Wage[a]	Life-cycle families			Altruistic family	
		Consumption	Labor supply[b]	Assets	Consumption	Labor supply[b]
		No social security benefit				
3	0.000	0.114	0.000	0.000	0.139	0.000
12	0.000	0.143	0.000	0.000	0.162	0.000
21	1.000	0.269	0.503	0.000	0.364	0.330
30	1.259	0.309	0.526	−0.701	0.401	0.386
39	1.423	0.343	0.523	−1.141	0.422	0.413
48	1.442	0.368	0.494	0.192	0.425	0.416
57	1.311	0.381	0.435	1.285	0.408	0.395
66	1.070	0.381	0.334	1.537	0.374	0.347
75	0.783	0.370	0.171	0.263	0.329	0.263
		Sixty percent replacement rate[c]				
3	0.000	0.109	0.000	0.000	0.145	0.000
12	0.000	0.137	0.000	0.000	0.170	0.000
21	1.000	0.261	0.518	0.000	0.373	0.313
30	1.259	0.300	0.540	−0.872	0.411	0.370
39	1.423	0.333	0.537	−1.680	0.433	0.398
48	1.442	0.357	0.509	−1.040	0.435	0.401
57	1.311	0.370	0.452	−0.888	0.418	0.380
66	1.070	0.370	0.354	−1.556	0.384	0.330
75	0.783	0.359	0.196	−0.126	0.337	0.244

Source: Authors' calculations.
a. Based on a wage of 1.0 for a 21-year-old.
b. Based on a full-time labor endowment equal to 1.0.
c. The social security benefit—the amount received annually by each person over the age of the initial benefit receipt—is 0.298 for life-cycle families and 0.395 for the altruistic family.

the late teens and reach peak labor supply of about 0.42 for the altruistic family member at age 48 and of about 0.53 for the life-cycle family member at age 30. These fractions are reasonable when compared to a full-time labor supply of 5,000 hours a year. The concentration of work in earlier years by life-cycle members again reflects their lower rate of time preference.

To finance their path of family consumption, life-cycle adults immediately begin to dissave; they do not begin to save until well into their thirties. They remain in debt until they are nearly 50, at which time they begin to accumulate assets to finance consumption during the later years when labor supply is low. (This low supply of labor late in life comes from the age profile of wages, which peaks in middle age and then declines until death.) The consumption and labor supply behavior of both types of family yields a net national savings rate equal to 7 percent of income at the assumed population growth rate of 2 percent a year.

Changing to an unfunded social security system affects the resources of members of life-cycle families and those of the altruistic family differently because of the method of benefit computation. In general, the present value of a person's benefits is far less than the present value of taxes paid, since the interest rate built into the pay-as-you-go system is the 2 percent population growth rate (a zero productivity growth in wages is assumed here) rather than the 5 percent after-tax return on capital. That is, the capacity of the economy to deliver a return in excess of contributions depends on the growth of the labor force that supports the system through payroll taxes. Since life-cycle adults work more than altruistic adults, they are hurt more by this characteristic. Because they work relatively more in their earlier years, they are penalized further by the fact that the shift of a dollar of earnings from a later to an earlier year raises the present value of social security taxes without affecting the value of *AIME* or benefits.

The size of this transfer may be measured by comparing the present value of social security taxes to social security benefits for a given individual. For the altruistic family member, taxes equal 0.76 in present value (about two years' earnings for a 21-year-old) and benefits equal 0.11, a difference of 0.65. For the life-cycle family member these numbers are 1.05 and 0.15, respectively, a difference of 0.90. Most of this difference is simply due to the fact that members of life-cycle families work more. This statement is based on the following features of this simulation experiment. In the second steady state, the income tax rate equals 30 percent, the same value as in the initial steady state. Coupled with the requirement that the net interest rate remain equal to the altruistic family's discount rate (0.05), this implies that the gross interest rate remains constant. That, in turn, implies a constant gross wage, and hence a constant net wage. Therefore, the net interest rate *and* wage rate are constant across these two steady states, so that the present value of social security taxes less benefits for the life-cycle family represents the loss in real income suffered by the family as a result of the social security system. This loss occurs both because of the intergenerational transfers to cohorts alive at the time of the system's initiation, and because the system treats life-cycle family members less favorably than altruistic family members within any age cohort. The effect of the resource transfer is to increase the aggregate annual consumption of the altruistic family by 2.8 percent and decrease its annual labor supply by 4.1 percent. For the poorer life-cycle families annual consumption falls by 3.3 percent and labor supply rises by 3.4 percent.

The advent of social security also alters the asset accumulation problem of life-cycle families. With the prospect of future social security benefits and with payroll taxes reducing disposable income, life-cycle adults now remain in debt for their entire lives. They use social security benefits to fund retirement consumption and pay off accumulated borrowing.

The Response to a Decline in Fertility

Recent declines in fertility have led to a projection of increased social security taxes to compensate for the decline in the size of the working population relative to the number of benefit recipients. To measure the effects of such a change, we simulate the change in the steady state of the economy with a social security replacement rate of 60 percent as the annual population growth rate drops from 2 percent to 0 percent. This corresponds to a decline in the total fertility rate per 21-year-old adult from 1.486 to 1.000. We consider the effect of this change first in the model just examined, with life-cycle families and the infinite horizon family each representing half the economy's population.

One issue that must be resolved in simulating the effects of such a fertility shift concerns the response of general government expenditures to the changing age structure of the population. Our standard assumption is that per capita expenditures are fixed, but one could certainly defend other views. The benefits of certain types of expenditures, such as national defense and highway construction, are hard to attribute to any narrow class in the population. However, expenditures on education redound largely to the benefit of people under 21 and are closely tied to the population of this age group. (We abstract here from the additional complexity that would arise if levels of government spending were permitted to influence private expenditure decisions.) For such expenditures, a decline in population growth would result in less government spending per capita. As an alternative to our assumption of constant government expenditure per capita, therefore, we also consider the case in which expenditures are based on the number of 21-year-olds in the population. Fortunately, most of the key results about the effect of demographic change on the social security system do not depend on which assumption is made here.

With per capita government expenditure fixed, the drop in population growth increases the social security tax necessary to finance a given replacement rate. Based on a 60 percent replacement rate, payroll taxes must rise from 7.3 percent to 12.9 percent. Part of this tax increase is mitigated by a drop in the income tax, from 30.0 percent to 27.6 percent. The present value of payroll taxes less social security benefits rises from 0.65 to 0.97 for members of the altruistic family and from 0.90 to 1.71 for members of life-cycle families. (A similar result occurs if we assume revenues per 21-year-old are held constant. The social security tax rises to 12.9 percent, though the income tax falls more, to 21.9 percent, in response to the decrease in the proportion of 21-year-olds in the working population.)

It must be stressed here that the drop in the ratio of working to retired population produces not only an increase in social security taxes but also an increase in per capita consumption. There are fewer children per adult, which allows an annual increase of nearly 3 percent in the levels of annual consumption by members of life-cycle families (whose labor supply is virtually unaffected), and over 14 percent for members of the infinite horizon family (whose labor supply declines at the same time). The greater increase in annual consumption of infinite horizon family members reflects their larger relative holdings of wealth in the new steady state.

An obvious alternative to increasing social security tax rates is to cut the social security replacement rate. Simulations for both assumptions about the pattern of general government expenditure suggest that a replacement rate of between 30 and 40 percent would be needed to maintain the balance with tax rates unchanged. With other government expenditure per capita fixed, a 40 percent replacement rate yields a social security tax rate of 8.6 percent, while a 30 percent replacement rate yields a tax rate of 6.4 percent. In both cases the income tax remains constant at 27.6 percent. In the second case the steady-state incidence of this benefit cut falls largely on members of the altruistic family, who have their net (of benefits) lifetime social security tax burden reduced from 0.97 to 0.52, while members of life-cycle families have their burden reduced from 1.71 to 0.82.

Another policy option is raising the minimum age at which benefits could be received. For either assumption about government expenditures, the age of initial benefit receipt needs to be raised from 65 to between 68 and 70 to forestall tax rate increases. With per capita government expenditure fixed, the social security tax declines to 9.1 percent when the retirement age goes up to 68, and 6.7 percent when it goes up to 70. The incidence of such changes is similar to those connected with benefit cuts; the net lifetime social security tax drops to 0.55 for altruistic families and to 0.87 for life-cycle families when the retirement age goes up to 70.

Another way the government could avoid raising the payroll tax would be by accumulating a social security trust fund, as suggested by Feldstein, among others.[16] We find that a trust fund equal to 6.2 times one year's social security benefits would be needed to prevent the payroll tax from rising. At current U.S. levels, this would mean a fund of about $1.4 trillion.

Models including altruistic families with time preferences of the kind described in the appendix usually exhibit small long-term changes in factor rewards. The gross marginal product of capital, and hence the gross wage rate, can change in the long term only to the extent that the income tax rate changes, since the *net* return to capital is fixed at the rate of time preference of altruistic families. Thus if per capita government expenditures are fixed and the income tax rate falls only to 27.6 percent from 30.0 percent, the gross wage rises by only 1.15 percent. In a pure life-cycle model, a decrease in population growth could lower the size of the working population relative to the number of elderly with accumulated savings, driving up the gross wage rate and mitigating the increase in payroll taxes. To test this hypothesis and examine the sensitivity of our previous findings, we consider the effects of a drop in population growth from 2 percent a year to 0 percent in a pure life-cycle model. For simplicity, we also ignore children in these simulations and assume a time preference rate of 0.015. (We used this value in our earlier simulations of the life-cycle adult model because it produced sensible baseline estimates of key economic variables.) We also assume that per capita government expenditures remain fixed. Our results suggest that the hypothesized rise in wages does not occur. Rather, the before-tax wage *declines* by 1.23 percent. An increase in government consumption per worker and a concomitant increase in income taxes appear to explain this result. With the drop in the birthrate, social security taxes rise from 7.1 percent to 13.1 percent of labor income, both values similar to those obtained from our previous model simulations. Simulating the effects of benefit cuts and retirement age increases again suggests that a replace-

16. Martin Feldstein, "Facing the Social Security Crisis," *Public Interest*, no. 47 (Spring 1977), p. 97.

ment rate of between 30 and 40 percent or a retirement age of between 68 and 70 would be needed to maintain the original social security tax rate. In all these simulations the income tax varies little from its original value of 30.0 percent, ranging between 29.3 percent and 31.9 percent. Thus our results about the effects of a decline in fertility do not seem sensitive to assumptions about the existence of a bequest motive among some people.

To summarize the findings of this section: assumptions about the pattern of government expenditure or the presence of a bequest motive have little impact on the simulated effects of a drop in fertility on the social security system. Social security taxes would nearly have to double to meet promised benefit levels; avoiding this increase would require a rise in the retirement age to between 68 and 70, or a cut in the replacement rate by almost 40 percent. In each case this would mean a cut in per capita benefits of almost one half. Only a substantial trust fund, presumably between $1 trillion and $2 trillion, would make such a cut unnecessary.

Conclusions

This study of social security and demographic change suggests, somewhat paradoxically, that necessary adjustments of social security policy variables to demographic change will be greater, but less painful, than previously expected. Although social security tax rates could double over the next sixty years if taxes are simply adjusted annually to meet benefits, the reduction in the ratio of dependent children to adults may permit future generations to finance a greater level of lifetime consumption and leisure than can current generations. This is true even if no growth in productivity occurs.

In the presence of demographic change, individual indicators such as potential levels of social security tax rates can provide misleading impressions about overall future welfare. One example is the national savings rate; the same simulations that indicate long-term increases in per capita output as economies head towards zero population growth show the national savings rate dropping from 7 percent to 0 percent. (As is well known, an economy without population growth or technological change will, in the long run, have a constant capital stock and hence no net savings.) Clearly a broad understanding of the course of all economic indicators is required to properly evaluate the response of social security to the demographic transition.

This paper has concentrated mainly on the long-term effects of demographic change; understanding the short-term, transitional effects of demographics and policy is perhaps even more important. Those issues and the analysis of additional social security policy alternatives provide a significant topic for future research.

Appendix: Some Technical Aspects of the Simulation Model

The lifetime utility of each single adult is given by the nested, constant elasticity function

$$
(5) \qquad u_A = \left(\frac{1}{1-\gamma^{-1}}\right) \sum_{a=21}^{75} (1+\delta)^{-(a-21)}
$$
$$
\times (C_a^{1-\rho^{-1}} + \alpha l_a^{1-\rho^{-1}})^{1-\gamma^{-1}/1-\rho^{-1}},
$$

where l_a and C_a are the adult's leisure (out of a unit labor endowment) and consumption at age a and δ, α, ρ, and γ are taste parameters. A large value of δ, the household's pure rate of time preference, indicates that a greater fraction of lifetime resources will be consumed in the early years of adulthood. The term α is an intensity parameter, determining the share of leisure in total expenditures on goods and leisure, given prices. The terms ρ and γ are the individual's elasticities of substitution between consumption and leisure in the same period, and between consumption (or leisure) in different periods, respectively. For all simulations in this paper, we set $\alpha = 1.5$, $\rho = 0.8$, and $\gamma = 0.25$. These values are based on estimates culled from the relevant literature.[17] Values of δ vary across different simulations.

In versions of the model where children are explicitly considered, each adult has N children at age 21, and in the case of no bequest motive, he seeks to maximize the utility of his immediate family, which consists of himself plus his children until they reach adulthood. The adult's utility of children is

$$
(6) \qquad u_C = \left(\frac{1}{1-\gamma^{-1}}\right) \sum_{a=21}^{40} f(a-20)(1+\delta)^{-(a-21)}
$$
$$
\times (C_{a-20}^{1-\rho^{-1}} + \alpha l_{a-20}^{1-\rho^{-1}})^{1-\gamma^{-1}/1-\rho^{-1}},
$$

17. See the discussion in Auerbach and others, "Efficiency Gains from Dynamic Tax Reform."

where $f(a - 20)$ is the utility weight given to children aged $a - 20$ and C_{a-20} and l_{a-20} represent children's consumption of goods and leisure. The parameters δ, ρ, γ, and α always correspond to those in equation 5 for any given simulation.

The budget constraint facing an adult with children at age 21 is

$$(7) \quad \sum_{a=21}^{75} \left(\prod_{s=22}^{a} [1 + r_s(1 - \tau_{ys})] \right)^{-1} \left((1 - \tau_{ya})w_a e_a(1 - l_a) - T_a \right)$$

$$+ \sum_{a=a_R}^{75} \left(\prod_{s=22}^{a} [1 + r_s(1 - \tau_{ys})] \right)^{-1} B_a$$

$$+ \sum_{a=21}^{40} \left(\prod_{s=22}^{a} [1 + r_s(1 - \tau_{ys})] \right)^{-1}$$

$$\left((1 - \tau_{ya})w_a e_{a-20}(1 - l_{a-20}) - T_{a-20} \right)$$

$$\geq \sum_{a=21}^{75} \left(\prod_{s=22}^{a} [1 + r_s(1 - \tau_{ys})] \right)^{-1} C_a$$

$$+ \sum_{a=21}^{40} \left(\prod_{s=22}^{a} [1 + r_s(1 - \tau_{ys})] \right)^{-1} C_{a-20},$$

where r_s is the gross interest rate, w_a is the standard wage rate, and τ_{ys} is the proportional income tax rate when the adult is age s. The terms T_a and B_a represent, respectively, social security taxes paid and benefits received by a person age a. Benefits are received after age a_R. In the individual's maximization problem T_a and B_a are treated as lump-sum payments and receipts. The term e_a is included to reflect the accumulation of human capital. These terms describe how many units of "standard" labor an age a individual supplies per unit of leisure forgone in any given year. Thus, $w_a e_a$ may be interpreted as the individual's gross wage rate. The human capital profile e is normalized so that $e_{21} = 1$; $e_a = 0$ for $a \leq 12$, and rises linearly from 0.3 at age 13 to 1.0 at age 21. After age 21 e_a rises and then falls off somewhat following the pattern estimated by Welch.[18]

In simulations without children, the last term on each side of the inequality (equation 7) is set to zero.

For an adult with no bequest motive, the problem is to maximize

18. Finis Welch, "Effects of Cohort Size on Earnings: The Baby Boom Babies' Financial Bust," *Journal of Political Economy*, vol. 87 (October 1979), pp. 575–81. The details of these calculations may be found in Auerbach and others, "Efficiency Gains from Dynamic Tax Reform."

nuclear family utility (either equation 5 or, if children are present in the model, equations 5 and 6) subject to the budget constraint (equation 7). To model bequests, we simply assume that one individual maximizes the discounted sum of all nuclear family utilities subject to the aggregate budget constraint facing all such families taken together. That is, the objective is

$$(8) \qquad W = \sum_{t=1}^{\infty} (1 + \delta)^{-t} (u_t^A + u_t^C),$$

where $u_t^A + u_t^C$ is the lifetime utility of an adult who reaches age 21 in year t.[19] With the definition of u^A and u^C from equations 5 and 6, equation 8 may be rewritten as

$$(9) \quad W = (1 - \gamma^{-1}) \sum_{t=1}^{\infty} \sum_{a=21}^{75} (1 + \delta)^{-(a+t-21)} \left(C_a^{t(1-\rho^{-1})} + \alpha l_a^{t(1-\rho^{-1})} \right)^{1-\gamma^{-1}/1-\rho^{-1}}$$

$$\times \sum_{t=1}^{\infty} \sum_{a=21}^{40} (1 + \delta)^{-(a+t-21)} \left(C_a^{t(1-\rho^{-1})} + \alpha l_{a-20}^{t(1-\rho^{-1})} \right)^{1-\gamma^{-1}/1-\rho^{-1}},$$

where C_a^t and l_a^t are the age a consumption and leisure of an adult who is 21 in year t, and C_{a-20}^t and l_{a-20}^t are the consumption and leisure of that adult's children in the same year.

Besides the overall budget constraint, we impose the requirement that labor supply can never be negative; that is, if the notional demand for leisure, l, exceeds one, the individual must "retire" for that period, supplying zero labor. We attach the Lagrange multiplier u_a to this labor supply constraint at each age a.

To solve for the life-cycle nuclear family's consumption and leisure profiles, we differentiate the Lagrangian based on the relevant utility functions and budget constraints (equations 5, 6, and 7) to obtain first-order conditions with respect to consumption and leisure at each age. These may be combined for l_a and C_a to yield[20]

$$(10) \qquad l = \left(\frac{w_a^*}{\alpha} \right)^{-l} C_a \qquad a \geq 21,$$

where $w_a^* = w_a e_a (1 - \tau_{ya}) + \mu_a$ is the effective after-tax wage at age a

19. An alternate way of modeling altruism would be to assume that each adult maximizes the discounted sum of his utility and that of his children, his children's children, and so on, or

$$(u_t^A + u_t^C) + (1 + \delta)^{-20} (u_{t+20}^A + u_{t+20}^C) + \ldots .$$

20. The details of these calculations may be found in Auerbach and others, "Efficiency Gains from Dynamic Tax Reform."

(including the shadow wage term μ_a). Combination of the first-order conditions for successive values of a yields

(11) $$C_a = \left(\frac{1 + r_a(1 - \tau_{ya})}{1 + \delta}\right)^{\gamma}\left(\frac{v_a}{v_{a-1}}\right)C_{a-1} \qquad a > 21,$$

where

(12) $$v_a = \left(1 + \alpha^{\rho}w_a^{*1-\rho}\right)^{\rho-\gamma/1-\rho}.$$

For families with children, equation 10 also relates leisure to consumption for ages 1 to 20, while the equation corresponding to 11 is

(13) $$C_{a-20} = \left[\left(\frac{1 + r_a(1 - \tau_{ya})}{1 + \delta}\right)\left(\frac{f(a - 20)}{f(a - 21)}\right)\right]^{\gamma}\left(\frac{v_{a-20}}{v_{a-21}}\right)C_{a-21} \quad a > 21.$$

These first order conditions and household budget constraints are solved using nonlinear techniques for utility maximizing time paths of consumption and labor supply.

Comment by Michael J. Boskin

The task of constructing a general equilibrium model with fifty-five overlapping generations is enormous. In their previous papers Auerbach and Kotlikoff looked exclusively at households with no bequest motive, truly life-cycle households whose adults live fifty-five years, from the age of 21 to 75. They modeled both the preferences of those people for consumption of goods and leisure and the production sector of the economy. They assumed that all markets cleared in each period. Given the budget constraints and some other assumptions, they could solve for the optimum consumption and leisure over the life cycle for these households. When a policy is changed or some other event occurs that disturbs an initial equilibrium, different cohorts will be affected in various ways because they are in different stages of their life cycles. For example, old people will have accumulated savings and be in the process of dissaving. Young people will have few assets or none at all and will be planning for a longer future than will the elderly.

This paper makes two interesting and important innovations. First, the authors explicitly model the effects of children in two ways. For people who are life-cycle planners, they model the utility value of children and the concern of parents for the consumption and leisure of children until the children leave home at age 20, when they form new households. In addition, they introduce a segment of the population that has infinite horizons in the sense that it maximizes the sum of discounted utilities of its offspring over an infinite horizon of future generations.

For most of the paper, the authors assume that half the population is of the pure life-cycle type and the other half is of the infinite-horizon type. The single most important effect of adding infinite-horizon households is that the long-run interest elasticity of supply of the capital stock is infinite. The real rate of return will be unchangeable in the steady state. The authors are also interested in other types of heterogeneity in the population, but they have done well to have got this far.

Second, the authors introduce a pay-as-you-go wage-indexed social security system into their model. People start paying into the system when they start working at age 21. They "retire" at some future date and collect benefits equal to 60 percent of an average of their lifetime indexed earnings. Total benefits divided by current wages yields the tax rates on earnings. That tax rate in turn affects individual budget constraints, saving behavior, labor supply behavior, and so on.

At the beginning of the paper the authors present several results: an estimate of the unfunded debt of the social security system as of 1982 that resembles independent estimates by me and by the Social Security Administration; an estimate of the amount by which the replacement rates would have to fall or ages of eligibility for benefits rise to prevent tax rates from rising; and estimates that payroll taxes would have to increase from 7.3 to 12.8 percent to sustain benefits in a pay-as-you-go system. They also show that the present value of taxes minus benefits will increase greatly because of the difference between the biological rate of interest in the pay-as-you-go system and the assumed real after-tax return to saving and the rate of discount.

The model itself requires some simplifying assumptions to allow tractability and to keep the computer budget finite. First, the production technology assumes no technological change. The authors also exclude from their model all transfer payments other than social security as well as expenditures focused primarily on age groups other than the elderly, such as education. These omissions are significant if one is considering the effects of alternative responses to a rise in social security costs induced by a drop in birthrates.

The production function used in this paper has an elasticity of substitution of one. The particular value of the elasticity of substitution is especially important in looking at the transitional effects of changes in the growth rate of population or of other factors. I think it would be useful to experiment with lower values of this key elasticity because the authors are dealing with the transfer of hundreds of billions of dollars across generations.

In conclusion I would only reiterate the paper's results: that the reduction in population growth from 2 percent to zero suggests the need for large increases in tax rates to finance social security or for a large reduction in replacement rates. Alternatively, a very large trust fund—one about seven times annual contribution—could be accumulated to smooth out the tax increase.

Auerbach and Kotlikoff distinguish the effects of these changes on households of different types and at different ages. I am anxious to see the results for the transition stage. I think the authors have highlighted something that is significant and often ignored, the very different way people of different ages or with different typical lifetime earnings and savings profiles will be treated under any general change in the social security system.

Paul N. Courant, Edward M. Gramlich,
and John P. Laitner

A Dynamic Microeconomic Estimate
of the Life-Cycle Model

The life-cycle model is one of the most commonly used and most difficult to verify in economics. It is widely used to make predictions about the distributional incidence of consumption taxes, the long-term labor supply impact of transfers, and the short-term macro impact of temporary tax cuts. The model is based on the idea that households make decisions about consumption over their entire lifetimes, and in making these decisions take into account the resources they will have available over their entire lifetimes. Thus the model places formidable requirements on households in that it is assumed that consumers can make long-term forecasts of income and wealth with a high degree of confidence. Given that households are able to make such forecasts, the model predicts behavior that often differs quite strikingly from those that assume households behave in a more mechanical or shortsighted manner.

But for all its elegance and rationality, the life-cycle model has not tested out very well. Efforts by macroeconomists to show that temporary tax cuts have very little effect on aggregate demand (as they should in the life-cycle model) are quite inconclusive and ambiguous, even when done with the meticulous care of Modigliani, more than anyone else the father of the model.[1]

We owe an enormous debt of gratitude to Deborah Laren, who programmed the complex panel data routines used here. We have also benefited from the comments of members of the macroeconomics workshop at the University of Michigan and participants at the Brookings Conference on Retirement and Aging.

1. See Franco Modigliani and Charles Steindel, "Is a Tax Rebate an Effective Tool for Stabilization Policy?" *Brookings Papers on Economic Activity, 1:1977,* pp. 175–209. The important preceding articles are Franco Modigliani and Richard Brumberg, "Utility

Nor have efforts to test the life-cycle model with cross-sectional microdata worked out very successfully. Mirer; Blinder, Gordon, and Wise; Kurz; and King and Dicks-Mireaux all found, with different data sets, that wealth does not appear to decline among the aged, as it should in a true life-cycle model view of the world. Blinder, Gordon, and Wise also showed that aged white men systematically underprovide for their consumption at older ages, perhaps explaining why they do not systematically decumulate assets they do not have. Further, Kotlikoff as well as Blinder, Gordon, and Wise found that social security taxes reduce the accumulated savings of middle-aged men, but not by as much as would be predicted by the model.[2]

If there is a problem with the life-cycle model, it would seem to be not in its internal logic, which is unassailable, but in its information requirements. As one illustration, Davies could rescue the finding of underdecumulation of wealth of the aged by introducing uncertainty about length of life.[3] It would not be surprising if the attenuated effect of social security accumulations could also be explained by the fact that middle-aged households simply do not know the full size of their future implicit benefits from social security. They would certainly also be unclear about the rate of return to be realized from their asset stocks and the interest rate likely to be charged on any new borrowing. Thus the model may not test out very well simply because consumers do not have a very accurate picture of their future income.

In this paper we try to explain household consumption with a different

Analysis and the Consumption Function: An Interpretation of Cross-section Data," in Kenneth K. Kurihara, ed., *Post Keynesian Economics* (Rutgers University Press, 1954), pp. 388–436; and Albert Ando and Franco Modigliani, "The 'Life Cycle' Hypothesis of Saving: Aggregate Implications and Tests," *American Economic Review,* vol. 53 (March 1963), pp. 55–84.

2. Thad W. Mirer, "The Wealth-Age Relation among the Aged," *American Economic Review,* vol. 69 (June 1979), pp. 435–43; Alan S. Blinder, Roger H. Gordon, and Donald E. Wise, "Social Security, Bequests, and the Life Cycle Theory of Saving: Cross-Sectional Tests," National Bureau of Economic Research Working Paper 619 (Cambridge, Mass.: NBER, January 1981); Mordecai Kurz, "The Life Cycle Hypothesis and the Effects of Social Security and Private Pensions on Family Savings," Stanford University Working Paper 335 (Stanford University, May 1981); M. A. King and L-D. L. Dicks-Mireaux, "Asset Holdings and the Life-Cycle," *Economic Journal,* vol. 92 (June 1982), pp. 247–67; and Laurence J. Kotlikoff, "Testing the Theory of Social Security and Life-Cycle Accumulation," *American Economic Review,* vol. 69 (June 1979), pp. 396–410.

3. James B. Davies, "Uncertain Lifetime, Consumption, and Dissaving in Retirement," *Journal of Political Economy,* vol. 89 (June 1981) pp. 561–77.

form of the life-cycle model. We view households as making plans from some date forward, based on information they could reasonably be expected to have at that date. Then a bit of history unfolds, the household information is seen to be incomplete, and a new plan is made. The household goes through life in this way, continuously updating its information, reprogramming, and, in what is most important for our story, changing its consumption in a way that could not otherwise be rationalized within the life-cycle model.

To implement this view of the life-cycle process, we estimate the life-cycle model with longitudinal microdata. Most previous empirical attempts to implement the model have used either time-series macrodata or cross-sectional microdata. Macrodata can be used to test micro hypotheses only in a very incomplete manner, and cross-sectional data cannot be used to examine the reprogramming phenomenon because reprogramming simply cannot be observed in cross sections. Longitudinal, or panel, data for individual households do not have these weaknesses and provide a good basis for trying to implement our version of the life-cycle model. The specific data series used is the Panel Study of Income Dynamics, the only longitudinal survey with enough information to measure the variables we are interested in, a long enough time series to give realistic time patterns of income and consumption changes, and a sample of households of all ages.[4]

The life-cycle model and the panel study could be used to test any number of hypotheses about family behavior. Because the problems in examining any one question are substantial, we focus here on just one aspect of household behavior—the consumption-saving decision. We treat labor income and family size as exogenous in this paper, recognizing that of course neither assumption would be appropriate in a more general view.

As a final introductory comment, we note that our method for dealing

4. The Panel Study of Income Dynamics is described in a number of different references, perhaps the most complete being James N. Morgan and others, *Five Thousand American Families—Patterns of Economic Progress,* vol. 1: *An Analysis of the First Five Years of the Panel Study of Income Dynamics* (University of Michigan, Institute for Social Research, 1974). For testing life-cycle models, these data have been used by Thomas E. MaCurdy, "An Empirical Model of Labor Supply in a Life-Cycle Setting," *Journal of Political Economy,* vol. 89 (December 1981), pp. 1059–85; and by Robert E. Hall and Frederic S. Mishkin, "The Sensitivity of Consumption to Transitory Income: Estimates from Panel Data on Households," *Econometrica,* vol. 50 (March 1982), pp. 461–81.

with reprogramming may have useful applications for dynamic household microsimulations. Such microsimulations are beginning to be used to investigate the long-term implications of tax, social security, and even macroeconomic policies. But in most cases these simulations have very little behavioral content because the equations that describe behavior are of the mechanical form that the life-cycle model was developed to criticize almost thirty years ago and do not imply any long-term household planning. Should our reprogramming model be used in a dynamic microsimulation, the household would gain new information as the microsimulation (time) proceeds and use that information to revise behavior in a more sensible manner.

The first section of the paper presents a simple and typical life-cycle model, assuming no uncertainty. The model implies a cross-sectional equation explaining consumption levels and a time-series equation explaining consumption growth rates. We note that both the cross-sectional and time-series models require very accurate knowledge of the future, and allow only for steady income growth over time. We then show how continuous reprogramming permits estimation of a version of the model that is much less restrictive. The second section describes the panel study data used to implement our version of the life-cycle model. The third section contains the main empirical parameters for both the cross-sectional and time-series equations. As expected, the two ways to estimate parameters of the underlying utility function yield different answers for many population groups, and the section then uses an empirically estimated reprogramming scheme to see if these differences can be resolved.

Once it is recognized that households are likely to revise their lifetime plans as new data about their lives become available, it makes sense to develop models of life-cycle behavior in which households are assumed to know from the outset that they are planning under uncertainty. The fourth section of the paper presents a simulation model of household behavior under such assumptions. Explicit recognition of uncertainty does change the way in which we interpret some of our results, and it may also provide the beginnings of a more realistic way to simulate life-cycle behavior in future work.

The Standard Life-Cycle Model with No Uncertainty

The basic idea behind the life-cycle model is that households plan rationally over time, attempting to maximize lifetime utility subject to lifetime constraints on wealth. In the case that has been most analyzed,[5] the household is assumed to face a perfect capital market with a constant real interest rate, to know the time path of its future earned income, and to know its date of death. Under these assumptions, plus the further assumptions that future utility is discounted at a constant rate and that the elasticity of substitution between consumption in any two periods is constant, the household maximizes

$$(1) \qquad M = \frac{1}{1 - \delta} \sum_{t=0}^{T} \frac{C_t^{1-\delta}}{(1 + \rho)^t} + \lambda \left[A_0 + \sum_{t=0}^{T} \frac{Y_t - C_t}{(1 + r)^t} \right],$$

where C_t is family consumption in year t, Y_t is after-tax family earned and transfer income (all income not from assets), r is the after-tax real interest rate, A_0 is the initial level of family net worth, and T is the year of death. The maximization problem could be expanded to include a target bequest level, but we omit that term because without a theory of how bequests are determined, such an inclusion would not change anything important.

The parameter δ gives the curvature of the indifference curves between C_0 and C_t. The larger δ is, the lower the elasticity of substitution is between consumption in different periods. A value of $\delta = 0$ implies that the utility function and indifference curves are linear. When $\delta = 1$, the utility function takes the familiar logarithmic form. And when $\delta > 1$, values that have often cropped up in the literature (see, for example, Davies),[6] indifference curves between C_0 and C_t have even greater curvature. Because we cannot isolate estimates of δ in this paper, we do calculations for assumed values of 1, 1.5, and 2.

The parameter ρ represents the household's subjective rate of time preference as derived from the utility function. If the consumers optimize the timing of consumption, the marginal rate of substitution between consumption now and consumption t years from now is $(1 + r)^t$. The role of ρ in this optimization is simply to determine how steeply consumption must rise or fall over time for this optimization condition to hold. While the internal rate of the preference is often assumed to be positive because families are presumed to desire consumption more now than later, we know of one careful psychological experimental study by Lathrop, who found generally negative values of ρ even for aged groups,

5. See, for example, Blinder, Gordon, and Wise, "Social Security, Bequests, and the Life Cycle Theory of Savings."
6. Davies, "Uncertain Lifetime, Consumption, and Dissaving in Retirement."

who would seem to have the highest rate of time preference.[7] Moreover, even if ρ were close to r, ρ could still be negative if r is negative, and the real after-tax rate of return facing consumers has typically been negative in recent years. Hence we make no a priori presumption one way or another—ρ could be positive or negative, greater or less than r.

The standard way to solve this maximization problem is to make some assumption about future income, for example, that it grows at a constant rate g. This implies

$$(2) \qquad\qquad Y_t = Y_0(1+g)^t,$$

which can be substituted into the budget constraint and solved to yield Modigliani's consumption function

$$(3) \qquad\qquad C_0 = a_0 A_0 + a_1 Y_0,$$

where

$$(4) \qquad\qquad a_o = \left[\sum_{t=0}^{T} (1+r)^{t[(1/\delta)-1]}(1+\rho)^{-t/\delta}\right]^{-1}$$

$$a_1 = a_0\left[\sum_{t=0}^{T}\left(\frac{1+g}{1+r}\right)^t\right].$$

Estimating equation 3 allows one to make inferences about the underlying utility parameters in equation 4. Equation 3 can be and has been estimated either with cross-sectional data at a point in time or with macroeconomic time-series data.

Suppose for simplicity that r, the after-tax real interest rate, is zero and that $\delta = 1$. If ρ is also zero, the coefficient of net worth (a_0) in equation 3 will be $1/(T+1)$—higher for older families than younger families because the assets have to be spread over fewer living years— and completely independent of projected income growth. The coefficient of income (a_1), on the other hand, will depend in an important way on projected income growth, being higher for those families who are optimistic about their prospects and do not feel the need to save for future shortfalls.

Another way to solve the model is to concentrate not on the level of consumption, but on the slope of the consumption path. This procedure

7. John W. Lathrop, "Preferences for Consumption Streams over Time: Some Experimental Results" (Ph.D. dissertation, University of Michigan, 1979).

involves simply finding the consumption first-order conditions from equation 1 and expressing them as ratios:

$$(5) \qquad C_t = C_0 \left(\frac{1+r}{1+\rho} \right)^{t/\delta}.$$

If $r = \rho$, the family's consumption level will be stable over time. If $\rho > r$, the family's subjective rate of time preference exceeds the market premium for delaying consumption, and the family will shift consumption to the present, showing declining levels of consumption over time. This decline will be less (in algebraic terms), the larger δ is. On the other hand, if $\rho < r$, consumption rises over time, but by less the larger δ is. One advantage of our empirical approach is that in addition to fitting a cross-sectional consumption equation like equation 3, we can also fit a time-series equation like equation 5 for individual households to see if the two estimates of ρ and δ are consistent.

Should the parameter estimates from the cross-sectional and time-series versions of the life-cycle model differ, a logical explanation is that households acting according to equation 3 will experience changes in their independent variables between period 0 and period t, leading to changes in consumption not envisioned in the cross-sectional relationship.

To deal with this problem, we introduce a simple reprogramming model. Let us suppose that in any year t the family makes its income forecast out to T and computes

$$(6) \qquad \hat{F}_0 = \sum_{t=0}^{T} \frac{\hat{Y}_t}{(1+r)^t},$$

where $\hat{Y}_t$ is forecast income in year t. This expression can replace equation 2 in the cross-sectional solution of the model, yielding

$$(7) \qquad C_0 = a_0(A_0 + \hat{F}_0) + a_2(Y_0 - \hat{Y}_0).$$

The expression for a_0 is the same as given above by equation 4—now it is applied not only to A_0 but also to the discounted sum of future incomes. But another term is tacked onto the consumption function, a term not implied by the life-cycle theory. If Y_0 exceeds $\hat{Y}_0$, this "unanticipated" income may also influence current consumption. Next year it will be known and presumably worked into an updated forecast of $\hat{F}$, but this year it may also influence consumption. Both the unanticipated income term and the recomputed forecast term could lead to rising time-series consumption levels even if $\rho > r$.

In our reprogramming section, therefore, we experiment with different plausible rules to forecast $\hat{F}$ for subsamples of the population. These calculations also lead to estimates of $Y_0 - \hat{Y}$. We then can test whether unanticipated income has an independent impact on consumption, over and above the computed value of $\hat{F}$ and the given value of A. If it does and if $\hat{F}$ has its expected positive impact on consumption, the family is updating its information set and changing observed consumption levels in a way that would not be describable within either the cross-sectional or time-series views of the world.

The Sample

The model was estimated with the Panel Study of Income Dynamics, a longitudinal household survey with 5,000 families initially that extended for thirteen years (1967–79). After deducting those who dropped out of the sample, those units where the identity of the head often changed, and those for whom data were incomplete for other reasons, we had usable data for about 5,300 households—2,500 white male-headed families, almost 1,300 nonwhite male-headed families, and slightly more than 1,500 female-headed families. The increase in the initial sample is due to the fact that whenever the sons, daughters, or wives of the initial families split off to form their own units, they were just added to the sample, with records kept on both the parent unit and the split-off unit. Nonwhite and female-headed families are proportionately more numerous than in the population at large because the sample was designed for poverty analysis (originally sponsored by the Office of Economic Opportunity before that agency's demise) and contains an oversample of the low-income population.

The Data

The panel study contains fairly complete family income data, broken into labor and transfer income, income from assets, and taxes of various sorts. The models discussed above require us to use Y_t, after-tax disposable income less capital income. This we computed by making the appropriate subtractions and deflating by the level of consumer prices to convert to real terms (1972 dollars). The models also require us to measure C_t and A_t, variables that are harder to determine.

We can measure A_t for a family as follows. An estimate of the value of housing equity, the most important component of net worth for most households, is reported in the panel study. Income from assets—interest, dividends, trust funds, and royalties—is included as one sum. To determine the stock of these assets, we divided asset income by the before-tax nominal interest rate that we assumed households received on the assets. These asset stocks were then deflated by the consumption price deflator in the national income accounts (NIA) to put them in real terms and added to real housing equity to determine real net worth. In performing these calculations, we assumed that wealthy families would earn higher interest rates than families with little wealth. Hence we divided through by the nominal passbook rate paid by savings and loan institutions for the first $300 of asset income and the higher Aaa corporate bond rate for asset income in excess of $300 per year.

Consumption is then measured by the identity

$$(8) \qquad Y_t - C_t \equiv A_{t+1} - A_t - HKG_t,$$

where A_{t+1} refers to end-of-year assets, A_t to start of year, Y_t' refers to total disposable income (including capital income), and HKG_t refers to housing capital gains. If our sample members had invested in assets on which interest payments change when interest rates change, such as savings and loan deposits, our asset series will omit capital gains and allow the identity to be used without error. If they had invested in long-term securities on which interest payments did not change, we will necessarily treat some capital gains or losses as household savings and misstate household consumption.[8]

The most serious capital gains problems should refer to housing equities, however. We used the NIA housing price deflator in a given year to measure and deduct housing capital gains from the change in net worth before deriving household saving and consumption.[9]

To derive these numbers, we needed, and used, time-series data on individual households. Often when a household first split off from its parent unit and formed a new sample observation, one or more of the three variables—Y, C, or A—moved erratically. To prevent transitional

8. That is to say, when nominal interest rates rise, the value of assets on which interest payments are fixed falls. We would mistakenly attribute this drop to a rise in consumption.

9. Another potential problem is that the consumption measured by this technique is close to the NIA version of consumption. The models may work better with a service flow concept of consumption, where expenditures on durables are deducted (as investment) but service flows from the cumulated stock of durables are added in. Such a calculation could be made for automobiles, but not for other durables in the panel study. We did not have a chance to do so, even for autos, for this paper.

Table 1. Income and Consumption Data from Panel Study of Income Dynamics Compared with National Income Accounts Data[a]

Variables in 1972 dollars per capita

	Panel study	
Item	Disposable income	Consumption
Constant	−1,269.0	863.0
	(8.4)	(1.7)
NIA disposable income	1.12	. . .
	(29.2)	. . .
NIA consumption	. . .	0.66
	. . .	(4.7)
R^2	0.99	0.71
Standard error	46.6	127.9
Number of observations (N)	13	11
Data period	1967–79	1968–78

Sources: National income accounts data are from the relevant tables in the *Survey of Current Business;* the panel study data are determined by blowing up sample observations with the Institute for Social Research weights.

a. The numbers in parentheses are absolute *t*-ratios.

measurement problems on these new split-offs, we kept all newly formed units out of our sample for two years to let their variables stabilize before treating them as if they were on their life-cycle path. Some units recorded negative values of Y in some years—these we did not trust, and we eliminated these units from the sample. For some units our identities implied negative values of A or C—we also eliminated these units to avoid potential measurement bias. These deletions left the usable sample sizes referred to above.

Before trying to use data on individual households to estimate the life-cycle models, we checked to see if our microdata were consistent with corresponding aggregate data. To do this, we used sample weights worked out by the Institute for Social Research (the group that managed the study) to blow up our income and consumption series to per capita estimates for the U.S. population, in 1972 dollars. We compared these to the corresponding series in the national income accounts with regressions of the form

(9)
$$Y_t'(PSID) = f[Y_t'(NIA)]$$
$$C_t(PSID) = f[C_t(NIA)],$$

where $Y(PSID)$ refers to disposable income in the panel study, $Y(NIA)$ to disposable income in the national income accounts, and so forth. The results are shown in table 1. The equation for income, extending over the entire thirteen-year sample, shows a close relationship between the panel study and the NIA series (the coefficient of $Y'[NIA]$ is close to one and the R^2 is very high), implying relatively little survey measurement error for the microdata. The equation for consumption, dropping the first and last years because of equation 8, shows a reasonably close correlation with its macro series, though, as might be expected, our computations and data manipulations and omissions do appear to have led to some measurement error (both the coefficient of $C_i[NIA]$ and the R^2 are lower than in the $Y'[NIA]$ equation).

Microeconomic Estimates of the Life-Cycle Model

Cross-Sectional Consumption Function

Our first effort to implement the life-cycle model is to estimate the cross-sectional consumption function in equation 3. Since the coefficients in equation 3 depend on the age of the household, the equation was estimated separately for each of five different age classes of the three demographic groups. The estimates for the 1978 cross section are shown in table 2. The fit of these equations is fairly good, with the R^2 averaging about 0.50 for white male-headed families and 0.75 for non-white male-headed families and female-headed families.

The coefficients for income and net worth are the complex expressions given in equation 4 and do not mean much on their own. To determine the underlying utility parameters of interest, we must make some restrictive assumptions. Regarding r, in 1978 the after-tax real interest rate was below zero for most households. We arbitrarily set r at zero in solving equation 4, though we will use more accurate values in our reprogramming models that we report on later. For the aged group, g can also be taken to be zero, which, on substituting into equation 4, means that T can be found by

$$(10) \qquad\qquad T = \frac{a_1}{a_0} - 1.$$

These values of T are computed for the aged class and used (with appropriate average ages) to find T for all other classes. This finding implies that younger households are assumed to anticipate the same age

Table 2. Cross-Sectional Consumption Functions, Panel Study of Income Dynamics, 1978

Age class	Sample data			Regression					$\delta = 1.0$	$\delta = 1.5$
	N	Head's average age	$\bar{Y}$	a_o	a_1	R^2	T^a	g^a	ρ^*	ρ^*
White male-headed families										
65 and over	284	72	6,065	0.22	0.75	0.48	4	0	-0.126	-0.183
50–64	502	56	12,104	0.26	0.65	0.59	20	-0.016	-0.026	-0.038
36–49	553	43	13,332	0.29	0.96	0.53	33	-0.008	0.005	0.008
26–35	824	30	11,280	0.30	0.81	0.50	46	-0.001	-0.008	-0.012
25 and under	318	22	8,365	0.30	0.97	0.63	54	0.005	-0.006	-0.009
Nonwhite male-headed families										
65 and over	86	73	5,216	0.10	0.94	0.89	9	0	-0.013	-0.020
50–64	272	56	8,556	0.16	0.85	0.82	26	-0.011	0	0
36–49	290	43	10,240	0.33	0.86	0.57	39	-0.008	-0.002	-0.002
26–35	417	30	9,489	0.35	0.86	0.76	52	-0.003	-0.003	-0.004
25 and under	222	19	6,271	0.36	0.97	0.94	63	0.004	-0.005	-0.007
Female-headed families										
65 and over	303	75	3,333	0.18	0.86	0.67	5	0	-0.057	-0.084
50–64	353	57	5,284	0.22	0.71	0.68	23	-0.013	-0.016	-0.024
36–49	348	43	6,763	0.16	0.92	0.89	37	-0.013	0.008	0.012
26–35	285	30	5,870	0.25	1.16	0.80	50	-0.002	0.008	0.012
25 and under	224	21	4,783	0.15	0.95	0.91	59	0.001	-0.003	-0.004

Source: Basic data on which equations were run were taken from the panel study.

a. Average until end of life at T, where T is computed under assumption that $g = 0$ for aged class. For each nonaged group, g is the constant growth rate that gives the same discounted future income until death as the actual $\bar{Y}$ path.

of death as do older households, an assumption that is not strictly in accordance with mortality tables, but should not lead to very great errors.

The value of g comes from the sample income statistics on the left side of the table. A white male-headed household in the 26–35 age class has an average age of 30 and an average income ($\overline{Y}$) of \$11,280. The average growth rate of income, until the end of life, is calculated by finding the constant g value that should be inserted into equation 2 to yield the same discounted future income until death (at age 76) as the actual $\overline{Y}$ path. The reprogramming model we deal with later incorporates more sophisticated techniques for estimating future income.

Computing T and g from the data in this way allows us to take the a_1 coefficients and find (ρ, δ) pairs, shown on the right side of the table for the assumed values of δ. These ρ values are computed in the same way as the g values—as constant rates until end of life—and they should be interpreted as average subject time preference rates for the families. Apart from the puzzling values for aged white males and females, the time preference rates range from -0.03 to $+0.01$ when $\delta = 1$, with a slightly higher variance around zero when δ is assumed to be 1.5. The approximate stability of ρ is reassuring because end-of-life ρ values should not change from group to group (though the coefficients in the life-cycle model will change). The calculations were all done with the income coefficient, a_1, because many families had zero entries for net worth, and those coefficients were estimated with less precision.

Time-Series Consumption Growth

The next step is to estimate the time-series relationships in equation 5. To do so, we computed for each family the average annual growth rate of consumption from their first year with usable data to their last, and we present the median value of this average growth rate for the whole sample in table 3. The means are not shown but are slightly higher. The sample size is smaller than that used in table 2 because now we need a time series for each family to compute the average annual growth rate, and we do not have time-series information on all households used in the cross-sectional sample.

The implied values of ρ taken from equation 5 are also shown in the table. In doing these calculations, we again set $r = 0$; if r is in fact negative (see below), the calculated values of ρ in equation 5 will be

Table 3. Consumption Growth Rates and Life-Cycle Parameter Estimates, Panel Study of Income Dynamics, 1968–78[a]

Age class	N	Median C_t/C_{t-1}	$\delta = 1.0$ ρ	$\delta = 1.5$ ρ
White male-headed families				
65 and over	165	0.980	0.024	0.031
50–64	346	1.005	−0.005	−0.008
36–49	351	1.031	−0.030	−0.045
26–35	428	1.036	−0.035	−0.052
25 and under	51	1.083	−0.077	−0.113
Nonwhite male-headed families				
65 and over	71	1.003	−0.003	−0.005
50–64	197	1.021	−0.021	−0.031
36–49	192	1.033	−0.032	−0.048
26–35	204	1.039	−0.038	−0.056
25 and under	31	1.076	−0.071	−0.104
Female-headed families				
65 and over	146	1.015	−0.015	−0.022
50–64	230	1.001	0.001	0.002
36–49	190	1.008	−0.008	−0.012
26–35	111	1.020	−0.020	−0.029
25 and under	27	1.045	−0.043	−0.064

Source: Same as table 2.
a. Assumes that $r = 0$.

lower than those shown in table 3. Recall that a value of $\rho < 0$ implies that people willingly will sacrifice \$1 of present consumption for less than \$1 of future consumption and for progressively less the longer consumption is deferred. For aged male-headed families of both races, household consumption declines at a slow rate, and the implied estimate of ρ is close to the value implied in the cross-sectional tests. For females, household consumption grows relatively slowly, and the implied values of ρ, while generally negative, are not very different from those shown on the cross-sectional tests. But for the nonaged male-headed families of both races, household consumption rises, implying (when $r = 0$) that ρ is negative, with computed values ranging from −0.01 for the older groups to −0.11 for the younger groups. Thus the cross-sectional and time-series estimates of the life-cycle model yield different estimates of consumers' time preferences, and the time-series estimates of time preferences are usually negative.

The balance of the paper is devoted to attempting to resolve the different results obtained by the two procedures and attempting to account for the disquieting finding that subjective rates of time preference are usually negative in the time-series estimates. It goes without saying that we could have data problems, but it is not obvious how these would generate any inconsistencies: the same data gave one set of results in a cross-sectional and a time-series context. It could also be that the simple life-cycle assumptions used here caused problems. That is precisely why we introduce reprogramming in the next section. There is also a well-known econometric difference between cross-sectional and time-series results: in a cross section a household is assumed to behave like a richer household once the household's income rises, but our time-series models are more realistic because they can relax that assumption. This matter too is best analyzed within a reprogramming model. Finally, there are several more technical possibilities that we check out at this point.

Since the results are essentially the same for nonaged white and nonwhite male-headed families, we have tried to resolve the inconsistency only for the former group (which has a larger sample, with less oversampling of low-income families). We first split the nonaged white sample into groups with and without a college education, to provide further detail on the nature of the inconsistency. The results, shown in the top part of table 4, do reduce the differences between the time-series and cross-sectional estimates. The biggest growth in consumption came for young whites with college, but statistics for this group are not reliable both because college attendance distorts measured consumption patterns and because the continuous time-series sample is very small. Omitting this group from the calculations leaves an implied value of ρ going from zero to -0.04 when $\delta = 1$, and from zero to -0.06 when $\delta = 1.5$. The inconsistency still exists but is not as large.

A second attempt to resolve the inconsistency also allows another check on our consumption data. If there were random measurement error in disposable income, assets, interest rates, or housing capital gains in equation 8, our consumption series would also contain random measurement error, and the consumption growth rates could be misstated. This possibility can be investigated by writing equation 8 in terms of three-year changes: three-year cumulated disposable income less the corrected change in assets over a three-year period equals three-year cumulated consumption. These three-year consumption figures are then compared, and their annual growth rates are computed in the bottom panel of table 4. The estimates of ρ are still generally negative, but the range is slightly reduced. Now ρ goes from 0.01 to -0.03 when $\delta = 1$ and from 0.02 to -0.05 when $\delta = 1.5$. The inconsistency still exists, but again it has been slightly mitigated.

Finally, we investigate the possibility that our measured rates of time

Table 4. Consumption Growth Rates and Life-Cycle Parameter Estimates, Nonaged White Male-headed Families, Panel Study of Income Dynamics, 1968–78[a]

Age class	N	Median C_t/C_{t-1}	$\delta = 1.0$ ρ	$\delta = 1.5$ ρ
		One-year definition of saving		
With some college				
50–64	100	1.002	−0.002	−0.003
36–49	126	1.031	−0.030	−0.045
26–35	193	1.035	−0.034	−0.050
Without college				
50–64	238	1.006	−0.006	−0.009
36–49	209	1.036	−0.035	−0.052
26–35	198	1.041	−0.039	−0.059
25 and under	37	1.045	−0.043	−0.064
		Three-year definition of saving		
With some college				
50–64	100	1.002	−0.002	−0.003
36–49	117	1.029	−0.028	−0.042
26–35	70	1.031	−0.030	−0.045
Without college				
50–64	236	0.990	0.010	0.015
36–49	199	1.028	−0.026	−0.039
26–35	89	1.034	−0.033	−0.049

Source: Same as table 1.
a. Assumes that $r = 0$.

preference reflect the fact that households face borrowing constraints that prevent them from getting on their desired, high early consumption life-cycle path. If these constraints are present, we would observe rising consumption paths that reflect the borrowing constraints and not the true internal rate of time preference. This possibility is tested by splitting the sample into wealthy and nonwealthy groups, as is done in table 5. The first and fourth panels of the table compute ρ for households where net worth (averaged over time) exceeds $30,000 in 1972 dollars, a level that should remove borrowing constraints for most families. Even these families show negative values of ρ, ranging from zero to −0.055 just as before. The implied ρ values *are* slightly less negative than for the nonwealthy (with net worth less than $15,000, in panels 3 and 6) of a given age, indicating that borrowing constraints may play some role in determining our observed ρ values, but the differences are not very great.

The result of each of these corrections, then, is to whittle away at the basic time-series, cross-sectional inconsistency we have demonstrated.

Table 5. Consumption Growth Rates and Life-Cycle Parameter Estimates, Nonaged White Male-headed Families, 1968–78[a]

1972 dollars

Age class	N	Median C_t/C_{t-1}	$\delta = 1.0$ ρ	$\delta = 1.5$ ρ
With some college				
1. Net worth more than $30,000				
50–64	46	1.012	−0.012	−0.018
36–49	27	1.022	−0.022	−0.032
2. Net worth more than $15,000				
50–64	81	1.001	−0.001	−0.002
36–49	64	1.026	−0.025	−0.038
26–35	24	0.995	−0.005	−0.008
3. Net worth less than $15,000				
50–64	19	1.004	0.004	0.006
36–49	62	1.036	−0.035	−0.052
26–35	169	1.036	−0.035	−0.052
Without college				
4. Net worth more than $30,000				
50–64	54	1.009	−0.009	−0.013
36–49	16	1.020	−0.020	−0.029
5. Net worth more than $15,000				
50–64	129	1.006	−0.006	−0.009
36–49	76	1.031	−0.030	−0.045
6. Net worth less than $15,000				
50–64	109	1.000	0.000	0.000
36–49	133	1.037	−0.036	−0.053
26–35	184	1.037	−0.036	−0.053
25 and under	36	1.039	−0.038	−0.056

Source: Same as table 2.

a. Assumes that $r = 0$.

But though this inconsistency is mitigated, a big difference remains between the implied internal time preference rates of −0.01 that one finds when estimating cross-sectional micro equations and the implied rates of −0.03 to −0.06 that one finds from time-series data. We now see if a theoretical revision involving reprogramming can shed some more light on the issue.

Reprogramming

The first step in building a reprogramming model is to describe how a household might make its income forecast; the next is to show how it might use that forecast.

We have three different forecasting variants. In the first households are assumed to expect their present real income to continue until end of life:

(11) $$\hat{Y}_t = Y_{t-1},$$

where $\hat{Y}_t$ is the forecast income for year t. Households following this rule use no information about anticipated age-earnings profiles in deriving their expected income levels.

The second rule is more elaborate. Households are assumed to forecast their own future income to behave like that of people of similar race, sex, and education. They are forecasting on the basis of a cross-sectionally estimated age-earnings profile. They would not be exactly on this cross-sectional profile at any time, but we assume they expect to return to it gradually by the relation

(12) $$\hat{Y}_t - Y_{t-1} = b(\bar{Y}_t - Y_{t-1}),$$

where $\bar{Y}_t$ is the average income for all white males of the same age and educational attainment as the head of the household making the forecast in that year and b is the adjustment parameter.[10] If $b = 0$, this rule reverts to the simple rule where the observed age-earnings profile is irrelevant as in equation 11. If $b = 1$, the household expects to return immediately to the age-earnings profile. Between these extremes, very quick or very gradual adjustment could be found. The properties of this equation can also be illustrated by solving it to

(13) $$\hat{Y}_t = b\bar{Y}_t + (1 - b)Y_{t-1},$$

showing that this gradual adjustment relation is tantamount to making a weighted average forecast, where the adjustment parameter b is the weight given to the age-earnings profile prediction of family income.

The third rule is more elaborate yet. Equation 12 gives a one-period gradual adjustment equation, but one might also expect that the initial position is a weighted average of this period's income and last period's, as in

(14) $$\hat{Y}_t - [wY_{t-1} + (1 - w)Y_{t-2}] = b[\bar{Y}_t - wY_{t-1} - (1 - w)Y_{t-2}],$$

which solves to the estimating equation

---

10. In this forecasting rule families are assumed to ignore the impact of general productivity change in shifting the age-earnings profile up over time. At least in the 1970s this impact should not have been very large. Moreover, in general it would add only a slight trend to equation 12 or 13.

(15) $\hat{Y}_t - Y_{t-2} = b(\overline{Y}_t - Y_{t-2}) + (1-b)w\,(Y_{t-1} - Y_{t-2})$.

If $Y_{t-1} = Y_{t-2}$, equation 15 solves to equation 12; but if not, equation 15 shows added backward income smoothing.

However people make forecasts, current life-cycle consumption depends on the entire discounted future stream of $\hat{Y}_t$, not just on the current value. Since only Y_{t-1} will be known when this future stream is forecast, the forecasting equations 11, 12, or 15 must be moved forward in time by recursive substitution. The family uses one of these equations to forecast $\hat{Y}_t$ and then substitutes $\hat{Y}_t$ into the forecasting equations to find $\hat{Y}_{t+1}$ and then $\hat{Y}_{t+1}$ to find $\hat{Y}_{t+2}$, and so forth. As this recursive substitution is made, the influence of expected values of $\overline{Y}_t$, observed from an examination of today's age-earnings profile for groups with like educational attainment, becomes very important for equations 12 or 15, while the influence of Y_{t-1} on future $\hat{Y}_t$ declines exponentially (except under the first reprogramming rule). In determing $\hat{F}_0$, Y_{t-1} will have a strong effect only if b is very low.

To estimate the basic reprogramming consumption function in equation 7, we need estimates of the forecasting parameters and an expression for the age-earnings profile. These data are as follows:

With some college
Expression for $\overline{Y} = 8{,}500 + 515(Age - 23) - 10(Age - 23)^2$, Age $= 23, \ldots 77$
  One-period forecast (equation 12): $b = 0.24$
  Two-period forecast (equation 14): $b = 0.24$, $w = 0.73$

Without college
Expression for $\overline{Y} = 6{,}000 + 507(Age - 21) - 9(Age - 21)^2$, $Age = 21, \ldots 77$
  One-period forecast (equation 12): $b = 0.13$
  Two-period forecast (equation 14): $b = 0.09$, $w = 0.71$

The age-earnings profiles for families in which the head does and does not have some college are expressed as second degree polynomials in age, measured with panel study data for 1974 (the arbitrarily chosen year in which we begin this reprogramming exercise). We assume that families could observe these $\overline{Y}_t$ values and their own previous incomes, and then estimate the values of b and w that minimize the squared forecast error in predicting their own income for 1974. These parameter values are also shown in the above table. For the one-period forecasting model, the adjustment parameter b in equation 13 ranges from 0.13 to 0.24. For the two-period model the adjustment parameter is slightly lower while the weight of Y_{t-1} in the expression w in equation 14 is from 0.71 to 0.73.

Table 6. Reprogrammed Consumption Functions for Nonaged White Male-headed Families, No Change in Family Income Expected, 1975–78[a]

| | | | | | | | | Parameters implied by coefficients on[b] | | | | |
| | | Regression coefficients | | | | | | A' | | $\hat{F}$ | | $a_2(Y - \hat{Y})$ |
Age class	Pooled N	Constant	A'	$\hat{F}$	H	$Y - \hat{Y}$	R^2	$\delta = 1$ ρ	$\delta = 1.5$ ρ	$\delta = 1$ ρ	$\delta = 1.5$ ρ	C
With some college												
50–64	384	5,121.7 (5.4)	0.273 (14.1)	0.018 (9.6)	0.050 (1.7)	0.777 (7.5)	0.50	0.375	0.637	-0.081	-0.106	-0.058
36–49	584	7,692.0 (8.7)	0.289 (18.0)	0.007 (9.5)	0.116 (4.2)	0.705 (6.4)	0.46	0.406	0.694	-0.070	-0.089	0.010
26–35	800	5,490.6 (10.2)	0.247 (16.7)	0.004 (11.8)	0.103 (5.5)	0.957 (11.8)	0.48	0.328	0.554	-0.058	-0.071	0.023
Without college												
50–64	920	3,757.9 (10.8)	0.191 (17.9)	0.023 (22.7)	0.059 (3.7)	0.866 (14.8)	0.56	0.232	0.386	-0.063	-0.082	-0.015
36–49	1,200	4,231.4 (13.2)	0.276 (23.2)	0.011 (24.9)	0.107 (8.2)	0.946 (20.1)	0.63	0.381	0.644	-0.051	-0.063	0.012
26–35	828	4,262.6 (16.1)	0.190 (14.0)	0.006 (23.1)	0.055 (5.1)	0.847 (16.8)	0.59	0.235	0.289	-0.046	-0.056	0.036
25 and under	228	4,096.0 (9.6)	0.628 (8.3)	0.004 (10.9)	0.193 (5.2)	0.886 (11.1)	0.71	1.689	3.463	-0.045	-0.055	0.040

Source: Same as table 2.
a. The numbers in parentheses are t-statistics.
b. Assuming $r = -0.03$ for the groups with college and -0.025 for those without.

These estimates then permit us to estimate the reprogrammed consumption function as in equation 7 for 1975–78. As new information becomes available on Y_{t-1} for the 1975–78 period, forecasts for both $\hat{Y}_t$ and $\hat{F}_t$ are updated, but the estimated values of the $\overline{Y}_t$ polynomial and of b and w are retained.

As a final point, the interest rate used to discount this income stream (as in equation 6) is the after-tax nominal rate less the anticipated rate of inflation. In this calculation, individual marginal personal income tax rates, as recorded in the panel study, were used as the tax rate, and an average of three previous years' inflation rates was used as the inflation factor. With these assumptions, the sample average values for r were about -0.03 for those with college and -0.025 for those without, the difference attributable to the higher marginal tax rates for the former group.

The reprogrammed consumption function estimates are shown in table 6 for the simple variant where households expect no change in income, table 7 for the one-period forecasting model, and table 8 for the two-period forecasting model. In each case a constant was added to the regression, A was decomposed into financial assets (A') and net equity in owner-occupied housing (H), the coefficients on A and $\hat{F}$ were not constrained to be the same, and the unanticipated income term included in equation 7 was added. Both the coefficients on A' and $\hat{F}$ were used to calculate implicit values of ρ (by equation 4).[11] The values of r used in making these calculations were the sample average values reported above.

Relatively few differences occur among the three income-forecasting variants of the consumption function. The fit is actually best in the first equations with no income forecasting (table 6), next best in the equations with two-period income forecasting (table 8), and worst in the equations with one-period income forecasting (table 7).

For each of the three models the amount of unanticipated income is high, and its coefficient is high. That the amount is high means that even our two-period forecasting equation leaves much income unanticipated; that the coefficient is high, and in particular so much higher than the coefficients of A or $\hat{F}$, means that under the life-cycle assumptions

11. We did not calculate values of ρ implied by the coefficient on H because imputed consumption of housing is included in our construction of C. For most groups, the coefficients on H fall within the range of rent to value multipliers we used in constructing C, and thus can be interpreted as simply measuring part of the dependent variables.

Table 7. Reprogrammed Consumption Functions for Nonaged White Male-headed Families, One-Period Family Income Forecast, 1975–78[a]

								Parameters implied by coefficients on[b]				
								A'		$\hat{F}$		$\dfrac{a_2(Y - \hat{Y})}{C}$
		Regression coefficients										
Age class	Pooled N	Constant	A'	$\hat{F}$	H	$Y - \hat{Y}$	R^2	$\delta = 1$ ρ	$\delta = 1.5$ ρ	$\delta = 1$ ρ	$\delta = 1.5$ ρ	C
With some college												
50–64	384	6,255.9 (4.4)	0.272 (13.5)	0.017 (4.3)	0.072 (2.4)	0.843 (7.7)	0.46	0.373	0.633	−0.085	−0.111	−0.001
36–49	584	9,837.7 (7.0)	0.283 (17.2)	0.005 (2.8)	0.140 (5.0)	0.975 (8.6)	0.44	0.395	0.672	−0.083	−0.109	0.033
26–35	800	9,478.0 (10.7)	0.236 (15.4)	0.001 (1.7)	0.118 (6.2)	1.114 (13.1)	0.45	0.309	0.520	−0.094	−0.125	0.028
Without college												
50–64	920	3,113.1 (6.1)	0.185 (16.0)	0.025 (14.2)	0.084 (4.8)	0.874 (13.6)	0.48	0.223	0.370	−0.057	−0.072	−0.037
36–49	1,200	4,837.6 (7.9)	0.297 (22.0)	0.009 (9.1)	0.176 (12.4)	0.932 (17.2)	0.53	0.422	0.718	−0.059	−0.076	0.008
26–35	828	5,910.0 (11.3)	0.183 (11.0)	0.003 (7.1)	0.094 (7.2)	0.812 (13.1)	0.38	0.224	0.371	−0.066	−0.085	0.025
25 and under	228	5,193.9 (6.1)	0.699 (7.8)	0.002 (3.2)	0.290 (6.9)	0.885 (9.0)	0.59	2.322	5.133	−0.062	−0.080	0.047

Source: Same as table 2.

a. The numbers in parentheses are t-statistics.

b. Assuming $r = -0.03$ for the groups with college and -0.025 for those without.

Table 8. Reprogrammed Consumption Functions for Nonaged White Male-headed Families, Two-Period Family Income Forecast, 1975–78[a]

| Age class | Pooled N | Regression coefficients | | | | | | Parameters implied by coefficients on[b] | | | | |
		Constant	A'	F̂	H	$Y - \hat{Y}$	R^2	A' $\delta = 1$ ρ	A' $\delta = 1.5$ ρ	F̂ $\delta = 1$ ρ	F̂ $\delta = 1.5$ ρ	$\frac{a_2(Y - \hat{Y})}{C}$
With some college												
50–64	384	5,877.7 (4.3)	0.277 (13.8)	0.017 (4.8)	0.069 (2.4)	0.904 (7.5)	0.47	0.383	0.651	−0.085	−0.111	−0.003
36–49	584	9,088.7 (6.6)	0.284 (17.2)	0.005 (3.3)	0.148 (5.3)	0.954 (8.1)	0.43	0.397	0.676	−0.083	−0.109	0.030
26–35	800	9,161.1 (10.5)	0.242 (15.8)	0.001 (2.0)	0.124 (6.5)	1.164 (13.3)	0.45	0.319	0.539	−0.094	−0.125	0.033
Without college												
50–64	920	3,124.1 (6.9)	0.140 (17.0)	0.026 (17.0)	0.072 (4.3)	0.918 (14.3)	0.52	0.153	0.255	−0.054	−0.067	−0.036
36–49	1,200	3,628.0 (6.8)	0.295 (22.6)	0.011 (13.0)	0.165 (11.8)	0.922 (17.5)	0.55	0.418	0.711	−0.051	−0.063	0.010
26–35	828	5,366.6 (11.3)	0.184 (11.6)	0.004 (8.8)	0.089 (7.2)	0.890 (14.5)	0.43	0.225	0.374	−0.058	−0.074	0.035
25 and under	228	5,092.5 (6.6)	0.715 (8.4)	0.002 (3.5)	0.291 (7.2)	0.882 (9.8)	0.62	2.509	5.656	−0.062	−0.080	0.054

Source: Same as table 2.
a. The numbers in parentheses are t-statistics.
b. Assuming $r = -0.03$ for the groups with college and -0.025 for those without.

households appear to regard this income flow as recurrent. In the parlance of the rational expectations literature, households are behaving as if even the two-period forecasting rule is not giving efficient forecasts of income. But what does not jibe with rational expectations logic is that the contribution of unanticipated income to consumption does *not* fall as the income-forecasting equation uses more information and becomes more efficient (using the rational expectations meaning of that word). In a comparison of this contribution, in the right column of the three tables, it can be seen that the contributions are least, and the coefficients are least, for the most simpleminded forecasting equation.

The picture that emerges from all this is that households consume on the basis of very simpleminded income forecasts. In fact, the model that best explains consumption is that households forecast no change in their income at all, even in the face of systematic evidence that income does change over time. Should this finding be substantiated with other bodies of data and for other types of time-related behavior, one can imagine significant changes in the ways that economists formulate and model household behavior where future expectations are important.

Perhaps the most striking result of the regressions is that the coefficients on A' and $\hat{F}$, which should be identical according to the life-cycle model, are significantly different from each other for all groups and for all forecasting rules. Moreover, while the coefficients on $\hat{F}$ imply values of ρ that are somewhat more negative than the time-series estimates of tables 3, 4, and 5, the coefficients on A' imply values of ρ that are positive and that appear to be implausibly high. For all of the college-educated groups, the subjective rates of discount implied by these coefficients exceed 0.30 when δ is unity and exceed 0.5 when δ is 1.5. Moreover, even if we ignore the youngest noncollege group, for whom the estimated coefficients on A' appear simply bizarre, the regressions imply that households consume on the order of a quarter of their financial assets each year.

It is hard to know what to make of these results. Trivially, we conclude that households treat financial assets and the present value of future earnings very differently, contrary to the hypothesis of the standard life-cycle model. In the next section of the paper, we show that uncertainty about future labor income can help explain the negative values of ρ implied by the coefficients on $\hat{F}$; yet the coefficients on A' remain implausibly high in and of themselves. One possibility, which we have not yet been able to explore, is that households that have any financial assets at all are simply more prone to consume than those that do not, perhaps because such households are generally more secure about their futures. In this interpretation, the coefficients on A' are high because the mere presence of any financial assets shifts the consumption function upward.

In any event, the majority of households in the sample have essentially no financial assets at all, and for all but the most elderly college-educated group the median ratio of A' to F is less than 1 percent. (For the top group it is all of 2.5 percent.) Thus, even though the coefficients on A' are high and have high t-statistics, A' accounts for only a very small fraction of total consumption compared to $\hat{F}$. Because of this, and because the data in tables 3, 4, and 5 imply rising consumption over time, we conclude that the negative estimates of ρ derived from the coefficients on $\hat{F}$ are more reliable than the positive estimates derived from A'.

As noted above, the values of ρ implied by the coefficients on F in the reprogramming model are even more negative than those implied by either cross-sectional or the simple time-series versions of the model. Because our measurement of ρ comes from calculations of consumption growth in the presence of known values of r (we do not independently observe ρ), an important reason for this result is that in the reprogramming model we use negative values of r (derived from the data) rather than simply assuming that r is zero, as we did earlier. These ρ values run from -0.045 to -0.125, suggesting (as before) that the household consumption path will be rising even when reprogramming is taken into account. To put this another way, the time-series, cross-sectional inconsistency mentioned above is clearly resolved in favor of the time-series estimates—if anything, even the time-series estimates of ρ were not negative enough.

These results then yield three reasons why household consumption rises over time, with the importance of the three varying for different groups. Because our new estimate of ρ, with careful assumptions about g and r, is strongly negative, the perfect-forecast life-cycle path given by equation 5 is rising for all groups. Added onto this finding is the reprogramming term. Members of the oldest group habitually overpredict their income—that is, they assume no change when they should anticipate declines—whichever forecasting model they use. For them, average unanticipated income is negative, the contribution to consumption is negative, and then next year the recomputed $\hat{F}$ will be lowered. Therefore, the basic trend in household consumption given by the negative ρ is offset, and the consumption path is quite stable. But for the other groups, all three forecasting variants systematically underpredict income, causing a one-shot rise owing to the unanticipated income term and then a sustained rise as $\hat{F}$ is recomputed. For these groups all three forces point in the direction of rising consumption paths, even when real interest rates are negative.

Although our main empirical efforts have been devoted to resolving an inconsistency between microeconomic time-series and cross-sectional consumption models, we should mention that macroeconomics too may have played some role in shaping our actual results. Over the 1975–78 period real per family consumption rose an average of 2.3 percent per year, faster than in years immediately before or after this period. Had we estimated the reprogrammed function over this longer span, our growth rates of consumption would have been smaller and our estimates of ρ would presumably have been closer to r. The degree to which income was underpredicted in general would perhaps be lowered also.

The Life Cycle with Uncertainty

The final step in the process tries to incorporate uncertainty into a life-cycle model. Previously we allowed life-cycle planners to make new forecasts when the old ones were seen to be wrong, but we had not worked uncertainty explicitly into the process. When we add uncertainty, about both labor incomes and interest rates, two more rationales for the empirically observed rising consumption paths surface.

A Theoretical Life-Cycle Model with Uncertainty

Let us suppose that we have a family that will live for only two periods. If C_0 is current consumption and C_1 is next period's consumption, the family's lifetime utility is

$$(16) \qquad U(C_0) + E[U(C_1)],$$

where $U(C) = C^{1-\delta}/(1 - \delta)$ as before. We assume that there are no completely risk-free assets in the economy, implying that the interest rate on current savings is a next-period realization from a random variable $\tilde{r}$. Let current and next-period income be Y_0 and Y_1.

Suppose first that there is an interest rate but not income uncertainty. If we let next period's labor income equal zero for simplicity, a young family must solve

(17) $$\frac{\text{Max}}{C_0}\left(U(C_0) + E\{U[(1 + \tilde{r})(Y_0 - C_0)]\} \right),$$

which yields

(18) $$C_0 = Y_0 / \left(1 + \{E[(1 + \tilde{r})^{1-\delta}]\}\right)^{1/\delta}.$$

If we were to remove the variance of $\tilde{r}$ without changing its mean,

(19) $$C_0^* = Y_0 / [1 + (1 + \bar{r})^{(1-\delta)/\delta}].$$

Comparing equations 18 and 19, we recognize that $C_0^* > C_0$ when $(1 + \bar{r})^{1-\delta} < E[(1 + \tilde{r})^{1-\delta}]$, or when $\delta > 1$. In words, variance in $\tilde{r}$ leads families to save more to guard themselves against future realizations of $\tilde{r}$, but the more they save, the larger the percentage of their lifetime assets they expose to risk. The two considerations just balance when $\delta = 1$; then the optimal level of C_0 is the same with or without variance in $\tilde{r}$. But when $\delta > 1$, as many argue it is, the first consideration dominates the second, families save more with variance in $\tilde{r}$, and stochastic consumption paths are rising. (Recall that $\delta > 1$ implies a very sharp curvature for the $C_0 - C_1$ isoquants. That is, the elasticity of substitution between consumption in different periods is less than one, implying that consumption plans are not very responsive to known and certain changes in interest rates.) Uncertainty in $\tilde{r}$ will then provide one explanation for rising consumption levels, as long as $\delta > 1$.

We then examine the case in which next period's labor income is positive and has a random variation, while there is no interest rate uncertainty. The first-order condition becomes

(20) $$C_0^{-\delta} = E\{(1+\tilde{r})[(Y_0-C_0)(1+\tilde{r}) + \overline{Y}_1]^{-\delta}\}.$$

If $\overline{C}_0$ is the maximizing value of C_0 in the nonstochastic case (when $\overline{Y} = E[\overline{Y}]$ is substituted for $\overline{Y}_1$), $\overline{C}_0 > C_0$ whenever $\delta > 0$. In this case the qualitative result does not depend on δ: for all values of $\delta > 0$, second-period income uncertainty leads to more first-period saving and a rising consumption path, as families try to ensure themselves against future income fluctuations. This income uncertainty has the same effect as a reduction in the internal rate of time preference and forms another reason why it might be sensible to observe negative values of ρ in nonstochastic models of consumption.

A Simulation Model

These two rationales for rising consumption paths are illustrated by a highly simplified simulation model. A family is assumed to live six periods and draw an expected annual labor income of $10,000 for the first four periods. There are two types of income uncertainty: transitory and persistent. These uncertainties are reflected in the income equation

$$(21) \qquad Y_t = 10,000 + \bar{v}_t + \bar{u}_t,$$

where $\bar{v}_t$ is independently and identically distributed (iid) with mean zero and standard deviation σ_v, while $\bar{u}$ follows a random walk process,

$$(22) \qquad \bar{u}_t = \bar{u}_{t-1} + \bar{x}_t,$$

where $\bar{x}_t$ is iid with mean zero and standard deviation σ_x.[12] We also allow for shocks in r independent of $\bar{x}_t$ and $\bar{v}_t$.

Using numbers resembling those in Hall and Mishkin,[13] we set $\sigma_v = 1,930$ and $\sigma_x = 1,220$. This implies, roughly speaking, that a family with a mean next-period income of $10,000 has seven chances in ten of experiencing an actual income between $7,720 and $12,280 and nineteen chances in twenty of an income between $5,440 and $14,560. As in our nonstochastic models, we assume that at time t the family observes Y_t and can separately identify v_t and u_t, or tell temporary from permanent shocks. The mean of $\bar{r}$, $\bar{r}$, is set equal to zero, meaning that we assume no net real return on saving, on the average. We set $\sigma_r = 0.03$, implying that a family has seven chances in ten of realizing, over one period, a return between -3 and 3 percent on its savings, and nineteen chances in twenty of realizing between -6 and 6 percent. We then use dynamic programming to generate consumption functions for each of the six periods of life. The consumption functions plus our distribution assumptions for $\bar{r}$, $\bar{v}$, and $\bar{x}$ allow us to assign probabilities to different levels of

---

12. In other words, realizations $v_t, v_{t+1}, \ldots$ for the shock term v will be independently derived samplings from a common random variable, and the same will apply in the case of $x_t, x_{t+1}, \ldots$. Notice that with the so-called random walks (see equation 22) a current u reflects the sum of all previous shocks x. Thus a realization of x_t affects u_t and, with the same potency, $u_{t+1}, u_{t+2}, \ldots$. In equation 21, on the other hand, after time t, v_t no longer plays any role.

13. "Sensitivity of Consumption to Transitory Income."

Table 9. Life-Cycle Consumption Simulation
Dollars

Life period	Mean income	Mean asset holdings beginning of period	Mean consumption	Mean C_t/C_{t-1}
$\delta = 1.0$				
1	10,000	0	5,921	...
2	10,000	4,079	6,677	1.128
3	10,000	7,403	6,802	1.019
4	10,000	10,600	6,879	1.011
5	0	13,720	6,861	0.997
6	0	6,861	6,861	1.000
$\delta = 2.0$				
1	10,000	0	5,802	...
2	10,000	4,198	6,803	1.172
3	10,000	7,396	6,769	0.995
4	10,000	10,630	6,890	1.018
5	0	13,740	6,866	0.996
6	0	6,870	6,870	1.000

Source: Authors' simulations as described in the text.

asset holdings at each age. Using these probabilities, we can then derive mean asset holdings and consumption figures.

Table 9 shows mean asset profiles with the parameters specified above. In the absence of any uncertainty, households would consume their earnings of $40,000 ($10,000 in each of their four working periods) equally over the six periods they live; hence each of the consumption levels would be $6,667 per period. With uncertainty, utility-maximizing behavior implies extra saving early in life and an average lifetime consumption growth rate of about 3 percent. Most of this saving comes in the first period. Consumption in the last three periods is approximately the same.

Table 10 enables us to compare consumption and asset figures for different amounts of risk. As expected, the interest rate uncertainty has little effect on household saving. The variances for $\bar{x}$ and $\bar{v}$ are more important. Because shocks in x affect a family's income contemporaneously and in the future (see equation 22), whereas a shock in v has an influence only currently, we would anticipate that variance in x would matter more than variance in v. In fact, the table implies that for each unit of increase in σ_x^2 a family's average (per period) asset holdings rise by one-third more than for each unit increase in σ_v^2.

As our theoretical demonstration indicated, income uncertainty of

Table 10. The Effects on Consumption of Reducing Different Types of Uncertainty
$\delta = 1$

Life period	Mean consumption			
	Given parameters	Halve σ_v^2	Halve σ_x^2	Halve σ_r^2
1	5,921	6,115	6,007	5,920
2	6,677	6,680	6,700	6,676
3	6,802	6,776	6,786	6,801
4	6,879	6,822	6,848	6,880
5	6,861	6,804	6,830	6,861
6	6,861	6,804	6,830	6,861
Average mean asset holdings	7,112	6,988	7,047	7,112
Lifetime consumption growth rate	0.030	0.021	0.026	0.030

Source: Same as table 9.

the type we have considered does seem to cause consumption profiles to rise with age. The amount depends on what sort of stochastic variance is being assumed, but generally reductions in σ_v^2 and σ_x^2 will reduce the average slope of household consumption paths. Reductions in σ_r^2 seem to make virtually no difference, although this might change if we allowed much longer life spans or permanent as well as temporary random changes in r. While anticipated income uncertainty does explain the empirical results described above, this explanation alone is unlikely to suffice because even big alterations in the anticipated variance of income lead to relatively modest changes in the slope of the consumption path as long as δ is close to one.

Conclusions

This paper has attempted to construct a life-cycle consumption model that deals with various types of information gaps and to estimate the model with longitudinal panel data. Without information gaps of any sort, panel data illustrate an apparent inconsistency in the life-cycle model. Cross-sectional consumption function coefficients on income are such that the implicit household rate of time preference, ρ, is close to zero (or at least close to the assumed value of r). Time-series examinations of individual household consumption paths show in general that consumption rises over time, as if ρ were negative.

Several refinements might resolve the inconsistency. Disaggregating the data more finely—by computing consumption over a three-year period, eliminating families that might have borrowing constraints, and eliminating families showing large consumption growth as they get out of college—plays a small role. Constructing a reprogramming model of consumption behavior plays a larger role, but only partly because the reprogramming term lets families adjust to a new consumption plan as new income data arrive. Even when reprogramming of this sort is included, all families still show rising consumption paths and implicitly a negative internal rate of time preference. The inconsistency is, in effect, resolved in favor of the time-series estimates of family consumption behavior. Moreover, the reprogramming model generates a new inconsistency: it shows that households treat lifetime income very differently from the way they treat financial assets, contrary to the predictions of the life-cycle model.

The other way to explain the rising consumption profiles, with which we have only begun to experiment, is by constructing a full-blown stochastic dynamic programming model with uncertainty. Interest rate uncertainty plays a small role in determining the slope of the consumption path in such a model: there is an insurance motive for saving more to protect against the uncertainty, but it is approximately offset by the fact that added saving adds to income variance when the interest rate is variable. However, in our examples income uncertainty does lead rational families to save more to protect themselves, and this fact could explain some of the observed growth in household consumption and partly rationalize our negative values for ρ.

Finally, we recall that the consumption-saving decision is only one of many that could be modeled in this way. We have devised two approaches for life-cycle planning under uncertainty—approaches that seem to reflect reality yet are simple enough to be used in dynamic simulations. Even on the question we are looking at, consumption-saving, it would be necessary to experiment with different and more elaborate household income forecasting schemes and to work in the influence of pension wealth and perhaps interest rate intertemporal substitution. The approach should also be tried for different data periods to see if reprogramming behavior is dependent on the growth or cyclical position of the economy. Moreover, the same approach should be extended to other aspects of household behavior, such as labor supply, to see if the same type of behavior explains other important household decisions.

Comment by John B. Shoven

This paper is an extended attempt to test the life-cycle model empirically. Although economists have found this model appealing, it has played to mixed reviews when the data are examined. The paper highlights the inconsistencies between the results of time-series analyses of the life-cycle model and cross-sectional studies, and attempts to reconcile these results by positing a reprogramming model in which households revise their lifetime plans as more information comes in.

The authors' argument for a reprogramming version of the life-cycle model is valid but probably not new. In fact, I can think of no other alternative formulation: I believe that this has always been the essence of the life-cycle theory. The point is that families have to maximize the lifetime utility with whatever information they have; if additional information comes, they want to reformulate the plan. Although the model may always have rested on this view, empirical applications have seldom examined reprogramming because the requirements for data are formidable. Researchers need to follow people longitudinally to assess what information they acquire and how it affects behavior.

The authors take a rather narrow view of the information families use in reprogramming. Their families project labor income using the appropriate age-earnings profile. Then the families reprogram each period according to how their income or earnings come out relative to their projections. Presumably, a family could do better than that. For instance, a family should be able to separate income changes that result from changes in wage rates from those that result from working overtime. The family also has other information. For instance, children are born, marriages and divorces occur, doctors deliver verdicts on good or bad health, and investments may do well or poorly. Any of these kinds of information, not recognized in the authors' model, might be sufficient cause for reprogramming.

The authors use data from the Panel Study of Income Dynamics for the period 1967 to 1979. The authors here concentrate on the saving-consumption behavior of these households. The sample is overrepresentative of nonwhite households, of female-headed households, and particularly of households with low incomes because the study was originally designed for poverty analysis and was sponsored by the now defunct Office of Economic Opportunity. The explicit assumption of the life-cycle model—that households face perfect capital markets with the same borrowing and lending rates—is particularly inappropriate for this population. Such people may anticipate rising income, and their true preferences may be such that they would like to have a consumption profile that grows less steeply with time then their income profile, but liquidity constraints may deny them this opportunity. Many of us find the life-cycle model intuitively appealing for some groups in the population, but unfortunately it is not these groups.

I now turn to the data. What one needs is data on income, consumption, and wealth over time. Perhaps the authors really extract from the Panel Study of Income Dynamics all and only the information it contains, but I fear they may have found more.

Let us start with the data on wealth. The panel study contains estimates of housing wealth but only of income from such sources as interest, dividends, trust funds, and royalties. The authors capitalize the income flows from financial assets by dividing the first $300 of capital income by the savings and loan passbook savings rate and the remainder of capital income flows by the Aaa bond rate. I think this approximation is rough. Dividends, for example, represent real income (which should be capitalized with a real discount rate) while interest represents nominal income (which should be capitalized with a nominal discount rate). But the authors' procedure treats them alike. Furthermore, they ignore retained earnings. They do not mention social security wealth or other forms of pension wealth—the main forms of wealth for at least the older households in the sample. Automobiles represent a surprisingly large fraction of household wealth, particularly for the poor, but automobiles are not included in their statistics.

The treatment of home equity is also tricky. During the 1970s many people had mortgages at interest rates that fell increasingly below market rates, resulting in shrinkage in the present market value of mortgage debt. But the importance of this fact depends on how long a household is going to keep this below-market instrument. Should mortgage debt be carried at redemption or market value? The difference there could change the net housing equity a great deal.

The burden of all of these remarks is that I have little faith in the household wealth that the authors use in their analysis. In fact, I have far less confidence than I would if they had used wealth data from the Retirement History Survey.

Turning next to the consumption data, I would point out that there are not any consumption data in the panel study. We can, of course, infer consumption from the identity that consumption is equal to income less saving. Income is reported, and saving equals the change in wealth, corrected for some capital gains items. In other words, the authors derive consumption by subtracting the asset values that I just suggested were unreliable and probably biased from the relatively good data on income reported in the panel study. To try to reassure themselves, the authors run their derived consumption series on GNP consumption figures (table 1). I was not reassured. The coefficient on GNP consumption is significantly different from zero, but it is also significantly different from one. I cannot be sure how much information is contained in these data.

Leaving the data and turning to the results, I find that the central issue is how to reconcile the seemingly inconsistent results generated by time-series and cross-sectional estimates. The variable on which the authors focus is ρ, the rate of time preference or bonus that a household must receive to postpone \$1 of current consumption. In effect, they stipulate values for each of the other variables—g, the growth of earnings; r, the rate of interest; T, the length of the lifetime households are assumed to expect; and δ, the curvature of the iso-utility curves—and calculate the value of ρ that most closely approximates observed behavior.

The cross-sectional estimates of ρ cluster around -0.01, indicating that people have negative time preference; they would be indifferent to the choice between \$1.00 of consumption today and \$0.99 next year. This result is surprising, as economists think most people require a reward to defer consumption. If this result is a surprise, the time-series estimates are shockers. These estimates are even more negative, clustering in the range from -0.04 to -0.12. These results explain the observed fact that the consumption of young people in the sample is growing fast, 8 percent for the youngest white male-headed families and 4 percent for other groups. This growth occurs in the face of a zero real interest rate. The only way within their model that the authors could reconcile this fact with the assumed values of the other parameters is by asserting that people prefer future to present consumption.

Unfortunately, the estimates of ρ based on cross-sectional and time-series data are very different, not only from the expected positive values but also from each other. The need to reconcile these results brings the authors to their reprogramming model. Each person views his income as depending, in the long run, on an age-earnings profile, but current earnings influence the forecasts. They estimate alternative parameters showing the degree to which the deviation of actual income from these profiles influences consumption.

I worry about their methods. If one is looking at couples, only the male may be working now, but the household may anticipate at some point in the future that both spouses will be working. Factors such as that are omitted from this model, but they are likely to be important in fact.

The estimates of ρ resulting from this effort at reconciliation are large and negative (about 8 percent) and are consistent with the time-series results. For these equations, the authors use the after-tax interest rates for each household, a better procedure than that used earlier. Some of the other results are a bit surprising. The coefficient on the expected present value of wealth is quite low. The marginal propensity to consume unanticipated income, in contrast, is quite high, 0.8 or higher.

Taken together, these results do explain the growing consumption profiles, but the implied motivations of people are odd. The rate of time preference seems to be negative, indicating that people prefer future to present consumption. Thus saving is considered attractive even though people face a negative rate of return because, net of tax, real interest rates are negative. But people are continually surprised by getting more than they expected. These surprises cause people to keep raising their estimates of their lifetime wealth, and therefore their consumption goes up.

What does one learn from this paper, assuming for the moment that my abiding doubts about the data are without substance? Was the purpose of the paper to test the life-cycle model, or was it to determine what parameters reconcile the model with the data? I think the paper is more the latter than the former. If so, do these parameter estimates increase or decrease one's sense that the life-cycle model is realistic? Mine is decreased because I find implausible the rate of time preference of -8 percent.

In short, a way has been found to reconcile the model with observed behavior, but making it consistent leads to some implausible parameter estimates. Overall, this paper indicts, rather than supports, the life-cycle model.

The Painful Prescription

HENRY J. AARON and
WILLIAM B. SCHWARTZ

For three decades the cost of hospital care has been rising faster than inflation or the growth of population. The continued development of sophisticated technology, as well as rising incomes and aging of the population, promises further increases in health care expenditure. A large part of this growth has gone for dramatically effective diagnostic and therapeutic advances. But a growing share has gone for the purchase of services that produce perceptible, but marginal, benefits at high cost. Both federal and state governments have passed legislation to try to hold down spending, but their efforts have been piecemeal and not generally effective. By contrast, Britain has managed to curtail the real growth of medical expenditures and spends barely half as much per capita on hospital care as does the United States. These budget limits have forced the British to make difficult choices.

In this book Henry J. Aaron and William B. Schwartz examine how the British have made those choices and draw inferences about how Americans would respond should they undertake to sharply reduce growth of medical spending. After describing the British health care system, they examine ten important medical procedures, comparing the British and American levels of care. They find that Britain provides less than the United States of some services, such as hemodialysis and coronary artery surgery. In other cases, such as radiotherapy for cancer patients, Britain provides the same amount of care. The authors then discuss the values that motivate rationing decisions and analyze the responses of British patients and physicians. In the final chapter they consider how rationing would work in the United States—what form it might take, what benefits might be given up, and what American reactions might be. Enforcement of a limit on medical spending will be much more difficult in the United States than in Britain because American patients have come to expect that all possible beneficial care will be made available to them.

Henry J. Aaron is a senior fellow in the Brookings Economic Studies program and professor of economics at the University of Maryland; William B. Schwartz is Vannevar Bush University Professor, professor of medicine at Tufts University, and senior physician at the New England Medical Center. This volume is the twenty-third in the Brookings Studies in Social Economics series.

161 pp./1984/cloth and paper

Sheila R. Zedlewski

The Private Pension System to the Year 2020

The U.S. retirement income system consists of social security, many separate pension programs for private employees, a program for government employees, and private savings. Private pensions have been studied extensively of late because they form an increasing share of retirement income. People who have pensions as well as social security benefits enjoy a much higher standard of living in retirement than those without pensions. Because few expect social security to be liberalized, many are looking toward the private pension system to raise future retirement income.

Currently only a minority of the retired population has a private pension. For example, in 1979 just 16 percent of single persons and 32 percent of married couples aged 65 and over had some income from private pensions.[1] A worker may not become entitled to a pension for several reasons. First, not all private employers offer pension plans. In 1978, for example, about one-half of all wage-and-salary workers aged 25 and over were covered by a private plan.[2] Second, coverage does not

Many people made important contributions to the development of the microsimulation model used for the projections in this paper. I am particularly grateful to James Schulz of Brandeis University, who pioneered the work to provide a full microsimulation of private pension plan provisions for the original DYNASIM model; Richard Wertheimer, who managed the model's development at the Urban Institute; Gary Hendricks, who initiated the effort to redesign the original version of the model for more effective use in retirement policy analyses; Jon Johnson, who redesigned the computer system at the institute; and Al Gillespie, who supplied valuable programming assistance.

1. March 1980 Current Population Survey; and Employee Benefit Research Institute, *Retirement Income Opportunities in an Aging America: Income Levels and Adequacy* (Washington, D.C.: EBRI, 1982), p. 34.

2. See President's Commission on Pension Policy, *Coming of Age: Toward a National Retirement Income Policy* (Washington, D.C.: The Commission, 1982), p. 13.

ensure benefit entitlement in old age. A covered worker must meet the plan's participation rules, which usually impose standards on age and tenure for plan entry and include a minimum hours requirement to maintain participation. Workers who are eligible to participate must also meet the plan's vesting requirements to ensure their future retirement benefits.

Some recent changes in the rules governing entitlement should result in significant increases in pension eligibility. Already coverage of workers has doubled since 1950, and plan participation rules have also been liberalized so that fewer covered workers are excluded. The 1974 Employee Retirement Income Security Act (ERISA) imposed a set of minimum standards on plan participation and established some minimum standards for vesting rules. The net effect of the new rules should be an increase in private pension income for future retirees.

However, workers could benefit from additional improvements in pension plan provisions. The lack of universal coverage affects some groups of workers more than others. For example, 60 percent of male wage-and-salary workers aged 25 and over were covered in 1978, compared with 38 percent of their female counterparts. Moreover, a worker who experiences frequent breaks in service may either fail to meet vesting requirements, or receive a very small pension because the benefit is usually based on earnings and service during employment with no adjustment for wage or price growth until the time of retirement. In addition, pension benefits are rarely adjusted for general wage or price growth during the period of retirement. Thus even workers who manage to secure benefit eligibility find that the value of the pension declines over time. During the 1969–75 period of high inflation, for example, older retired people with private pensions experienced a significant decline in real income.[3]

This paper presents the results of a set of microsimulations of the private pension system that (1) project the effects of recent changes in pension rules and (2) test the effectiveness of several changes in these rules. Three pension rule changes were simulated: (1) universal coverage for all private sector employees, (2) portability of pension credits from one job to another, and (3) price-indexing of benefits for retirees.

The Urban Institute's dynamic simulation of income model (DYNA-

---

3. Roberta Barnes and Sheila R. Zedlewski, "The Impact of Inflation on the Income and Expenditures of Elderly Families," Urban Institute Research Report 1401-01 (Washington, D.C.: Urban Institute, October 1981).

SIM) was used to make the projections.[4] A 60,000-person sample from the 1973 Current Population Survey was aged to the year 2020. The aging process included procedures to simulate all the main demographic and labor market events in sample members' life histories. These simulated data were saved and used to project social security and private employer pension benefits. The simulations demonstrate the use of microsimulation in the area of retirement income analyses. This model allows one to run controlled experiments to measure the effects of alternative policies. The three pension scenarios illustrate the kind of experiment one can perform; they are not policy suggestions. The main projections of the simulations are the following.

—Under present pension rules, between 1982 and 2020 there will be a dramatic growth in the number and proportion of older people who have private employer pensions, and retirement income from these pensions will more than double for people 65 and over.

—Under the full price-indexing scenario, the benefits rise significantly. For example, in 2020 the benefits of men 68 through 71 and men 72 and over are 43 percent and 96 percent higher, respectively, than under the base run.

—Under the universal coverage scenario, women benefit the most. In 2020, 60 percent of women 65 through 71 receive an employer pension, compared with 40 percent under the base run. The comparable figures for men are 75 percent and 65 percent.

—Under the portable pension scenario, the real levels of employer pension benefits rise even more than under the base run.

Methodology

The DYNASIM system has two principal models. The first, the family and earnings history (FEH) model, simulates annual demographic and

4. This model has developed over many years at the Urban Institute. Its first implementation is described in Guy Orcutt and others, *Policy Exploration through Microanalytic Simulation* (Urban Institute, 1976). The most recent version is described in "The Dynamic Simulation of Income Model," vol. 1 (revised): Jon Johnson, Richard Wertheimer, and Sheila R. Zedlewski, "The Family and Earnings History Model," Urban Institute Project Report 1434-03 (November 1983); and vol. 2: Jon Johnson and Sheila R. Zedlewski, "The Jobs and Benefits History Model" (Urban Institute, December 1982).

labor force behavior. Included in the demographic simulation are leaving home, death, birth, marriage, divorce, geographic mobility, education, and disability. Labor force behavior includes labor force participation, hours worked, hours unemployed, and annual earnings. The main output of this model is a set of longitudinal demographic and labor force histories for each person in the sample. The second, the jobs and benefits history (JBH) model, simulates a job history and a retirement benefits history for each person in the sample, using the longitudinal history files produced by the FEH model as its input. The JBH model then simulates job change, industry, employer pension coverage and participation, retirement age, social security benefits, and pension benefits.

To obtain the estimates presented here, a sample of the U.S. population was aged to the year 2020 by using the family and earnings history model. Successive surveys of the population were taken during the simulation to produce cross sections of the population for 1982, 2000, and 2020. These files were used as input in the jobs and benefits history model, and social security pension benefits were projected for people 58 and over in each of the target years. Benefits were projected first by simulating the current system throughout the period, then by altering the pension model to simulate three different scenarios—universal coverage for all private sector employees, portability of pension credits within the private pension system, and indexing of private pension benefits. In each one all other assumptions were held constant, although events that are interdependent may change. For example, higher pension benefits or their wider dissemination may decrease the average age at retirement.

Creation of an Earnings History File

As mentioned, the family and earnings history model makes population and economic projections by predicting major demographic and economic events for each person in the simulation in a way that closely approximates actual social and economic life processes. For instance, everyone in the sample population is exposed to a probability of dying each year based on his or her sex, race, age, education, marital status, and, for women, parity. Similarly, labor force participation is determined by age, race, sex, marital status, disability status, presence of young

Table 1. Main Events Simulated by the Family and Earnings History Model

Event or characteristic	Principal determinants
Birth	Marital status, age, race, education, number of previous live births
Death	Age, race, sex, education, marital status, parity of women, current year
First marriage	Age, race, sex, education, hours worked, wage rate, transfer income, current year, year of birth
Remarriage	Age, sex, marital status (widowed or divorced), current year, year last marriage ended
Divorce	Age, race, disability status, unemployment status of husband, earnings of wife, length of marriage, year of marriage, current simulation year
Education (probability of advancing a grade)	Age, race, sex, education of head of family, number of grades completed
Geographic location (region and size of SMSA)	Age, sex, education, and marital status of family head or single individual, duration of marriage, region and current SMSA size
Disability	Age, race, sex, education, marital status, whether disabled in previous year
Labor force participation	Age, race, sex, presence of disability, whether participated in previous year, other income, marital status and presence of child under six for women, aggregate unemployment rate
Hours of labor supplied	Age, race, sex, education, marital status, presence of child under six, expected wage, labor force supply in previous year
Hours of unemployment	Age, race, sex, education, marital status, presence of child under six, unemployment in previous year, aggregate unemployment rate
Wage rate	Age, race, sex, education, marital status, region, disability status, wage in previous year, aggregate level of income

children in the family, and past labor force participation. Thus the model produces, one year at a time, the life history of each person in the sample.

Table 1 lists the events simulated in the FEH model and the main factors determining the outcome of each event. The basic substance of the model is an extensive set of functions that range from probability tables to equations based on regression analysis. The functions may be structured either to take into account certain strong correlations in the probability of an event occurring, or to capture the results of sophisticated behavioral analysis.[5]

5. The interested reader will find the details of all these functions in Johnson, Wertheimer, and Zedlewski, ''Family and Earnings History Model.''

SIMULATION DATA BASE. The 1973 Current Population Survey matched with social security earnings records (CPS-SER) was used as the initial simulation population, drawing a statistically representative, self-weighted population of 60,000 people from the survey. (This survey is the most recent data base representative of the entire U.S. population with matched social security earnings records.) The social security benefits model uses these earnings history data to calculate benefits, and the FEH model updates the history each year. The historical information (1950–72), of course, has a declining effect on the results of the benefits model over time.

PROJECTION ASSUMPTIONS. The initial 1973 CPS-SER data file was then aged to 2020. Each event in the model is simulated on probabilities, according to the parameters embedded in each module. But some important *aggregates* of the model, such as birthrates, mortality rates, and labor force participation rates, were lined up to either known historical data or external projection series. Thus the paths for some aggregates were controlled, but the operating characteristics of the model determined the distributions for each of the events simulated.

This process of targeting the simulation of certain events was accomplished by examining the unadjusted DYNASIM predictions to historic or projected time series and calculating adjustment factors to apply to the individual probabilities. First, all events were aligned to available historical data; then aggregate model outcomes were adjusted to closely approximate some future aggregate trends, using the assumptions in the 1981 report of the Trustees of the Old-Age and Survivors Insurance Trust Funds.[6] The model outcomes approximate the intermediate set (II-B) of demographic and economic assumptions, which are neither optimistic nor pessimistic regarding the likely future fiscal health of the old-age, survivors, and disability insurance program.

The II-B assumptions that were followed are:

—fertility rates rise from the current level of about 1.8 births per woman to 2.1 in 2005;

—mortality rates improve by 0.59 percent a year until 2005;

—ultimate labor force participation rates reached by 2000 decline

---

6. *1981 Annual Report of the Board of Trustees of the Federal Old-Age and Survivors Insurance and Disability Insurance Trust Funds* (Government Printing Office, 1981). For data listed below, see pp. 29, 32, and 75–76.

slightly for men (0.4 percent) and rise by 8.4 percent for women from 1980 levels;

—the aggregate average unemployment rate declines gradually from 1981 to an ultimate rate of 5 percent by 1999;

—the real increase in earnings rises to an ultimate rate of 1.5 percent a year by 1995.

MODEL OUTCOMES. The family and earnings history model produces reasonably accurate projections of various forms of behavior when it is used to project for the period 1973–77. This span of years follows the year of the initial population file and results of actual behavior are, of course, available. A comparison of what the model "predicts" with what actually happened is a useful test of the model.[7]

Based on this method of evaluation, the FEH model forecast earnings with a high degree of accuracy. For the five years 1973–77 the model's projections differed from social security earnings records by an average of 2.4 percent for white men, 2.0 percent for white women, 1.2 percent for nonwhite men, and a less creditable 4.6 percent for nonwhite women.

Looking into the future, the model projects little change in birthrates, a decline in mortality rates among those 65 and older by about one-third between 1980 and 2020, a gradual increase in labor force participation of women of all ages and of men 65 and older (especially between 1980 and 2000), and a steady increase in real earnings (1.4 percent a year for white males and nonwhite females, 1.3 percent for nonwhite males, and 1.2 percent for white females).

The lifetime earnings patterns produced by the FEH model are satisfactory for the estimation of social security and pension benefit accruals. The model works especially well for white males, because they are most likely to have the continuous work histories that are easy to model with available longitudinal data. The model works less well for groups that have traditionally less predictable earnings patterns, because

7. A sample of longitudinal earnings history data from the Social Security Administration's records through 1977 matched to records on the March 1976 CPS was used for comparison with simulated earnings histories produced by the FEH model. These comparison data are not totally satisfactory for validating the FEH results since they include only earnings derived from covered employment. However, they were the most comprehensive earnings histories available at the time for this purpose. The period covered by the data is 1973–77. (See Johnson, Wertheimer, and Zedlewski, "Family and Earnings History Model," for a fuller discussion of these results.)

it is difficult to capture the factors that affect the labor supply of these groups.[8]

Projections of Jobs and Benefits Histories

The jobs and benefits history model was used to augment the earnings histories with simulated information about each person's employment history, including job characteristic and retirement benefit information. The job characteristics simulated are industry attachment (one of the twelve major industries), tenure (length of time on each job), and coverage under the social security and private employer pension systems; the retirement benefit information simulated includes social security benefits, employer pension benefits, and the date of pension acceptance.

For workers under 58, the model simulates job change, and if a job change takes place, an industry for the new job. Subsequently, the model either updates social security and pension plan participation information, or, for job changers, stochastically determines whether the new job has a pension plan and which type of plan it is.

For workers 58 and over, the simulation is more complex. It is assumed that a worker's decision to accept a pension or retire is based on the potential retirement income that he or she could receive.[9] The explanatory variables in the retirement decision functions are social security and employer-pension-reduced and full-retirement-benefit indicators, the loss (gain) in social security and pension wealth if retirement is delayed one year, social security wealth, employer pension wealth, current earnings, disability status, and marital status. The model first determines whether the worker stays on the same job, then whether job leavers take a new job or quit the labor force. People who leave their

8. Robert Meyer and Richard Wertheimer at the Urban Institute have completed a new model of labor supply for the DYNASIM system that uses thirteen consecutive years of data. Their model of lifetime employment patterns employs a multivariate probit model, a significant technical improvement over the current model. A permanent error component is included that should improve the estimates for the groups that to date have been more difficult to model.

9. This part of the JBH model is based on the work of Richard Burkhauser and Joseph Quinn as part of an Urban Institute contract with the U.S. Department of Labor to explore the effect of increasing the mandatory retirement age. A full discussion of the theoretical development and estimation is given in James R. Storey and others, "The Effects of Raising the Age Limit for Mandatory Retirement in the Age Discrimination in Employment Act" (Urban Institute, 1981).

current jobs are awarded employer pensions (if they are eligible) and social security benefits (if they pass the social security earnings test).[10]

SOCIAL SECURITY RETIREMENT BENEFITS. The social security benefits model calculates a history of benefits for each person in the population: retirement benefits, spouse benefits, disability benefits, and children's benefits. It selects a type of benefit based on critical events in each person's life. That is, age can trigger the retirement benefit simulation, an incidence of disability can trigger the simulation of disability benefits, and the death of a spouse can trigger spouse benefit processing.

The retirement benefit simulation calculates a potential benefit for each person in the sample once he or she reaches the minimum retirement age and has the required numbers of quarters of covered earnings. The model uses a person's simulated earnings history to calculate a benefit, in a way similar to that used by the Social Security Administration. This benefit may or may not be assigned to that person, depending on the final labor force decision made by the retirement model.

PRIVATE EMPLOYER PENSION BENEFITS. The simulation of private employer pension benefits also tries to emulate the current administrative climate surrounding these plans. But this task is much more difficult than for social security because pension provisions vary widely. Indeed, there are more than 500,000 private employer plans in existence today.[11] The main features of pension provisions—rules governing participation, vesting, retirement age, benefit formula, and survivors—are represented in the model. The rules that apply to an individual worker are simulated on a stochastic basis. Thus the model tries to capture the variability in plan provisions and applies these to the worker's earnings histories to estimate private pension benefits.

10. All of the job characteristics simulated (industry, pension coverage, and partic- ipation) are reassigned for job changers. However, a deficiency exists within this retirement process because the model has no provision to resimulate hours of work and earnings for those who change jobs. If an older person leaves his or her current job and takes another, his or her simulated earnings are those assigned in the FEH model simulation. This is unrealistic, of course, because older people who take a pension from one job and move to another are apt to adjust their work schedules or job responsibilities and, therefore, their earnings. See, for example, Alan L. Gustman and Thomas L. Steinmeier, "Partial Retirement and the Analysis of Retirement Behavior," National Bureau of Economic Research Working Paper 763 (Cambridge, Mass.: NBER, September 1981). But because workers in this age group change jobs infrequently (that is, most workers will accept a pension and leave the labor force), this model deficiency should not severely affect my results.

11. James Schulz and others, "Private Pension Benefits in the 1970s" (New York: McCahan Foundation for Research in Economic Security, March 1982).

The pension model has two principal components.[12] The first simulates plan coverage and participation and assigns a broad type of pension plan—single-employer defined benefit, multi-employer defined benefit, or defined contribution—to participating workers. The second component calculates a benefit for each participating worker who leaves a job with a vested status.

The first model component therefore operates as an integral part of the job assignment process. Workers are assigned to new jobs, and perhaps a pension plan, because their work history indicates a labor force participation entry or exit or because they change jobs. The probabilities of pension coverage and participation vary among workers depending on their industry attachment, earnings level, sex, hours worked per year, and tenure. Participating workers are assigned to one of the three types of pension plans according to their industry.

The second component of the pension model assigns the characteristics of a pension plan to a vested worker who leaves a job or is eligible for retirement. Workers who participate in a pension plan accrue years-of-service credits as the simulation proceeds. If years of service equal or exceed the simulated vesting requirement at the time of job exit or retirement,[13] the worker is guaranteed a pension from that job. The model includes ten types of defined benefit plans and a general defined contribution plan. A basic formula and other key characteristics of a plan (such as early and normal retirement age) are assigned stochastically to workers in defined benefit plans. These characteristics represent the wide variability that exists among defined benefit plans rather than a set of specific plans.[14]

The model accumulates career contributions plus interest for each year of service for workers in the defined contribution plan. The stock of accumulated contributions plus interest is converted into a life annuity that pays constant retirement benefits. The model assumes an annual contribution rate of 7 percent of salary and a nominal rate of interest of

12. The model is briefly outlined here. Appendix A shows some of the key parameters and their sources.

13. For defined benefit plans the vesting requirement may be one of the three major options permitted by ERISA (full after ten years, graded to reach full vesting after fifteen years of service, or full vesting when age and years of service equal forty-five; for defined contribution plans vesting is immediate).

14. For a full history and description of the original design for the DYNASIM model, see James Schulz and others, "The Economic Impact of Private Pensions on Retirement Income," a report to the National Science Foundation (Washington, D.C.: NSF, 1977).

7 percent. Benefits are based on accumulated contributions and assumptions regarding specific age-sex life expectancy.

The pension benefit may be adjusted for early retirement reductions, joint and survivors' annuity options, maximum years of service limitations, and minimum benefit provisions.[15] The benefit is paid whenever a worker retires. The parameters of the pension model do not change over time, but underlying distributional changes in the sample can cause the incidence of different provisions to change. All dollar constants used in benefit formulas are assumed to be price-indexed.

The model does not assume that the benefits of retirees are price-indexed during the retirement period. Since this assumption is extremely conservative, one of the scenarios shows the difference that full price indexing of employer benefits would make. In reality, most surveys find that private employer pension benefits are adjusted on an ad hoc basis over time, but these increases have fallen short of the increases in prices experienced by retirees.[16] Plans may adjust benefits over time in various ways, such as a flat dollar increase for all retirees, a dollar increase for each year of service, or a percent of current pension benefit adjustment. But because representative data on increases made by pension plans do not exist, and because increases are almost never guaranteed to retirees, the base case simulates nonindexed benefits.

The simulation exercise is primarily intended to demonstrate the value of a microsimulation model for examining the long-range effects of a change in the current pension climate. Thus the absolute values of projected pension benefits are primarily used only as baseline values against which alternative scenarios can be compared. Obviously, there is considerable interest in improving these baseline values so that this capability can be used to project the likely retirement income of future cohorts with more certainty.

Results

This section presents the results of the baseline projection and the three private employer pension scenarios. The baseline simulation

15. See Johnson, Wertheimer, and Zedlewski, "Family and Earnings History Model," for a full description of the provisions simulated.
16. Bankers Trust Company, *Corporate Pension Plan Study: A Guide for the 1980s* (New York: Bankers Trust, 1980).

assumed that the administrative rules governing private pensions today persist through 2020. Alternative A projects the consequences of requiring pension coverage of all private sector workers (universal coverage). Alternative B projects a pension plan feature that permits employees to take their earned credits to a new job, provided that the new employer has one (portable credits). Alternative C requires that private pension benefits be indexed to the change in prices (benefit indexing). These alternative administrative rules are assumed to begin in 1983. No other assumption differs. Thus the only responses to these pension changes will be those that are built into the model. For example, an increased incidence in private pension benefits is likely to decrease labor supply of older workers because this response is explicitly built into the retirement decision model.

The three scenarios are not forecasts of actual pension legislation. Enactment of universal coverage or portability of pension credits would probably change the entire pension environment.[17] These scenarios, instead, examine the adequacy of future pension benefits and demonstrate microsimulation.

Baseline Projection to 2020

Between 1982 and 2020 both social security and private pensions will grow rapidly even if no changes in policy are made (see table 2).[18] From a much smaller base, pensions grow at a higher rate, but social security remains larger and accounts for more income growth than pensions do. Men derive a larger part of their retirement-type income from private pensions than women do, and this pattern persists.[19] Pensions grow

17. See the President's Commission on Pension Policy, *Coming of Age*, for a discussion of possible legislation.

18. These projections do not take account of the small social security benefit reductions enacted in 1983.

19. Table 2 shows a much higher growth in social security benefits for younger retirees (62–64) than for older ones (65 and over). This anomaly is caused by a combination of the effects of a transition to the wage-indexed benefit system and the fact that price adjustments for retirees have exceeded wage increases in recent years. That is, benefits for many of the older persons in 1982 were calculated under a more generous system (those who were first eligible before 1979 were fully grandfathered) and then indexed to fully compensate for price increases. But everyone in the younger age group retired under the newer wage-indexed system (the oldest in this category were first eligible in 1980), which incorporated lower wage-replacement ratios. Actually these younger persons are also affected by transition rules, but the guarantee is not as generous, so that most do better under wage indexing. The last two columns of table 2

Table 2. Average Retirement Benefits for People Aged 62 and Over, 1982, 2000, 2020
1980 dollars unless otherwise specified

Age and sex	Average benefit			Percent increase	
	1982	2000	2020	1982–2000	2000–20
	Social security[a]				
Men					
62–64	3,949	5,791	8,061	46.6	39.2
65–67	5,084	5,573	7,865	9.6	41.1
68–71	4,972	5,526	7,831	11.1	41.7
72 and over	4,138	4,589	6,571	10.9	43.2
Women					
62–65	2,637	3,233	4,674	22.6	44.6
65–67	3,115	3,452	4,808	10.8	39.3
68–71	3,219	3,362	4,992	4.4	48.5
72 and over	3,271	3,558	4,594	8.8	29.1
	Private pensions				
Men					
62–64	2,334	3,703	4,974	58.7	34.3
65–67	1,876	3,509	4,521	87.0	28.8
68–71	1,736	2,835	4,518	63.3	59.4
72 and over	601	1,419	2,586	136.1	82.2
Women					
62–64	1,141	1,602	1,865	40.4	16.4
65–67	846	1,584	1,897	87.2	19.8
68–71	771	1,103	1,776	43.1	61.0
72 and over	259	586	1,047	126.3	78.7

Source: DYNASIM baseline projections.
a. Includes retirement and survivors' benefits.

especially rapidly during the first half of the simulation period.[20] The growth in pension coverage and ERISA rules governing vesting and participation causes an increase in the number of benefits awarded.

Table 3 shows the dramatic growth in the proportion of the elderly with a pension. The model projects that more than 60 percent of men and about 40 percent of women aged 62 and older are likely to have a pension benefit in 2020.

show the relative growth in benefits from 1982 to 2000 and 2000 to 2020. These data indicate that when people retire under the same system rules (2000 to 2020), benefit levels increase at about the same rate among all age groups.

20. These results must be viewed with some caution, however, because pension benefits assigned in the early years of the simulation are highly dependent on data imputed to people in the original 1973 CPS data files. On the other hand, one would expect to see a very significant growth in average pension benefits over the period, for reasons discussed earlier.

Table 3. Percent of People 62 and Over with a Private Pension Benefit, 1982, 2000, 2020

Age and sex	1982	2000	2020
Men			
62–64	25.5	53.3	61.8
65–67	31.1	54.1	64.8
68–71	34.1	55.0	66.1
72 and over	25.2	42.7	63.1
Women			
62–64	8.7	23.1	38.6
65–67	11.2	24.3	40.6
68–71	12.2	22.5	41.5
72 and over	8.9	16.4	31.4

Source: DYNASIM baseline projections.

Table 4 shows the projected increase in real income from both private pensions and social security. Over the 1982–2020 period there are considerable improvements in the income distribution for people 62 and older. Although pensions constitute an increasing share of total income, they are still a minor fraction of the total. On average, pensions provide 25 percent of income for men and 10 percent for women by 2020, as shown in the table. By 2020, 58 percent of males aged 62 and older have combined income from social security and private pensions that exceeds $8,000 (in 1980 dollars), compared with only 6 percent in 1981. The income gains for women shown in table 4 are also significant. The proportion of women in the lowest two income categories, for example, declined from 74 percent in 1983 to 37 percent in 2020.[21]

Thus the DYNASIM model projects that public and private pension income will be a source of much more income for retirees than it is today. The model predicts about a twofold increase in pension recipiency rates for males and a fourfold increase for females. It also projects substantial real gains in average benefits for recipients.[22]

The Effects of Three Alternative Scenarios

By 2020 the changes in pension rules—universal coverage, portable credits, or indexing—all have major effects on coverage or benefit levels,

21. The benefits shown are on a one-person basis and do not account for the fact that many of these older people are married and have combined incomes.

22. The Pension and Retirement Income Simulation Model (PRISM) at ICF, Inc., projects similar growth in pension benefit recipiency rates and even higher future benefits

Table 4. Distribution of Income from Social Security and Private Pension Benefits, People Aged 62 and Over, 1982, 2000, 2020

Percent

Income (1980 dollars)	1982	2000	2020
Men			
Under 2,000	7.6	2.8	0.7
2,001–4,000	29.7	18.7	5.1
4,001–6,000	39.2	34.0	14.4
6,001–8,000	17.2	27.3	22.1
8,001–15,000	6.0	14.8	47.7
15,001 and over	0.3	2.4	10.0
Total	100.0	100.0	100.0
Average income	4,791	6,261	9,806
Percent from pension income	0.09	0.20	0.25
Women			
Under 2,000	20.2	13.8	5.2
2,001–4,000	53.6	49.7	31.3
4,001–6,000	22.5	27.6	33.1
6,001–8,000	3.2	7.3	18.2
8,001–15,000	0.5	1.5	11.6
15,001 and over	. . .	0.1	0.6
Total	100.0	100.0	100.0
Average income	3,186	3,665	5,241
Percent from pension income	0.02	0.06	0.10

Source: DYNASIM baseline projections.

or both. The percent of all people receiving a pension and the average benefits in the year 2020 are shown in figure 1. *Universal coverage* significantly increases the percent of the population with a private pension, and more for women than for men.[23] Because federal and state and local pensions are not included in the model, and persons who spent their careers in these sectors are included in the denominator, there tends to be an upper limit on the percent of the population likely to earn a private employer pension. About 17 percent of the labor force is in the government sector in any given year.[24] But many of those workers spend part of their lives in private employment and would earn private pensions

levels (including benefits from supplemental thrift and profit-sharing plans). Projections from PRISM can be obtained from Dave Kennell at ICF.

23. Note that the estimates are percentages of the entire aged population.

24. Valerie A. Personick, "The Outlook for Output and Employment through 1990," *Monthly Labor Review*, vol. 104 (August 1981), pp. 28–41.

Figure 1. Percent of People Aged 62 and Over with a Pension and Their Average Pension Benefits under Alternative Pension Systems, 2020

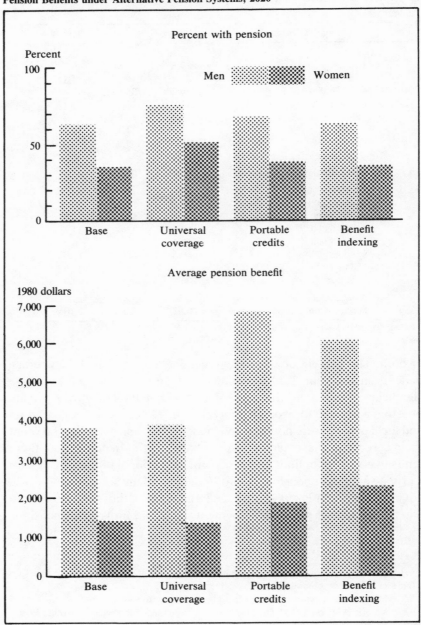

if coverage were universal. The percent of women with a private pension rises to about 51 percent in 2020, while 74 percent of the men have a pension in the 2020 universal coverage projection. Women remain less likely than men to earn a retirement benefit because fewer work and those who work are more likely to work part-time. Because existing plan participation and vesting rules are still in place, some private sector workers will still not earn a retirement benefit.

These results reemphasize the rapid growth in pension benefit receipt even if rules are unchanged. The proportion of men 62 and older with a pension is projected to rise from 28 percent in 1982 to 64 percent in 2020, a rise of 229 percent. For women the rise is 367 percent. Universal coverage adds another 10 percent more men and 15 percent more women. Thus for persons whose work histories permit them to meet the participation and vesting standards of at least one plan, current coverage will take us more than half the distance from here to universal coverage.[25]

Portability of credits increases coverage only slightly, but boosts real benefits dramatically. The average benefit increases 77 percent for men and 31 percent for women. Portability of credits helps people who earn pensions but who leave one or more jobs before becoming entitled or who leave jobs with a vested benefit that declines in real terms until the time of retirement (because it is based on nominal dollars earned while on that job).

Benefit indexing has no effect on coverage, but increases benefits to offset the effects of inflation. Although not shown by figure 1, indexing is increasingly valuable for older retirees for whom the steady erosion of benefits by inflation can be devastating.

Despite the significant effects on both coverage of private pensions and benefit amounts from the three changes in rules, the overall effect on income from pensions plus social security is rather modest (table 5). Most pension income continues to come from social security, not private pensions, even if the rules are changed for most retirees. Indexing and portability of credits enables about 9 percent of men who would otherwise fall into lower retirement income brackets to achieve or to sustain total retirement benefits above $15,000 a year (1980 dollars).

---

25. Private pension coverage rates are much higher for full-time wage and salary workers in the prime-age working groups than for the entire work force. See *Retirement Opportunities in an Aging America: Coverage and Benefit Entitlement* (Washington, D.C.: Employee Benefit Research Institute, 1981).

Table 5. Distribution of Income from Social Security and Private Pension Benefits under Alternative Pension Systems, People Aged 62 and Over in 2020 with Some Income from These Sources

Percent

Income (1980 dollars)	Base case	Universal coverage	Portable credits	Benefit indexing
Men				
Under 4,000	5.8	5.2	5.2	5.3
4,001–8,000	36.5	33.1	31.8	30.9
8,001–15,000	47.7	48.7	43.5	45.8
15,001 and over	10.0	12.9	19.5	19.0
Total	100.0	100.0	100.0	100.0
Women				
Under 4,000	36.5	33.8	35.0	34.2
4,001–8,000	51.3	52.2	50.8	50.2
8,001–15,000	11.6	13.2	12.7	14.0
15,001 and over	0.6	0.6	1.3	1.5
Total	100.0	100.0	100.0	100.0

Source: DYNASIM projections. Figures are rounded.

For women, the income distribution changes little because social security (which generally remains constant in each scenario) overshadows pension benefit changes. As table 4 shows, private pension benefits contributed only 10 percent of income, on average, for women in 2020. Universal coverage seems to help low-income women more than the other changes do.

Limitations of the Projections

There are several limitations to this methodology that may have important implications for these results. The first is that the model makes no links between job choice and pension characteristics of the job. For example, a worker may leave a job without regard to his or her vesting status on that job. Moreover, workers do not choose to take a new job because of its wage and benefit package. Unfortunately, enough research has not yet been done to permit the modeling of that behavior.

Another limitation is the lack of information on work behavior after a person leaves his primary career job and begins to receive a private pension from it. People near retirement age in the model base their job-exit decisions on information about their eligibility for a pension. This aspect of the model is derived from a behavioral model based on the retirement decisions of people in the Social Security Administration's

Retirement History Survey. That model simulates whether a person changes jobs or leaves the labor force in order to begin receiving pension benefits. But the work behavior of a person who changes jobs is based on that person's previous hours and wage-rate experience rather than on an explicit model of that behavior. Presumably, people who work after accepting a pension may exhibit work patterns different from those they had in their primary career jobs. In particular, hours of work or wage rates may differ significantly.

Some omissions in the model also present significant limitations. For example, the model lacks an asset accumulation model and a government pensions model. Thus the importance of such income cannot be taken into account. As additional retirement-related research is completed, these aspects of the retirement process can be incorporated. Another important task is to validate more fully the results from microsimulation model projections. The full implementation of these models is a relatively new phenomenon, and one needs to know how much confidence one can have in their results. It is hoped that this simulation demonstration will stir the additional interest and research support that is necessary to move forward with this kind of methodology.

Appendix A: Pension Model Parameters

As mentioned earlier, there are two main components of the DYNA-SIM private pension model. The first determines whether labor force participants are in a plan and assigns a basic type of plan to participants. The second determines whether a benefit should be calculated for job changers, labor force exiters, or potential retirees and calculates a benefit for persons who are eligible. The major parameters used in each of these model components are presented here.

Plan Coverage and Participation

Employer pension coverage is simulated each time a worker either changes jobs or enters the labor force. The coverage probability depends on a worker's sex, industry, and earnings level. The coverage probabilities used in the model are shown in table 6; they were estimated by using the May 1979 Current Population Survey, which included a pension questionnaire. As the coverage probabilities show, workers who

Table 6. Probability of Employer Pension Coverage in Various Industries, by Sex and Earnings

Industry	Earnings (1978 dollars)					
	Under 5,000	5,000– 9,000	10,000– 14,000	15,000– 19,000	20,000– 29,000	30,000 and over
Men						
Agriculture and fisheries	0.0713	0.2137	0.2974	0.3428	0.3453	0.7380
Mining	0.5167	0.7119	0.7719	0.8373	0.8707	0.9780
Construction	0.2265	0.2876	0.4691	0.6326	0.7739	0.6028
Manufacturing	0.3588	0.6181	0.7693	0.8615	0.8330	0.7745
Transportation	0.3570	0.3615	0.5446	0.8020	0.8373	0.9579
Communication and utilities	0.7678	0.7962	0.8232	0.9247	0.9632	0.9645
Trade	0.2502	0.3280	0.4902	0.6317	0.6719	0.8230
Finance, insurance, and real estate	0.3473	0.4891	0.6957	0.7125	0.7380	0.7230
Service	0.3197	0.5068	0.6629	0.7550	0.7415	0.6250
Number (weighted)	6,170,784	6,537,567	7,961,068	7,342,490	6,467,052	2,478,594
Number (unweighted)	1,651	1,759	2,255	2,015	1,771	735
Women						
Agriculture and fisheries	0.2219	0.1811	0.5853	. . .	. . .	
Mining	0.1604	0.4720	0.5082	0.5564	0.7514	
Construction	0.1653	0.2093	0.3611	0.4314	0.5664	
Manufacturing	0.4566	0.5292	0.7677	0.7406	0.9110	
Transportation	0.5251	0.4797	0.6019	0.8843	0.8301	
Communication and utilities	0.7055	0.7870	0.8984	0.9010	0.9259	
Trade	0.2277	0.4534	0.5844	0.6483	0.5217	
Finance, insurance, and real estate	0.4912	0.7063	0.7943	0.5959	0.7179	
Service	0.3238	0.6142	0.8079	0.8421	0.8056	
Number (weighted)	11,555,701	10,663,781	5,505,460	1,776,727	661,264	
Number (unweighted)	3,415	3,098	1,594	509	204	

Source: Current Population Survey, May 1979.

have high earnings are much more likely to be in a job with a pension plan than those with low earnings. Moreover, when earnings are held constant, the coverage probabilities for women are similar to those for men. In fact in some industries women are more likely than men to be in a job with coverage when earnings are held constant. For example, in the service industry, the coverage probabilities are higher for women than for men in all earnings categories—probably because men in this category are more likely to be self-employed than women and are therefore not covered by an employer's plan.

For all workers who are covered, a stochastic decision is made each

Table 7. Probability of Pension Plan Participation, by Age, Sex, and Tenure

Tenure (years)[a]	Age			
	Over 24	25–44	45–64	65 and over
Men				
Full-time				
Less than 1	0.5835	0.6855	0.7386	0.0000
1–3	0.7087	0.8680	0.8386	0.1438
More than 3	0.8360	0.9728	0.9780	0.8392
Part-time				
Less than 1	0.3173	0.5118	0.7722	0.0000
1–3	0.2172	0.3880	0.6566	0.0463
More than 3	0.5040	0.8723	0.8435	0.2766
Women				
Full-time				
Less than 1	0.4054	0.4893	0.5126	0.0000
1–3	0.5645	0.7591	0.7499	0.1286
More than 3	0.6732	0.9180	0.9469	0.7772
Part-time				
Less than 1	0.2951	0.4532	0.4167	0.0000
1–3	0.3560	0.4527	0.4028	0.0000
More than 3	0.4544	0.6348	0.5876	0.4447

Source: Current Population Survey, May 1979.
a. Full-time is 1,000 or more hours of work a year; part-time is less than 1,000 hours.

year to determine whether they are eligible to participate in their employer's plan. These probabilities, also derived from the May 1979 CPS, are modeled on the basic rules established by ERISA, which allow employers to exclude from coverage employees who do not meet minimum standards for participation. For example, employees who work less than 1,000 hours a year, those who are under 25, and those who are 25 or more and who have not yet completed one year of service (or in plans with immediate and full vesting, three years of service) may be excluded from participation. Table 7 shows the plan participation probabilities for covered workers.

All workers who are participating in a pension plan are assigned to one of four categories of plans: single-employer defined benefit plan, multi-employer defined benefit plan, single-employer defined contribution plan, and multi-employer defined contribution plan. These categories refer to some general distinctions that exist among employer plans. The plan may either specify a final benefit formula (the defined benefit plan) or specify the extent of payment into a pension plan so that benefits are based on the amount of total contributions (the defined

Table 8. Cumulative Probability of Assignment of Plan Type for All Pension Plan Participants, by Industry

Industry	Single-employer defined benefit	Multi-employer defined benefit	Single-employer defined contribution	Multi-employer defined contribution
Manufacturing	0.674 (.674)	0.751 (.077)	0.981 (.230)	1.00 (.019)
Mining	0.455 (.455)	0.773 (.318)	0.955 (.182)	1.00 (.022)
Finance	0.576 (.576)	0.591 (.015)	0.985 (.394)	1.00 (.015)
Construction[a]	0.198 (.198)	0.724 (.526)	0.725 (.078)	1.00 (.198)
Transportation, communication, and utilities	0.425 (.425)	0.692 (.267)	0.945 (.253)	1.00 (.055)
Trade	0.299 (.299)	0.505 (.206)	0.969 (.464)	1.00 (.031)
Services	0.324 (.324)	0.493 (.169)	0.944 (.451)	1.00 (.056)

Source: For private industries the probabilities were calculated from ICF estimates of the distribution of pension plans and participants in 1975, from "A Private Pension Forecasting Model" (Washington, D.C.: ICF, Inc., October 1979).

a. Agriculture is treated in the same way.

contribution plan). The single-employer plan covers the employees of one employer; the multi-employer plan, more than one employer. The latter usually covers a broad type of union employee.

The probabilities shown in table 8 are used to distribute pension plan participants among the four plan categories. Because data in this area are sparse, published data on participants by plan category and broad industry group were relied on to calculate these probabilities. The categories are used later to assign a benefit formula to a worker. Ideally one would be able to assign a plan to every covered employee, so that participation rules could be connected with the type of plan. Participation is likely to vary among plans because ERISA defines different participation rules for different plans. For example, plans with full and immediate vesting (usually defined contribution plans) may have different age-of-entry rules than plans that have a longer vesting period.

Pension Benefits

The private pension model calculates a benefit for workers who participate in a plan if they leave their current jobs or when they reach either early or normal retirement age, given that they achieve a vested status. Workers participating in defined benefit plans are stochastically assigned either a full vesting after ten years of service or a graded vesting rule. Both the graded fifteen-year service rule (25 percent after five years, with 5 percent additional vesting for each of the next five years and 10 percent additional for each of the next ten years) and the rule of 45 (50 percent vesting when age and service total forty-five years) permitted by ERISA are represented in the model. For workers participating in defined contribution plans, the simulation model assumes full and immediate vesting.

Determinations of normal and early retirement eligibility are functions of age, years of service, and industry. The probabilities used for these functions were estimated from the 1974 Bureau of Labor Statistics Survey of Defined Benefit Plans.[26] The actual benefit formula is assigned to a worker only after he or she leaves a job (either because of a job change or labor force exit) and meets these eligibility criteria.

The model represents a set of defined benefit plans and a prototypical defined contribution plan. The four broad types of plans included are a flat dollar times years of service plan, a nonintegrated percent of earnings times years of service plan, an integrated percent of earnings plan, and a "split earnings" plan (table 9). In the formulas that are earnings based, the highest five-year average of workers' earnings in the last ten years was used. In reality, many plans simply use the last five years or the last ten years (which are usually the highest years in nominal dollars) or career earnings. But the most common earnings measure used in the 1979 Bureau of Labor Statistics Survey was an average for the last or best five years (or less) of work. The use of this kind of measure for earnings has been increasing,[27] whereas formulas using career earnings have been decreasing significantly. The highest five-year average measure is used to minimize the effects of stochastic variations in annual earnings over time and to have a common standard for workers with earnings-based formulas.

Workers in defined benefit plans are stochastically assigned one of these benefit formulas according to the probabilities shown in table 10.

26. These probabilities are omitted because of space limitations. See Johnson and Zedlewski, "Jobs and Benefits History Model," for a complete description of the model.

27. Schulz and others, "Economic Impact of Private Pensions on Retirement Income," found that 64 percent of workers subject to earnings-type formulas in 1979 were in plans using the five (or less) years measure, up from 50 percent of plans in 1974.

338   Sheila R. Zedlewski

Table 9. Defined Benefit Plan Formulas Used for Benefit Projections

Formula	Specification
	Single-employer plan participants
1	Flat dollar benefit times years of service
2	Percent times highest five-year average earnings out of last ten years times years of service
3	Percent times highest five-year average earnings out of last ten years times years of service minus social security offset
4	Percent (1) times highest five-year average earnings out of last ten years for earnings up to step 1, plus percent (2) times highest five-year average earnings out of last ten years for earnings exceeding this step
5	Formula 1 or 2, whichever is higher
6	Formula 1 or 3, whichever is higher
7	Formula 1 or 4, whichever is higher
	Multi-employer plan participants
1	Flat dollar benefit times years of service
2	Percent times highest five-year average earnings out of last ten years times years of service
3	Formula 1 or 2, whichever is higher

These probabilities were based on the 1974 BLS Survey of Defined Benefit Plans. As the data show, plan participants in the manufacturing, mining, and construction industries are most likely to have a nonearnings benefit formula. In addition, almost all multi-employer plan participants have this kind of formula assigned. On the other hand, a split-earnings formula is most common for the service and finance industries. Schulz found that the more recent 1979 BLS data basically reconfirmed these proportions of workers by formula type and industry.[28]

The final elements of the benefit formulas are the values for the dollar constants used in the nonearnings formulas and the percentages used in the earnings-based formulas. Table 11 shows the median values used, by industry. The simulation model actually includes a distribution around these values for each industry to capture the wide variability in formulas in existence today.

Appendix B: Comparisons of DYNASIM and PRISM Projections

A comparison of the DYNASIM base case projections with projections from another pension forecasting model supports the finding that

28. Schulz and others, "Private Pension Benefits in the 1970s."

Table 10. Probability of Assignment to a Benefit Formula for Workers in a Defined Benefit Plan, by Plan Type and Industry

Industry	Benefit formula[a]						
	1	2	3	4	5	6	7
Single-employer plan							
Manufacturing	0.430	0.036	0.060	0.173	0.173	0.056	0.072
Mining	0.537	0.022	0.052	0.264	0.023	0.102	. . .
Construction	0.981	0.011	. . .	0.008	. . .	. . .	. . .
Transportation	0.366	0.099	0.229	0.113	0.031	0.140	0.022
Communications and utilities	0.023	0.134	0.027	0.169	0.588	0.040	. . .
Trade	0.260	0.125	0.179	0.285	. . .	0.065	. . .
Finance, insurance, and real estate	. . .	0.085	0.274	0.494	0.053	0.035	. . .
Service	0.054	0.167	0.139	0.459	0.054	0.009	0.044
			(1)	*(2)*[b]	*(3)*		
Multi-employer plan							
Manufacturing			0.967	. . .	0.033		
Mining			1.000	. . .	. . .		
Construction			0.925	. . .	0.075		
Transportation			0.975	. . .	0.025		
Communications and utilities			. . .	. . .	1.000		
Trade			0.855	. . .	0.145		
Finance, insurance, and real estate			. . .	. . .	1.000		
Service			0.896	. . .	0.104		

Source: 1974 Bureau of Labor Statistics Survey of Defined Benefit Plans.
a. See table 9 for description of benefit formulas.
b. This formula is never assigned alone, but only as an alternate to formula 1.

one should expect to see significant real income gains for retirees in the future if the pension system remains as generous as it is today. The Pension and Retirement Income Simulation Model (PRISM) of ICF, Inc., seems to project even more significant increases in benefit levels but similar increases in recipiency rates for private pensions.[29] Unfortunately the bases for comparing the results of the two models are not identical, so one can get only a general impression of the differences.

Table 12 shows some results from both models. Note that the PRISM estimates are for *unmarried* men and women, while the DYNASIM

29. Dave Kennell supplied some unpublished PRISM results that he felt were the most comparable to the DYNASIM projections. The PRISM projections were also made using 1982 actuary's assumptions regarding macroeconomic variables.

Table 11. Median Dollar and Percent Constants Used in Defined Benefit Formulas, by Industry[a]

Industry	Formula 1 (1974 dollars)	Formula 2 (percent)	Formula 3 (percent)
Single-employer plan			
Manufacturing	6.50	0.50	1.25
Mining	7.50	1.25	0.50
Construction	6.50	1.25	0.50
Transportation	6.50	1.25	0.50
Communications and utilities	1.50	0.75	1.75
Trade	6.50	0.75	1.75
Finance, insurance, and real estate	6.50	1.25	0.50
Service	1.50	1.25	0.50

Industry	Formula 1 (1974 dollars)	Formula 2 (percent)
Multi-employer plan		
Manufacturing	5.50	0.50
Mining	7.50	1.25
Construction	3.50	1.25
Transportation	6.50	1.25
Communications and utilities	5.50	0.75
Trade	7.50	0.75
Finance, insurance, and real estate	5.50	1.25
Service	3.50	1.25

Source: Same as table 10.
a. See table 9 for description of benefit formulas.

results include all men and women. The projection years and age-group comparisons are also not identical. The general indications are that both models predict substantial increases in the proportion of older persons likely to have private pensions in the future. DYNASIM shows higher growth for all men probably because married men—who are excluded from the PRISM estimates—have higher pension recipiency rates than nonmarried men. The effect is the opposite for women: married women tend to have lower pension recipiency rates than unmarried women (because they are more likely to have shorter work histories). Thus the DYNASIM recipiency rate projections are lower for all women than the PRISM model's projections for unmarried women. The PRISM average

Table 12. Projected Retirement Income from Social Security and Private Pensions according to DYNASIM and PRISM Models, Selected Years, 1982–2020
1980 dollars unless otherwise specified

	DYNASIM, ages 65–67			PRISM, age 65		
					1995–	
Item	1982	2000	2020	1985	2005	2015
Men						
Social security	5,084	5,573	7,865	4,401	5,733	7,875
Private pension	1,876	3,509	4,521	3,903	6,160	7,438
Percent receiving						
private pension	31.1	54.1	65.0	29.3	48.5	49.3
Women						
Social security	3,115	3,452	4,808	3,002	3,992	5,532
Private pension	846	1,584	1,897	2,321	2,287	3,756
Percent receiving						
private pension	11.2	24.3	40.6	11.7	30.2	46.5

Source: PRISM data from David Kennell, "Baseline Projections of the Pension and Retirement Income Simulation Model" (ICF, Inc., 1982).
a. Includes retirement and survivors' benefits.

benefit level projections, however, are about 40 percent higher than the DYNASIM projections.

There are several reasons why these differences should be expected. The PRISM model simulates supplemental plans for all participating workers, while DYNASIM simulates only a basic plan for workers. From 40 to 60 percent of participants have one of these plans in the PRISM model, and these supplemental plans tend to be generous and have quick vesting. Thus one would expect the effect of this difference in modeling to be significant. Other differences between the two models also tend to result in higher benefit projections for PRISM than for DYNASIM. The PRISM projections assumed that plan constants would rise with real wages rather than with prices as in the DYNASIM model. PRISM assumes a shorter vesting schedule and assumes that no job change occurs within two years of the vesting point. Finally, basic modeling strategies contribute to these results. PRISM includes the characteristics of 350 actual plans, while DYNASIM assigns individual plan characteristics stochastically. Thus there is no control in the DYNASIM model over assigning some workers to plans that tend to be generous in all respects. A final difference to note is that PRISM's estimates (which assume price adjustments during retirement according to the past experience of the plans represented) are for 65-year-olds, whereas the DYNASIM results are for 65- to 67-year-olds, who have already suffered some real declines in benefits during retirement years.

Comment by Paul N. Courant

For people like me who are not experts on microsimulation, this paper is a useful guide to how such models work and how simulations are actually made. The results both indicate the uses to which microsimulation models can be put and illuminate important policy questions concerning private pensions. The paper provided me with a basis for understanding how microsimulation is carried out, and I think it would provide a similar service for any other interested reader.

This model works in two stages. First, the family earnings history model generates a labor force and demographic history for a sample of the U.S. population, spanning the years from 1973 to 2020. The data generated are then used as input for the jobs and benefits history model. At this second stage, pension and social security benefits for each person are computed. In both stages people are assigned probabilities, year by year, of moving from one status to another. These probabilities may be derived from econometrically complex behavioral equations or in much less sophisticated ways.

In the family earnings history model, for example, one begins with a sample of 60,000 people who are representative of the population in 1973. Members of this sample get married, have children, get divorced, die, and do other things at rates based on behavioral equations or rules of thumb. This process continues up to 2020. To make sure that the model is not going off track, one must align the sum of all these actions with externally generated estimates. In this case the external estimates come from the 1981 report of the social security actuary. It is hoped that the internal detail will describe with reasonable accuracy what would happen if the aggregate estimates turn out to be the same as the externally generated estimates. In addition, one can compare more detailed estimates for smaller groups with actual historical data for periods after the beginning of the simulation (1973 in this instance), but before the present (1982). By these standards the model does well for white males, but somewhat less well for other groups.

The obvious question is whether a model that behaves well for the first five or ten years will continue to behave well for the next thirty or thirty-five. It is easy to imagine a dynamic process that tracks the true world for the first period and then goes way out of line for the next thirty. I do not have any sense of how one looks for that kind of a problem in this model and tries to prevent it from happening. Certainly the dismal history of macroeconomic models that track the past faithfully and are useless as forecasting tools gives one pause.

Armed with labor force and family earnings histories, one then goes to the jobs and benefits history model, where one learns which industry people work in, how often they change jobs, what their social security and pension coverage is, and when they retire. I am troubled by the apparent fact that movement among jobs by people under age 58 does not seem to be influenced by the pension characteristics associated with those jobs. The precise relationship between pensions and labor turnover may be uncertain, but there is strong reason to think that some such relationship exists. The model treats people over age 58 as being smarter (which may well be true), and these people do base their decisions on whether and when to retire in part on the value of their income and other resources, including pension entitlements.

The treatment of people under 58 remains disturbing. People who lose jobs do not simply have a chain of probabilities hung around their necks. They know something, however imperfectly, about their pensions, and that knowledge should influence their job choices. But the model does not allow for those possibilities. Moreover, they may be different in other relevant ways from people who do not lose jobs.

As far as the simulations are concerned, I have no empirical sense as to what the numbers should look like. But I would like to raise several issues. First, two minor questions. Why are the social security benefits of 62- to 64-year-olds so different from those of other groups among the elderly in 2020? Why does indexing increase the benefits of 62- to 64-year-olds so much in 2020 even though they will not have been drawing benefits for very long?

More important, however, are the limitations of the simulation method itself. The policy changes that are being simulated are large and important, and in all likelihood they would alter behavior. If pension credits were fully portable, for example, job turnover might well be affected. Yet, by its very nature, the model is unable to take account of these possible responses. The model implicitly assumes that the conditional probabilities of various individual economic choices will be unaffected by policy. In short, just the kind of responses that economists have most to say about are often ruled out by assumption.

Finally, large policy changes are likely to have macroeconomic effects. It would make no sense to try to put the entire enterprise sector into a model of this kind. But it would be desirable to take some account of the macroeconomic effects on microeconomic behavior.

Conference Participants

with their affiliations at the time of the conference

Henry J. Aaron *Brookings Institution*

Joseph Anderson *ICF, Inc.*

Alan J. Auerbach *Harvard University*

Martin Neil Baily *Brookings Institution*

Michael Boskin *Stanford University*

Barry P. Bosworth *Brookings Institution*

Gary Burtless *Brookings Institution*

Paul N. Courant *University of Michigan*

Sheldon Danziger *University of Wisconsin*

Peter A. Diamond *Massachusetts Institute of Technology*

Joseph Friedman *Abt Associates*

Harvey Galper *Brookings Institution*

Edward M. Gramlich *University of Michigan*

Thomas A. Gustafson *U.S. Department of Health and Human Services*

Giora Hanoch *Columbia University*

Jerry A. Hausman *Massachusetts Institute of Technology*

Robert H. Haveman *University of Wisconsin*

Marjorie Honig *Hunter College*

William C. L. Hsiao *Harvard School of Public Health*

F. Thomas Juster *University of Michigan*

Laurence J. Kotlikoff *Yale University*
John P. Laitner *University of Michigan*
Frank Levy *University of Maryland*
William McNaught *General Accounting Office*
Sally R. Merrill *Abt Associates*
Robert A. Moffitt *University of Wisconsin*
Alicia H. Munnell *Federal Reserve Bank of Boston*
Joseph P. Newhouse *Rand Corporation*
Larry Ozanne *Congressional Budget Office*
Joseph A. Pechman *Brookings Institution*
Anthony J. Pellechio *U.S. Department of Health
and Human Services*
Sherwin Rosen *University of Chicago*
Louise B. Russell *Brookings Institution*
Saul Schwartz *Tufts University*
John B. Shoven *Stanford University*
Timothy M. Smeeding *University of Utah*
Eugene Smolensky *University of Wisconsin*
Raymond J. Struyk *Urban Institute*
Michael K. Taussig *Rutgers University*
Barbara Torrey *Office of Management and Budget*
Jacques van der Gaag *World Bank*
Jennifer L. Warlick *University of Notre Dame*
Harold W. Watts *Columbia University*
Richard Wertheimer *Urban Institute*
Douglas A. Wolf *Urban Institute*
Barbara L. Wolfe *University of Wisconsin*
Sheila R. Zedlewski *Urban Institute*

Index

Aaron, Henry J., 1, 148n, 200n

Aged. *See* Elderly

Age of retirement, 6–7; decline in, 138; defined, 99, 102, 138; effect on benefits, 141–42; factors influencing, 101, 133–34, 158–60; health and, 7, 8, 101, 105, 109, 110, 113–15, 118–19, 127, 133, 158–59, 173; labor supply response to, 138; longevity and, 173–74; preretirement wages and, 160; retirement income onset and, 102–03, 105; social security benefits and, 9, 10–11, 135, 137, 143, 147, 155, 164. *See also* Life-cycle utility model

Akerlof, George A., 26n

Ando, Albert, 280n

Annual Housing Survey, 224, 227

Assets: income from, 287; liquid versus illiquid, 203, 207, 210, 216, 220, 223; private retirement, 151, 153, 155, 173; role of children in accumulation, 258

Auerbach, Alan J., 16, 257n, 260n, 262n, 263n, 273n, 274n, 275n

Avrin, Marcy, 258n

Balcer, Yves, 47n

Barnes, Roberta, 316n

Barro, Robert J., 257n, 260n

Bartel, Ann P., 30n

Barton, M., 136n

Becker, Gary S., 27n

Benefits, private pension: indexing of, 316, 325, 326, 331; projection, 20–21, 317, 331; types of plans for, 337–38

Benefits, social security disability; basis for determining, 75; effects of changing, 86–87, 95; effects of terminating, 79–85, 94, 95–96; stigma cost, 76; work status choice versus, 5, 67–68, 75–79

Benefits, social security retirement: effective, 144; equity effects of reducing, 190–92, 194–95; equity effects of taxing, 188–90, 191–92, 194–95; formula reforms proposed for, 164–65, 167–68; illiquidity, 143–44, 161; indexation, 10, 143, 195, 196; labor supply response to, 136, 137; projection, 20–21, 320, 323, 326–28; retirement test applied to, 144–46, 162–63; time of retirement and, 7, 8, 9, 10–11, 111, 113, 115–17, 125–27, 133, 134, 165, 167, 259

Bequests: in capital formation, 257; and unfunded social security system, 257, 261

Bergstrom, Albert R., 108n

Berndt, E. K., 111n

Bilderback, R., 199n, 224n

Blinder, Alan S., 28n, 117n, 137n, 141n, 280, 283n

Bloom, David E., 253n

Boskin, Michael J., 117n, 118, 126, 136n, 258n

Brown, Mary A., 65n

Brumberg, Richard, 197n, 279n

Budget constraint: consumption and work decisions from, 257, 260, 261; payroll tax effect on, 262; postretirement working hours and, 146; social security, 142–43, 146, 157–58

Bureau of Labor Statistics, 49, 58, 188; Survey of Defined Benefit Plans, 337, 338

Burkhauser, Richard V., 28n, 136n, 177n, 187n, 322n

Burtless, Gary, 9, 10, 28n, 30n, 137n, 143n, 147n, 148, 205n, 262n

Cagan, Phillip, 218n

Carlson, Diane A., 200–01n

CEX. *See* Consumer Expenditure Survey

Chamberlain, Gary, 239, 240, 248

Children, and life-cycle consumption behavior, 258, 261, 273–74, 276–77

Chirikos, Thomas N., 115n

347